THE ACTS OF
THE APOSTLES

VOLUME 31

THE ANCHOR BIBLE is a fresh approach to the world's greatest classic. Its object is to make the Bible accessible to the modern reader; its method is to arrive at the meaning of biblical literature through exact translation and extended exposition, and to reconstruct the ancient setting of the biblical story, as well as the circumstances of its transcription and the characteristics of its transcribers.

THE ANCHOR BIBLE is a project of international and interfaith scope. Protestant, Catholic, and Jewish scholars from many countries contribute individual volumes. The project is not sponsored by any ecclesiastical organization and is not intended to reflect any particular theological doctrine. Prepared under our joint supervision, THE ANCHOR BIBLE is an effort to make available all the significant historical and linguistic knowledge which bears on the interpretation of the biblical record.

THE ANCHOR BIBLE is aimed at the general reader with no special formal training in biblical studies; yet, it is written with the most exacting standards of scholarship, reflecting the highest technical accomplishment.

This project marks the beginning of a new era of co-operation among scholars in biblical research, thus forming a common body of knowledge to be shared by all.

William Foxwell Albright
David Noel Freedman
GENERAL EDITORS

THE ANCHOR BIBLE

THE ACTS OF THE APOSTLES

INTRODUCTION, TRANSLATION AND NOTES

BY

JOHANNES MUNCK

REVISED BY

WILLIAM F. ALBRIGHT and C. S. MANN

Doubleday & Company, Inc.

Garden City, New York

ISBN: 0-385-00914-3
Library of Congress Catalog Card Number 66–20918
Copyright © 1967 by Doubleday & Company, Inc.
First Edition
Tenth Printing
1981

Dedicated to
the Faculty of Divinity at the University of Oslo
as a token of my gratitude

PREFACE

The task of the exegete is to understand a text, its author, and its first readers. He must understand, but he must neither philosophize nor preach. However important these later processes may be, a text must be understood before it is used for purposes of philosophy or preaching. Otherwise purely arbitrary decisions will take the place of that understanding which restricts the exegete's use of the text to what is real and possible.

Everyone who writes a commentary on Acts must express his gratitude to the editors and authors of *The Beginnings of Christianity* for their outstanding work, and for the advance their book has signified and still signifies for all later work within this field.

Sigfred Pedersen, Reader in New Testament exegesis, has contributed greatly to the present book, especially through his translation into Danish of the Greek text of Acts, and has improved the book considerably in every respect. Dr. Ingeborg Nixon and Professor Johanne Stochholm have translated into English respectively the text of Acts, and the introduction and commentary, and American friends have helped to perfect the English version. Karin Bøgely and Erna Thode have made fair copies of the manuscript at its various stages, and have thus been of great assistance in completing the book. To them all, my warmest thanks for their help.

I should like to dedicate my book to the Faculty of Divinity at the University of Oslo, in gratitude for the degree of Doctor Theologiae *honoris causa* conferred upon me at the university's jubilee in 1962.

January 1965   *Johannes Munck*

During the fall term of the academic year 1964–65, my husband Johannes Munck was Visiting Professor of New Testament at Princeton Theological Seminary, where he gave a series of lectures drawn from his commentary on the Book of Acts. This circumstance provided him with a welcome opportunity to go over the text of his manuscript. Having attended all his lectures, I can testify to the eagerness and enthusiasm with which he availed himself of this opportunity to revise his work. He was well along in these labors, and had even written the preface, when he was interrupted by illness. The final editing of the manuscript, including especially the translation of the Greek text, was undertaken by Professor W. F. Albright, general editor of the Anchor Bible, and his assistants, Drs. C. S. Mann and Leona G. Running.*

My warm thanks are due to: my husband's colleagues and students, especially the doctoral candidates at Princeton Theological Seminary, who befriended us; Northern Baptist Theological Seminary in Oakbrook, Illinois, where my husband, having left Princeton at the beginning of February, gave his last lectures, and where his colleagues there, especially Professor Robert P. Meye, sustained him through the days when the first signs of serious illness appeared; Pacific Lutheran Theological Seminary in Berkeley, California, where we received the most generous and sympathetic hospitality, but where my husband had to abandon all plans for lecturing on the West Coast. We had to make a hasty departure from the United States and return to Denmark. Only twelve days later, on February 22, 1965, Johannes Munck died peacefully in Aarhus.

Above all I wish to express my gratitude to the General Editors of the Anchor Bible, Professors W. F. Albright and David Noel Freedman for their never-failing kindness, and to Eugene Eoyang, of Doubleday and Company, for his amiable and untiring help in preparing the present volume.

Aarhus, 1965   *Elisabeth Munck*

* All additions to the text are marked in an appropriate manner in the volume, and attributed to the "General Editors."

CONTENTS

CONTENTS

INTRODUCTION

I. THE ACTS OF THE APOSTLES AND THE GOSPEL OF LUKE

In the Bible, Acts follows the gospels and precedes Paul's epistles, but Acts was originally the second part of a single work, of which the first part was the Gospel of Luke. When this work was included in the New Testament the two parts were separated. (The present arrangement in the Bible puts the gospels in one group, the letters in another, while Acts takes its place between the two, with the Revelation of John after the letters.)

Even though the two parts of the work were separated, they still show signs of having belonged originally to one continuous work. Unlike the three other gospels, Luke opens with a preface (i 1–4). This preface, like that of Acts, is addressed to Theophilus, and on beginning Acts (i 1) the author once more addresses himself to Theophilus by referring to the first part of his work. These features, not usually found in primitive Christian literature, indicate both the author's Greek cultural background, and his effort to write his two-part work in such a way that it could be read by the educated public.

The preface to the whole work sounds entirely Greek. Luke[1] says that many people have already tried to give an account of all that had happened among "us" in accordance with the tradition handed down from all those who in the earliest days had been eyewitnesses[2] and servants of the Word. Here we find, behind Christian expressions, traditional phrases from contemporary Greek prefaces. Just as others had undertaken this task, so too would Luke. His reference to earlier written accounts is conventional and no proof of earlier gospel publications or written accounts of apostolic times. It must also be stressed that nothing is said about the character and extent of the work of his predecessors, so

---

[1] Luke is the name in general use for the author of the two-part work. Later, in Part IV of this Introduction, the value of the early church tradition concerning Luke's authorship will be examined. On the name "Luke," see Appendix I.

[2] On "eyewitnesses," see Appendix II.

that the reference does not necessarily posit the existence of gospels similar in length and character to Luke's but may simply mean that others had written down parts of the tradition previously transmitted by eyewitnesses. Nor does the reference to his predecessors indicate or prove Luke's dependence on them. Luke is simply aware of their existence; this is all that can be safely inferred from the text. Nor does he criticize their efforts. When Luke took pen in hand he did so because, like the others, he felt there was a task to be performed.

Luke himself was not *from the very beginning* an eyewitness to what is related in the Gospel or in Acts, but he writes in the preface that his task was to write down everything he had heard. This means that he wrote down everything carefully. Whether or not he witnessed the events described in the later chapters of Acts he does not say; in his preface he is concerned only with establishing the truth of all that he is transmitting.

Luke addresses Theophilus, a man otherwise unknown to us, as an official of high rank. At the time books intended for the general public were dedicated to a single person, who might be able to contribute to the costly dissemination of an otherwise unknown work or who perhaps had some connection with the purpose of the work. At any rate, Luke records that he undertook the writing so that Theophilus might realize that what had hitherto been known only to him was true and certain.

The two-part work, Luke-Acts, probably had no title. If analogies are sought within Christian literature one finds that the other three gospels are also without title and author's name. It is only posterity that has provided them with titles and the authors' names. In Greek literature, which Luke strove to emulate in his work, an old tradition existed to the effect that a single poem or a single prose work always appeared without title or author's name. Traditions about how a single work should be named were slow to develop. The Epistle to the Hebrews is an example of a literary work composed in the Greek manner, appearing at the outset without title and author's name.

Even though the work first appeared without a title, the oldest testimonies to its existence, originating as late as the second half of the second century, give a very different picture. The two parts of the work, now separated as two independent books, had acquired separate titles. The first part was given a title similar to those of the other canonical gospels: The Gospel according to

Luke. The second part was named The Acts of the Apostles by the church father Irenaeus in his long work *Against Heresies* written toward the end of the second century (III.xiii.3 f.) and in the anti-Marcionite prologue to Luke (ca. 160–180). A third testimony from this period is contained in the Muratorian Canon (ca. 170–190) which, like the two others, mentions Luke as the author of both the Gospel and Acts.

The title—Acts—was at that time applied to historical works, and to eyewitness accounts. As it cannot be traced back to the author of the two-part work but is attributable to a later age, the title is no more than interpretation. As such it deserves as much consideration as any later interpretation, for it goes back to a period when people knew Greek and were better able than we are to judge Greek style, but when, at the same time, there was a tendency to misunderstand primitive Christianity. This was because the writings of the Apostolic Age were often—against all probability—considered to reflect a standard of higher education, and the apostles were assumed, in consequence, to have written in correct Greek.

Though generally known and mentioned, the close relationship between Luke and Acts is, nevertheless, frequently forgotten in subsequent discussions of the books themselves. The relationship between Luke and Acts is acknowledged at the outset, but seldom brought to bear thereafter: Luke is a gospel and Acts is a narrative about the apostles, and one treats them separately. Yet the prefaces at the beginning of Luke and Acts show that the author wrote one immediately after the other, ending the first volume and starting the second with the ascension.

Since this connection between the two books is one of the few known facts about Acts, one should never allow more hypothetical assumptions concerning Luke and Acts to overshadow it.

II. THE CONTENT OF THE ACTS OF THE APOSTLES

Chapter i. The book opens with a preface to the second part of Luke-Acts, referring to the end of the first part: the risen Christ meets his apostles and orders them to stay in Jerusalem, to await the Father's promise of the outpouring of the Holy Spirit (1–5). Their question as to whether Jesus will now restore the kingdom to Israel is dismissed. The gift of the Holy Spirit will make them his witnesses from Jerusalem to the ends of the earth. Such are Jesus' last words before he is lifted up into heaven where, according to the two angels who appear to the apostles, he will remain until his return to earth in the same manner (at the end of the world). Whereupon the eleven apostles, all of one mind, join in prayer with the women and Mary, mother of Jesus, and with his brothers (6–14). Peter proposes that in order to fill the place left vacant by Judas a new twelfth apostle be admitted to the group—to be chosen among those who have been with Jesus from the beginning of his ministry till the day of his ascension—to bear witness with the Eleven to his resurrection. Lots are drawn and the choice falls on Matthias (15–26).

Chapter ii. On the day of Pentecost the disciples are filled with the Holy Spirit, whereupon they begin to speak in other languages.[3] As the people are bewildered and confused by this (1–13), Peter comes forward to explain that what has happened is the fulfillment of an Old Testament prophecy. It is Jesus, killed by the Jews, but raised from the dead by God as the Old Testament foretold, who has after his ascension given the Holy Spirit to them (14–36). The audience is exhorted to repent and to receive baptism (37–40). Three thousand are baptized, and the founding of the church is accompanied by "wonders." The life of the church is characterized by common ownership of all property and common participation in temple services and in the celebration in their homes of a common meal (41–47).[4]

[3] On the significance of this, see the note on Pentecost in Appendix III.
[4] On the organization of the early Christians, see note in Appendix IV.

Chapter iii. Peter together with John cures a lame beggar in the temple (1–10); Peter, addressing the people, explains that this miraculous cure has been brought about in the name of Jesus, the prophet whose coming was foretold in the Old Testament, to whom God's covenant with Israel and all the prophets have pointed (11–26).

Chapter iv. The Sadducees place the two apostles under arrest (1–4); the next day, after Peter explains what has happened, they realize that the miracle cannot be denied, but that it is important to forbid the disciples to mention the name of Jesus. Peter will not promise to submit, whereupon the Sadducees again threaten Peter and John but then release them (5–22). Upon their return to their own people, all join in prayer (23–31). Once more the life of the early church is described as characterized by common agreement and common ownership of property: those who had any possessions sold them and gave the money to the apostles to help the needy. Barnabas is one of these (32–37).

Chapter v. The married couple Ananias and Sapphira give money, too, but they retain some for themselves. When Peter reproaches them for having lied against the Holy Spirit, the husband falls down dead and so, a little later, does his wife (1–11). The life of the church is marked by the miracles of the apostles and by the fellowship of its members (12–16). The Sadducees now lay hands upon all twelve apostles and put them under arrest, but an angel releases them, so that they appear the next morning, teaching in the temple. Then they are brought before the Sanhedrin and reminded not to teach in the name of Jesus. Peter again insists (as in iv 19–20) that they must obey God rather than man. A Pharisee and Scribe, Gamaliel, persuades the council to change its plan to kill the apostles by referring to earlier religious movements in which the death of the leader brought those to an end. The same, he maintains, will happen in this case, unless this movement is inspired by God. The apostles are beaten and afterward released, whereupon they continue their activities (17–42).

Chapter vi. A disagreement between the Hellenists and the Hebrews over the maintenance and support of widows leads the Twelve to suggest that a council of seven members be established to relieve the apostles of the burden of social duties (1–6). Of the Seven who are named, Stephen is singled out for his preaching and miraculous signs. He is opposed, and false witnesses are introduced who accuse him of speaking against the temple and the law of Moses (7–15).

Chapter vii. Before the Sanhedrin, Stephen delivers a speech characterising Israel as the people who were always disobedient to those sent to them by God, including finally Jesus. For a long time, he adds, the people were without any rights to the holy land and without a temple (1–53). Infuriated by his words, the people drive him out of the city and stone him to death (54–1a).

Chapter viii. Persecution of the church now rages in Jerusalem, Paul taking an active part, and all except the apostles flee (1b–3). Their flight provides an opportunity for missionary preaching: Philip, one of the Seven, preaches in the capital of Samaria and baptizes many, causing Peter and John to come there to pray for the new Christians that they may receive the Holy Spirit. Simon Magus—at first Philip's rival, later his disciple—is rejected by the apostles when he wants to buy the power of transmitting to others the power of the Holy Spirit (4–25). Philip is ordered to take the road that leads from Jerusalem to Gaza, where he speaks to and baptizes an Ethiopian courtier. Philip ends his journey in Caesarea (26–40).

Chapter ix deals with the calling of Paul. In the course of his persecution of the Christians, he travels to Damascus but is confronted outside the city by the risen Christ. Ananias, acting as an intermediary between Jesus and Paul, cures Paul's temporary blindness and baptizes him (1–19a). Immediately after his baptism, Paul preaches in the synagogues of Damascus, but when the Jews plan to kill him, he is lowered over the city wall during the night and flees to Jerusalem. Barnabas leads him to the apostles, but here also plots are laid against his life, so he continues his flight to Tarsus (19b–30). Now the persecution is ended and Peter travels to Lydda, where he heals a lame man, Aeneas, and on to Joppa, where he raises a woman, Tabitha, from the dead (31–43).

Chapter x. While staying with Simon, the tanner, in Joppa, Peter receives a message from Cornelius, a centurion in Caesarea, who has been exhorted by an angel to send for the apostle and listen to his teaching in his house. Peter had earlier been told in a vision to convert Jew and Gentile alike, so he goes with the messengers to the house of Cornelius the Gentile; and when, during his speech, the Holy Spirit is manifestly given to the Gentiles present, they are baptized.

Chapter xi. Rumors of this event alarm the church in Jerusalem

and upon his return to that city Peter has to give an account of
the event and of the clear signs he received from God, that
justified his action toward Gentiles (1–18). The persecution following Stephen's death has now inspired missionary efforts in
places as distant as Phoenicia, Cyprus, and Antioch (in Syria).
In Antioch, Jews from Cyprus and Cyrene have also preached
to the Gentiles and gained a great many followers. Barnabas (himself from Cyprus) is sent to Antioch where he proves himself a
sympathetic and active worker for the church, and sends for Paul
to share his work (19–26). Some prophets from Jerusalem arrive
in Antioch, and one of them, Agabus, predicts a great famine. A
collection is at once taken, and Barnabas and Paul carry the money
collected to Jerusalem (27–30).

Chapter xii. King Herod Agrippa I persecutes the church. He
executes the apostle James and arrests Peter. Before Peter's execution can be arranged, he miraculously escapes from prison and
leaves Jerusalem. The persecutor does not escape God's just
punishment; at the height of his power, the king is struck by a
terrible disease and dies. Barnabas and Paul return to Antioch
together with Mark.

Chapter xiii. In Antioch the Holy Spirit marks out Barnabas and
Paul for a mission (1–3) which first takes them to Cyprus where
they appear before the proconsul Sergius Paulus (4–12). From
Cyprus they embark for Asia Minor, where Mark leaves them.
Paul preaches to the Jews at the synagogue in Pisidian Antioch
(13–41). When the Jews oppose the apostles, they start preaching
to the Gentiles, until persecution by the Jews forces them to leave
(42–52).

Chapter xiv. In Iconium also the Jews express their unbelief,
and the apostles flee to Lystra (1–7). There they cure a lame
man, leading the people to assume that they are gods. Later the
Jews of the two towns cause a break in their missionary activities
(8–20). After a stay in Derbe, the apostles return to the towns
which they had previously visited and appoint elders for their
churches. Then they return to Antioch (21–28).

Chapter xv. A dispute between disciples from Judea and the
Antioch church over the necessity of circumcising Gentiles who
have become Christians, leads Barnabas and Paul to go to Jerusalem to meet Peter and James, the Lord's brother, and the church
there (1–5). While Peter and James are in favor of the Gentiles
being exempt from circumcision, James proposes that the new

converts be asked to keep a few rules; the proposal is accepted (6–21) and is announced in a letter to the disciples in Syria and Cilicia (22–33). Barnabas and Paul have a sharp dispute over Mark as a traveling companion and Barnabas returns to Cyprus (35–41) with Mark.

Chapter xvi. Paul, now accompanied by Silas, travels to the old mission fields near Antioch and in Asia Minor, where he circumcises his companion, Timothy, and delivers to the churches the decrees from Jerusalem (1–5). The Holy Spirit prevents the apostles from going farther into Asia Minor. Not until they reach Troas does Paul have a vision about their further travels: they are to go to Macedonia (6–10). At Philippi, Paul preaches in the Jewish place of prayer outside the city gate. After he has won to the faith Lydia, and a slave girl who has a gift of soothsaying, Paul and Silas are put in prison. By means of a miraculous earthquake during the night they are set free and taken into the house of the prison guard, who is baptized with his household. Paul and Silas leave Philippi the next morning (11–40).

Chapter xvii. In Thessalonica, the Jews force Paul from the newly founded church (1–9), and also force him to leave the next town, Berea (10–15). Paul comes to Athens, where he is active among both Jews and Gentiles (16–21), and delivers an address to the court of the Areopagus (22–34).

Chapter xviii. In Corinth, where he encounters his future helpers Aquila and Priscilla, Paul preaches for some time in the synagogue, but leaves it to preach to the Gentiles. An attempt by the Jews to have Paul arraigned before the court fails when Gallio, the proconsul, refuses to hear their complaint (1–17). The apostle journeys to Ephesus and Caesarea on his way to Jerusalem (18–23), while a new helper, Apollos, preaches, first in Ephesus, later in Corinth (24–28).

Chapter xix. In Ephesus, Paul baptizes disciples of John the Baptist (1–7) and preaches at first only in the synagogue but later to all the inhabitants of the city and of the province for a period of two years. As a healer, Paul overcomes all those who practice magic to effect their cures (8–20). Paul, who has decided to return to Jerusalem through Macedonia and Greece, and from there to Rome, is faced with a silversmiths' demonstration against his work. They consider that he attempted to deprive the goddess Artemis and her temple of all honor (21–40).

Chapter xx. Paul now travels through Asia and Macedonia to

Corinth; and instead of taking ship from there to Palestine, he doubles back with a large group by land, because of a Jewish conspiracy against his life. He does not take ship until he reaches Philippi (1–6), and goes by way of Troas (7–16) to Miletus. There he addresses the elders from Ephesus and takes his leave of them (17–38).

Chapter xxi. Paul reaches Ptolemais and Caesarea where, in Philip the evangelist's house, the prophet Agabus predicts Paul's imprisonment and hardships in Jerusalem (1–14). There they are joyfully welcomed by James and the elders who, in their concern over the Jewish reaction to Paul's arrival, suggest that Paul demonstrate his maintenance of Jewish customs by participating in the purification of four men who are under a Nazirite vow (15–26). This demonstration of Paul's loyalty to Judaism misses the mark. Jews from Ephesus provoke the mob to attack Paul and kill him. He is rescued by soldiers of the Roman tribune who carry him to safety. On the way to their barracks, Paul is given permission to address the crowd (27–40).

Chapter xxii 1–29. Paul tells about his call near Damascus, but when he adds that he has been sent from Jerusalem to the Gentiles (1–21), the mob once more clamors for his death. The tribune therefore orders him brought into the barracks; thanks to his Roman citizenship, he is exempt from interrogation under the lash (22–29).

Chapter xxii 30 and xxiii. The next day Paul is sent before the Sanhedrin to be questioned, to clarify the Jewish accusations for the civil authorities, but the meeting ends in chaos (xxii 30 – xxiii 10). A conspiracy against Paul's life is revealed by his nephew to the tribune, who sends his prisoner to Caesarea, where the Roman procurator Felix receives him (xxiii 11–35).

Chapter xxiv. The Jewish authorities then present their accusations against Paul before Felix in Caesarea, but the meeting ends with the court's postponement of the case (1–23), and nothing happens on it for two years. Felix, who is about to be replaced as procurator by Festus, leaves Paul in prison in order to curry favor with the Jews who had accused him of misgovernment (24–27).

Chapter xxv. Soon Festus goes up to Jerusalem, where the Jewish authorities ask him to send Paul to them, with the intention of having him assassinated (just as they had intended doing during his earlier imprisonment in Jerusalem). At Festus' request their proposal is brought before the court in Caesarea, but when Paul is asked whether he is willing to stand trial in Jerusalem, he requests that an appeal be made to the court of Caesar in Rome (1–12). A visit by King Agrippa results in another meeting of the court at Caesarea, as Festus needs information about the case for a report to be sent along with Paul to the Emperor (13–27).

Chapter xxvi. Paul thus secures an opportunity to present his case to the court presided over by Agrippa in Rome. He speaks of his call near Damascus and of the activity that followed. The ground of his faith as a disciple of Jesus is the same as it was when he was a Pharisee (1–23). Festus and Agrippa agree that Paul is not guilty of the charges brought against him, but the appeal to the Emperor will have to stand (24–32), since he has claimed it.

Chapter xxvii. From Caesarea Paul embarks with other prisoners for Rome. It is late in the year and the voyage is slow. South of Crete the ship runs into trouble and is battered by a storm. Paul predicts that the ship will be wrecked but that all the people on board will be saved. After running aground on an island they manage to get ashore without loss of life.

Chapter xxviii. The island is identified as Malta, and the stranded men are well received. To the surprise of all the spectators, Paul escapes death from a snake bite and he cures several persons. After a stay of three months, they leave the island and sail to Puteoli, whence the last stage of the journey is made on foot. In Rome, Paul is received by the Christians and given permission to live in a rented house with a soldier guarding him (1–16). The apostle's attempt to convert the Jews in Rome fails. Once more, and for the last time, he acknowledges his people's unbelief and announces that he will turn to the Gentiles (17–28). Paul lives in Rome as a prisoner for two years but is not hindered in his missionary work (30–31).

III. LUKE'S LANGUAGE AND STYLE

Examination of the language and style of Luke in both his Gospel and the Book of Acts has illuminated the differences between him and the other New Testament authors. But two factors must be kept in mind if such an examination is to remain firmly based. Many are of the opinion that in his gospel Luke is dependent on Mark. It is, however, more correct to assume that Luke is dependent on oral tradition and also on the earliest written notes of parts of this tradition. In one form or another oral tradition underlies all the gospels. Hence it is important that we regard Luke's work not merely as an adaptation of the Marcan source, but rather as a stylistically more elegant version of the tradition about Jesus. It is likewise important to emphasize the fact that Luke is dependent on oral tradition and possible written sources, not only in Luke but also in Acts. He cannot freely invent or shape his story, but is a transmitter of tradition.

At the time of the New Testament events, Greek was the universal language of the eastern part of the Roman Empire.[5] It was the language of government, literature, commerce, and communications. In contrast to Latin in the West, which supplanted the native tongues of the conquered peoples and survives in the Romance languages, the dissemination of the Greek language in the eastern areas was neither strong nor lasting. The native tongues continued to exist side by side with the universal language and survived as languages of individual countries.

Then as now Greek existed in two separate forms: literary Greek and popular, or illiterate, Greek. Literary Greek was a continuation of classical Greek, and although it was no longer in colloquial use, this traditional but somewhat archaic language was still looked upon as the natural medium for literary work. If an epic was to be written it had to be composed in Homeric hexameters, a

[5] On the customary languages of the Jews in this period, see Appendix IX.

philosophical treatise had to imitate Plato, in a tragedy, the
choruses had to be in the Doric dialect.

Gradually a considerable divergence developed between the traditional language and popular colloquial language. We may imagine
a Greek author, perhaps a Greek-speaking Semite, using the Hellenistic language in everyday life, but in his literary production
making a determined effort to imitate models from the classical
works and frequent use of his grammar and dictionary. Thus it is
natural that in time people began to use the Hellenistic common
language as a written language. A realm of literature came into
existence written in a so-called "illiterate" language. Purely literary works were written in the classical language, but technical
works and writings with a wider appeal for the common people
(such as Artemidorus on dreams in the late second century A.D.)
were written in less ambitious literary style, even if still intended to
be Attic Greek.

Thus when New Testament language is said to be "popular"
or "illiterate," one must remember that the dividing line set between
the literate and the illiterate languages differs greatly from that
posited in our modern world. Purely literary works (and hence,
pure Greek) were reserved to a small group, while the popular
language was the property of everyone, including the literary
author when he talked with his family. But as in the development
of the language on Greek soil, the two languages began to merge.
The literary author, whom we have just seen in his home, would
be quick to insert a few classical expressions in his conversation
with other educated men. Like Luke, he would speak different
kinds of Greek with different kinds of people, depending on the
topics and the participants in the conversation. Or, to give another
example: Paul's letter to the Romans is indeed "popular" and
"illiterate" but its subject matter precludes our shedding light on it
from the papyrus letters of ordinary people.

It is here that Luke differs from most New Testament authors.
His knowledge and his skill with language are so great that he can
vary his account and his language. He avoids certain words used
by other evangelists, probably because he thought them too common. The best example of his talent for variation is found in Luke
i–ii, where his preface (i 1–4), composed in Greek literary style,
is followed by a description of the birth and childhood of John
the Baptist and of Jesus written in a completely different style.

This example leads us to another aspect of the Greek language in New Testament times. As we have seen, this common language was already spoken by non-Greek populations who were obliged to use a universal language. This was the case in Palestine: the native language, Aramaic, was itself a language known throughout the East, yet at this time Greek was dominant to such an extent that many people considered it to be the future universal language of the East—to be spoken in addition to their native tongue. Two scenes in Acts illustrate bilingual situations. In xiv 8 ff., Paul preaches the Gospel in Lystra (Asia Minor) in the usual Greek. But when the listeners are carried away by the healing of a cripple among them they use their native Lycaonian tongue (xiv 11). In xxi 40 ff., Paul starts speaking from the steps leading up to the fortress of Antonia. From the moment the excited crowd realizes that he is addressing it in Hebrew—and not, as had been expected, in Greek—it becomes "even more quiet" (xxii 2).

In such bilingual areas as the Semitic countries a merging of the universal language with the native tongue was possible. This is the reason for the controversies among scholars over "semitisms" in the New Testament. A semitism is more than the use of a Semitic word or of a Semitic but non-Greek idiom in Greek. The term can also be applied to idioms existing in both Greek and Semitic, which in the New Testament occur with a frequency characteristic of Semitic. As the New Testament books were early written records of a religious message first delivered in Aramaic, all kinds of semitisms may occur, including the new use of a Greek word to cover content hitherto expressed only in Semitic.

Luke is aware of such semitisms but is not overly anxious to use them. Thus he does not like the word "Amen," which he uses only a few times—whereas Matthew uses it five times as often and Mark twice as often. Luke's attitude to latinisms (i.e., the introduction of Latin words and expressions into Greek) is similar. He avoids Latin words used by the other evangelists for instance "quadrans" (Luke xxi 2 and parallels [hereafter abbreviated par.]) and "census" (xx 22 par.).

It does seem peculiar, however, that Luke should use semitisms—they must be considered, therefore, as deliberate additions to the style of his work. The above-mentioned example, Luke i–ii, demonstrates how Luke in describing the earliest events of the redemption story, namely, the births of John the Baptist and of Jesus, transmits these tales in idioms that must be considered

Semitic. In Luke's case it is not a question of *native* semitisms disclosing the author's Semitic origin and his rather limited knowledge of Greek; on the contrary, it is a question of *biblical* semitisms, that is, semitizing idioms which originated in the translation of the Hebrew Old Testament into Greek, the translation known as the Septuagint (LXX). Luke has deliberately chosen such biblical expressions in order to illuminate themes which he considers a continuation of what is found in the Old Testament. This procedure shows that he behaves like the Greek authors who write in the classical style, but with one decisive difference; namely that to Luke, the Septuagint is a classical work and a literary model.

To read Acts through from beginning to end is like traveling in mountainous Switzerland, a land sharply divided into separate areas which has nevertheless been molded into a whole both by nature and by human effort. Although there are different population groups with different languages and cultures, a common life with its own special characteristics is nevertheless comprised. With Acts, the individual chapters have, similarly, their own character both with regard to form and content, but they are united in a work that is infused and unified by the purpose of the author (see p. 3).

IV. LUKE AS AUTHOR OF THE ACTS OF THE APOSTLES

The earliest church tradition, from the second half of the second century, states that Luke and Acts were written by Paul's fellow worker, the physician Luke (see p. XXXII). It has in recent times been stressed that this tradition must be reliable since it would be unusual to ascribe the authorship of these two books to such a relatively unknown person as Luke. But after examining these considerations, offered to prove the reliability of the tradition, one must remember that it was possible, in the primitive church, to reach the same point of view from the same considerations *without* any earlier tradition.

It has been considered reasonable to assume that Acts was written by a man who was a fellow worker of Paul, a Gentile Christian, and a physician. We shall now examine these three assumptions to see whether they can be maintained and whether they substantiate the tradition of authorship.

It is entirely reasonable to assume that Acts was written by a fellow worker of Paul, for the second part of the book dealing with Paul's missionary work reveals a more direct knowledge of the events than the first twelve chapters, which deal with the primitive church in Palestine. And as many of these events are concerned with pioneering missionary work in parts of the world where no Christian had ever been, it does seem reasonable to look for the author among Paul's fellow workers. In addition, it is logical to look for him among the fellow workers not mentioned in Acts. This argument is bound up with the assumption that the "we" source (see p. XLII) can be traced directly to the author, whom we find speaking in the first person, whereas the other fellow workers are mentioned in the third person. This seems a likely assumption if Acts is considered to be almost contemporary with the events it describes.

In our later consideration of the purpose of Luke-Acts (Part VII), we have assumed that Luke wrote his work for a definite purpose during Paul's trial. This is in agreement with the assumption mentioned above, that the author of the "we" source accompanied Paul to Rome. If the author was Luke, then he had the opportunity in Rome to write precisely such a work as Acts. We cannot be absolutely certain that he did with our present knowledge, but we are obliged to choose the most probable explanation.

The suggestion is sometimes made that the author of Acts might have been another of Paul's fellow workers, of whom we hear a good deal in Acts and the letters (although several of the workers mentioned in the letters are not referred to in Acts—Demas, Luke, and Titus). Supposing Titus, for example, to have been the author of Acts, we should have expected him to use the "we" form in writing of the council in Acts xv, if that council was identical with the meeting which Paul mentions in Gal ii 1 ff. Further, if Titus were the author of Acts, then he would be Paul's messenger to Corinth (II Cor ii 13, vii 6, 13, 14, viii 16, 23, xii 18). But though Titus was closely associated with the collection taken for the poor in Jerusalem, he is not mentioned as accompanying Paul from Greece in Acts xx 4. In fact, almost any "fellow worker" might be considered as a possibility—the author of Acts has not left us enough information.

The view that the author of Acts was a Gentile Christian is one of the many opinions held by the Tübingen School, founded by F. C. Baur in the first half of the nineteenth century, from which scholars have not yet emancipated themselves. This school made a sharp distinction between Jewish and Gentile Christianity in the churches founded by Paul, and was therefore obliged to maintain that a man showing sympathy for the mission among the Gentiles belonged to Gentile Christianity. As will be shown below, such sympathy was common in the primitive church even among the Jewish Christians in Palestine; accordingly this argument must be considered of no value.

If it were to be applied at all to a more modern view of primitive Christianity, it would be a matter of maintaining that the author's extensive knowledge of the missions to the Gentiles excludes the possibility of his belonging to Jewish Christianity in Palestine. But we shall see later (p. LI) that, especially within Jewish Christianity, great sympathy for missions to the Gentiles did not imply any active participation in them. These missions were carried on in distant places and Paul and his companions were the ones who, from time to time, brought news of the Gentiles' acceptance of the Gospel (see p. LI).

However, even if the author did not belong to Palestinian Jewish Christianity, it is still not necessary to assert that he belonged to Gentile Christianity; for Gentile Christianity as such did not exist at all at this early date. To be sure, the Gospel had been preached to Gentiles and accepted by them, but this did not result in a Gentile Christianity. It must be realized that Gentile Christians are Gentiles who have become Christians. But the term "Gentile Christianity" also means more than that. It would mean that the converts were embracing a special type of Christianity. Not until two generations later was it possible for a Christianity to develop among the Gentiles that clearly dissociated itself from the Christianity held in common by Jews and Gentiles, the Christianity preached in the Apostolic Age. The apostles and missionaries who took the Gospel to the Gentiles were Jews, some of them Palestinian Jews. Paul was a Jew with a Palestinian background, even though he came from Tarsus in Cilicia. Although we find in his company fellow workers who were former Gentiles, they were in their faith and preaching dependent on Jewish Christianity as they encountered it in Paul and other Jews, who had been won over to Christ and sent as apostles to the Gentiles.

A comparison can be made with the experience gained by church missions in more recent times. In general the Gospel preached to the populations of the mission field has been characterized as "European" or "American" Christianity and a considerable amount of time has passed before an indigenous form of Christianity, influenced by life in the respective countries, has developed.

By "Jewish Christianity" we mean the Christianity found in the first churches formed in Palestine by Jews believing in Christ. They were Jewish, not only in a national sense, but because they were also influenced by the Jewish origin of Jesus and the apostles. As long as no other form of Christianity (as for instance, later Gentile Christianity) existed, Jewish Christianity was considered identical with Christianity; only later did the Jewish character of primitive Christianity become evident. "Jewish Christianity" is a genuine designation of content, separating the primitive believers from the Gentile Christianity of the second century. It has nothing to do with the Judaizing movement, which was an heretical Christianity which sought to extend Christianity by requiring that Christians also be Jews who are circumcised and keep the law of Moses.

As far as primitive Christianity is concerned "Gentile Christianity" posits something which never existed outside the thought of the Tübingen School.

Just as in recent times Christian missionary work has been unable to produce an Indian or Chinese Christianity in the first or second generation, so primitive Christianity in the first and second generation of converted Gentiles was likewise unable to produce a Gentile Christianity significantly different from that which the new Christians received from the Jewish-Christian missionaries, who were the apostles to the Gentiles.

The Tübingen view of "Gentile Christianity" has been based on, among other things, the misunderstandings and exaggerations of Paul's message by his Gentile Christian converts. The Corinthians' talk of liberty and the Galatians' enthusiasm for the first apostles and the church in Jerusalem developed from Paul's teaching on these points. But his congregations misunderstood what he said, interpreting it in a way which Paul had to repudiate. At this juncture the only thing that can be said with confidence about the author of Acts is that he shared Paul's enthusiasm for the mission to the Gentiles and that he knew a great deal about the first decades of this missionary work.

Our understanding of the author of Acts as a Gentile Christian— in the sense that he has great sympathy for and insight into the mission to the Gentiles—may be said to enhance the likelihood of the first premise that he was one of Paul's fellow workers. But the denial of the existence of an early Gentile Christianity, separate from Jewish Christianity, enlarges the field where we must search for the author of Acts. For it is not necessary for him to have been a Gentile Christian in order to show sympathy for the mission to the Gentiles or to know a great deal about the work in the Gentile mission field in Paul's time. We should be able to find the author among Paul's fellow workers, whether they were Jew or Gentile by birth.

The third assumption about the author of Acts, that he was a physician, provides an argument for the belief that Luke the physician wrote Acts. In his book *The Medical Language of St. Luke* (1882), W. K. Hobart was the first scholar to present weighty arguments in favor of the author's being a physician, a physician who used a medical vocabulary and was particularly interested in Jesus' acts of healing. While admitting that Hobart tried to prove too much, A. Harnack wanted to prove the same (*Lukas der Arzt*

[1906], pp. 122–37). His thesis was based on parallels from medical texts which many scholars have found convincing. In his book *The Style and Literary Method of Luke* (I [1919], pp. 39–72), H. J. Cadbury reported on his own testing and checking of this material. He compared Luke with other Hellenistic authors known not to be physicians, and found most of the supposed medical terms in their works. Even when the word list was reduced to its most striking examples, these can be found in Josephus, Plutarch, Lucian, and in the Septuagint. Thus the evidence that the author of the two-part work was a physician is not conclusive, and it can no longer be proved decisively that since the author was one of Paul's fellow workers who was a physician, he must therefore be Luke the physician. Yet, the possibility remains that he may nevertheless have been a physician. Cadbury is right in stating that we are unable to make assertions about what a physician of apostolic times could not have written. The fact remains that among Paul's fellow workers the authorship may be ascribed to several besides Luke.

It is not necessary to suppose that the author of Acts was either a physician or a Gentile Christian, and the evidence which we have is such as to preclude certainty. But it is quite unnecessary to dismiss the early Christian traditions of New Testament authorship as being without foundation or validity. It is safer to accept the traditions and ask whether in the written sources there is any supporting testimony and, if so, what value can be placed upon it.

One more argument between scholars remains, the one which rejects Luke's authorship and also the view that the author had been one of Paul's fellow workers. This argument stresses the discrepancies existing at some points between the accounts in Acts and in Paul's letters. As will be seen later (p. 84), during his first visit to Jerusalem after his experience near Damascus, Paul met only Peter and James, the Lord's brother, a fact which he confirmed by oath (Gal i 18–20). According to Acts ix 26–30, he was introduced to the apostles by Barnabas and was then received into the congregation. If Acts xv is a description of the same meeting that Paul mentions in Gal ii 1 ff., various discrepancies persist. The account of Paul's visit to Jerusalem (Acts xi 30, xii 25), must then be based on an error, as according to Gal i 18–ii 1, no more than two visits were made to the apostles in Jerusalem.

In historical sources from other fields such discrepancies are no surprise to the scholar, nor do they make him doubt the historical reliability of the accounts except at a few points where they directly contradict each other. But many New Testament scholars adopt a very stringent attitude when no complete agreement exists among the different accounts, regardless of the fact that perfect agreement would be suspect or proof of artificial construction.

Similarly, critical remarks are made about the picture of Paul presented in Acts which, according to the critics, contradicts the conception of Paul gained from his letters. So it is said that the author of Acts cannot have been a man close to Paul. Several of the contradictions here mentioned appear to be more in line with a modern conception of Paul as the austere champion of Paulinism, an arm chair theologian and not a human being. Hence, Paul's attitude toward the Law and circumcision is mentioned, and an account in Acts (xvi 3) is singled out in which Paul causes Timothy to be circumcised. Although Paul indicated in his letters (Rom x 4 ff.; Gal iii 10 ff.) that the coming of Christ signified the termination of the Law, yet he still participated in the purification of four Christians in the temple at Jerusalem (Acts xxi 20 ff.) in order to demonstrate that it was not true that he taught Jews outside Palestine to abandon the law of Moses. The critics have also been annoyed by the description in Acts (xxiii 6) of Paul maintaining at his trial that he is a Pharisee.

These points are understandable when one imagines Paul as a man with feet firmly planted on the ground, who, for this very reason, may appear full of contradictions. But some of the points made are more easily explained than would appear from the evidence given above. Thus Timothy must be considered a Jew, and Paul did not teach the Jews that they should not have their children circumcised, but he *did* teach them that they would be saved through Christ. He therefore allowed them to follow such popular customs as were not considered necessary for salvation. But he forbids the circumcision of his Gentile Christian audience, for they would then deem circumcision necessary for their salvation in addition to Christ. Like the Christians in Jerusalem, Paul held sacred the temple and such customs (including a Nazirite vow—Acts xviii 18) as were not in conflict with Christ. Not only did Paul want to be a Jew to the Jews so that he could win Jews, to be to those under the Law as one under the Law (though not himself under the Law) to win those under the Law (I Cor ix 20);

he also in relation to Christ felt himself to be a Jew and an Israelite. And for him the church is God's Israel.

A few details in the Acts picture of Paul are surprising in their
individuality; their unexpectedness has the ring of truth. When the
authorities in Philippi wanted to release Paul and Silas after they
had spent a night in prison, Paul says, no doubt to the astonishment
of everybody, "They have, without trial, publicly beaten us, who
are Roman citizens, and put us in prison. Do they now want to
release us secretly? No, on the contrary, they must themselves
come and lead us out" (xvi 37). We likewise notice the words
exchanged between Claudius Lysias and Paul in the fortress of
Antonia, when Paul was to be interrogated under flagellation.
Told that Paul is a Roman citizen, the tribune says naïvely, "I
bought this citizenship for a great sum of money," whereupon Paul
answers, "But I am a citizen by birth" (xxii 28). The same frank
way of speaking by a man who perhaps went a little too far in his
self-assertion is encountered in the trial scene before the Sanhedrin,
when the high priest orders those who stand beside the prisoner
to strike him on the mouth. Paul reacts with the words, "God
will strike you, you whited wall; you sit in judgment on me according to the Law, and contrary to the Law you order that I
shall be struck" (xxiii 3). Our fourth and last example concerns
Paul as a member of the convoy of prisoners aboard a ship on
her way to Rome. Against his advice they have left Kaloi Limenes
and have sailed straight into a storm. After the ship drifts with the
current and hunger and fear of death beset those on board, Paul
steps forward to give them courage and confidence. During the
night God has revealed to the apostle that he will save them all.
Paul begins his joyful message with the following words, seemingly
superfluous, but not for him, "Men, you should have been guided
by me, and not have sailed from Crete, then you would have
escaped these troubles and losses" (xxvii 21).

These are the traits of a living human being with his own individual features. It is not the portrait of a saint or of a bloodless
ideal, but a portrait so striking and convincing that it seems to be
drawn from life. One who could so describe Paul must have known
him intimately and loved him.

V. THE SOURCES OF LUKE'S TWO-PART WORK

In the treatment of Luke's sources, it is customary to separate the two parts of the work (see p. xv) as if Luke had always been associated with the Gospel, and Acts had always had an independent existence. This leads to the regrettable result that the two parts of the work are treated separately, with no adequate consideration of their interrelatedness. It is obvious that this method is incorrect.

Luke is discussed in connection with Matthew and Mark, as if Luke were an independent gospel and not the first part of a continuous work. Many scholars follow in their studies the traditional two-source theory according to which Matthew and Luke are based on Mark and on an oral source (Logia or Q). Alternatively, a four-source theory is sometimes taken as a basis. According to this theory the two later evangelists, in addition to Mark and Q, each used his own particular source; these have been called M and L, from the names of the two evangelists. The latter theory gives rise to a difficulty in that the arguments presented in its favor can equally well be applied against it. If more than two sources existed, why then stop at four? Would not such a complex problem as that of the parallels and differences among the gospels be more likely to be solved by an equally complex theory? In that case the obvious solution would undoubtedly be another variation of the multiple-source theory.

In this respect, too, the strange conservatism characteristic of New Testament research for the last two generations prevented radical doubt about the correctness of the traditional solution. This is best seen in Germany in the appearance of the *Formgeschichtliche* (form-critical) school at the end of the First World War. Scholars of this school, turning against the research done about the person of Jesus up to that time, attempted to trace the beginnings of gospel tradition, and to analyze its earliest form in oral tradition, and did not imagine that the traditional solution to the gospel problem would in time be subject to challenge while their work was in progress.

If the traditional solutions of the source problem are accepted, the scholar knows in advance how Luke worked when he wrote his first volume. The practical application of these theories suggests that he could look into the books lying on Luke's desk while he wrote. By comparing Mark and Luke the relationship between Luke's source and his own adaptation of it can be conveniently studied. It is possible to twist and turn the words and to find not only Luke's stylistic improvements on his source but also his theological point of view.

But it has been established that Acts is actually a continuation of Luke. It is important therefore not to make too great a distinction between the first part and its continuation. The parallels of Luke with the other three gospels incline many to dispense with Acts as a continuation of Luke. Yet, if we are to understand Luke, we must instead wonder why on earth the other evangelists stopped after the resurrection of Jesus and did not include the subsequent events for which oral tradition also existed.

On the whole, our three gospels (including Luke separate from Acts) follow the tradition about Jesus up to the account of the empty tomb (Matt xxviii 1–10; Mark xvi 1–8; Luke xxiv 1–11 [12]). From this point on there is no settled tradition but each one of the gospels gives its own account. Luke and Matthew have this in common, that they both take up the subject of the spread of the Gospel throughout the whole world (Luke xxiv 44–49 and Matt xxviii 16–20). As is well known, Mark's account suddenly breaks off. Generally one talks about a missing leaf, because of the common opinion that Mark resembles Matthew. But the missing part may have been a longer part of a roll or several pages of a codex, and we do not know what might have been written on them. The last words of Matthew contain Acts in a nutshell. Mark may—perhaps in a way different from Luke's— have continued his record of oral tradition about apostolic times. A gospel is a Christian innovation and it cannot be expected that its form would have been established at the very beginning. On the contrary, one would expect that the earliest gospels began and ended in different ways and that preservation of, or change in, the tentative forms of oral tradition also occurred in very different ways.

If Acts also sprang from oral traditions which were recorded

only sporadically when Luke wrote his preface to his entire work
(Luke i 1–4), we must reckon with Luke using the same procedure with regard to the material in Acts as he does in the
Gospel. Thus Luke and Acts originated in Luke's writing down of
oral tradition, which he had found in the Pauline churches of
Asia Minor and Greece and in the Palestinian churches he had
visited at the end of Paul's third journey. We learn from the
preface in Luke that, before he wrote this work, he knew, or at
least knew of, written records of traditions both about Jesus and
about the apostles, but we do not know the kind or the extent of
the attempts made by his predecessors.

In earlier days one reckoned with distinct written sources for
Acts. In recent times one has grown more skeptical. One realizes
that Luke used sources, but this does not mean that they can be
separated. A growing uncertainty reigns therefore concerning the
details of his use of sources. This has caused most scholars to
see a decisive difference between the use of sources in Luke and
in Acts since they think that Luke, in his Gospel, worked with
clearly defined, written sources.

This new view of the source situation in Acts derives chiefly
from dissatisfaction with the suggested division of sources. There
is yet another view, one that stresses the difference between the
use of sources in the two parts of the work from a theological
point of view. It is perhaps characteristic that historical judgments
rely more often on theological judgment than on historical arguments.

It was Martin Dibelius (*Aufsätze zur Apostelgeschichte*, 1951)
who started a new trend in Acts research. He was of the opinion
that in the case of Acts no tradition existed corresponding to the
tradition behind the gospels. Thus Luke does here not appear as
transmitter of tradition but as author. For this reason one cannot
pursue *Formgeschichtliche* studies in Acts but only critical investigations of style. Dibelius introduced the trend in research
which culminated in Ernest Haenchen's commentary, *Die Apostelgeschichte* (13th ed., 1961), in which the aim is to explain
Acts as a work of Luke the author, one who deals highhandedly
with the material he found and invents new tales for the edification
of the church. Implicit in the work of Dibelius and Haenchen
are two theses: one, that there was no preaching about the apostles
in the primitive church, the other, that what is historical cannot be
edifying.

These modern German views and their effect on the exegesis of Acts must be rejected. As it would take too much space to deal with the second thesis, I imagine that it may be sufficient to present a rebuttal of the first thesis only, namely, that one did not preach about the apostles in the primitive church. If this can be proved wrong, it will then be obvious that the early church found historical material edifying.

Jacob Jervell has demonstrated (*Studia Theologica* 16 [1962], 25–41) that it is wrong to maintain with Dibelius and Haenchen that there is no possibility of a tradition about the apostles which might have existed alongside the tradition about Jesus. An examination of Paul's letters proves that prevailing conditions were favorable to the formation of a tradition from apostolic times.

Accounts of the acts of the apostles and the faith of the church have their place in the preaching and life of the church. Thus in Rom i 8, Paul gives thanks to God that the faith of the Roman church is preached all over the world, and in I Thess i 8 ff., we see that a church's faith as such can constitute the content of the message. "The word of the Lord" is identical with the faith of the Thessalonians. The "word" is here, by that very faith, fused with those who hear it. The same is the case in II Cor iii 1–3, where the Corinthian church constitutes for Paul, his letter of recommendation, Christ's letter to the world, in contrast to the Law, which is written on stone tables. Thus the Pauline gospel, including the Corinthians' faith, is a letter of recommendation (see Col i 4).

When Paul mentions that he has fully preached the word of God (Rom xv 19; Col i 25; cf. II Tim iv 17), it is by means of his missionary work among the Gentiles (on the grace of God, see II Cor iv 15; I Cor xv 10).

Other points of view are expressed in II Thess i 4, where Paul gives an account of the Thessalonians to the other churches he founded. The faith of the church in Thessalonica is a confirmation of God's calling of Paul. Moreover, to Paul the Gospel is a comfort to sufferers. God, from whom all comfort comes (II Cor i 3 ff.), can through a sufferer, through the church's steadfastness in the faith, comfort others. This is seen in I Thess iii 6, where Timothy returns to Paul bringing him *the gospel* of the faith and love of the Thessalonians. It is correct to maintain with Jervell that here Paul speaks about bringing the Gospel. A connection exists between the apostle and the church, which explains this allusion (I Thess ii 19; cf. II Cor i 14; vii 3; Philip ii 16; cf. II Cor vii 4–13).

What we have found in the *paraclesis,* invocation, is also found in the *parenesis,* exhortation. In II Cor viii–ix, we find Paul telling the Corinthians about the churches in Macedonia where he has formerly stressed the goodwill of the Corinthians (viii 1 ff., ix 1 ff.). Thus the collection for the poor in Jerusalem provides the opportunity of spreading information about the different churches, including the church in Jerusalem. Just as Christ, who though he was rich, became poor for our sake so that by his poverty others might become rich (viii 9), so the poverty of a church can make many rich (viii 2). The gift made by a church is a manifestation of its attitude to life (ix 12 ff.). Everybody has heard of the Roman church as an example of obedience (Rom xvi 19). An apostle may himself serve as a model, and to follow an apostle is to follow God; and churches, in becoming imitators of the apostles and of the Lord, may also become examples (I Thess i 6 ff.). This exalted role of the apostle is not dependent on the purely historical person but on the charismatic figure serving as an exemplar.

Just as Paul speaks of the churches he established, so in the same way accounts must have been given about the church in Jerusalem. The church in Thessalonica was undoubtedly an example to the churches in Macedonia and Achaia, but the church of Jerusalem was the original model (I Thess ii 14). The Thessalonian church knows about the persecutions it has suffered and about its relation to its Jewish countrymen (I Thess ii 14–16). For God's word started from Jerusalem (I Thess ii 14; cf. I Cor xiv 36) and the Gentile Christians owe this church a debt of gratitude for having shared its spiritual gifts (Rom xv 26–27).

We also find that the tradition about Jesus and the tradition about the apostles cannot be separated. Our Lord's appearance before Peter and the Twelve (I Cor xv 3 ff.) was part of the original *kerygma.* The Gospel, which here is given in a mighty condensed form, contains both the account of the death and resurrection of Jesus and the account of the revelations to Peter and the apostles and perhaps also to a large number of members of the primitive church. Paul can take it for granted that Peter and the twelve apostles are known to the churches. "What Paul transmits is the preaching of the primitive church, which at the same time is a preaching on the primitive church. What Paul has received from men is God's word, which also speaks of men" (Jervell, p. 39).

Jervell is in this way able to show that favorable conditions existed for the formation of a tradition about apostolic times. The preaching which took place was about the apostles and about the rise of the individual churches. The congregational life in faith was used in *paraclesis* and *parenesis*. The particular events of apostolic times form an inseparable part of all forms of Christian preaching and instruction, and for this reason the basic assumption of the scholars of the "form-critical" school must be rejected.

As Luke had at his disposal an abundance of material both about Jesus and about apostolic times, the conception of Luke as an edifying author maintained by Haenchen, must be dropped. In Haenchen's view, Luke shaped what he knew or thought he knew into tales which were not based on his sources or on his personal experience, but were the result of his theological ideas. For instance, as he regards Paul as a holy man, who as such must have performed miracles, Luke speaks of healings which Paul is supposed to have performed. But no attention is paid to the fact that wonders performed by the apostle are mentioned not only in Acts but also in Paul's letters (see Rom xv 17–19; II Cor xi 21–xii 12).

This view is even more to be deplored as we have historical material demonstrating the inventive narrative technique of an edifying author of that time. Two edifying miracle stories have been preserved within Greek-speaking Jewry, namely, III Maccabees and Aristeas. When Luke's work is compared with Aristeas, the difference between an account of events and an edifying story can be clearly seen. The author of Aristeas speaks of Jerusalem and Palestine in such a way that it must be assumed that he has never been there or read descriptions of the conditions there. Apart from the fact that he seems to have acquired some of his incorrect information from the Old Testament, he is describing an ideal country and an ideal city. With regard to Egypt it is a different matter, for he did know the conditions there. One must suppose that he looked into the archives in order to write the edict of liberation of the Jewish slaves (Aristeas xxii–xxvii) as convincingly as possible, but its content is freely invented and its form shows characteristics that do not belong in a Ptolemaic edict. In this respect Acts is very different. The historical events related may be influenced by the author's purpose in writing his work; but on the whole they bear the stamp of reality which is the property of history, rather than of the historical novel.

The discussion started by Dibelius and further developed by

Haenchen must be considered a return to theories advanced by the Tübingen School in its time (see p. XXXVII). Again Acts is treated as though it were a *Tendenzschrift*, a piece of propaganda whose purpose supposedly distorts history or replaces it with free invention. All the arguments advanced in the period between the two hypotheses (Tübingen and Dibelius) in proof of the historicity of the account are forgotten.

In a study of the possible sources of Acts three problems in particular are to be examined: the account of the history of the primitive church in the first half of the book, the so-called "we" passages, and the speeches.

a. It was generally assumed that the author was further removed from the events in the earliest history of the church (i–xii) than from those which he later described (xiii–xxviii), and therefore the source problem in the first part of Acts was treated separately. Moreover it was thought that repetitions could be found, the same material being used in the account more than once. These repetitions went back to different sources originating in Jerusalem, Caesarea, and Antioch (in Syria). Individual passages were also put together and ascribed to sources according to the principal figures appearing in them, for instance, the apostle Peter and the evangelist Philip. As has been mentioned before (p. XXXVIII), these separations of sources have in recent times met with a growing skepticism or at any rate with a growing reserve on the part of scholars.

b. The so-called "we" source, comprising a series of texts in Acts, related in the "we" form, is another problem. After the account of the departure from Greece of Paul and his companions (xx 4), we learn that "These went ahead, and waited for us at Troas" (xx 5). The passages in question are the following "we" texts: xvi 10–17, xx 5–xxi 18, xxvii 1–xxviii 16. It was formerly assumed that, in these passages, Luke used as his source an eyewitness account which he inserted into his version without removing the no longer appropriate "we"; or that the author of Acts was identical with the eyewitness speaking in these passages. It has been thought that the use of the "we" form is an artificial change from the general use of the third person in Acts. Thus this change is supposed to have no connection with the sources of the work but to be a purely stylistic variation. This assumption does not seem convincing. As the use of "we" is not a generally used stylistic feature of Luke's work but limited to the journeys from Troas to Philippi, from Philippi to Jerusalem, and from Caesarea to Rome, it is difficult to assume that, as now suggested, it is only an expression of a literary trend and not meant to indicate an historical state of affairs.

The "we" source takes the narrator from Asia Minor to Philippi, later from Philippi to Jerusalem and, via Caesarea, to Rome. It would be pedantic to limit the "we" source simply to those verses in which this pronoun is used without considering the context. So it is natural to allow the first use of the "we" source to include the last part of the journey in Asia Minor and the stay in Philippi. The same holds for chapters xx–xxviii where the word "we" is not used between xxi 18 and xxvii 1, but it is reasonable to suppose that the intervening part, the account of Paul's trial in Jerusalem and Caesarea, is also covered by the "we" source.

It has been common practice to ascribe these "we" passages to Luke and thence assume that we know that he stayed several years in Philippi, accompanied Paul from there to Jerusalem, and stayed close to Paul during the trial in Palestine and Paul's journey to Rome. The alternative is that Luke used an account here which originated with another of Paul's fellow workers. As it must be assumed that the accounts of Paul's journey to Macedonia and Greece after his departure from Philippi depend in any case on other people's reports, these accounts would have been taken over without use of the "we" form. Thus there is reason to maintain that the "we" source goes back to the author of Luke-Acts.

c. The speeches in Acts have for a long time been thought to be the work of Luke. Similarly, the speeches in the Greek historical works express their authors' opinions rather than those of the speaker. This very summary verdict on the Greek historians cannot be applied to Luke without reservation. Obviously Luke did not have reports of the speeches, in the modern sense of the word, which he was able to use in the writing of his work. It is likewise obvious that he has given the speeches the form in which we now have them, but it cannot be assumed as a matter of course that Luke, who in the larger part of his entire work is a faithful transmitter of tradition, should use a completely different procedure in the speeches in the second part of his work.

Just as we compared the individual chapters of Acts to the various sharply differentiated valleys and landscapes in Switzerland which in spite of everything have common characteristics, so we must ascribe to the speeches in Acts both their individuality and their coherence in context. An author bent on edifying his readers would probably have seen to it that complete conformity was established between the individual speeches. But Luke did not do this; he did not want to write an "edifying" book; nor do the speeches differ for the sake of variation. For Luke really knew something about what was being said and done in apostolic times.

In some speeches the individual stamp is much in evidence; for instance in Stephen's speech in vii 2–53 and in Paul's speeches in xiv 15–17 (Lystra), xvii 22–31 (Athens), and xx 18–35 (Miletus). The history of biblical research shows how difficult it has been to consider Stephen's speech as something Luke freely invented. For some time Paul's speech before the court of the Areopagus was considered an alien element in Acts, originated by another author. And it is commonly admitted that Paul's speech in Miletus is related to the Pauline letters.

The close agreement between Peter's speeches in Acts (ii–v, x–xi) and Paul's speech in xiii 16–41 (in Pisidian Antioch) was early observed. In the case of Peter, Luke must have been dependent on the information he could gather from other fellow workers associated with Paul who, including Paul himself, were in contact with Jewish Christianity in Palestine or from Palestinian Christians whom he met during his sojourn of several years in Palestine. Paul's speech in Pisidian Antioch has resemblances to Peter's speeches in the preceding chapters but not to the Lystra, Athens, and Miletus speeches (xiv 15–17, xvii 22–31, and xx 18–35). This is not surprising, as these speeches were delivered to Gentiles and Gentile Christians while the speech in Antioch, like Peter's speeches, was addressed to Jews. While one must maintain that there is a tradition behind the speeches in Acts, including those in the first part, it may here be more justifiable than it is usually to consider in regard to Peter's speeches whether this traditional material was connected with the actual situations to which it was attached. This does not hold for the Pentecost address (ii 14–36), for on such an occasion words are more apt to be remembered; whereas speeches such as iii 12–26, iv 9–12, v 30–32, and x 34–43 could more easily have been reconstructed on the basis of a general knowledge of Peter's sermons.

If Luke had a wider tradition on which to draw in the speeches in Acts, one may well ask if resemblances cannot be traced back to the author's purpose in writing his work. He who selects can

in so doing take into account his literary aim, so that the speeches
selected, and their themes, will show more agreement than would
appear in the material as a whole. During Paul's trial, the resurrection of Jesus is a decisive point in the accused man's account
of the relationship between Judaism and Christianity. And even if
the circumstances in which Peter's speeches are delivered provide a
quite natural opportunity to speak about the resurrection of Jesus,
it is of value to notice that this theme of the early chapters corresponds to an important point in Paul's trial and therefore to
Luke's purpose in writing the two-part work.

VI. THE TIME OF COMPOSITION

Since Luke's work forms a whole, one may assume that Luke and Acts were written at the same time. It has been customary among many scholars to base the dating of Acts on Luke and to adhere in the case of Luke to the general views concerning the mutual relationship of the first three gospels. Regardless of whether one favors the two-source or the four-source theory (see p. xxxvi), it is not possible by the use of either to arrive at a definite date of composition. Therefore Luke's two-part work must be dated on the information to be gained from the work itself. Later investigations will then show whether the relative dating of the gospels agrees with the results attained by the dating of Luke-Acts.

The earliest date for the writing must obviously fall after the last events related in Acts, that is, the two years Paul spent as a prisoner in Rome following his appeal from Caesarea to the court of Caesar. (Of course the work may well have been started within the two-year period in Rome or even a little earlier, but it was not published until the Roman imprisonment could be included in the work.)

Determination of the latest date for the writing presents greater difficulty. In this case, the above-mentioned relative dating of the first three gospels has influenced the late dating of Luke. It has been urged by modern scholars, as a further argument in favor of Luke's being written late in the first century, that in Jesus' prophetic account of the destruction of Jerusalem, the author has given a detailed picture of the siege of Titus in A.D. 70 that corresponds closely to the actual course of events as it is known from the Jewish historian Josephus. On this hypothesis Luke (xix 43–44, xxi 20, 24) must have been written after A.D. 70.

It is true that in this matter Luke differs from Matthew and Mark, but in his account the words of Jesus are filled with references to Old Testament prophecies about Jerusalem's siege and destruction, the death of its inhabitants and their exile among the

Gentiles (see C. H. Dodd, "The Fall of Jerusalem and the 'Abomination of Desolation,'" *Journal of Roman Studies* 37 [1947], 47–54). As Luke's accounts of the future do not go beyond these Old Testament predictions—they have even kept the exact wording of a few of these—the prophecies of Jesus that he presents are not his adaptations of passages from Mark and Matthew but independent predictions reinforcing Old Testament prophecy. The alleged agreement in detail with the Roman siege of A.D. 70 is therefore wholly unconvincing and it becomes much more reasonable to date the composition of Luke before A.D. 70.

Scholars have also tried to find proof of a late date of composition in the suggestion that Luke depended on a work by Josephus, *The Jewish Antiquities* (hereafter abbreviated *Ant.*) XX.5, which was not available till the nineties. In his speech before the Sanhedrin (Acts v 34 ff.), Gamaliel (Paul's teacher) attests that there were popular leaders in earlier times who had been considered dangerous, but that the danger had disappeared upon the death of these leaders. Gamaliel's purpose is to show that the disciples of Jesus can no longer be considered dangerous, because their leader had been executed by the Romans. Gamaliel gives two examples; one is Theudas, whose rebellion occurred under the procurator Cuspius Fadus, that is, in the middle of the forties. This is strange since Gamaliel was supposed to have delivered his speech a decade earlier, in the thirties.

Even stranger is the second example; Judas the Galilean; Gamaliel refers to him as coming "after" Theudas whereas his rebellion occurred as early as A.D. 6–7. Here, then, Luke appears to have been mistaken. Attempts have been made to explain away the mistakes by asserting that at this point Luke depended on Josephus who named the two rebels in the same order, and that he, reading carelessly, supposed the order given by Josephus to be chronological and expressed this in Gamaliel's words. As Luke is in agreement with Josephus only as regards the order, an assumption of literary dependence is not very likely and does not help to establish a late date of composition.

Further consideration shows how forced this argument is. While Luke's and Josephus' remarks about Theudas have a few traits in common, there is no proof at all that Luke is dependent on Josephus where Judas the Galilean is concerned. His death is not mentioned by Josephus, nor is the dispersal of his followers after his death. Only an unusually careless reader of the *Antiquities* would be likely to miss the fact that Judas' followers played an important part in Palestine after his death and continued to do so till the destruction of Jerusalem. Josephus actually lists them as a fourth party, side by side with the Essenes, Sadducees, and Pharisees (*Ant.* XVIII.1).

Thus, while the arguments in favor of a late date of composition for Luke-Acts are unconvincing, several cogent reasons can be stated in favor of an early dating. Only those based on Acts will be discussed.

a. As is well known, Acts contains much information on existing conditions at the time of Paul, and much on the geographical, historical, and political conditions in Palestine, as well as in many Roman provinces. This detailed information and the imposing gallery of Christians of the first generation, and of contemporary kings and procurators presented in the work are of such a nature that they could not have been obtained at a later date. It is wrong to think that large parts of this material are figments of the author's imagination, produced from a desire to illustrate his theological ideas. An author of moral tales would choose a very different procedure: he would not include many details without theological significance, which might arouse suspicion about the historical nature of his work.

It is therefore reasonable to maintain that this information is reliable and must have originated with an author roughly contemporary with the circumstances he describes. It cannot be denied that it is not possible in all cases either to confirm or to deny the correctness of the information Luke provides. But it is possible to confirm its correctness in a few cases. To be sure, later writers may often be guilty of anachronisms, but the lapse of time involved in Luke's case is so slight as to make this factor negligible. After all, Luke was alive at the time of the events he records, and had a lively recollection of those he witnessed.

In the account of Paul's stay in Corinth, Gallio the proconsul is mentioned. At the beginning of the fifties when Paul was there, Achaia was a province of the Senate, governed by a proconsul, but even as late as A.D. 44 Achaia and Macedonia were united under an imperial legate. The mention of politarchs in Thessalonica refers to a title most often used in Macedonia for non-Roman magistrates in the cities. Luke's mention of Iconium illustrates the new information provided by Ramsay about conditions in Asia Minor in apostolic times (see p. LVI). Geographically Iconium as well as Lystra and Derbe is part of Lycaonia, but in Acts, Iconium is not mentioned as a Lycaonian city. This can be observed in xiv 6, where Paul leaves Iconium and flees to "the cities of Lycaonia—Lystra and Derbe—and the region round them." For a long time it was thought that Luke was in error about this, but Ramsay has shown that the official Roman dividing line was not recognized by the people of Iconium, so that Luke's words are an expression of local judgment with regard to the relationship between Phrygia and Lycaonia.

b. The second argument in favor of an early date of composition is the prominence of Paul in Acts. One half of Acts deals with his life and work; it comprises the most important—one might say climactic—part of the book. A late author would have been unable to ascribe so much importance to the apostle. The same thing can be said about such an author's readers, who naturally would question the need for attributing so much importance to Paul.

Thanks to Paul's letters and Acts, we now know a good deal about the apostle and can form a picture of his importance in the history of the primitive church—a picture different from the one in the last third of the first century. With the rapid march of history, the problems Paul had had to struggle with had been solved. Even if the solution found was not always the one proposed by Paul, it often depended on his contributions. Paul, though often not fully understood, had won such a tremendous victory that he was no longer of current interest, so of course he appeared to be either obviously right or quite out-of-date. At the *end* of the first century the controversies of Paul must often have seemed irrelevant to the contemporary scene. They are, however, a faithful record of their own time.

Another chronological datum can be obtained by noticing that Luke wrote his work without making use of Paul's letters. This would seem to indicate that no collection of the letters was available in his time—which also speaks in favor of an early date of composition. Luke, being without the most important source dealing with Paul and all primitive Christianity, makes mistakes about details documented in Paul's letters. Nor can we expect Luke to present a flawless description of Paul. He is capable neither of presenting a picture corresponding to the one-sided understanding of modern scholars, nor of entirely avoiding following sources not in complete agreement with the apostle's own words in the letters.

Luke may also have understood Paul in a way that differed from
Paul's understanding of himself, but what makes his presentation
attractive is precisely the independent picture drawn of the apostle,
with features which would have been noticed only by a contemporary observer.

From the scanty material available, we are able to conclude
that in the second half of the first century the twelve apostles
were recognized by the Christians as the true leaders of the church,
carriers of the tradition concerning Jesus from the beginning, and
true apostles to the Gentiles. In those days the oldest was considered the truest and the most important; therefore Jesus' earliest
disciples had the highest authority. After them the Old Testament
was the most important proof of the age of Christianity, because
Moses was older than Pythagoras and Plato. Moreover, the earliest
disciples, the twelve apostles, had been sent forth by Jesus "to
proclaim from the housetops" what had been whispered in their
ears (Matt x 27). Therefore they became carriers of the tradition,
handing it down to posterity. Thus, to be sure, the twelve apostles
provided some leadership to the primitive church and were directly
or indirectly carriers of the tradition; but they were not—certainly
not all twelve of them—of such importance in leading the church
or in the history of transmission as posterity claims.

It is, on the other hand, difficult to see how according to later
tradition they could also have been apostles to the Gentiles. We
know from Paul that Peter was called to be an apostle to Israel,
just as Paul himself was the apostle to the Gentiles (Gal ii 7),
and Luke knew that Peter had preached to Gentiles at the house
of Cornelius (Acts x). This isolated event did not lead to missionary work among the Gentiles, but later became of importance
to the Jerusalem congregation's view of its mission to the Gentiles.
But the great reinterpretation of the history of primitive Christianity
is of a later date. This is bound up with the process of recording
and spreading the tradition of Jesus, a process incomprehensible
unless the Pauline and other Gentile-Christian churches had absorbed traditions of Jesus which they were eager to disseminate.

Paul was the originator of this development. He liked to talk
about the earliest apostles and about Jerusalem, although all this
was distant in time and place and had no connection with the
daily life of the Gentile-Christian congregations. Jervell's account,
mentioned above (p. xxxix), made us aware that the Pauline
churches had extensive knowledge about the apostles and the Jerusa-

lem church. These accounts of distant Jewish Christianity are misinterpreted by the Galatian Judaizers (see p. LXIII) in such a way that they deny the agreement and co-operation actually existing between Peter and Paul. In Corinth too, there were people who gave their adherence to Peter, as though his teaching differed from Paul's (I Cor i 11–13, xv 11).

We are ignorant of the details about the further phases of the development; we know only the final result. The twelve apostles become apostles to the Gentiles; they are described just as Paul is described; their journeys and wonderful deeds are depicted in imitation of the canonical Acts. According to later accounts, they meet in the upper room in order to divide up the whole world among themselves and they set forth to convert the Gentiles, ending as martyrs after many trying experiences. Such a picture of the Twelve has no room for a thirteenth apostle. Paul was, indeed, eminently successful in leaving his own stamp on the twelve apostles, as they are pictured in the later sources, but at the same time he was forgotten, and the acts of which his modesty forbade him to speak have instead provided the relatively unknown apostles, who preach only to the Jews in Palestine, with laurel wreaths.

c. This must be seen in connection with the fact that the Gentile Christian churches had completely forgotten their antecedents. It is in this case not so much a question of the men who carried the Gospel to the Gentiles but of the strange, slow development which the church had to undergo in order to undertake missions to Gentiles.

Jesus had been sent to Israel in Palestine (Matt xv 24), and he sent his disciples to the Jews there, but specifically forbade them to go to Samaritans or Gentiles (Matt x 5–6). After the death and resurrection of Jesus, his disciples continued this work in Jerusalem and preached to Jews only. When persecutions after Stephen's death forced the members of the congregation to flee to other lands, missionary work among the Gentiles was started in Antioch where Paul, who had received his call as a missionary to the Gentiles at Damascus, also shared in this work (Acts xi 19–26). Disagreement in Antioch caused Paul and Barnabas to return to Jerusalem, where they learned that Peter at one time had preached to some Gentiles at the house of Cornelius in Caesarea. This isolated event had had no effect (Acts xv 1 ff.), but now it was taken as a precedent and made the congregation take a positive stand with regard to missions to the Gentiles in far-distant Syria. As late as Paul's return to Jerusalem, the congregation there is found to be well-disposed toward missions to the Gentiles but just as passive about them as earlier (Acts xxi 17 ff.).

This rather surprising but historically reliable picture has been preserved by Luke, but it was lost in the church's picture of its own past, which appears to be modeled on Matthew in that after his resurrection, Jesus sends his apostles away from Palestine to go to the Gentiles and make them all his disciples (xxviii 18-20). There may have been many reasons for this situation. The mission to the Jews was futile, as Paul declared in Rom x 5-21, and the nature of the Christian church, as being chiefly made up of Christian Gentiles, was given emphasis by the destruction of Jerusalem in A.D. 70, a destruction which probably also led to the complete obliteration of early Jewish Christianity as well as to that of the Essene community at Qumran. Later it was not possible to remember and to understand that at the outset the church had considered the conversion of Israel its most crucial task. In this respect Jewish Christianity and Paul had been in agreement. But now it was thought that from the start the bringing of the Gospel to the Gentiles had followed a straight course. Therefore Luke's account testifies to his having lived and written during the Apostolic Age, when all this was contemporaneous to him.

d. Formerly, scholars liked to stress the picture presented in Acts of the friendly attitude displayed by the Roman authorities toward the Christians. It was the Jews who were the persecutors and the Romans who stopped the persecution. This no doubt gives a correct picture of the situation as it was to begin with, when the Romans still looked upon the Christians as a sect within Judaism, a recognized religion (*religio licita*).

It seems strange that in biblical research no scholars have considered for what period this picture of the time before Nero's persecution would have remained significant. In this persecution of A.D. 64, the Christians were persecuted as adherents of an illicit religion, namely Christianity. Whether under Nero an edict had been issued against the Christians or whether their persecution can be classified as police investigation (*coercitio*), it is hard to see how, after this, memories of the past could have held any significance for anybody. For such a picture of what is no longer valid cannot possibly serve as an apology before the Roman authorities. And the evaluation of Christianity as a Jewish sect, formerly applied to it by the Roman authorities, could not be renewed. Rome's decision could not be recalled except for weighty reasons, and the two parties concerned had no desire to change their mutual relationship. Jewry insisted upon the segregation of the Christians and the Christians in turn considered themselves adherents of an independent religion not connected with Judaism.

The only time when the picture of the Roman state's originally friendly attitude toward the Christians would have been worth recalling to people's minds was the time when it was still valid but in danger of being lost. And this means that it was the time of Paul's trial, after he had made an appeal to the court of Caesar. Then it was necessary to present a picture of the conditions as they had existed till then, and to argue in favor of Christianity as a genuine expression of Judaism, a continuation of the classical line in Israel: Moses and the prophets, Messiah and the resurrection of the dead.

e. Finally, it is a matter of some consequence that the assumption of an early date of composition, in the period between Paul's first two years in Rome and his execution, provides a reasonable solution to the problem posed by Acts' strangely abrupt end. From chapter xx onward the predictions of Paul's hardships and death occur, but after the author has thus prepared his readers for the apostle's death, the account suddenly breaks off without indicating the outcome of the trial. Did his trial, as we should expect, end with the death of the apostle or was he acquitted to continue his work for a few years, until his execution in Rome during the reign of Nero? It is a reasonable assumption that this question is not answered because it could not be answered. Acts closes in Rome two years after Paul's arrival there. The trial is not over. Will it end with the sentencing of the apostle or will he be acquitted? Would it be possible for Luke's work to influence the verdict by presenting a picture of Christianity and of Paul, which would enable Paul to continue his work as apostle to the Gentiles?

A survey of other explanations that have been offered will emphasize the value of the suggestion just made. It has been proposed that the length of the papyrus roll could have forced the author to stop when he did—hardly a convincing argument when one considers that the papyrus roll could have been increased by pasting new leaves onto it. No external circumstances forced the author to stop.

Another proposal suggests that the author intended to continue his work in a third volume. This is possible, but without evident basis. Nor can one discern any sensible reason for ending this volume at that particular point. A third explanation maintains that with Paul's arrival in Rome, Luke had fulfilled his purpose in writing this part of the work. But to this the objection can be made that Rome is certainly not "the ends of the earth" mentioned in Acts i 8. Nor does primitive Christianity, which from Jerusalem spread westward within the Roman empire, consider Rome its goal. Rome did not become a Christian center of decisive importance until a later stage in the development of the church had been reached.

There are other explanations for the abrupt end of Acts. It is said, for example, that in an apologetic work addressed to the Roman authorities it would be thought tactless to mention the execution of Paul by the Romans, and consequently this fact was omitted. Or it is suggested that if Paul had spent two years in Rome without his accusers having appeared before the court of Caesar, their failure to appear would have caused the suit to be discharged, resulting in Paul's release.

All these and other explanations of the same kind are undermined by the fact that Luke did prepare the reader for the death of Paul in his work. It is therefore unlikely that he would have deliberately avoided an account of Paul's death.

Since certain points in Luke's work clearly indicate an early date of composition—at the beginning of the sixties—there is good reason to favor that date. It is simply not possible to use relative chronologies based on internal comparisons among the gospels as arguments against an early date for Luke-Acts, until the datings proposed either by source critics or members of other schools can be demonstrated beyond cavil to have a firmer foundation than is at present the case.

VII. THE PURPOSE OF LUKE'S WORK

The purpose of Luke's two-part work must be determined without regard to the present position of the Gospel of Luke or to the title The Acts of the Apostles (added to Acts at a later date), with its associations concerning the genre of the book. We shall try to deal with the two parts in their original connection, in an attempt to find a purpose for the work that would seem reasonable to the people of the first century. In the preceding part, we saw that the usual late dating of Acts is not likely to be correct, and for this reason we are obliged to work with a date of composition somewhere between Paul's two-year stay as a prisoner in Rome, as related in Acts xxviii 30–31, and his death during the reign of Nero (probably some time before the persecution of Christians began in Rome).

Looking back upon the history of biblical research, we find that the Tübingen School (see p. xxx) was of the opinion that Acts is a piece of propaganda intended to represent an adjustment of the original contrast between Jewish and Gentile Christianity. According to this view, the marked contrast between the two, to which the earliest Christian writings testify, grew gradually weaker in the course of the first two centuries, so that the history of the primitive church ended with a compromise between them in the form of "the old Catholic church."

Acts is actually an example of the compromise between the two contrasting groups, for it describes Peter, the representative of Jewish Christianity, and Paul, the apostle to the Gentiles, no longer as contrasting but as parallel figures.

Acts, the Tübingen School maintained, was such a conciliatory piece of propaganda, that it was completely unhistorical. If information of an historical nature was to be found there, it was badly distorted and for that reason not reliable; therefore the book was not supposed to have been written until the first half of the second century.

Ironically, this purely academic reconstruction of the history of the primitive church assumed its greatest importance through works written against such a reconstruction. In the case of Acts, two men should be mentioned who, each in his own way, helped to guide biblical research into fruitful fields.

The first is William Ramsay (1851–1939), a Scottish archaeologist who became aware of the Tübingen School's view of Acts as unhistorical through his journeys in Asia Minor and his studies in Roman history. When he found that various pieces of information in Acts were actually correct and could not have been easily accessible at a later date, Ramsay posed the question of how a later author could possibly be absolutely correct in his statements about conditions that existed around the middle of the first century. He concluded that Acts could not have been written in the second century, and that the precise statements about even relatively unimportant matters could be explained only on the assumption that the author was a contemporary of Paul, and had known the regions in which the apostle traveled either from personal experience or from the oral reports of others. We have already given an example (p. XLVIII) of such an observation made by Ramsay.

The other scholar is Adolf Harnack (1851–1930). Like Ramsay, Harnack was convinced of Luke's personal knowledge of the events recorded. According to Harnack, Luke the physician was the author of the "we" source and Paul's companion (see p. XLII). In his dating of Acts (and Luke), Harnack ascribes the date of composition to Paul's Roman imprisonment, that is, to the early sixties.

Ramsay and Harnack and many of their contemporaries thought of Luke as an historian. This was before the eschatological point of view had been introduced in biblical research, before anybody would think it strange that primitive Christianity, like classical Greece, had found its historian. And the idea that Luke was an historian who tried in Acts to give an account of the history of the primitive church has much to recommend it. Nonetheless, it is wrong. The juxtaposition of Luke and the Greek historians, so often suggested, serves only to show up their differences. The only thing that really links them together is their honest determination to relate what they thought had happened. Luke possessed enough Greek culture so as to be thought in a modest degree to resemble the Greek historians. But his real concern lay outside the Greek world, namely, in his allegiance to a Christianity deeply rooted in the Old Testament. Though he used his skill in matters of language and style to write a work which could be read by educated Greeks, that was not his sole purpose (see p. xxv f.).

It has been suggested that Luke intended his work to be an apology. Since the days of liberal theology, an apologetic point of view has frequently manifested itself in New Testament studies. But its adherents failed to pay attention to the fact that liberal theology's conception of apologetics cannot be applied to the New Testament. Confronted with the lofty view of culture held by their contemporaries, liberal theologians wanted to demonstrate that religion is the core of all culture, and that Christianity is the highest of all religions. They aspired in this way to defend Christianity. These apologetic works clearly fix a norm. One knows in advance where the highest value is to be found, and one then asks whether one's own religion, considered inalienable, is to be included in this highest value. The norm fixed is generally used as a basis for defending Christianity, and this object is attained by furnishing a description of Christianity which is as close as possible to the norm. Primitive Christianity had no knowledge of such a fixed norm and, moreover, showed no interest in apologetics. It was not on the defensive but on the offensive. Its outward spread was accompanied by a desire for expansion and was not concerned with any inward accommodation to Jewry or to the new Hellenistic mission fields. One can say with Paul that one has "become everything to everybody, so as by all means to save some of them" (I Cor ix 22), but such missionary practice has nothing to do with apologetics.

Greek culture did not become important to Christianity until the appearance of the Christian apologists in the second century, and in the Alexandrian catechetical school, where we find men like Clement and Origen in full possession of the highest culture of their age. They, just as their more or less known predecessors, recognized the fixed norms of Greek culture. But we do not find in them anything corresponding to the view taken by modern liberal apologists or their successors to whom "modern man" has become a dogmatically fixed norm.

Thus it cannot be assumed that Luke's purpose is of an apologetic nature. In one respect only is it possible to speak of an apologetic purpose, namely, when apologetics is defined in such a way that one can consider Paul's trial a defense of Christianity that confronts the accusations brought against it, a defense which stresses its relation to the Old Testament and the people of Israel as well as the Christians' spotless reputation within the Roman state. In this connection, it seems obvious that such a defense used Roman law as a fixed norm: there has been no transgression of the law by the Christian mission. No agreement with the Jewry of that time was the prime consideration. On the contrary, from the very beginning this Jewry is thought of as a hostile power which causes the Romans to crucify Jesus and which later persecutes Paul and the Palestinian Christians. As a result, the Jews find themselves in disagreement with their sacred books as well as with their God and his Messiah. Thus the two-part work shows that, from the annunciation of the birth of Jesus to Paul's trial, there is a coherence within which God, at one and the same time Israel's Lord and the Father of our Lord Jesus Christ, prepares his salvation in many different ways but is hindered and prevented from this by unbelieving Israel. Thus only part of the Jews followed Jesus, later to be joined by the Gentiles to whom God also sent his gospel of salvation.

These points are indicative of the real purpose. It is in *this* particular sense an apology—presenting a defense of Christianity and Paul—and as such it may have played a part in Paul's trial in Rome. It is unfortunate that practically nothing is known to us about the court of Caesar (see p. LXXX), and there is little hope of finding documents which might throw light on such a case. Luke's work may have been one such document. On the other hand, it may have been a work issued without any direct relation to the court of Caesar, in order (at a critical time, in connection with Paul's trial) to clarify the position of Christianity within Jewry and within the Roman empire. In both cases the unknown Theophilus may have been a member of the court of Caesar and the use of his name may indicate the author's purpose with the work (see p. XVI).

Luke's work contains no legal argumentation. It deals with the history of Christianity and Paul's life and work, without departing from history in order to proceed to formal categories of law or to attempt a remodeling of the facts of the case into a pattern acceptable to the court of Caesar. The New Testament enjoins Christians, when before a court of justice, to bear witness, and states that the Holy Spirit is speaking through the accused (cf. Matt x 17–20; Acts iv 8). Therefore the accused Christian is preaching the Gospel; but this cannot be called a legal defense in the ordinary sense of the word. If this, as applied to the Christian martyr, provides a close definition of the character of the work, it will not then be essential to know whether it was presented to the court or issued for general publication as a document accessible to everybody.

To consider the work from this point of view we must first notice that Luke starts his account in the temple of Jerusalem. During the service an angel appears to Zechariah and promises that the precursor of the Messiah will be born (Luke i 5 ff.). One cannot help but notice, especially in light of the end of the work, that Zechariah, this earliest representative of Israel, is unbelieving. Just as later, the Jew Elymas became blind (Acts xiii 6 ff.), so Zechariah loses his gift of speech. The accounts that follow, concerning John the Baptist and Jesus, take place in the temple or in Jewish homes where the praise of God ascends in hymns inspired by the Old Testament. This is the opening of the account that ends at Paul's trial with the question of whether or not Christianity is Judaism.

Acts, like the Gospel, begins at the center of Jewry—the temple. It speaks of the revelation of the risen Christ to his disciples and of their first days without Jesus (i–xii). They walk in the temple, which to them is both the place of prayer and the place where they preach to other Jews. Early in Acts, their preaching shows great results among the people (ii 41—three thousand baptisms, iv 4—five thousand), but the temple authorities persecute the disciples just as they had persecuted their master. Thus the relationship between the Christian congregation in Jerusalem and their Jewish countrymen is one of open conflict.

Just as Paul's call is mentioned three times in Acts, so a scene in which Paul preaches to Jews and is rejected by them occurs three times (xiii 14–51, xxi 40–xxii 23, and xxviii 17–28). In the first two scenes this rejection turns into persecution. We find in this the same theme as in the account of Jesus in Nazareth (Luke iv 16–30): the Gospel is preached to Jews who soon turn against such preaching and reject it. We are confronted with this situation in Paul's sermon in the synagogue in Pisidian Antioch, in his address to the crowd from the steps leading to the fortress of Antonia (where the speech is delivered during a short pause in an already tempestuous episode), and in Paul's reception of the Jews in Rome.

These accounts and speeches plainly show the unbelief of the Jews, but the repetition of the theme makes it obvious that their unbelief does not deter Jesus, the apostles, or Paul from bringing the Gospel to them. As Jesus died at the instigation of the Jews, his resurrection provided his disciples with new motives for missionary work among the people in Palestine, as seen in the early chapters of Acts (iv 32–36, 38–39, iii 13–26, iv 10–12, 27–30, v 30–31, x 39–42, xiii 30–39). And no experience, such as the one in Pisidian Antioch, can make Paul give up his principle of beginning his mission work in every city at the synagogue (e.g., xiv 1). We can be quite certain that if Paul had been acquitted by the court of Caesar, he would have continued his work in the Jewish synagogues.

But when the Jews had heard the Gospel and refused it, Paul turned to the Gentiles, and again and again it appears that they heard the Gospel with great eagerness and were won over to Christ. As will be seen later (p. 105), what Paul did represented a new departure within the primitive church, the development of which was so slow in Palestine that even by the end of Acts, the church had only reached the stage of recognizing a mission to the Gentiles, but not of Jewish Christian participation in such work.

It is important to note—both with regard to the court of Caesar and to our present understanding of primitive Christianity—that Luke describes the stages of this development in order to explain that it was not the work of man but of God. The earliest disciples remained loyal to their master and continued his work among the people of Israel, the only work to which Jesus had been called (see p. L–LI). They were not frightened by the fate that Jesus and his work had suffered, but through their faith in his resurrection gained courage and power to take up and continue Jesus' preaching to the Palestinian Jews. Even though they had killed Jesus, the risen Lord was still intent on winning Israel for the Gospel.

Missions to the Gentiles were not within the horizon of these early disciples. However, God revealed to them that the Gentiles too must hear the Gospel (xi 5–12, 16–17). And forced as they were to flee from the persecutions started by their enemies, during their flight some of them became missionaries to the Gentiles (xi 19–21). We may suppose not only that such visions and revelations were convincing to the Christians, but also that they may have been of a certain value in a court of justice of that time. Members of the Sanhedrin, at any rate, took Paul's account of his call seriously—as seen by their words in Acts xxiii 9: ". . . what if a spirit spoke to him, or an angel . . ."

It is worth noticing that although Luke, with his special attitude, or theology—as it is now called with considerable exaggeration— did not produce or remodel the material which he found in the tradition, he selected precisely those passages from the rich material at his disposal.

In this respect he is obviously close to Paul. For in his letters Paul dealt with the same problems discussed in Acts, namely, that Israel was unbelieving first when Jesus preached and later when the apostles were the preachers (Rom ix–x). Nevertheless, the apostles sent to the Jews continued their preaching of the Gospel to deaf ears (Rom x 5–21). The Gentiles on the other hand became believers, and their faith became, in God's plan, a means to arouse Israel to believe (Rom xi 11–32). Paul saw all these changing phases of the history of God's salvation as an expression of God's will and work. God conquered all opposition to the salvation of Israel, although the Israelites themselves were their own worst enemies by their resistance to God and his Christ.

VIII. PRIMITIVE JEWISH CHRISTIANITY

For a long time scholars have thought of early Jewish Christianity as a congregation of Jews who in piety and observance of the Law, did not differ from other Jews, but did differ in their expectation that the crucified Jesus would return as the Jewish Messiah.

According to these scholars, just as all Jewry was engaged in missions to the Gentiles, so were the Jewish Christians, and it was as important to them as to other Jews to persuade the Gentiles to be circumcised and to observe the law of Moses. In this respect the Jewish Christians differed from Paul and other missionaries who baptized Gentiles without demanding that they first become Jews and live in accordance with the precepts of the Law.

These scholars further maintained that Jewish Christianity in its struggle against Paul showed a great and inexplicable leniency. It was, for instance, willing to accept such a compromise as the Decree (Acts xv 20, 29) of the so-called Apostolic Council in Jerusalem. But whether they were leading apostles or people unknown to us, Paul's adversaries sent forth a steady stream of Jewish Christian emissaries to the Pauline churches, for the purpose of winning over the converted Gentiles to the Jewish Christian point of view and to separate them from Paul.

All these assumptions had been taken over from nineteenth-century research without thorough examination, and they are not correct. In the first place, Judaism is not a proselytizing religion. To be sure, in Acts Luke described the synagogues in the Hellenistic cities as having a nucleus of Jews surrounded by proselytes and god-fearing Gentiles who—in accordance with the general interest in Oriental religions characteristic of the time—had deliberately chosen Judaism (e.g., xiii 43, xvii 4). The conditions thus described were not caused by missionary work among the Gentiles. While a few Gentiles wanted to embrace Judaism, the large majority of those whose interest had been aroused remained in a much looser relationship to Judaism. As in earlier and later ages, and at the time of Jesus, Judaism was never a missionary religion. It accepted a number of proselytes but was never interested in converting the Gentiles. It was unsympathetic toward the idea of missions as outlined by Jesus when he ordered his disciples to go out into the whole world and make disciples of all the Gentiles (Matt xxviii 19–20).

The main sources of our knowledge about relations between the Jews and the primitive church are to be found in the New Testament. They can be divided into three groups: Paul's letters, the tradition about Jesus as set forth in the four gospels, and the tradition about apostolic times as preserved in Acts.

The most important source is Paul's letters. They were written at almost the same time as the events they deal with, and by a man in a leading position who experienced the apostolic period at close range; he is thus a primary source to be preferred to all later reporters. Paul can therefore be relied on in his instructions to the Galatians, who assumed that the earliest apostles and the congregations of Judea preached circumcision and observance of the law of Moses (Gal i 10, v 11, vi 12–13). According to Paul, the truth of the matter is that there was no decisive difference between the leaders in Jerusalem and himself. Just as the apostle, in his non-polemical utterances, always mentions the leaders of Jewish Christianity with understanding and sympathy (e.g., I Cor ix 5), so he is, when polemics are involved, also capable of confirming their close agreement with him with regard to missions to the Jews and to the Gentiles (Gal ii 1–10).

All the adversaries (whom previous research has thought to be emissaries from Jewish Christianity in Jerusalem, inimical to Paul) were actually local adversaries. The Judaizers of the Epistle to the Galatians were not Christians from Jerusalem, but Galatians who had adopted the heretical teaching that salvation through Christ is not sufficient but that in addition the Gentiles must become Jews, allow themselves to be circumcised, and promise to observe the law of Moses (Gal v 2–3, 11–12, vi 13 ff.). According to I Corinthians, the members of the Corinthian church, who were not Judaizers, were taken with Peter, actually unknown to them, and proclaimed him their master (I Cor i 12). According to II Corinthians, they had allowed themselves to be impressed by visiting Jewish Christian apostles, who were not proselytizers for Judaism. Later, they tried to enlist the support of the congregation (x 12–18, xi 13–15) at a time when Paul had secured a resumption of the famine-relief collection, with which he departed for Jerusalem. Although the Roman church, to whom Romans is addressed, was not faced with the conflict which the struggle against the Judaizers had revealed in the Galatian churches, yet the conflict and its lasting results have set their stamp on this Christian manifesto. Paul composed it just before his journey to Jerusalem, which was intended to be the beginning of his Roman visit preceding his mission to Spain (Rom xv 14–33). From this it can be seen that Paul thought of Jerusalem as a center with which he had cordial relations, a center not involved in missionary activity to the Gentiles; yet he looked upon it with great sympathy. (Cf. my book, *Paul and the Salvation of Mankind* [1959], Chs. IV–VII.)

In turning to the next source of Jewish Christianity found in the Bible (i.e., the tradition about Jesus found in the four gospels), we realize of course that they are not direct sources of Jewish Christianity. But since the church was convinced that the words of Jesus were also of lasting validity for itself, the tradition underwent an adaptation which must be considered unintentional. Not so much by addition as by interpretation, the sayings of Jesus remained of current interest to his disciples in their somewhat changed situation.

In the account of the temple tax (Matt xvii 24–27), Jesus asks: Who is obliged to pay it? Here we see a contrast between the children of God, who are free, and the aliens who must pay the temple tax, and this contrast is applied by Jesus to the Christians and the Jews. The former are children of God, while the Jews are alien to him and therefore rightly obliged to pay a tax to his temple in Jerusalem. In these words of Jesus, we have early evidence of primitive Jewish Christianity's attitude toward Judaism: the Christians are the children of God, the other Jews are alien to God. Already as early as this, we encounter the church's view of itself as God's people, the true Israel, distinct from the Jews.

This fundamental attitude manifests itself in the careful preservation of Jesus' words about Jewish religious customs which he and the Jewish Christians challenge (Matt vi 1–18, ix 14–17 par., xii 1–8 par., xii 9–14 par.; Luke xiii 10–17, xiv 1–6), in interpreting the Law (Matt v 21–48, xv 1–9 par.), and in assuming the law of Moses is the basis of what God himself desired (Matt xix 1–12 par.). From all this a picture emerges of early Jewish Christianity as a movement obviously different from Judaism, and with a new understanding of God's revelations in the Old Testament. It is precisely in their picture of Jewish Christianity that the gospels show the decisive differences existing between it and Judaism, differences that go back to Jesus. And just as the early Jewish Christianity preserved Jesus' words about the Jewish faith and practice because they were of importance to it, so also were Jesus' words about persecution preserved because they were of current interest to the primitive church.

This difference between Jewish Christians and other Jews did not cause the former to undertake missions to the Gentiles. Jesus was said to have forbidden his disciples to go to the Samaritans and Gentiles (Matt x 5). We also have many words from Jesus where the original Jewish emphasis is kept (Matt v 47, vi 7, 32, xviii 17, xxiv 9, 14) as further evidence of the fact that both Jesus and the earliest Jewish Christians considered Gentiles to be outside their field of operation (cf. p. LI). On a few occasions Jesus did help Gentiles who asked for his assistance, such as the Roman centurion in Capernaum (Matt viii 5–13 par.) and the Canaanite woman (Matt xv 21–28 par.). These accounts were preserved and developed within the tradition. The story of the Canaanite woman in Matthew was thus understood to be a fundamental discussion of the question of whether Gentiles can participate in the Gospel, while the tradition behind Mark (vii 24–30) started with a positive answer to this question, but asked whether Gentiles should not wait until Israel had received the Gospel.

In this way a clear difference can be seen between the missions among the Jews carried out by Jewish Christianity, and the missions to the Gentiles carried out by Paul and others. There is no decisive difference with regard to the understanding of the nature of Christianity, and the Jewish element in Jewish Christianity had been devalued to nothing more than popular customs without any reference to salvation. Only with respect to the attitudes toward missionary work can a decisive difference be observed, in that primitive Jewish Christianity only continued Jesus' work among the people of Israel.

It was the faithful Jewish missionaries who, according to Paul in Rom x 16, cried out with Isaiah, "Lord, who has believed what we have told?" And it is they who realized God's will to save Israel in the words, "The whole day I stretched out my hands to a disobedient and obstinate people" (Rom x 21). In this quotation from Isa lxv 2, it is not their disobedience that is stressed but God's firm will to save Israel. The account of Peter's call after a miraculous haul of fish (Luke v 1–11) echoes Paul's words. The tired Jewish missionaries may well have cried out, "Master, we worked all night and caught nothing," but at the request of Jesus they nevertheless continue, "as you tell me to do it, I will put down the nets" (v 5). And the miraculous haul of fish follows as a fulfillment of their expectation of the saving of Israel.

Our third source for primitive Jewish Christianity is in Acts, where traditions about the Apostolic Age are preserved. If in Palestine primitive Jewish Christianity perished during the war between Israel and Rome (A.D. 66–71), then—apart from the tradition about Jesus in the gospels—its traditions perished with it and we are obliged to rely on the accounts given in Acts, whose value can be demonstrated by comparing them with those in Paul and the gospels.

The picture preserved in Acts of the early church in Jerusalem clearly differentiated it from Jewry. Like John the Baptist and Jesus, the early church considered the Jews to be its mission field. It preached about Jesus and about salvation through him (ii 38–40). The Christians attended the temple, as did their Jewish fellow countrymen, but they had in addition their own meetings, their own meals with celebration of Holy Communion for those who had been baptized, and their own system of caring for their poor (ii 44–46). Thus it is not only their expectation of the coming of the crucified Jesus as the Jewish Messiah that differentiates them from other Jews. As the Lord of the Christians, Jesus Christ made them in every respect different from the Jews. This is best seen in the fact that the Jews persecuted the Jewish Christians as they had persecuted Jesus (iv 23–30).

The Jewish Christians engaged in missionary work among the Gentiles no more than did the Jews. Thus when Peter in Acts x was invited to visit Cornelius, the Gentile in Caesarea, he was completely unprepared and unwilling to go. Only after his vision of the clean and unclean beasts was he willing to seek out Cornelius, who had been told by an angel to send for Peter to be a guest in his house. When Peter saw the Holy Spirit come upon the Gentiles assembled there in the same way as it had earlier with the Jewish Christians (x 47, xi 15), he agreed to have them baptized.

But there were no further developments. Peter did not continue to proselytize among the Gentiles. The church in Jerusalem, which had insisted that the apostle report on his visit to a Gentile (xi 1–18), calmed down and likewise did nothing. The story of Peter and Cornelius lived on, just as did the accounts of Jesus' meetings with the centurion in Capernaum and with the Canaanite woman. But no matter how interesting these events may have been, as indicated by their actually having remained in the tradition, they produced no immediate effect. They dealt with matters of no current interest at that time.

In its early days the Christian church was not described as an institution that prepared its future according to a plan and deliberately initiated new developments. As Acts clearly states, God controlled it in a peculiarly sovereign manner and allowed events themselves to overtake the apostles and the congregation in Jerusalem, who only afterwards attempted to analyze and evaluate the events. After Philip the evangelist had carried on missionary work in Samaria, Peter and John went there (viii 14 ff.); and after a mission to the Gentiles had been started in Syrian Antioch, Barnabas was sent there (xi 22 ff.). Later, Jerusalem does not interfere in the work begun by others, limiting its intervention to cases in which members of the Jerusalem church, such as Philip or the Hellenists in Antioch, were concerned. After Paul started missionary work among the Gentiles, he went to Jerusalem. The congregation in Jerusalem was said to be ignorant about happenings in the mission field until Paul arrived to inform them of his activities. About this, Paul and Acts are in agreement.

As Jewish Christianity did not proselytize among the Gentiles, it did not know in advance what should be required of a Gentile who had come to believe in Christ. The problem came to Jerusalem from outside, from distant Antioch where Paul and Barnabas were at work. Christians from Judea passing through Antioch had been astounded to meet uncircumcised Christians (Acts xv 1 ff.), just as on another occasion "some from James" had been shocked at finding that in the congregation at Antioch, Jewish Christians, Jewish fellow countrymen, sat down and ate in common with Gentile Christians who, from a Jewish point of view, were Gentiles (Gal ii 12). Whereupon Paul and Barnabas went up to the apostles and the elders in Jerusalem to explain to them the demands made by the Christians from Judea. These demands were rejected by Jerusalem. Circumcision and observance of the

Law cannot be required of Gentiles. The brethren from Judea had not been spokesmen for Jewish Christianity, but had acted on their own responsibility. Instead, only a few requirements (cf. p. 138) were adopted, and representatives of the Jerusalem church were sent to confirm the position taken by it. There were, according to Acts (xv 5), former Pharisees who in Jerusalem raised the same claim as had been raised in Antioch, but they formed an unimportant minority.

The accuracy of Luke's account of the Apostolic Council in Acts xv has been in doubt—and rightly so. For we possess an account of a meeting in Jerusalem that resembles the Apostolic Council but shows important deviations; and as it was Paul, one of the leading participants in the meeting, who wrote this account (Gal ii 1–10), Luke cannot have been right in every detail. Thus Paul cannot be assumed to have shared the responsibility for the Apostolic Decree, of which he did not make use later in the churches, as seen from I Cor viii–x.

In spite of differences, the two accounts are in agreement in essential matters. Jerusalem approved of mission work among Gentiles faraway from Jerusalem and Palestine, in which no one from Jerusalem had any intention of participating. Formerly scholars had difficulty in understanding this attitude. When something appears to be completely incomprehensible, it usually means that a reasonable explanation for it has not been found. It then becomes a matter of re-examining the sources in order to uncover an explanation there. This is possible, because in the sources we find no Jewish Christianity nearly identical with Judaism. Through its faith in Jesus, the Jewish Christian church deviated from Judaism to the extent that it had no intention of requiring circumcision and the observance of Moses' law of converted Gentiles.

We have observed this in Paul's writings; now we are also faced with it in Acts. In Gal ii 14 ff., Paul recounts what he said to Peter in Antioch when the latter had led all the Jewish Christians to withdraw from participating in meals with Gentile Christians. Paul talks about what "we Jewish Christians" do and think, but he is nevertheless not speaking in his own name. Paul certainly had not come to believe in Christ through his own conviction that man will not be saved by his performance of deeds prescribed by the Law. In his case it was Christ who led him to reject salvation through observance of a law which he had formerly done his utmost to obey (Philip iii 4–11). The Jewish Christians, to whom Paul alludes in

Gal ii 14 ff., were Peter and the Palestinian Jewish Christians. And in Acts xv 7–11, Peter in his speech at the Apostolic Council maintains the same position. Christian Jews cannot demand that Gentiles observe the Law neither they themselves nor their ancestors had observed. This view of the Law as a demand that cannot be fulfilled is not a Jewish but a Christian one. It presupposes Jesus' interpretation of the Law, in which it is not enough to obey the sixth commandment against killing; one must also never have been angry with another human being (Matt v 21–22).

With such an attitude toward the Law, it is obvious that Jerusalem had never demanded that Gentiles converted to Christ should become Jews, allowing themselves to be circumcised and promising to observe the Law in its entirety. And what appears from the account of the Apostolic Council is confirmed by the rest of Acts. The Law and circumcision are most frequently mentioned in a polemical context where Jews attack Christians like Stephen (vi 13–14) or Paul (xviii 13) (cf. p. LXIII), or are mentioned indirectly in James' words (xxi 20–24; cf. xxi 28). Apart from the two above-mentioned passages, xv 1 and 5, where small minorities raised demands about circumcision and observance of the Law, Paul's attitude toward Jewish law and customs is mentioned several times (xxii 3, xxv 8, xxviii 17), usually to demonstrate his conformity with his pharisaical youth.

The infrequency of Pauline references to the Jewish law and circumcision need not surprise us: what *is* surprising is that circumcision and observance of the Law are not mentioned in the places where, according to earlier scholarship, it would be natural to expect them. When Peter most reluctantly accepted Cornelius' invitation, his problem was: How can a Jew enter a Gentile's house (x 28–29)? And when he decided to baptize the Gentiles in Cornelius' house, he did not add: after they have been circumcised and have promised to observe the Law. When the congregation in Jerusalem was shocked by Peter's behavior in Caesarea, it was not because he had failed to make these demands, but because "You have entered in among uncircumcised men, and you have eaten with them" (xi 3).

All this indicates that Jewish Christianity had been liberated by Jesus from the Law in the Jewish sense of that word, because it read the entire Old Testament as a story about Jesus Christ. The two elements characteristic of Jewish Christianity are found in the account given in Acts of the Apostolic Council. Peter denied

that one could demand circumcision and observance of the Law
from the Gentiles. And James, the Lord's brother, voiced in his
speech Jewish Christianity's view on missions: God will first rebuild David's fallen house, that is, convert Israel by means of the
mission to the Jews, and through this it will then be made possible
for all Gentiles to seek the Lord.

This apparently paradoxical way of thinking is, as frequently
happens, historically accurate. A third factor must be added,
namely, that like Paul, Jewish Christianity would like to have been
everything to the Jews and those under the Law so as to win
them for the Gospel. Great caution was required in the official
abandonment of the lawful way of life that formed a necessary
basis for living among the Jews. A radical departure from the law
of Moses could, to a missionary sent to Israel, be a possible hindrance in the establishment of further contacts with the Jews and
in his opportunity to evangelize them. This point of view may,
therefore, have had something to do with Peter's suddenly changed
behavior toward the congregation at Antioch (Gal ii 11 ff.). Paul's
sharp words to the effect that Peter's fear of those who were
circumcised might possibly mean that Peter feared losing the possibility of continuing his missionary work among the Jews, if he
became known as one who did not obey the Law in his intercourse
with Gentiles.

IX. PAUL'S TRIAL

With Paul's trial in Jerusalem and in Caesarea, and his later appeal to the court of Caesar in Rome, the account in Acts certainly reaches its climax—a climax, however, not entirely unexpected. From its earliest days the Christian church had suffered persecution in Jerusalem and Palestine, and later Paul had met with opposition in the Hellenistic cities of the Roman empire from Jews who had rejected the Gospel (e.g., I Thess i 5–6, ii 14–16; Acts xvii 1–8, 13).

Paul's life as a missionary in Asia Minor and Greece frequently brought him into contact with the local authorities. As early as the time of his visit to Cyprus, he had become involved in a religious discussion with Sergius Paulus, the proconsul (Acts xiii 7–12). Later, he had been imprisoned by the authorities in Philippi (xvi 19–24, 35–39), and had stood before the court of the Areopagus in Athens (xvii 19–33). In Corinth, accusations against him were brought before the court held by Gallio, the proconsul.

This experience in Corinth (xviii 12–17) is worth noting because it was characteristic of the difficulties which Paul encountered, and because it came to an end in a way that clearly distinguishes it from the Jerusalem trial. The Jews were the persecutors (as in ix 22–25, 29–30, xiii 50–51, xiv 2, 4–6, 19), and their conflicting statements and mockery had already led to a break between the synagogue and Paul and to his entering upon an intensive mission among the Gentiles (xviii 6). The Jews therefore attempted to have him sentenced in Gallio's court by accusing him of trying to persuade the people to honor God "against the Law." Before Paul had had time to say anything, Gallio answered this point. If there had been any question of a criminal offense, he would have allowed the Jews to present their case to him. But, as the matter at issue was concerned with doctrines, names, and Jewish law, they would have to make their own decision. Gallio did not want to judge such issues.

His answer was right. A Roman court would not interfere with the Jewish religion and the right of Jewish authorities to judge their own cases. But this unsuccessful attempt to strike at Paul through a Roman court leads straight on to the Jerusalem trial. "Against the Law" (xviii 13) he had tried to persuade people to honor God, but the expression is ambiguous. If this referred to the Jewish law, as Gallio thought, his refusal to hear the case was correct. But if the apostle in his missionary work had transgressed Roman law, then the Romans would have had to pay attention to the Jewish accusations. And a religious movement "against" the Jewish law would be no part of Judaism, a religion the Romans recognized (see p. LII). In that case, Christianity would also be against the Roman law.

This is an important point, because the Roman state was apprehensive of the new religions which in the course of the preceding centuries had invaded the empire from the East (see p. LXXVI) and settled in Rome, the capital (cf. Tacitus *Annals* XV.44). Several of these Oriental religions had suffered Roman persecution until, after a time, they were allowed to spread within the empire. But no Oriental religion was exposed to periods of persecution so long and savagely as Christianity.

The trial in Jerusalem, like so many other episodes of persecution, began with an unruly crowd (cf. xvi 22, xvii 5–6). Jews from Ephesus had recognized Paul and their Gentile—now Christian—townsman, Trophimus, in Jerusalem. This made them believe that Paul had brought Gentiles into the temple, thereby desecrating their holy place (xxi 27–29). In their consternation they called for assistance to the crowd outside the temple which, becoming excited, came very close to lynching Paul. He was saved from death by Roman soldiers, but the episode did not, as on previous occasions (see xvi 35 ff.), end with peace and order in the city the next morning nor with the discharge of the man from Tarsus by the Roman authorities.

The brief tumult in the temple had died down, and the Ephesian Jewish authority in Jerusalem took over the case and pursued it through the years following. In this way, firm support had been established for an attack on Paul which otherwise might have lost its force in the course of a few days.

We learn of the Jewish charges against Paul from direct reports of the accusations and from Paul's refutations. The outcry of the Ephesian Jews (xxi 28) had already indicated the essential points in later charges: everywhere he taught against the people, the Law, and the temple. He had, moreover, brought Greeks into the temple (Gentiles were forbidden entrance to the temple apart from the "Court of the Gentiles," and a Gentile who entered the temple and was caught, suffered the death penalty). On the one hand, Paul was accused of a specific crime—namely the bringing of Gentiles into the temple—and on the other, of a general transgression—preaching all over the world against the Jewish people, the law of Moses, and the temple in Jerusalem. The same accusations that were once brought against Jesus (Matt xxvi 61 par.; cf. Acts vi 14) and Stephen (Acts vi 11, 13) were now brought against Paul.

The Jewish charges were formulated by an advocate, Tertullus, in this manner (xxiv 5–6): that Paul had stirred up trouble among the Jews all over the world and that he had desecrated the temple (cf. xxi 28). Later, before Festus in Caesarea, the Jews made "many serious charges" against Paul, none of which they could prove (xxv 7, cf. xxv 18–19). The two conspiracies against Paul's life (xxiii 12–15, xxv 3) are indicative of certain doubts among the Jews on the outcome of the trial.

Paul's speeches and remarks during his trial provide us with more information. In his speech from the steps leading to the fortress of Antonia (xxii 1–21) Paul told about his life, from the time of his studies in Jerusalem and his persecution of the Christians to his meeting with Christ near Damascus and his mission to the Gentiles from Jerusalem. Paul's trial before the Sanhedrin (xxii 30–xxiii 10) presupposed an account of his call to become an apostle, for some of the Pharisees present were heard to say, ". . . What if a spirit spoke to him, or an angel . . ." The trial before Felix (xxiv 1–23, particularly vss. 10 ff.) gave Paul occasion for pointing out that he was not guilty of the disturbances that had taken place in Jerusalem. His arrival at the temple as a pilgrim bringing gifts to his people had not been the cause of the disturbance. The Ephesian Jews who had initiated the episode were important witnesses and should have been summoned to testify. One would suppose that they were able to throw light on the charge concerning the desecration of the temple, as well as on the charge that Paul had provoked disturbances outside Palestine.

At his trial before Festus (xxv 6–12) two years later, Paul's answer to the Jewish accusations was that he had committed no offenses either against the law of the Jews, against the temple, or against Caesar (xxv 8). And after his appeal to the court of Caesar, he took the liberty of mentioning that Festus was well aware of the fact that he had committed no offense against the Jews (xxv 10). Upon Agrippa's arrival at Caesarea, a meeting of the court was arranged where Paul was given an opportunity to speak (xxv 13–xxvi 32). Only indirectly did he refer to the Jewish accusations, but at a meeting with the Jewish leaders in Rome (xxviii 17–23), he stressed that he had committed no offense against the people or the rules of their fathers (xxviii 17).

In other statements Paul throws light on the intention behind the Jewish charges. As a Christian, he had not ceased being a Jew. His faith was not very different from what he believed as a Pharisee and what had been added was caused by the fulfillment of the Old Testament promises in Christ, who from the time of his Damascus experience had had command over his life and activities (xxvi 19–21). Whereas in missionary preaching the account of the apostle's call had been a paradigm of God's unmerited grace toward the sinner (Rom xv 17–19; I Cor xv 8–10; cf. I Tim i 12–17), in the trial it was considered from another angle, that is, as a revelation from the time of birth and later affected by the revelation of Christ, as in Gal i 15–16.

As we have seen, Paul's meeting with a heavenly being was mentioned as early as his questioning before the Sanhedrin. In xxiii 6 Paul began with these words, "I am a Pharisee, son of Pharisees, I am being tried because of the hope and the resurrection of the dead." Before Felix, Paul made the following statement, "But this I admit to you, that in accordance with that 'way,' which they call sectarian—so I worship the God of my fathers, believing all that is written in the Law and the Prophets, and trusting in God, as do also these men here, that there will be a resurrection both for the righteous and for the unrighteous" (xxiv 14–15). In his speech before King Agrippa, the apostle described his youth as a Pharisee until the event of the heavenly vision which he from then on had obeyed (xxvi 4–20). Toward the end of his speech, he mentioned that as Christ's emissary he had said "nothing but what both the prophets and Moses have spoken of as something that was to come: that the Messiah must suffer, that being as the first to rise from the dead, he would bring light both to the people and to the nations" (xxvi 22–23). Paul then turned to the proofs of this to be found in Old Testament texts. Paul returned to this matter once more in a remark he made in his speech to the Jews in Rome, where he said that it was "for the sake of the hope of Israel that I am in chains" (xxviii 20).

Paul made these statements in order to prove that he and his preaching followed the central line in Judaism, that is, the Messiah and the resurrection of the dead (see xxiii 6, xxvi 6–8, 23; the reference to xxiii 6 in xxiv 21 mentions only "the resurrection of the dead"). A revelation had shown him that this expectation of Israel had now been fulfilled and he was convinced that through Christ he had become a Jew or an Israelite in the most fundamental sense of the word. As we know from Paul's letters, the church was Israel (Gal vi 16), and its most important task was the conversion of the Jewish people to Christ (Rom ix–xi). The later separation of Judaism and Christianity, now so obvious to us, was not at that time recognized by the Christians. They had accepted the Roman view of Christianity as a Jewish sect, as an imperfect definition of the church, which actually was the true continuation of God's people, or Israel. Both Palestinian Jewish Christianity and Paul had lived in the hope that the unbelieving Jewish people would soon be converted to Christ.

This conviction became of special importance in Paul's trial because it showed that in dealing with both Jews and Romans, Paul was anxious to establish his own as well as Christianity's natural position within Judaism. Official Jewry held a different opinion. By its unceasing persecution of the Christians, it had shown that it did not recognize them as proper Jews, and in its case against Paul, it took the opportunity to submit its view of Christianity to a decision by a Roman court of justice.

The Romans would have to adjudicate the case and, according to the Jews' plan, make the Jewish point of view legal within the Roman empire. But the Romans were inclined to dismiss the case as being an internal Jewish concern, as Gallio had done earlier. This can be seen from Claudius Lysias' letter (xxiii 25–30), stating that he had found Paul indicted with regard to their law, but not charged with anything that might lead to a death sentence (xxiii 29). Gallio had expressed the same ideas in almost the same words (xviii 14–15). Felix, the procurator of Caesarea, shelved the case for two years and was thought both to have wanted money from Paul and to curry favor with the Jews by leaving him a prisoner in Caesarea (xxiv 25–27). Felix had already acquired such a bad reputation that these accusations against him were easily credited. Festus, his successor, worked quickly but apparently with no great understanding of this difficult case (xxv 20). When Paul appealed, Festus still knew so little about the case that he did not know what to write in the accompanying report (xxv 26). He was nevertheless convinced that the apostle had "done nothing deserving the death sentence or chains" (xxvi 31; cf. xxv 25). As was the case with Claudius Lysias, the Jewish accusers had also disappointed him by producing religious controversial issues about a certain Jesus who was dead but who Paul had asserted was alive (xxv 18–19). After Paul's speech in chapter xxvi, both Agrippa and Festus agreed that he was not guilty of criminal charges. It was therefore with regret that Agrippa ended by saying, "This man could have been released if he had not appealed to Caesar" (vs. 32).

The practice until that time of treating the Christians as a Jewish sect made one Roman after another make light of Paul's case. Since he was not guilty of crimes, he ought to be released. But to the Jews, the decisive question was whether Paul was a Jew and Christianity inside the Jewish religious community, or whether he was an apostate Jew and his religion a new Oriental religion outside Judaism, and for this reason not covered by Roman approval as a "recognized" religion (see p. LII). This was the problem which the Roman officials at first did not see, but which in itself could lead to the death sentence for Paul and to the eradication of Christianity. It did not take the Romans long to grasp the new approach to this problem and decide the case in accordance with the wishes of the Jews (cf. ch. x). From then on, Christianity was considered a new Oriental religion, which the Roman empire did not recognize but persecuted. It was the Christian name itself (*nomen ipsum*)—and not the crimes of which the Christians were accused—that was a punishable offense (cf. Pliny *Letters* X.96–97).

According to Agrippa, the appeal was a dangerous recourse for the prisoner who could otherwise have been released by Festus. His words must be understood in the same way as other utterances predicting Paul's death in Rome. It is interesting to consider the point in the trial at Caesarea when Festus' question made Paul appeal to the court of Caesar. It has been customary to think that this appeal was caused by the procurator's question as to whether Paul would be willing to stand trial before him in Jerusalem. If so Paul may have had several reasons for appealing his case to Caesar. The last time he stood before a procurator, his case had been postponed indefinitely and Paul had already turned his eyes

toward Rome (Rom i 10–15, xv 23–24). Was he to suffer a slow
death in a Palestinian prison? Or might the possibility that in
Jerusalem he could be put to death without legal trial have led
to this decision? It has, however, been suggested that Paul's case
in Jerusalem would have been adjudicated not by Festus (this
detail has been omitted in Acts xxv 20—it is probably only a
Lucan variant), but by the Sanhedrin. If so, Paul's reason for
appealing his case was clear: he could not have expected fair
treatment there. But this suggestion is, all in all, not very likely to
be correct.

By the end of his stay in Ephesus, Paul had already turned his
thoughts to Rome (xix 21); he had planned a visit there after
his journey to Jerusalem (Rom xv 25–28). His imprisonment and
trial brought a change in his situation, but as early as the time in
Jerusalem, Christ in revealing himself to him had promised him
that, as he had testified to God's works before the authorities in
Jerusalem, so he should testify before the authorities in Rome also
(Acts xxiii 11). On his voyage to Rome an angel appeared to him
with this message: "Fear not, Paul! You are to appear before
Caesar" (xxvii 24). The importance of Paul's testifying before
Caesar was emphasized as the main reason for God's protection
of the ship: the prediction that all the people on board—we know
there were two hundred and seventy-six persons—would get safely
ashore was only of secondary importance. Jesus and the primitive
church attached great weight to the testimony before the authorities: it would become a "testimony before them and the Gentiles"
(Matt x 18; cf. Mark xiii 9–11). Paul could work for the Gentiles
even as a prisoner. The appeal gives him an opportunity to testify
before the Emperor.

Luke's description of Paul's trial was influenced by his firm
conviction of Paul's innocence: he had not profaned the temple
or provoked disturbances all over the world. It was with a clear
conscience that Paul professed the faith of his forefathers as expressed in the Old Testament.

Characteristic of Luke's picture of Paul during his trial is its
similarity to the trial of the accused Jesus. Just as the story of his
passion occupied the key position at the end of the gospels, so
also did the account of Paul's trial in Acts. And just as the suffering
of Jesus was foretold by the prophets, so Paul's imprisonment
and hardships had been predicted. As early as his call near Da-

mascus, it was said, "and I will show him all he is to suffer for my name's sake" (ix 16). On the third journey, Paul said in his speech at Miletus to the elders from Ephesus, that in every city the Holy Spirit predicted that chains and tribulations awaited him and that the Ephesians would not see him again (xx 22–25). We have an example of such a prophecy in the prediction of Agabus that Paul would be imprisoned by the Jews in Jerusalem and handed over to the Gentiles (xxi 11). This expression that the Jews would hand him over to the Gentiles is found in almost the same words in the predictions of the sufferings of Jesus in the gospels (Matt xx 19 and par.; cf. "handed over to men" in Matt xvii 22 and par.). But while Jesus actually was handed over to the Romans by the Jews, the same did not happen to Paul, who was rescued by Roman soldiers when a group of angry Jews was about to lynch him outside the temple (xxi 31–33), as correctly stated by Tertullus (xxiv 6). One is reminded of xxi 11, and in xxviii 17 it is stated that Paul had been handed over to the Romans as a prisoner from Jerusalem. In both these passages, the parallel between Jesus and Paul has colored the expressions, although the actual events do not resemble each other.

Both at Jesus' trial and at Paul's, we find Jews and Gentiles, procurators and the Herod family, co-operating. The Jews were endeavoring to have the prisoner sentenced, and the Romans while not wanting to be used by them, were yet obliged to serve Jewish interests.

As Jesus was, at first, charged with having said that he would destroy the temple and rebuild it, so Paul was also, at first, charged with having committed an offense against the temple by bringing Gentiles into it. During their trial both Jesus and Paul were involved in an episode with the high priest. In John xviii 22–23, it is stated that Jesus was struck in the face by one of the guards because he thought his answer to the high priest irreverent. And in Acts xxiii 2–5, the high priest commanded one of the guards to strike Paul on the mouth. These charges of having committed an offense against the temple give way to the real charges—in the case of Jesus for having pretended to be the Messiah, and in the case of Paul for having provoked disturbances among the Jews all over the world.

The case against Paul, which with dragging slowness led to his death, must have been a terrible strain for such a restless worker. He was in prison and could not do the work which Christ had assigned to him as the apostle to the Gentiles. Here also we must imagine that Paul had asked to have his freedom restored, but Christ made him realize that his grace was sufficient and that his strength was made perfect in weakness (II Cor xii 9). Paul's letters testify to the imprisoned missionary's participation in missionary work (e.g., Philip i 12–14, 30) and we find the positive evaluation of his sufferings in his thoughts about his testimony before Caesar.

X. LUKE'S TESTIMONY

If it is true that Luke wrote all he knew and then put his pen aside, his two-part work was finished at the end of the two years in Rome (Acts xxviii 30; see p. XLIX). We cannot help thinking about the events that followed, which Luke did not know about and which we thus do not know about either. For events that are known to us do not occur in a vacuum but in the context of other events. Where our knowledge is lacking, we must attempt to reconstruct what may have happened, in the hope that this reconstruction will make us understand better what we do know. We shall therefore in this part proceed very guardedly to combine the description of Paul's trial in Acts with other information we have.

To begin with, let us suppose that the apostle's case was tried before Caesar's court and that the verdict was either acquittal or death. Tradition tells us that Peter and Paul were both executed in Rome during the reign of Nero, but we do not know the exact dates of these events (cf. I Clement v; Ignatius *Romans* iv 3; Eusebius *Ecclesiastical History* II.xxv.6 ff.) There may possibly have been an interval between the trial related in Acts and Paul's execution, but it is not very likely. As the persecution begun under Nero in A.D. 64 presupposes a definite separation between Judaism and Christianity, and as according to Acts, Paul's case turned upon this problem (see p. LXXII), it is natural to suppose that the definite separation goes back to Paul's trial before Caesar's court and that its verdict led to Paul's execution.

We have very little definite information concerning the procedures of the Roman imperial court of law or of the administration of justice at the time of Paul. Roman law was not codified until later and even then it does not throw much light on the problems raised by the account in Acts. No one has yet collected the material presented by historians and others to elucidate the procedure of this court. To be sure, little of this material is of real value as an exact description of this institution. These considerations ought to be kept in mind by those who have ascertained with regret that on decisive points Luke's description of the trial is not very accurate. In this he is like other Greek authors who have mentioned such legal cases. That is why in an earlier part (p. LVIII), we were obliged to speak hypothetically about the possibility of presenting documents to Caesar's court. What follows is therefore subject to great uncertainty.

Paul's case involves a problem both religious and political, namely, whether the appearance and development of Christianity is a genuinely Jewish development, which would make the Jews' rejection of the Christians an unreasonable act, or whether it constitutes a break with Judaism, which would mean that Christianity is an Oriental religion independent of Judaism, and thus considered by the Romans suspect and dangerous. In a court of law, it would be important for the Christians to demonstrate that Christianity appeared in Palestine as a fulfillment of the Old Testament prophecies, and that a number of Jews, and in particular the Jewish authorities, had not accepted this but from the beginning attempted to crush the movement by persecuting and killing Jesus, its leader. After the death of Jesus, the persecution continued; the early congregation in Jerusalem was subjected to it as was also the first mission to the Gentiles outside Palestine. Luke's work corroborates this persecution (see p. LX). In addition it relates how both the history of Jesus and that of the church were accompanied by signs and wonders and other manifestations of God's will (e.g., Acts ii 22, iv 29–30, v 12), so that it is plainly seen that Israel's God has guided Jesus and the apostles right up to Paul's trial. Thus it is self-evident that the other Jews were not guided by the Old Testament or by God's will, but had erred in rejecting the genuine continuation of Israel's religion.

The problem handed over to Caesar's court was not an easy one. The division of a religion into two movements poses the question as to which of the two is advancing the original religion, and is, therefore, the correct continuation. At any rate, this is the point that the Christian part of Jewry had to stress in a possible plea to the court: that Christianity was the genuine continuation of Israel's religion. A comparison can be made with the situation of the reformed churches at the time of the Reformation. They had to try to demonstrate that the church of Christ was continued in them and not in the parts of the hitherto united Western church that had refused to let the Gospel renew them.

The burden of proof seems to have been much easier in the case of the Jewish religious community: it could claim that it was the organized form of religion in the temple and for the majority of the people, and that it was the (at any rate apparently) unchanged continuation of what had once been given. A Roman court, in its desire to maintain peace and order in the state, would find it easy to ask the political question: How many Christians are there, how many Jews? As the Jews were, on the whole, unbelievers, there is no reason to doubt that the case must have suffered from a lack of balance from the very beginning, and that it ended with Christianity's being considered a distinct and separate Oriental religion which could not be included in Judaism and therefore could not claim its privileges. This attitude is clearly shown in Nero's persecution, which was directed against the Christians but not against the Jews (see Suetonius *Life of Nero* XVI.2).

But when Luke wrote his work, the matter had not been decided. In Acts the Christian party to the case argued that Jesus and the church constitute the great act of God: Israel's religious culmination as the means of salvation for both Jews and Gentiles, and that thus Christianity was a divinely fulfilled Judaism, intended for all men. Now this last point, namely, that Christianity was intended for all men, might have had an adverse effect on the court's view of Christianity. Custom had already established the cult of the Emperor as the unifying faith of the world, in other words the population of the whole Roman empire.

Judaism claimed for itself only that it was a religion for Jews, and in addition, for a few Gentiles who had gained admission to the Jewish religious community (see p. LXII). Despite all its peculiar features that created political difficulties from time to time, Judaism came within a category of religions which the Romans could understand and fit into their political system. It was the category of folk religions, inside which each people had its own religion and its own gods. The Romans maintained that these various gods were basically the same, and recognized Jupiter, Juno, Venus, and the others everywhere. To be sure, such an identification could not be successfully established with the Jewish religion, which—just as consistently as the Christian church did later—struggled to maintain that its God was the only one. At the beginning, as is plain from Acts, Christianity seemed only another

Jewish sect. By the end of Acts, Christianity could not be considered by any informed person as a specifically Jewish movement.

For Christianity was aimed at all mankind and wanted to win
all men, not for Judaism, but for Christ. A religion which from
the beginning addressed itself to the populations of the entire Roman empire caused a completely new kind of difficulty, because,
as we have already mentioned, emperor worship provided a religion which was certainly intended to serve as a means of unification among the highly varied population groups and their widely
differing religious beliefs and customs.

That is why the mission to the Gentiles was a key point in
determining the Roman empire's attitude toward the new religion.
In its mission to the Gentiles a Jewish sect, namely Christianity,
had revealed its intention of carrying its message to the ends of
the world. To put it in a nutshell: the new religion had one definite
aim; the spread of Christianity as the religion of the empire. In
a political sense such an aim may be considered as an attempt at
usurpation. To a court of jurists and statesmen, that was what
was behind the will to win all peoples for Christ. The practical
and serviceable solution implemented by the Roman state was in
danger of being subverted. Emperor worship was to the state a
means for the unification under its rule of all the peoples of the
world by what it considered to be a convenient and minimal intervention in their lives. Concessions that could be granted to the
Jewish religion, with its ethnic limits, could not be granted to Christianity, with its ethnic illimitability. As Christ had fallen, so Paul also
had to fall, and many others after him, for Rome was endangered
wherever the mission to the Gentiles was successful. A choice had
to be made between Christianity and Rome, unless one dared to
replace emperor worship by Christianity—a solution later chosen
by Constantine the Great and his successors.

At the time of Paul, the considerations had not so wide a scope
as we outline here, mainly because no one had thought that
Christianity would have much of a chance to hold its own here on
earth. Then as now, many people were of the opinion that Christianity was an ephemeral phenomenon. And even if Paul's work
in particular had spread Christianity throughout the Roman empire from its modest beginnings in Palestine, it had not caught the
attention of many people and few reckoned with its continuation.
Who of that time can be supposed to have possessed the foresight
—to guard as the historian must against hindsight—that Rome

would be the one to fall and not Christianity, that it would no longer be the Jews who persecuted the Christians but, alas, the Christians who persecuted the Jews.

Finally, it should be stressed once more that Luke told what he knew and gave his testimony. Christianity is a continuing revelation to Israel, in which Christ carries God's salvation beyond the limits of the people and country of Israel, offering it to all men, Jews as well as Gentiles. Although Luke and Paul differ on many points, in his testimony Luke reveals his relationship to Paul, without whose thoughts his more modest performance would not have been possible. It is testimony, not a legal defense. The more dangerous side of Paul and of Christianity, that is, the mission to the Gentiles, is not minimized and the case is not presented primarily to persuade. In the same way as the Christian martyr uses his trial as an occasion to bear testimony before the authorities (see p. LVIII), so in his work Luke appears as a witness, not as an advocate.

XI. THE TEXT OF ACTS

In connection with the text of Acts, there are matters of such great importance that they must be mentioned even in this brief account. With respect to all New Testament writings, variations exist between different manuscripts and between different groups of related manuscripts, but it is rare that the texts of the various groups are as unlike or contradict each other as plainly as in the case of Acts.

The "Western" text contains such independent and interesting readings that it has for a long time been considered by some scholars as the original text.

The Western text is represented by Codex Bezae,[6] a sixth-century manuscript now in Cambridge, England. This manuscript, which is bilingual (Greek and Latin), contains nearly all of Acts in a decidedly Western form. Apart from this, the most important sources of the Western text are the margin in the Harclean Syriac and the early African version in Latin. These sources are often not fully preserved, and other manuscripts which confirm the Western text do not always offer reliable testimony. Thus the Western text does not appear clearly in definite manuscripts but must be approximately determined by means of extensive materials.

At present it is the generally accepted opinion that the Western text is not the original text of Acts, but that it came into existence at an early date and soon won acceptance throughout the Christian world. It may very well contain readings older than those we find in other texts, but such passages were probably not originally "Western" at all, but unchanged readings from a still earlier time, preserved in Western manuscripts.

Even if the "Neutral" (Egyptian) text cannot be considered as the earliest text and is also a recension, there is still a tendency to

6 The "Western" text normally means readings supported by Codex Bezae, the old Latin and Syriac versions, together with certain late Greek manuscripts showing textual recensions of an unusual type.

prefer its readings in many passages where the Western text shows a strong deviation from it. The translation of the text of Acts in this book is based on Nestle's *Novum Testamentum Graece,* which is strongly influenced by the Neutral text.

In the NOTES to Acts that follow, attention has been drawn in several passages to problems of textual criticism where variations between the Neutral and the Western texts are of importance for an understanding of the content. Because of the need to limit such references, it has not been possible to draw a fully adequate picture of the problems in textual criticism. There is actually a great deal of material, but most of it is so uncertain and so difficult to explain without detailed references to Greek and Latin, that it has been omitted here. Otherwise the material presented would have assumed such dimensions that it would have been quite out of proportion to its usefulness in examining the problems of the text.

Some examples of characteristic Western readings may be noted here:

a. Precise statements in the text: In xii 10 the apostle Peter and the angel "went down six steps." In xix 9 it is stated that Paul taught in Tyrannus' school (in Ephesus) "from the fifth till the tenth hour." In xxvii 5 the voyage along the coasts of Cilicia and Pamphylia is said to have lasted "fifteen days."

b. A number of Western texts help to explain discrepancies in the other texts of Acts. They thereby have the effect of being the result of a revision. In xiv 2, the other texts speak about the Jews being incited to persecution, but this persecution does not really get started until xiv 5. In vs. 2, the Western text has added "but the Lord gave peace quickly," so that the difficulty in the Neutral text has disappeared: the persecution had two stages with a pause in between. In xiv 19 in the Neutral text, the stoning of Paul occurs very suddenly, while the Western text, by making additions about the missionaries' stay in Lystra, presents a more acceptable picture of the missionary period in this city.

c. Theologically important alterations occur in Western manuscripts and give the impression of being later adaptations of unbiased texts. Thus in xv 20, 29 (the Apostolic Decrees), the Western text adds the Golden Rule in a negative form. In xv 2 the Western text is obviously correct (both syntactically and logically) in stating expressly that the visitors from Jerusalem selected the men who were to go to Jerusalem and consult the apostles. In the quotation from Joel in ii 17–21, the Western text shows a series of variants from the text of the Septuagint (chiefly preserved in the Neutral text) which make the text of the quotation better suited to the occasion. Thus in both vs. 18 and vs. 19 of Joel ii the end is omitted.

SELECTED BIBLIOGRAPHY

It must be emphasized that this list is not meant either to be exhaustive or to satisfy the needs of the scholar. What is here suggested is intended for the general reader interested in following up the kind of problems touched on by the late author in the course of his commentary.

Avi-Yonah, Michael, and Emil G. Kraeling, *Our Living Bible,* New York, 1962. This is an excellent work, copiously illustrated, covering both Testaments historically, socially, and religiously, grounded on the best interpretation of archaeological evidence—indeed, it might with justice be called the general reader's archaeological handbook to the Bible.

Cadbury, Henry J., *The Making of Luke-Acts,* New York, 1927.
————ed. with Kirsopp Lake, and F. Foakes-Jackson, gen. eds., *The Beginnings of Christianity,* Vols. IV and V, New York, 1933. Both the above works always appear in bibliographies of scholarly works on Acts. The first exercised, and to some extent still exercises, wide influence on the study of Luke's work.

Conzelmann, Hans, *The Theology of St. Luke,* tr. by Geoffrey Buswell, London, 1960. This book reflects the somewhat unexpected marriage between existentialism and neo-Hegelianism which has characterized so much German religious writing in the past decade. However, the book is often referred to in other works which the student might consult, and so is included here. It is not clear how seriously Conzelmann takes the element of eschatology in primitive teaching. Certainly he produces an interpretation of *parousia* which owes more to the Hegelian "synthesis" than to the Pauline "age to come" with which we may assume Luke to have been familiar.

Davies, William D., *Paul and Rabbinic Judaism: Some Rabbinic Elements in Pauline Theology,* London, 1948.
————*Christian Origins and Judaism,* London, 1962. The author of these two books is a specialist in the influence of Judaism on the primitive Christian community. The first title explains itself; the second is a collection of essays on various aspects of New Testament scholarship in the light of first-century Judaism.

Deissmann, Adolf G., *Licht vom Osten*, 4th ed., Tübingen, 1923. English translation: *Light from the Ancient East*, tr. by L. R. M. Strachan, New York, 1927.

――――*Paulus, Eine kultur- und religionsgeschichtliche Skizze*, Tübingen, 1925. English translation (of 2d ed.): *Paul, A Study in Social and Religious History*, tr. by William E. Wilson, New York, 1927.
These two books, by a leading authority in papyrology, and a very considerable authority on ancient literature, are valuable for the insights they provide on the interplay of linguistic and literary influences.

Dupont, Jacques, O.S.B., *The Sources of Acts: The Present Position*, tr. by Kathleen Pond, London, 1964. This is an important examination of the sources which various schools of thought have attempted to distinguish in the composition of Luke's work. As such, it is not only an important work of reference, but also materially useful in evaluating recent scholarly work. It contains important studies on "form criticism."

Filson, Floyd V., *A New Testament History: The Story of the Emerging Church*, New York, 1964. This is a book for anyone who is prepared to take some pains to come to grips with the historical background of the New Testament, and it is particularly good on the ministry of Paul.

Finegan, Jack, *Light from the Ancient Past: The Archaeological Background of Judaism and Christianity*, 2d ed., Princeton, 1959.

――――*Handbook of Biblical Chronology: Principles of Time Reckoning in the Ancient World and Problems of Chronology in the Bible*, Princeton, 1964. The first volume, admirably illustrated, is a fine book of reference. It is a mingling of history, archaeology, and the development of religion, and as such is a magnificent accomplishment. The second book, though indispensable for the scholar, is hardly a work for the general reader. There is, however, much information such a reader would gain from its discussions of various topics. The bibliography is excellent.

Grant, Robert M., *Gnosticism and Early Christianity*, New York, 1959. In view of all the attention now being paid to influences from outside on the early history of the Church, this book will repay both the student and the general reader willing to take the trouble to examine what is meant by "Gnosticism" in its varied forms.

Kee, Howard C., and Franklin W. Young, *The Living World of the New Testament*, Englewood Cliffs, New Jersey, 1957. This book covers the New Testament, and is a "popular" work in the very best sense.

Knox, Wilfred L., *St. Paul and the Church of the Gentiles*, New York, 1939.

――――*The Acts of the Apostles*, New York, 1948. It should be stressed that Knox's works were written before the first-century Jewish world had been so brilliantly illuminated by the discoveries at Qumran. But both books continue to be important as studies of the impact of the conversion of Paul on the primitive church.

Munck, Johannes, *Paul and the Salvation of Mankind,* tr. by Frank Clarke, Richmond, 1959. Toward the end of his life, and while writing this commentary on Acts, the late Johannes Munck grew more conservative in his attitude to Acts. The growth of a conservative approach to Luke's work is reflected in this book. With its many new approaches to the picture of the primitive Christian communities which we have from Paul's letters, this book serves to illuminate some of Munck's distinctive contributions to New Testament thought.

Nock, Arthur Darby, *St. Paul,* London, 1938 (latest ed. 1964). This book remains an important tool for the student. Nock was ahead of his time in understanding many of Paul's central themes and their background.

O'Neill, J. C., *The Theology of Acts in Its Historical Setting,* London, 1961. This book must be treated with caution in that matter of the dating of Acts. The author appears to treat the relations of Jews to Gentiles in the first century with more assurance than the evidence warrants. Moreover, there is but one reference to the Qumran material, and that of a peripheral character. There are, however, some useful insights into the theological preoccupations of Luke.

Ramsay, William M., *St. Paul the Traveller and Roman Citizen,* London, 1895. Ramsay's unrivaled knowledge of the topography and inscriptions of the first century made this a book of capital importance, and it may still be read with great profit. The book marked the beginnings of a serious effort to understand the historical framework of the latter part of Acts. It should be noted that when the book was published, there were no recognized *koinē* inscriptions; this is no longer the case.

Williams, C. S. C., *The Acts of the Apostles,* London, 1957. This commentary, intended for the general reader who is prepared to study further, comes to no conclusions of its own on the varied problems which Acts raises, but does make clear all the issues involved. The bibliography is excellent, and all the references are worth exploration.

PART I

1. THE PREFACE TO ACTS
(i 1-5)

I ¹ In my first book, Theophilus, I wrote about all that Jesus began to do and teach ² until the day when he was taken up (into heaven), after he had given instructions through the Holy Spirit to the apostles whom he had chosen; ³ and after his passion, he showed himself alive to them with many clear proofs, appearing to them during forty days and speaking about matters concerning the kingdom of God. ⁴ While he was in their company he enjoined them not to depart from Jerusalem, but to await what the Father had promised, which "you have heard about from me; ⁵ for John indeed baptized with water, but you shall be baptized with the Holy Spirit within a short time."

NOTES

i 1. On Theophilus see p. xvi.

from his first appearance (in King James Version). This is a translation of a Greek verb which literally means "began." Others therefore think that this verse stresses the fact that Jesus' ministry began during his life on earth, as related in Luke, and that it continued after his ascension, as related in Acts.

2. In the Greek text *through the Holy Spirit* is governed by *given his instructions* as well as by *had chosen*. In both cases the Holy Spirit is said to be functioning before the day of Pentecost. The *apostles* are the twelve disciples—now the Eleven—who had followed Jesus and whose names are given in i 13. The *Holy Spirit* plays a very important part in Acts but is described in different ways in the many sources used by Luke. The Holy Spirit prevented Paul from going to Bithynia (xvi 7), and later the apostle went to Jerusalem guided by the Holy Spirit, who at the same time foretold that chains and tribulations would await him there (xx 22-23). The whole church was filled with the Holy Spirit, who was sometimes regarded as a spiritual power and at other times as a visible and

audible manifestation, so that everybody was able to perceive that it was the Holy Spirit acting. It would hardly be correct to ascribe importance to whether or not the Holy Spirit is accompanied by the definite article, to attempt in this way to differentiate between different conceptions of the Holy Spirit in Luke's sources. Here we are trying to reproduce Luke's reading of his source; therefore the Holy Spirit is written throughout in one way, without any attempt to represent the varying forms: "a spirit," "the spirit," "the Holy Spirit."

3. *showed himself alive*. Like a similar expression in ix 41, a demonstration of the reality of the wonder. The *many clear proofs* refer to the events that followed the appearances of the risen Christ. The *forty days* is a frequently used approximate numbering (cf. xiii 31); Jesus, for instance, fasted for forty days and nights (Matt iv 2 par.); (cf. Mark i 13). There are also significant Old Testament connections to the days of the wilderness, etc.

4. Besides Luke xxiv 41–43 and John xxi 12–13, only Acts speaks of the meals of the risen Christ with his disciples; cf. "those witnesses . . . who ate and drank with him" (x 41).

the Father had promised. Used in Luke xxiv 49 and Acts ii 33, about the gift of the Holy Spirit. The disciples were to await this before leaving Jerusalem. Nevertheless, the account of primitive church history in Acts shows that the gift of the Holy Spirit on the day of Pentecost did not result in the eldest disciples leaving Jerusalem to take up their work at another place. Luke's interpretation of the Father's promise would therefore appear to be incorrect. In four other passages (ii 39, xiii 23, 32, xxvi 6), the expression "the promise" is used in another sense, namely, that of the coming of salvation to Israel. If we adopt this interpretation in the two passages mentioned above, they mean that when the promise of the salvation of Israel is fulfilled, then the twelve apostles should leave Jerusalem and go to the Gentiles. This promise has not yet been fulfilled.

5. A promise going back to John the Baptist (cf. Mark i 8 par.; John xxi 33; see also Acts xi 16), according to which it was the Holy Spirit which was new in Jesus and his disciples, would be fulfilled in a few days.

COMMENT

Acts opens with a preface addressed to the same Theophilus mentioned in the preface to the whole work in Luke i 1–4. The preface to Acts gives an account of the first volume, not however of the content of the whole volume, as is usually the case, but only of what is dealt with toward the end of this volume. The sequence of events described appears to be accidental. The account first mentions the ascension, then Jesus' appearing to the apostles during a period of forty days (the number is not mentioned in Luke). Jesus spoke to them of matters concerning the kingdom of God, which appears to be a common expression for giving Christian instruction, although it anticipates the question of the apostles in vs. 6. Jesus also joined them and once while so doing, enjoined them to remain in Jerusalem until the Holy Spirit had been given to them. The features of the preface are to be found in Luke xxiv: the ascension in vss. 50–51; the appearances in vss. 15–16, 30–31, 36; Jesus speaks of his passion both in vss. 25–27 and vss. 44–47; he eats with his disciples (vss. 41–43) and in connection with this he orders them to remain in Jerusalem until "they are clothed with power from on high" (vs. 49). The accidental order does not conceal the fact that this passage deals with decisive matters which link the first part of the work with the second, namely: Jesus in his life on earth with his apostles, his passion, death, and resurrection; and finally with the Holy Spirit, already present before his ascension and for whose coming the apostles must wait in Jerusalem.

2. THE MISSION TO THE WORLD AND
THE ASCENSION
(i 6–14)

I 6 When they were all together again, they asked him, "Lord, are you at this time about to restore the kingdom to Israel?" 7 He said to them: "It is not for you to know the dates and times which the Father reserves to his own sovereignty; 8 but you will be empowered when the Holy Spirit comes upon you, and you will then bear witness for me in Jerusalem, and throughout the whole of Judea and Samaria, and to the ends of the earth." 9 When he had said this, he ascended as they watched, and a cloud removed him from their sight. 10 As they gazed up into the sky while he departed, behold, two men in white garments stood by them 11 and said: "Galileans, why do you stand looking up toward heaven? That Jesus who has been taken from you into heaven will come (again) in the same way as you saw him depart into heaven."

12 Then they returned to Jerusalem from the mountain called the Mount of Olives, which lies near Jerusalem, a sabbath day's journey away. 13 When they had come into the city, they went to the upper room where they were staying, Peter, John, James and Andrew, Philip and Thomas, Bartholomew and Matthew, James son of Alphaeus, Simon the Zealot, and Judas son of James. 14 They engaged in common prayer continuously with the women and Mary the mother of Jesus, and with his brothers.

NOTES

i 6–8. The disciples' question sounds as if they had misunderstood the Father's promise and thought it concerned the restoration of the kingdom to Israel. If so, the interpretation of the expression, outlined above, as the promise of Israel's salvation is a probable one. It is reminiscent of the disciples' questions about the coming destruction of the temple, Christ's second coming, and the end of the world (Matt xxv 3 par.). The beginning of Jesus' answer in vs. 7 recalls Matt xxiv 36 par.: the Father alone knows the time for the end of the world. Verses 6–8, perhaps in conjunction with vss. 4–5, form a farewell speech. Jesus gathered around him those close to him, giving them final decisive instructions before his departure.

9–11. The ascension had been told before in Luke xxiv 50–51, but as quietly as if it were a matter of saying good-by with a view to meeting again the next day.

12–14. *a sabbath day's journey* (Exod xvi 29; Num xxxv 5) was a little more than half a mile. The upper room has been identified with the place where the Holy Communion was instituted (Luke xxii 12), and with the house of Mary, the mother of Mark (Acts xii 12), but this is quite uncertain. The list of apostles deviates from that given in Luke vi 13–16 especially in placing John directly after Peter (cf. Peter and John in Acts iii 1, 3, 4, 11, iv 1, 13, 19, 23, viii 14).

COMMENT

It should not be surprising that after this account of the contents of the first part of Luke-Acts, which as mentioned above is certainly not written in the traditional Greek form, the following account of the content of the second part should also turn out to be something quite different. The problems that arise with the theory that Luke must have been a man of great culture and therefore a slavish imitator of ancient models (see p. xxv) need not worry us. It is not necessary to explain why Luke included this material where one would expect to find traditional forms and expressions, nor is it advisable to assume that a later editor removed Luke's classically formed preface in order to substitute the passages that follow. As a Christian, Luke had a completely new story to tell and that is why he could not use the established forms.

Here we find, instead of a summary of the content of the second part, a saying by Jesus corresponding to what was said in Luke xxiv 47–48 about preaching to all the peoples of the world, starting from Jerusalem, and what was said in Matt xxviii 19 where Jesus sent his eleven apostles out to the whole world to make the Gentiles his disciples. What corresponds to this in our text is that the thought of the restoration of the kingdom for Israel is replaced by the mission to the world, although it is not, as in Matt xxviii, clearly stated that the mission is to the Gentiles. The preaching of the Gospel in this passage in Acts could apply either to the Jews in dispersal or to all men. A further illustration of this problem is only gradually provided by Acts in the progress of the narrative which reveals Israel's unbelief and the Gentiles' openness to the Gospel. An account of the apostles' testimony in Judea is found in chapters ii–vii and in Samaria in chapter viii, but Acts deals chiefly with the mission to all the world, although Paul in his journeys did not in the literal sense of the word go to the ends of the earth.

After this saying of Jesus the ascension took place. Luke is never afraid of telling something more than once and in rather different ways. When a cloud hid Jesus from the eyes of the apostles, two angels interpreted what had happened, linking his ascension with his second coming. Upon their return from the Mount of Olives, the apostles went to the upper room where all the early disciples prayed together. A brief survey of the members of this earliest group follows.

3. THE TWELFTH APOSTLE IS CHOSEN AFTER
THE DEATH OF JUDAS
(i 15–26)

I 15 In those days Peter stood up in the midst of the brethren
(there was a gathering of about a hundred and twenty, persons known by name), and said: 16 "Brothers, that text had to
be fulfilled which the Holy Spirit foretold through the mouth
of David, concerning Judas who acted as guide to those who
arrested Jesus. 17 He was one of us, and had his place in this
ministry. 18 (This same man afterwards bought a plot of land
with the reward of his sin, and he fell headlong, and his body
was shattered so that his entrails poured out. 19 This had become known to all that lived in Jerusalem, so that this land was
called in their language Hakeldama, which means Field of
Blood.) 20 For it is written in the Book of Psalms:

> 'His homestead shall be desolate
> and there shall not be anyone living there';

and

> 'Another shall have his work of overseeing.'

21 Therefore one of the men who was with us throughout the
time when the Lord Jesus came and went among us, 22 from
the time of the baptism by John to the day when he was taken
from us—one of them should bear witness with us to his resurrection." 23 And they proposed two, Joseph called Barsabbas,
surnamed Justus, and Matthias. 24 And they prayed saying:
"Lord, knowing the hearts of all men, let us know which of
these two you have chosen 25 to fill the place in this apostolic
ministry which Judas left to go to his own place." 26 And
they drew lots, and the lot fell on Matthias, and thereafter he
was numbered with the eleven apostles.

NOTES

i 15–20. Jesus' acts and his suffering had been predicted in the OT. This also holds for Judas' betrayal and his later fate as well as for the coming election of his replacement. The references are found in two quotations from Psalms, namely, lxix 26, very freely quoted, and cix 8. First Peter speaks about Judas' fate, which had not been mentioned in Luke. He used his payment for the betrayal to buy a plot of land but fell headlong and lay there in his blood—which gave the plot of land the name "Field of Blood." Matthew (xxvii 3–10), however, offers another explanation of the name: Judas repented of his treachery and after throwing the money into the temple he went away and hanged himself. The chief priests were now faced with the difficult question of what to do with the ownerless blood money. When they bought a field with the money and turned it into a burial ground for strangers, it was named after the blood money and called the "Field of Blood." Papias (Fragment III in Bihlmeyer, *Die apostolischen Väter,* 1924) has still another account of Judas' horrible death, which recalls the death of Agrippa I (cf. Acts xii 23; Josephus *Ant.* XIX.343–52 [VIII.2]).

21–26. Eligible for service as an apostle were those disciples who had maintained a close connection with Jesus from the time of John the Baptist's ministry (cf. x 37) until the ascension, and consequently could bear witness to his resurrection. One is reminded by these words of the preface to the two-part work (Luke i 2): "eyewitnesses and ministers of the word." The congregation nominated two, of whom one, Joseph, was called Barsabbas, as was Judas in xv 22. The name Barsabbas has been found on one of the ossuaries from Talpioth (cf. E. L. Sukenik's most uncritical article in *The American Journal of Archaeology* 51 [1947], 351–65). It looks as if only two outside the apostolic group qualified, which meant that the demands were rigorous. After praying to God (or to Jesus), who knows the hearts of all men, the decision was made. The expression in vs. 26, *they gave them lots,* can be understood as voting by ballot so that it need not be a question of the drawing of lots. The apostles' number, twelve, seems to reappear in the number of members in the congregation, where there are about one hundred and twenty men (cf. vs. 15)

Comment

Here, a traditional account is inserted about the death of Judas and the election of Matthias to take his place. The vacancy is immediately filled which provides an opportunity for defining what an apostle is. The event is precisely dated as it occurred after the ascension, which ended the approximately forty days during which the risen Christ revealed himself to the apostles, and before Pentecost, which comes fifty days after Easter. In the congregation, Peter took the initiative by referring to Judas' death. His act and his miserable end had been foretold in the Old Testament. This man, who had been in apostolic service but had helped the persecutors to find Jesus during the night, had bought a plot of land for the money he received for his treachery, but had fallen down and been killed by his fall. As the Scriptures had foretold, he would not be able to live on his land, and another was to replace him in the group. What was required of his successor was that he had been one of the group of disciples from the beginning to the ascension, and thus, together with the other apostles, be able to bear witness to the resurrection. The congregation presented two candidates who met this requirement, and after prayers, Matthias became the new member of the Twelve.

Strangely enough Matthias is not mentioned anywhere else in the New Testament. The meaning of "apostle" in this account was not the original, which was a "designated messenger." By "apostle" Paul, our earliest witness, meant a man to whom the risen Christ had revealed himself and whom he had called to be a missionary to Israel or to the Gentiles. Luke is the first to link together the twelve disciples—and we follow him in calling them apostles—with the original meaning of the word "apostle" in the primitive church. It is worth noting that these witnesses never really left Jerusalem and Palestine. Their mission was to the people of Israel in the Holy Land. Other missionaries, apostles in the original meaning of the word and among them Paul in particular, were sent out and carried the Gospel all over the world.

While Luke used the word "apostle" six times about the twelve disciples around Jesus (vi 13, ix 10, xi 49, xvii 5, xxii 14, xxiv 10), the word is found only once in Matthew (x 2) and once in Mark (vi 30). John uses the word once, but not about the Twelve (xiii

16). Luke's concept of the word "apostle" seems to presuppose Paul's, and the difference with regard to this fundamental point is an important argument, one must concede, against the view advanced in this book concerning the relationship between Luke and Paul and concerning the time when Luke's work was composed (pp. XLVI ff.). As it is impossible in any view of the work to make everything agree, one is obliged to choose the view that provides the most likely solution to the largest number of problems.

4. THE PENTECOSTAL MIRACLE
(ii 1–13)

II ¹ When the day of Pentecost had begun they were all assembled in one place; ² and suddenly there came from heaven a sound like the rushing of a great wind, and it filled all the house where they were sitting. ³ There appeared to them tongues, like tongues of flame, distributed so that a tongue settled upon each one of them. ⁴ They were all filled with the Holy Spirit, after which they began to speak in other languages, as the Spirit gave them ability.

⁵ And there were Jews living in Jerusalem, devout men of every nation under heaven; ⁶ now, when this sound was heard, the crowds came flocking, and were struck with awe because each man heard them speaking in his own language. ⁷ They were filled with astonishment and said: "Are not all those who are speaking Galileans?* ⁸ How is it, then, that each of us hears them speaking his own language which he has heard from early childhood— ⁹ Parthians, Medes and Elamites, and those who come from Mesopotamia, Judea, and Cappadocia, Pontus, and the province of Asia, ¹⁰ Phrygia and Pamphylia, Egypt, and those parts of Libya that are near Cyrene, and Romans living here, ¹¹ Jews and proselytes, Cretans and Arabians—how is it that we hear them speaking of the great works of God in our own languages?" ¹² And they were all of them astonished and bewildered, and they said to one another: "What does this mean?" ¹³ But others taunted and said: "They are drunk on sweet wine!"

* Or "Christians"—i.e., "followers of the Galilean"; see Appendix III on Pentecost.

NOTES

ii 1–2. *All* may be the apostles, who from ii 14 appear before the people, but it is more likely to be the whole congregation. The first Pentecost may very well have been the occasion for a larger gathering of Galilean disciples of Jesus who, like their Jerusalem brethren, had met the risen Christ in their native district. This is the only certainty in an otherwise quite uncertain identification of the Pentecostal experience with the risen Christ revealing himself to more than five hundred brethren at the same time (I Cor xv 6). One has wondered whether there would be enough room in a private house for such a large assembly of god-fearing Jews, but the text maintains that it was an ordinary house.

3–8. The wondrous happening is described first as a movement and a sound and then as something visible to individual Christians or apostles. Just as the Jews spoke of the Law having been handed to seventy nations so an attempt has been made to find a similar thought in this passage, but what is significant is the fact that Jews, who had grown up with another language than that of Palestine, suddenly encountered the preaching about Christ in the language of their native country. It is an anticipation of what we know from the liturgy of the later church, that the Gospel of the feast is read in different languages.

9–11. The Jews themselves enumerate the peoples from Persia and Mesopotamia to Asia Minor and from there to North Africa—interrupted only by *Judea* (vs. 9) and *Romans living here, Jews and proselytes* (vss.10–11)—ending with the inhabitants of the desert regions and of distant islands (as in Jer xxv 22–24; Isa xi 11). Considerable uncertainty exists with regard to the wording of the text and the thought behind it.

12–13. The miracle cannot be explained and this uncertainty prepares the Jews for Peter's speech. So does the mocking suggestion that what was strange in this matter could be explained by too copious a use of wine at the opening of the festival.

COMMENT

In Acts as it has come down to us, the Pentecost miracle was the fulfillment of the promise to pour out the Holy Spirit upon the disciples. On the day of Pentecost as the Christian church was assembled for its service, a very loud rushing noise was heard round the house and the house was filled by it. The sound soon gave way to tongues of flame which settled on every Christian, as all were filled with the Holy Spirit, and upon its inspiration, they began to speak in other languages. [For another interpretation of these events, see note on Pentecost in Appendix III.] Jerusalem was a Jewish city of international character—during a festival, the visiting pilgrims contributed much to the city's claim to being the capital of the whole world—and in the crowds drawn by the miracle, there were Jews from all the countries and peoples of the world, who each heard the disciples preach on God's great acts in their own language. As the Christians were known to all as people who had moved to Jerusalem from Galilee no reasonable explanation for this miracle of languages could be found. Many did not find any explanation, and the usual mockers ascribed the many languages to the liberating effect of wine on the human tongue.

5. PETER'S PENTECOSTAL ADDRESS
(ii 14–36)

II 14 Then Peter came forward together with the Eleven, and raising his voice began to preach to them: "Jews and all you who live in Jerusalem, understand this, give me your attention! 15 For these men are not drunk, as you assume—it is only the third hour of the day— 16 but it is rather what was spoken by the prophet Joel:

17 'And it shall happen in the last days, says God,
    I will pour out my Spirit upon all flesh,
    so that your sons and your daughters shall prophesy,
    so that your young men shall see visions,
    so that your old men shall dream dreams;

18 even upon my slaves, men and women,
    will I in those days pour out my Spirit
    so that they shall prophesy.

19 And I will cause wonders to happen in the heaven above,
    and signs on the earth below,
    blood, fire, and billowing of smoke.

20 The sun will be turned to darkness
    and the moon to blood
    before the day of the Lord comes, the great and glorious day.

21 And it shall be that
    whosoever calls upon the name of the Lord will be saved.'

22 Israelites, listen to these words: Jesus of Nazareth, a man whom God has accredited to you by the powerful deeds, wonders, and signs which he performed through him in your midst, as you yourselves know, 23 this man who was handed over according to God's appointed plan and foreknowledge, you killed, when you had him crucified by heathen hands; 24 but God put an end to the agony of death and raised him up, since it

was not possible that he should be held captive by death. 25 For David said this about him:

'I saw the Lord always before me,
for he stands at my right hand,
lest I should be made to stumble.

26   Therefore my heart rejoiced,
and my tongue was jubilant with happiness.
Yes, my body will dwell in hope,

27   for you will not leave my soul in the kingdom of the dead,
nor will you allow your Holy One to see corruption.

28   You have taught me the ways of life,
you will fill me with joy in your presence.'

29 Brothers, it is possible to speak confidently to you of the patriarch David, for he is both dead and buried, and his tomb is with us to this very day. 30 Now, as he was a prophet, and (also) knew that God had sworn an oath to him to place one of his descendants upon his throne, 31 he foresaw and spoke of the resurrection of Christ: that he should neither be left in the kingdom of the dead, nor should his body see decay. 32 This Jesus was raised up by God, and of this we are all witnesses. 33 Now that he has been exalted to the right hand of God, and and has received from the Father that which was promised, namely the Holy Spirit, he has poured it out as you both see and hear. 34 For David did not ascend to the heavens, but he says himself:

'The Lord said to my Lord:
Sit at my right hand

35   until I make your enemies your footstool.'

36 The whole house of Israel shall now know for a certainty that God has made this very Jesus, whom you crucified, both Lord and Messiah."

NOTES

ii 14. The speech was addressed to Jews only and the Pentecostal miracle predicted the mission among the Jews all over the world.

15. *The third hour of the day* was 9 A.M., before the Jews had their first meal of the day. The twenty-four-hour period was divided into

twelve hours of night and twelve hours of day and the hours were counted from 6 P.M. and 6 A.M.

17–21. The quotation from Joel (ii 28–31) is a free rendering and exists in different versions in the Western and in the Neutral texts (see pp. LXXXV–LXXXVI). In the quotation, the pouring of the Holy Spirit over them all stresses that this happened to the whole Christian congregation in Jerusalem. *The Lord* in vs. 21 is Jesus (as in Rom x 13).

ii 19. Signs and wonders is a phrase that appears nine times in all from here to xv 12 and never after that.

22–24. *Jesus of Nazareth . . . whom God has accredited to you by the powerful deeds.* It is not indicated whether the powerful deeds had shown that he was the Messiah or "Messiah-elect." In the gospels, these deeds make up about half of what is said about Jesus. His death is at one and the same time determined by God and carried out by men, namely by the Jews to whom Peter was speaking. His death occurred with the assistance of the Romans who nailed him to the cross. The death of Jesus did not put an end to the connection between God and his chosen people, for through the resurrection of Jesus God had offered the Jews another possibility of believing in Jesus and participating in salvation (cf. ii 36, 38–39). Jesus could not be held fast by death, and God raised him up.

25–28. The quotation from memory of Ps xvi 8–11 is taken as a prophecy about the resurrection of Jesus. At the end of vs. 26 the LXX rendering *in hope* has been adopted and the psalm understood as expressing hope in the resurrection from the dead.

29–31. Peter proves that Ps xvi 8–11 does not refer to David himself. His tomb in Jerusalem is proof that he was not exempt from the ravages of death. At the time of Jesus the tombs of OT figures were objects of great interest, to which Jesus himself testifies by his words that "your fathers killed them and you are building the tombs of the prophets" (Luke xi 47–48 par.). The tomb of David, now shown in Israel, is of a later origin.

32–36. The apostles (cf. i 22) or the Christians bore witness to the resurrection of Jesus. After God had raised him to his exalted position, Jesus had received the Holy Spirit and had given it to the Christians as an initial step toward the salvation at the end-time. Up to then it had only been said that the Jews heard (ii 6 ff.), but now they were said both to see and to hear. It is not certain that Jesus' being named Lord and Messiah took place only after his crucifixion. What is stressed is clear testimony to this attribution. It is at any rate difficult to disregard that God vouched for Jesus by *powerful deeds* in vs. 22 and would not let his *Holy One see corruption* or let him leave his *soul in the kingdom of the dead* according to the quotations in vs. 27. According to Philip ii 6 ff., Jesus received the name that is above all names, the name of "Lord," after his death.

COMMENT

As in the gospels, and elsewhere in Acts, Peter is the representative of the Twelve and of the congregation in Jerusalem. Like everything else in the history of Jesus and of the primitive church, the miracle of languages that had just occurred was a fulfillment of an Old Testament prophecy, this time a prophecy of the prophet Joel (ii 28–32), which spoke of the pouring of the Spirit upon all flesh (i.e. all Jews) in the last days. Peter then turned to the matter that had come between Jews and Christians, namely, Jesus of Nazareth. The Jews had killed him, but God had thereupon raised him from the dead. For it was not possible that Jesus should be imprisoned by death. Proof of this is given in the Scriptures in Ps xvi 8–11, which David as a prophet had pronounced about Jesus. After his resurrection, Jesus had been exalted and sat at the right hand of God, had received the Holy Spirit from the Father, and had given it so that the audience had been able to see and hear its outward signs. David also spoke of the exaltation of Jesus in Ps cxl which cannot refer to David himself. By the pouring out of the Spirit, it was made known to the whole of the house of Israel that Jesus, whom they had crucified, had by God been made both Lord and Messiah.

6. THE GREAT BAPTISMAL ACT ON THE DAY OF PENTECOST
(ii 37–40)

II 37 When they had heard (this) they felt a deep grief in their hearts, so they said to Peter and the other apostles: "What shall we do, brothers?" 38 Peter (said) to them: "Repent and let each of you be baptized, calling on the name of Jesus the Messiah, that your sins may be forgiven, and then you will receive the gift of the Holy Spirit. 39 For the promise is to you and your children, and all those far away, as many as the Lord our God will call." 40 With many other words he thus set forth his case, and he exhorted them and said: "Let yourselves be saved from this vicious generation!"

NOTES

ii 38. The baptism, which Peter urged the repentant Jews to receive, comprises both the elements in the baptism of John the Baptist, and those in the Christian baptism (cf. i 5 and NOTE; xix 2–6). In this passage as well as later Luke reckoned with very large numbers of baptized Jews (cf. NOTE on iv 1–4).

40. *vicious generation.* This expression, found in Deut xxxii 5 and Ps lxxviii 8, is frequently used by Jesus—sometimes only in the form of "this generation" (Matt xi 16 par., xii 39, 41, 42 par., xvi 4 par., xvii 17 par., xxiii 36 par., xxiv 34 par.; Mark viii 38; Luke xvii 25).

COMMENT

The speech made the listeners feel penitent and they asked what they should do. Peter answered that they must repent, let themselves be baptized, receive forgiveness of their sins and the Holy Spirit. For the promise of the Holy Spirit concerns the Jews, including the Jews living far away in other lands, corresponding to the present situation of Jews in all the countries of the world. Luke gave only a brief excerpt of Peter's words and added the following quotation: "Let yourselves be saved from among this vicious generation!" Like Jesus, primitive Jewish Christianity considers the unbelieving Jews a source of perdition from which one must dissociate oneself to be saved.

7. LIFE IN THE GROWING CHURCH
(ii 41–47)

II ⁴¹ Those who had accepted his preaching were baptized, so that on that day about three thousand souls were added to them. ⁴² They persevered in the apostolic teaching and fellowship, in breaking bread, and in prayer. ⁴³ Awe came upon all, for many wonders and signs were done through the apostles. ⁴⁴ But all those who came to believe had all in common as a group; ⁴⁵ they sold both lands and other property, and distributed the money to all according to need. ⁴⁶ They continued to meet every day in the temple and, breaking bread at home, they ate their meals with joy and simplicity. ⁴⁷ They praised God and were well liked by all the people, and the Lord continued daily to add to the total of those who were saved.

NOTES

ii 41. Here a large number, three thousand, are baptized (cf. ii 47); the number increases to five thousand, in iv 4, with a further increase, mainly a large group of priests, in vi 7. See xxi 20 and NOTE.

42. This verse describes the special characteristics of the church. The apostles, witnesses to the resurrection, demonstrate what separates them from the other Jews. The common meals, and their prayers to Christ are only for the baptized. Cf. Appendix IV on the organization of the early Christians.

43. As was the case in all future missionary advances the word was accompanied by wonders (cf. iv 30, v 12, xix 10–12).

44–45. Just as Judas carried the common purse when Jesus walked with his twelve disciples (John xii 6, xiii 29), so everything was held in common by the larger group of disciples. The narratives inserted give a more detailed picture of the community of property in the primitive church. Barnabas was singled out as one who had sold a plot of land and had given the money for it to the apostles (iv 36–37). It would not have been necessary to stress this if "all of them" had done so.

46. This verse shows that the primitive church is in close connection with the temple in the same way as John the Baptist's and Jesus' close connection with it is shown in Luke i–ii; Acts iii 1 throws further light on vs. 46: the disciples took part in the hours of prayer at the temple and on certain occasions they spoke there (cf. iii 11 ff., v 20–21, 25).

47. Their relations with the people are good, just as in iv 33 and v 13. Acts xii 3 can be understood to mean that the people might change sides as they had in the case of Jesus.

COMMENT

The listeners whose hearts had been stirred by Peter's words were baptized and thus about three thousand were added to the small congregation of one hundred and twenty. And as they followed Peter into the church, so they continued to consider the apostles their preachers and teachers; those baptized met and had their meals together and prayed in common to Christ, their Lord. A fear fell on everybody inside and outside the congregation because of the wonders and signs that occurred in Jerusalem. The disciples held their property in common, sold both their land and their possessions, and distributed the money received to everybody in need. They appeared in full view of the public in the temple at the daily prayers as missionaries of Jesus. They also held daily meetings in their homes where their common meal was observed with joy and with praise of God. Therefore they were well liked by the people and day by day God allowed their community to grow.

8. HEALING IN THE NAME OF JESUS
(iii 1–10)

III 1 Peter and John went up to the temple at the hour of prayer, the ninth hour, 2 and a man who had been crippled from his mother's womb was carried up. Every day they laid him by the temple gate called Beautiful, so that he might beg alms from those who went into the temple. 3 When he caught sight of Peter and John as they were on their way into the temple, he asked for alms. 4 But Peter—together with John—gazed intently at him and said: "Look at us!" 5 And he looked earnestly at them, expecting to receive something from them. 6 But Peter said: "I have no silver or gold, but what I do have I give you. In the name of Jesus Christ the Nazarene, walk!" 7 And he seized him by the right hand and raised him up; and immediately his feet and ankles were strengthened, 8 and he leaped up and stood. He walked about and went with them into the temple, walking and leaping and praising God. 9 All the people saw him walking about and praising God, 10 and they recognized him as the man who had sat by the Beautiful Gate of the temple to beg alms, and they were filled with wondering amazement because of what had happened to him.

NOTES

iii 1. Peter and John walked together as in viii 14 ff. John, generally supposed to have been the son of Zebedee (Matt iv 21 par.), took no active part. Is this because the apostles were sent out two by two (cf. Mark vi 7; Luke x 1)? *at the hour of prayer, the ninth hour.* This was the second daily hour of prayer at 3 P.M. (cf. NOTE on ii 15).

2. The lame beggar had been a cripple all his life and was a well-known figure at the temple and in Jerusalem. We have no definite knowledge of a temple gate called the Beautiful, and our two main texts, the Neutral and the Western, differ from each other, so that it is

uncertain whether the gate was placed at the entrance to the temple grounds or as an entrance to the temple buildings.

3–6. The cripple did not ask to be cured but for alms, and the two apostles stared gravely at him and urged him to look at them. He was still thinking of nothing but his alms, when Peter's words revealed that he was confronting a man who, though poor, could give him more than he knew and who commanded him to walk. The words of command were, *"In the name of Jesus Christ the Nazarene, walk!"* These were the words and this was the name that made the authorities persecute the apostles (cf. iv 7, 10, 17–18, v 27–28).

7–10. We follow the different stages in the healing process. While giving the commands, Peter raised up the lame beggar and his feet and ankles were immediately strengthened so that he could use them. As if overwhelmed by these new and unknown possibilities, he leapt up, stood upright and praising God, followed the apostles into the temple. All the people recognized him and were filled with wonder (cf. ii 43).

COMMENT

A description of the apostles' testimony in Jerusalem in connection with the account of the day of Pentecost is begun in chapter iii. Peter and John went up to the temple to pray, but their meeting with a lame beggar led to his being healed in the name of Jesus. This gave Peter an opportunity to make a speech to the people (iii 11 ff.) in which he stressed that it was the name of Jesus Christ which alone had effected the beggar's healing. Thus the speech became a testimony to Christ, the Christ who had been killed but had risen. Peter's address led to persecution (iv 1 ff.). The authorities interfered in order to stop any preaching in the name of Jesus. The closest parallel to these accounts, which cover healing, speaking of Jesus, and persecution, is found in John, where it was Jesus himself who was present and who healed the sick (v 1–5, ix 1–39; cf. xi 1–44). These healings gave Jesus an opportunity to speak about himself and his relationship to the Father (v 19–47, vii 14–24; cf. x 22–30). And these speeches also led to persecution (v 16–18, vii 25–26; cf. x 31–39, xi 45–57). Even the setting was the same, namely, the temple and the streets of Jerusalem. In both John and Acts the beginning is marked by a healing performed by Jesus or in the name of Jesus. The healing becomes the subject of the preaching which ensues: a confession of Christ, in whose name God's power was brought to bear on the

sick person. In Acts, as in John, the persecutors are the Sadducees
and the chief priests of the temple. But on one point they differ: in
John, the Pharisees were considered Christ's enemies in strange al-
liance with the temple aristocracy. One point remains: in neither
book did the persecution achieve its goal. In John, the attendants
returned without any success (vii 32, 45–46); in Acts the apostles
were released again and continued their preaching in the name of
Jesus.

9. PETER'S EXPLANATION OF THE MIRACLE OF HEALING
(iii 11–26)

III 11 While he clung to Peter and John, all the people, filled with wonder, came running and surrounded them in the colonnade called Solomon's. 12 When Peter saw this, he began to speak to the people: "Israelites, why do you marvel at this, or why do you stare at us as if we had by our own power or holiness enabled this man to walk? 13 The God of Abraham, Isaac, and Jacob, the God of our fathers, has glorified his servant Jesus, whom you indeed handed over and repudiated in Pilate's presence when he wished to release him. 14 You repudiated the holy and righteous one, and you demanded that a murderer should be released to you. 15 But you killed the prince of life, whom God raised from the dead, as we bear witness. 16 Through faith in his name, Jesus' name has given strength to this man, whom you see and know, and the faith that is called out by him (Jesus) gave this man the full use of his limbs, as you can all see.

17 "Now, brothers, I know that you acted out of ignorance, as your leaders did too, 18 but in this way God fulfilled what he had made known beforehand through the mouths of all the prophets: that his Messiah was to suffer. 19 Repent therefore, and turn (to God), so that your sins may be wiped out, 20 in order that times of renewal* may come from the presence of the

* As it stands, the expression in the Greek which the RSV renders as "times of refreshing" is capable of translation. But whether one translates *kairoi anapsuxeōs* as "times (or seasons) of refreshing (or refreshment)," or by any other similar expression suggesting a period of respite, it remains to be asked what idea is conveyed by the phrase, and also whence originally it derived. (A somewhat similar idea is to be found in Luke xvi 24.) The phrase does not occur in the rabbinic literature, and as it stands is not a Semitic expression. However, the unpredictable nature of the rainfall in Babylon and Syria-Palestine, with consequent hazards for human and animal life, found expression very early in the inscriptions, myths, and even in

Lord, and he may send Jesus, whom he has chosen as your Messiah. 21 But heaven must receive him until the time of the re-establishment of all things, about which God spoke by the mouths of his holy prophets from the earliest days. 22 Moses said: 'A prophet like me will the Lord God raise before you from among your brothers; obey him in all that he may say to you. 23 But it shall happen that every man who does not obey this prophet shall be destroyed from among the people.' 24 And all the later prophets too, from Samuel onward, as many as spoke, have preached of these days. 25 You are the heirs of the prophets, you are included in the covenant God made with your fathers, when he said to Abraham: 'And through your family all the families on earth shall be blessed.' 26 God made his servant appear first to you, and he sent him to bless you when you—all of you—turn away from your wicked deeds."

---

the grave-furniture of the whole area. Egypt, with a wholly different situation climatically, conceived its "refreshing" in terms of cool breezes. But in both areas the idea is the same: prayer for, anticipation of, interludes of refreshment by which the human spirit may be fortified. (It is noteworthy that the phrase *locum refrigerii, lucis et pacis,* is still to be found in the Latin liturgy of the departed.)

The best study of the whole idea, and a study by no means yet superseded, is that of André Parrot, *Le "Refrigerium" dans l'au-delà,* Paris, 1937—W.F.A. and C.S.M.

NOTES

iii 11. Solomon's Colonnade, also mentioned in John x 23 and Acts v 12, was situated in the eastern part of the temple buildings.

12–15. The phrase *The God of Abraham, Isaac, and Jacob* appears in Exod iii 6, 15, and the expression *servant,* used in connection with the suffering servant of the Lord, appears in Deutero-Isaiah, in particular in lii 13 ff. In Acts, it appears in iii 13, 26, iv 27, 30. The Jews handed over Jesus to Pilate, opposing the latter's wish to release him (Luke xxiii 16, 22).

handed over appears to be a stock phrase in primitive Christian preaching (cf. I Cor xi 23). From the speeches in Acts, it becomes evident that sinful man often did God's will in such acts. The people's desire to have Barabbas and not Jesus released, furthermore, was mentioned. In Mark xv 7 and Luke xxiii 19, it was hinted that Barabbas was a murderer. The speech made use of contrast: *the holy and righteous one—a murderer—the prince of life—you killed—God raised from the dead.* Once more the apostles were mentioned as witnesses to the resurrection as in i 22, ii 32. "The Righteous One" was also a title for Jesus, vii 52, xxii 14. It may have been an early title used about Jesus. Later James the brother of the Lord was called "the Righteous One."

16. Refers to the faith of the cripple, not to that of the apostles, even though his faith—as well as that of many other persons healed—was hardly demonstrated. The sentence (vs. 17) is a good example of the difficult kind of language found throughout the whole chapter. With respect to these early chapters there is no reason to ascribe the differing linguistic forms to Luke. They can more naturally be referred to his sources, unknown to us.

17-18. Both the people and the authorities had acted out of ignorance, as already stated in Jesus' prayer on the cross (Luke xxiii 34) and repeated by Paul (I Cor ii 8); another parallel can be found in Acts xiii 27. As for the OT prophecies to which Peter and the others referred: the primitive church found many more passages dealing with the sufferings of the Messiah than we have been able to find.

19-21. The situation of the Jews was not without hope. They ought therefore to repent so that their sins might be wiped out and Jesus return in his glory bringing final salvation. Both Jews and Christians knew that there would be human participation in the fulfillment of salvation. The Jews maintained that Israel must first be converted, otherwise the Messianic age could not occur; in the NT it is stated that before the end could come, the Gospel must first have been preached to all ⁓peoples, Matt xxiv 14 par.; Acts i 8; II Thess ii 6-7. Just as the prophets had all foretold the sufferings of the Messiah, so they had also stated that he would stay in heaven until the end of the world. In contrast to the rapidly spreading modern insistence on a consequent eschatology in the NT, the last events before Christ's second coming are apparently seen as a definite interval between Jesus' life on earth and his return in glory. The prophets had foretold a number of things about changes in the relative strength of different powers, about the return of the exiles, about the exaltation of Jerusalem, and about the conversion of the Gentiles, and we find echoes of certain aspects of these OT expectations in what is said by Jesus and by his disciples about the last days before the second coming. Luke i 70 is a parallel to vs. 21.

22-24. Whether Moses' prophecy about a prophet like himself (Deut xviii 15 ff.) refers to Christ's second coming or to Jesus' first coming, is difficult to determine; vs. 23 corresponds to some extent to Lev xxiii 29. It may very well be a warning about the right attitude toward the coming Messiah, but may also be applied to what had already occurred; the same holds for vs. 26. But as the people did not, after all, obey him in his life on earth, there is reason to interpret the

THE ACTS OF THE APOSTLES

words as referring to Christ's second coming. We hear of the people's expectation of this prophet in John vi 14 and possibly in John i 21. The warning to those who did not obey the promised prophet shows that the Christians were the true Israel.

25–26. The present Jews were descendants of the prophets who predicted all this, and were partakers in God's covenant with Abraham which promised that through Abraham's family (Christ or the Jews) all the families on earth should be blessed (Gen xii 3 et passim; Gal iii 16 interprets "the family" as Christ). God had first addressed himself to them, whether this were done through Jesus on earth or through the returning Christ (cf. Rom xi 26: the deliverer will come from Zion). If one chooses to interpret vs. 26 as referring to the apostles' preaching of Christ there are a number of parallels: Mark vii 27; Acts xiii 46; Rom i 16, ii 10, all showing that the Jews would be the first to hear the Gospel and, after them, the Gentiles. This Jewish Christian view of missions (cf. p. LXV), we find once more in James' speech in Acts xv 13 ff., where the same assumption is made.

COMMENT

The first event, the healing, led to the next, Peter's speech, which was meant to explain what had happened. The crippled man had not been healed by the two men standing with him in the crowd but by the name of Jesus, for whose death the crowd present, together with all the Jewish people, must be held responsible. God had raised from the dead, him whom they had killed. They had, Peter went on, acted out of ignorance but at the same time God had fulfilled the predictions of all the prophets that his Messiah was to suffer. Therefore the Jews must have a change of heart and be converted, so that their sins could be wiped out and the times of renewal might come and Christ return. Even though a quotation from the Old Testament pointed out that every man who did not obey the Lord's prophet should be eradicated from the people, Peter's exhortation was full of optimism. He referred to God's promise to Abraham: "And through your family all the families on earth shall be blessed," and ended by saying that God had raised his servant first of all for them, and sent him to bless them when each one had turned away from his wicked deeds.

10. PETER AND JOHN ARRESTED
(iv 1–4)

IV ¹ While Peter and John were speaking to the people, the priests, the commander of the temple, and the Sadducees came upon them, ² indignant that they taught the people and preached resurrection from the dead through Jesus. ³ They laid hands upon them and placed them under arrest till the following day; for it was already evening. ⁴ But many of those who had heard the word believed, so that the number of the men became about five thousand.

NOTES

iv 1–4. The speeches in Acts are frequently broken off, but nevertheless constitute a whole and are in fact brought to a conclusion (ii 36?, v 33?, vii 54, x 44, xvii 32, xxii 22, xxvi 24). It is strange to find that the Sadducees are mentioned side by side with the priests and the Levite commander of the temple, the next in rank after the high priest, as the word is the name of a party and not of a function. In vs. 2 we find the usual statement made about the Sadducees that they were against the teaching of the resurrection from the dead (cf. xxiii 8; Matt xxii 23 par.). Like ii 41, vs. 4 indicates that Peter's speeches had produced excellent results. When compared with Paul's account of the unbelief of the Jews and the complete failure of the mission to the Jews (cf. pp. LIX–LXIII), these figures give the effect of being highly exaggerated.

COMMENT

While Peter was still speaking, the priests, the commander of the temple, and the Sadducees came upon them. The Sanhedrin, consisting of the leading priests, representatives of the old patrician families, and the scribes, were forgathering, their meetings presided over by the high priest. At the arrest of the disciples no mention was made of the healing, but the Sanhedrin was said to be indignant that Peter and John had taught the people and had preached resurrection from the dead through Jesus. So they were placed under public arrest until the following day. Then vs. 4: the number of those who had believed is now five thousand, the increase perhaps a consequence of the healing and the speech and in any case reason enough for official concern. Thus a link is provided for the persecution to come.

11. THE APOSTLES' DEFENSE BEFORE THE
SANHEDRIN
(iv 5–22)

IV 5 Next day the rulers of the Jews, their elders, and their scribes gathered in Jerusalem, 6 among them the high priest Annas, Caiaphas, John, Alexander, and all who were of the high priest's family. 7 They placed them before them and asked them: "By what power or by what name have you done this?" 8 Then Peter, filled with the Holy Spirit, said to them: "You rulers of the people and elders, 9 if today, because of a kindness to a sick man, we are asked by what means he was cured, 10 let it be known to all of you and to all the people of Israel, that it is through the name of Jesus Christ the Nazarene, whom you crucified, but whom God raised from the dead—it is through him that this man stands before you cured. 11 He is that stone which was rejected by you, the builders, but which has now become the cornerstone. 12 And there is no salvation through any one else. For there is no other name under heaven given to men through which we must be saved."

13 When they observed the boldness of Peter and John, and saw that they were unlearned in the Law and laymen, they marveled and recognized them as men who had been with Jesus; 14 and, seeing the man who had been cured standing beside them, they could give no answer. 15 They then commanded them to go outside, and thereafter consulted among themselves. 16 They said: "What shall we do to these men? That a clear sign has taken place through them is plain to all who live in Jerusalem, and so we cannot deny it. 17 But in order that rumor of it may spread no further among the people, let us forbid them with threats to say any more to anyone about this name." 18 They called them in, and commanded them on no account to preach or teach in the name of Jesus. 19 But Peter and John an-

97653

swered and said to them: "Judge for yourselves whether it is right
in duty to God to obey you rather than God. 20 We cannot re-
frain from speaking of that which we have seen and heard."
21 But they threatened them still more, and then released them,
being unable to punish them because of the people, who all
praised God for what had happened; 22 for the man on whom
this act of healing had taken place was more than forty years old.

NOTES

iv 5–6. Annas was high priest from A.D. 6–14 and was still known
because no less than five of his sons became high priests. No longer a
high priest at this time, he like others seems to have kept his title; the
title could be given to members of the families from which high priests
were chosen. The text seems to indicate that Annas was the officiating
high priest (cf. Luke iii 2), but this is not correct. Like Caiaphas, Annas
was known from Jesus' passion; and John who clearly recognized
Caiaphas as the officiating high priest (cf. xi 51), had Jesus first taken
before Annas (xviii 12–13). John may be one of Annas' sons who later
became high priest. Nothing is known about Alexander.

7. The question, *By what power or by what name have you done this?*
with its scornful tone and its reference to the healing recently performed,
recalls the question which the high priests and the elders had asked
Jesus: "What authority have you for doing as you do, and who gave
you this authority?" (Matt xxi 23 par.).

8. Peter spoke, *filled with the Holy Spirit.* Jesus had foretold that
under persecution (cf. p. LXV) his disciples should speak what would be
given to them by the Holy Spirit (Matt x 19–20 par.).

9–10. The answer that it was the name of Jesus Christ that had
healed the cripple was as it had been stated in Peter's speech in the
temple. And as in that passage, so it was stressed here that the Jews—or
the authorities—had had Jesus crucified but that God had raised him
from the dead.

11–12. In a metaphor borrowed from Ps cxviii 22, Jesus is compared
to the stone rejected by the builders that becomes the cornerstone
(cf. Matt xxi 42 par.). Peter once more maintained that salvation could
be gained not through Judaism but only through Jesus (cf. iii 19, 23).

13–14. The authorities did not know the two apostles, and wondered
why they—though unlearned in the Law—were so firm in their attitude,
until they realized that they were disciples of Jesus (which, according to
vs. 2, they already knew). The healed beggar presented a striking argument which threatened to silence the authorities.

15–17. Whereupon they ordered the prisoners to go outside, while they held their council. They were not able to deny that a powerful sign had occurred. Jesus' healings were thought of as facts which could not be denied but could be interpreted as acts of the Devil (cf. Matt xii 22–27 par.). This to them seemed to be the only way to stop the spread of the story of the healing. So they decided to forbid the apostles to speak in the name of Jesus. (It did not seem to have occurred to anybody to forbid their healing in the name of Jesus.)

18–22. The apostles were ordered not on any account to speak of Jesus, but their immediate reaction was to protest against this because they were bound to obey God and to speak of what they had seen and heard (cf. Acts xxii 15, xxvi 16).

COMMENT

Led by the high priests, the Sanhedrin met the next day and put the following question to the two apostles: "By what power or by what name have you done this?" Peter, filled with the Holy Spirit, answered—just as in his speech at the temple—that it was through the name of Jesus that the lame beggar stood healed before them. The council based its decision solely on the fact that the sign was known to all in Jerusalem and it could not be denied. The only way to fight the occurrence was to prevent them by threats from preaching or teaching in the name of Jesus. But although the apostles refused to obey the council, they were released, for the council could not punish them for something for which everybody in town was praising God.

12. THE CHRISTIANS PRAY FOR BOLDNESS
DURING THEIR PERSECUTION
(iv 23–31)

IV 23 After Peter and John had been released they returned to their fellows, and they told them all that the high priests and the elders had said to them. 24 When they had heard this they all raised their voices to God and said: "Lord, you who have created heaven, earth, the sea, and all that is in them, 25 you who by the Holy Spirit, through the mouth of our father your servant David, said:

'Why did the Gentiles boast,
and why did the peoples make plans in vain?

26   The kings of the earth stood in array,
and the rulers gathered together
against the Lord and against his Messiah.'

27 For truly they gathered together in this city against your holy servant Jesus whom you had appointed Messiah, both Herod and Pontius Pilate, together with the Gentiles and the tribes of Israel, 28 to do all that your hand and will had already determined should happen. 29 Now today, Lord, take notice of their threats, and grant that your servants may speak your word with all boldness, 30 in reaching out your hand in healing, and making signs and deeds take place through the name of your holy servant Jesus." 31 When they had prayed, the place where they were gathered was shaken, they were all filled with the Holy Spirit, and continued to speak the word of God with boldness.

Notes

iv 23–28. After their release, the apostles told their own people about the threats of the authorities and all joined in prayers to the Lord—they did not usually address God as "Sovereign"; Luke used it only in this passage and in Luke ii 29—the Almighty Creator (Exod xx 11; Ps cxlvi 6), as in xiv 15, xvii 24, who according to Ps ii 2 preserved his servants from the Gentiles and the people, from the kings and rulers of the earth. Psalm ii 2 had been fulfilled in Jesus' passion, in which Gentiles and Jews, kings (i.e. Herod Antipas; cf. Luke xxiii 6 ff.) and rulers (i.e. Pilate) were opposed to Jesus (cf. p. 18), whom God had appointed Messiah (it is not said when this was done). But what was instigated by these sinful people was only what God had willed.

29–31. At this point the Christians were faced with the same situation as Jesus had been when threatened by the authorities. The earthquake shaking their house came as a divine answer to their prayer, as a "Your prayer has been heard." The disciples were filled with the Holy Spirit, and continued speaking with the boldness for which they had prayed.

Comment

When the apostles were back among their own people, they told them everything that the authorities had said to them. And immediately all of them joined in prayer to the Creator of the world, who in the Psalms had already spoken about the futility of any opposition against the Almighty by the peoples and their rulers, as had been shown in the case of Jesus, God's anointed servant. They implored the Lord that despite the threats of the authorities, he would give his servants boldness to speak when he stretched out his hand to heal in the name of Jesus. After their prayer, the house where they had gathered was shaken and the disciples became filled with the Holy Spirit and they continued to speak the word of God with boldness.

13. COMMON OWNERSHIP OF PROPERTY AMONG THE CHRISTIANS
(iv 32–37)

IV 32 The band of those who believed had one heart and one soul, and not one of them said that anything that belonged to him was his own, but they had all in common. 33 And the apostles witnessed with great power to the resurrection of the Lord Jesus, and abundant grace (of the Lord) was upon them all. 34 Nor did any among them go in need, for those who owned land or houses sold them, and brought the money for what had been sold 35 and laid it at the feet of the apostles. It was then distributed to each man according to his need. 36 And Joseph, whom the apostles had surnamed Barnabas, which translated means "Son of consolation," a Levite, whose family was from Cyprus, 37 sold a field that he owned, and he came with the money and laid it at the feet of the apostles.

NOTES

iv 32–35. The whole of this passage (with vss. 36–37) deals with the common ownership of property in the primitive church. A break occurs only in vs. 33, which speaks of the apostles' testimony to the resurrection of Jesus (i 22, ii 32; cf. ii 42)—referring *with great power* to the wonders worked by the apostles (cf. iv 29–30)—and of the grace that had come to all Christians (cf. ii 47 where, however, the expression "were well liked by all the people" was used). We have previously heard about their property being held in common, namely, that the owners sold their property and distributed the money to the needy (ii 44–45). This is retold here in more detail and using the expression they *laid it* [the money] *at the feet of the apostles* (cf. iv 37, v 2). *Nor did any among them go in need,* the beginning of vs. 34, recalls Deut xv 4. An important question is whether common ownership of property was usual. The story of Barnabas might indicate that those who carried it into effect were few

enough to be named. Peter's words in v 4 show that the common
ownership of property was a voluntary affair. One also wants to know
whether the gifts were distributed only to members of the congregation.
The common ownership of property in Qumran was on a different
basis and of a different kind.

36–37. We meet Joseph Barnabas again in ix 27, xi 22, 30, xii 25,
and in chs. xiii–xv; and in Paul's letters I Cor ix 6; Gal ii 1, 9, 13;
Col iv 10. His surname, which the apostles were supposed to have given
to him, has been translated by "Son of request" (or of "consolation"),
but this cannot be right. The same holds for Elymas or Bar-Jesus in
xiii 8. Such impossible interpretations of Semitic names might be an
indication that Luke did not know Aramaic.

COMMENT

Those who had attained the faith held everything in common.
The apostles testified with great power to the resurrection of Jesus
and to the grace (of the Lord), so abundant upon them all. Nobody was in need, for those who owned anything sold it and gave
the money to the apostles to be shared by all, each man according to his need. Joseph the Levite, surnamed Barnabas, sold
a piece of land and placed the money received for it at the feet
of the apostles.

14. THE FIRST DEATHS IN THE CHURCH
(v 1–11)

V 1 A man named Ananias together with his wife Sapphira sold a field, 2 and with her knowledge, kept back part of the money for himself and then came with the rest and laid it at the feet of the apostles. 3 But Peter said: "Ananias, why did Satan fill your heart so that you lied to the Holy Spirit and put some of the money for the land aside for yourself? 4 Was it not yours as long as you owned it? After it was sold was not the money yours to dispose of? Why did you decide in your heart to act so? You have not lied to men, but to God." 5 As Ananias heard these words he sank to the ground and died, and great fear fell upon all who heard of this. 6 The young men rose, wrapped him, and carried him out and buried him.

7 It happened, about three hours later, that his wife came in, not knowing what had occurred. 8 Peter asked her: "Tell me, did you sell the land for so much?" She said, "Yes, for so much." 9 Peter said to her: "Why have you agreed to harass the Spirit of the Lord? Listen, the feet of those who buried your husband are at the door, and they shall carry you out." 10 And immediately she sank down at his feet and died; the young men came in and found her dead, and they carried her out and buried her by her husband. 11 Great fear fell upon the whole church and upon all who heard about these things.

NOTES

v 1–2. A married couple, Ananias and Sapphira, names in common use at the time, sold a plot of land, but without telling anybody they put aside for their own use part of the sum received, before they brought the remainder to the apostles. A just parallel is that of Achan who, according to Josh. vii 1 ff., misappropriated (here the same Greek word is used in the LXX) what had been dedicated to God and was killed together with his family.

3–6. In receiving the gift of money, Peter accused Ananias of having been lured by Satan into lying against the Holy Spirit (cf. vs. 9) and keeping back part of the money for the field. He had full possession of his land and the money paid for it at the sale. For the primitive church sinning against the Holy Spirit is the greatest sin. It would be forgiven neither in this world nor in the world to come (Matt xii 31–32 par.). Satan was behind this sin just as it was he who had entered into Judas Iscariot before the betrayal (Luke xxii 3; John xiii 2, 27). This was also the reason why church discipline was maintained by handing the guilty one over to Satan (I Cor v 5); in Acts there is no mention—as there was in I Cor v—of the possibility of salvation for the guilty one. In Corinth, death had snatched several people away because they had taken part unworthily in the Holy Communion (I Cor xi 27–30). With regard to this matter, see also Paul's severe words in II Cor xiii 2–7.

11. The word *church* occurs here for the first time in Acts. This early use has been doubted, because it is maintained that the Christians considered themselves part of Judaism at that time, as a kind of special synagogue. Primitive Jewish Christianity doubtless felt itself to be part of Israel, namely, the true Israel, the true inheritors of the patriarchs. They, however, assumed an independent and critical attitude toward the Jewry of the time, whose understanding and fulfillment of the law of Moses Jesus had criticized (e.g., Matt iii 7–10 par., v 17–48); like John the Baptist, he refused to accept the notion that they, being children of Abraham, would automatically attain salvation. This was the Jewry which killed Jesus and later tried to prevent the Christians from speaking and acting in the name of Jesus.

The Greek word for "church" is used in the LXX as a translation of the Hebrew word which precisely signifies "Israel as a congregation." The Christian use of the word "church" may have come from that. The earliest church must have consisted of more than one community, and even if the numbers given by Luke are treated with a certain caution, still the early Christians could not all have been assembled in one place. But the entity is the church, just as new Christian communities may indeed be called "churches" yet taken together or as individual representatives constitute the church. Jesus may have used the word "church" about the one that was to come. It is however not certain when he spoke the word to Peter: "You are Peter (rock) and on this Peter, I will build my church" (Matt xvi 18). The word "church" was probably spoken during the revelation of the risen Christ mentioned in Luke xxiv 34; I Cor xv 5. It requires the substitution of the present tense for the difficult future tense. In other words, the passage in Matthew caused a change from the normal biblical word of calling "Now I make thee" to the unusual "Sometime you shall be," but this agrees with Paul's word that Peter was called to be apostle to the circumcised (Gal ii 8), and accord-

ing to Paul, an apostle was called by the risen Christ. Thus Peter was the
rock on which Christ built his Jewish Christian church, whereas Paul
was the messenger traveling to the end of the world to induce all Gentiles
to believe in Christ and to undertake a pilgrimage to Jerusalem.

COMMENT

Chapter V opens with an account of a sale of property and the
handing over of the money to the apostles—in strange contrast
to the story of Barnabas. The same things seemed to occur, but
the married couple, Ananias and Sapphira, put aside some of the
money that they received for their property and place the remainder at the feet of the apostles. But he who lies against the
Holy Spirit can be detected by men who are filled with the Spirit.
Peter accused Ananias of lying against the Holy Spirit, whereupon
Ananias fell dead. When his unsuspecting wife confirmed that she
had connived in her husband's action, Peter pronounced her death
sentence. The death of this couple struck fear both in the Christians
and in people outside the church.

Some scholars have taken this account to be an example of
church discipline where the expulsion of the guilty one was followed by his death, as in I Cor v 5. Others have wanted to interpret the account as an attempt to explain to the Christians the
(to them surprising) fact that they would not all experience Christ's
second coming when the separation of the sheep from the goats,
of the tares from the wheat, would take place. In Matt xiii 30 it
was said, "Let them grow together until harvest time." But here
in Acts, it is a matter of such a great sin—a sin against the Holy
Spirit—that immediate church discipline and punishment must follow. It is correct that the earliest Christians did not think that all
of them would die. Therefore the deaths of some of the members
of the congregation called forth genuine grief in Thessalonica (I
Thess iv 13–18). In Corinth, it was thought that the wonderful
experience of receiving the gifts of the Holy Spirit was proof that
the resurrection had already taken place; it would not be necessary
to die and to rise again in order to gain the heavenly gifts (I Cor
xv; cf. I Cor iv 8–9). Paul impressed upon them the reality not
only of resurrection but also of death (xv 12–19); it was important
to tell them this for earlier, when it was mentioned that some of
the more than five hundred brethren had died (xv 6), the Corinthians

had not really believed that Christians would die. Jesus had foretold that "there are some of you that stand here who shall not taste death until they have seen the kingdom of God come with power" (Mark ix 1 par.), and when all the original disciples except John had died, the hope still lingered that he, the disciple whom Jesus loved, would remain until Christ's return (cf. John xxi 20–23)—but this hope failed too.

While we are more accustomed to gradations of agreement, the primitive church took it for granted that one must say either yes or no. If one associates with the holy—by the gift of grace from the Holy Spirit or by the pledge of one's money to God—then ordinary Christians, like Ananias or Sapphira, risk becoming involved in Satan's struggle with God, a struggle which only apostles and prophets are capable of.

15. SIGNS AND WONDERS BY THE APOSTLES
(v 12–16)

V 12 Many signs and wonders took place among the people through the ministry of the apostles. They customarily gathered together in Solomon's Colonnade. 13 At first no one outside their number ventured to join them, but the people in general held them in respect. 14 But still more were added who believed in the Lord, crowds of both men and women, 15 so that they even carried their sick out into the streets and placed them on beds and on litters, that as Peter passed by perhaps at least his shadow might fall upon one or another of them. 16 Indeed, even from the towns around Jerusalem the crowd came flocking with their sick and those who were afflicted with unclean spirits, and they were all healed.

NOTES

v 12–14. As in iii 12–16, the apostles did not heal, but healings were performed through their hands. The Christians foregathered—just as the witnesses to the healing of the lame beggar had (iii 11)—in Solomon's Colonnade, but during their persecution they were isolated, because the others feared the authorities. In vs. 11 another kind of fear was aroused by Peter's actions with regard to Ananias and Sapphira.

15–16. We learn later (xix 12) that after removing the scarves and garments that had touched Paul's body, people had carried them to the sick, who were then healed by them. We recognize a feature from the ministry of Jesus, namely that people brought sufferers to Jesus, often from a great distance, in the hope that God would save them (Matt iv 24–25 par., viii 16, xv 30 par., xxi 14). The remark that all the sick had been healed also occurred elsewhere (Matt iv 24, xii 15 par., xv 30 par.).

COMMENT

The passage v 12–16 is full of puzzles. Who were those who were gathered in Solomon's Colonnade: the apostles, yes, but who else? And what was their relation to the people? And does that relationship help to explain why many came to believe in Christ? Although it is impossible to offer a definitive interpretation of these verses, we shall assume that it was the Christians who were gathered in the temple and that it was the non-Christians who did not dare to join them in Solomon's Colonnade, because the Christians were persecuted by the authorities. The people at large, however, held them in respect, and in spite of everything, the membership of the church was increasing. Verse 15 is a continuation of the first sentence in vs. 12 dealing with the signs and wonders that had occurred through the apostles. But the intervening verses enable us to understand those who expected help through the power abiding in the apostles. It was the people at large who, believing in Peter's healing powers, carried their sick out into the street in the hope that the apostle's shadow would fall on them and heal them. Rumors spread from Jerusalem to the people of the neighboring towns, so that they too brought their sick and those possessed by demons and all of them were said to be cured.

Like Jesus, the apostles undertook healing and the exorcising of unclean spirits (Matt x 1 par.). Missionary preaching was accompanied by extraordinary healings (cf. NOTE on iv 16). In Acts, signs and wonders are seen to accompany Paul's bringing of the Gospel to a town (xiv 8–10, xvi 18, xix 11–12; cf. xiii 10–11). The Pauline letters confirm the Acts' account of the overwhelming power characteristic of the early missions (I Thess i 5; Gal iii 1–5; cf. I Cor ii 4–5; II Cor xii 12). There can be no doubt that the early church included such unusual events in its picture of primitive Christian expansion. Just as the audiences were moved by the word, so they came under the power of God, which was manifested in signs and wonders. It may be doubted that wonders ever happened, but the events which were taken by the first Christians to be signs and wonders cannot be denied.

16. THE PUBLIC ARREST OF THE TWELVE APOSTLES AND GAMALIEL'S ADVICE
(v 17–42)

V 17 However, the high priest came forward, and all those who were on his side, that is, the Sadducean party in that place, were inflamed with zeal, 18 and they laid hands on the apostles and placed them under public arrest. 19 But in the night an angel of the Lord opened the door of the prison, led them out and said: 20 "Go and stand in the temple and tell the people all about this way of life." 21 When they had heard this, they went into the temple at dawn and taught. As soon as the high priest and his followers had come, they summoned together the Sanhedrin, that is, the whole Israelite council of elders, and they sent word to the prison that they should be brought before them. 22 But when the deputies arrived, they did not find them in the prison. They returned and reported, 23 "We found the prison securely locked, and the guards standing before the doors, but when we opened them, there was no one there." 24 When they—the commander of the temple and the high priests—heard these words, they were perplexed about these men as to what might happen. 25 But someone came and told them: "Listen, those men you put in prison are standing in the temple teaching the people."

26 Then the commander of the temple together with his deputies went and brought them, but not by force—for they feared the people might stone them— 27 and they set them before the Sanhedrin, and the high priest questioned them thus: 28 "We expressly commanded you not to teach in this name, and now you have filled Jerusalem with your teaching and you seek to bring this man's blood upon our heads." 29 But Peter and the (other) apostles said in reply: "One must obey God rather than men. 30 The God of our fathers raised up Jesus,

whom you executed by crucifixion. 31 God has exalted him at his right hand as Prince and Saviour, to give repentance and forgiveness of sins to Israel. 32 Both we, and the Holy Spirit, which God gives to those who obey him, are witnesses to these things."

33 When they heard (this) they were seized with indignation and wished to kill them. 34 Then there rose in the Sanhedrin a Pharisee called Gamaliel, a teacher of the Law greatly respected by all the people, and he gave orders that these men should be taken outside for a short time. 35 Then he said to them (the other members of the council): "Israelites, beware of these men, whatever you intend to do. 36 For before these times Theudas came forward and said that he was somebody, and about four hundred men joined him. But he was executed, upon which all those who had followed him were dispersed, and nothing came of it. 37 After him Judas of Galilee came forward in the days of the registration, and he gathered a (large) following; he also perished and all those who had followed him were scattered. 38 As to this matter: I say to you, stay clear of these men and let them alone. For if this design or this work comes from men it will be destroyed, 39 but if it comes from God you cannot destroy them—in order that you may not come to be regarded as men who contend against God." They followed his advice, 40 summoned the apostles, had them beaten, and commanded them not to speak in the name of Jesus, after which they released them. 41 So they went out from the presence of the Sanhedrin, glad that they had been held worthy of disgrace for the sake of his name. 42 Every day in the temple and in their homes they did not cease to teach and proclaim Jesus as the Messiah.

NOTES

v 17–21a. It is difficult to translate the Greek expressions for arrest and imprisonment, for there are now different forms of imprisonment which were hardly to be found at that time. The use of *public arrest* is an attempt to avoid too precise a definition.

In Peter's later release from prison, the door appeared to him to open and close by itself; here it is an angel who leads the apostles out (xii 10).

21b–27. *the whole Israelite council of elders,* like *all about this way of life* (vs. 20), illustrates the high style which Luke found in his source. Here again the people represented a factor to which the Jewish authorities must pay attention in their treatment of the apostles (cf. ii 47, iv 21, v 13). It comes as a surprise that Luke, or his source, first tells us of the release of the apostles in a brief, only slightly detailed account and then, while the authorities were still presumably ignorant of what had happened, he presents the events in order and at length: the high priest and his retinue had arrived, summoned the council, and ordered the attendants to fetch the prisoners; the attendants had returned with a strange report, without having been able to carry out their order. The council was uncertain about what to do next until told that the men were teaching in the temple.

29–33. As earlier in iv 19, Peter and the apostles state that one must obey God rather than men. It is perfectly logical that the apostles could not obey "the men" who had killed Jesus the Messiah. Peter's speech confirms the words of the high priest at the end of vs. 28 (cf. Matt xxvii 25). A distinction is made between the authorities, who had killed Jesus, and Israel whose salvation Jesus, now sitting at God's right hand, makes possible. Just as in i 22, ii 32 ff., iii 15, Peter points out that the apostles—but in this case the Holy Spirit as well—were witnesses to the resurrection and the other events.

34–38. Gamaliel was a well-known Pharisee and teacher of the Law, a descendant of Hillel and himself a member of the Sanhedrin; later (xxii 3) to be revealed as Paul's teacher. The two examples Gamaliel cites are: (*a*) Theudas, who had persuaded a large crowd to follow him to the Jordan by promising them that he would divide the waters of the river and allow them to cross it dryshod. Theudas was killed by Fadus the procurator (A.D. 44–46) and his supporters dispersed. (Josephus *Ant.* XX.v.1). (*b*) Judas the Galilean, who was active during the census of the people and collection of taxes under Quirinius in A.D. 6 (Josephus *Jewish War* II.8.1). As the Zealots, the movement started by Judas, had not been dispersed at his death, this second example was badly chosen. Moreover, the chronological determination of the two examples precludes any suggestion that Gamaliel could have delivered his address in the form in which Luke reported it in Acts. (Nor can the attempt to bring Luke into agreement with Josephus by the assumption of a Theudas who lived before Judas be considered to carry much conviction.)

39. Previously scholars insisted on finding a reference to Euripides in *men who contend against God,* as they did also in Jesus' word to Paul "It will be hard for you to kick against the goad" (Acts xxvi 14). There is no reason to in either case. The phrase can readily have been formed

without recourse to Euripides, and the sentence is a Greek proverb older than the *Bacchae,* where Euripides uses it.

A possibility exists that Gamaliel the Pharisee may have been opposed to the Sadducees' wish to persecute the Christians. While the Pharisees appeared as opponents of Jesus in that part of the tradition laid in Galilee, they were not prominent during his stay in Jerusalem and disappeared completely from the passion story except in John, where they appear as an authority (e.g. the chief priests and the Pharisees, vii 32, 45, xviii 3), and even as a powerful faction preventing open confession to Jesus (xii 42), and in a single passage in Matthew, namely in xxvii 62. Otherwise the accounts of the passion in the first three gospels and Acts agree that the enemies of Jesus and of the primitive church respectively were the chief priests and the highest Jewish authority in Jerusalem. As Jesus had been there, and as later the primitive church had its center there, it was natural that the Jewish authorities in Jerusalem in their official capacity should have taken measures against the new movement. But it is important to note that the Pharisees have dropped out of their role—ascribed to them by the Galilean part of the Synoptic tradition—as Jesus' antagonists and persecutors, and that in Acts it is they who are against the persecution instigated by the Sadducees. Just as parallels have been previously found between John and Acts with regard to the sequence of healing–speech–persecution, so John has also a parallel to Gamaliel in the Pharisee Nicodemus (iii 1 ff., xix 39), who in vii 50–51 protests against the persecution of Jesus. But this should not make us forget that Jesus' relation to the Pharisees, like all hostilities, also covered a positive contact. Conversation was possible and necessary, both sides wanted a confrontation, which offered Jesus an opportunity for missionary work. In Acts xv, we hear of some former Pharisees who had embraced the Christian faith. The only Pharisee in the service of the chief priests was Paul, who had left Gamaliel and become an ardent persecutor of the Christians before an even more radical switch made him an apostle of Jesus.

40–42. The Sanhedrin limited itself to having the apostles scourged, just as Pilate had had Jesus scourged rather than go further (Luke xxiii 16, 22; John xix 1), and as the Jews were to have Paul beaten several times (II Cor xi 24). The apostles' joy at being persecuted for the sake of Jesus' name has its parallel in I Thess i 6 (cf. Luke vi 23).

COMMENT

This passage is in two parts. It begins with the arrest of the twelve apostles, vss. 17–27, well told in clear language but having the effect of an enumeration of details: the twelve apostles were arrested, released from their prison, and the next morning were

found preaching in the temple, from where they had to be fetched
to the Sanhedrin. All these events follow in quick succession, but
are not fully discussed, and their significance is not stressed. Something like this must also be said about vss. 28–33 which surprisingly
connect what has been told here with the preceding passages (iv
17–20): the Sanhedrin had forbidden the apostles to preach in the
name of Jesus. But the apostles had done exactly this, and had declared the Jewish authorities to be guilty of the death of Jesus. The
apostles answered that one must obey God rather than men. The
authorities had Jesus crucified, but God raised him up and placed
him at his right hand as Saviour in order to give repentance and
forgiveness of sins to Israel—as witnessed by the apostles and the
Holy Spirit. There is nothing new in this answer when compared
to earlier speeches in Acts.

A seeming repetition is not, necessarily, another account of the
same event. Events may also be repeated and this fact must be
remembered because for some time there has been a tendency in
New Testament research to identify persons, events, or parables
that might or perhaps might not be identical. In fact history is
full of fortuitous repetitions, and two people with the same name
are in many cases two different people; two events that resemble
each other, such as Peter's healing of a lame man at the temple
in Jerusalem (Acts iii 1–10) and Paul's healing of a lame man
in Lystra (iv 7–10) are not duplicates any more than the wedding
of the king's son (Matt xxii 1–14) and the great supper (Luke
xiv 16–24) are different versions of the same parable. On the one
hand, it is possible to underestimate Jesus' power of artistic creation in the parables, and on the other, it is possible to underestimate
the possibility of a number of versions. As a scholar one cannot
take it for granted that the material is to be reduced to the fewest
occurrences, which were simply told in different ways.

After the apostles' plea before the Sanhedrin, there was a new
development that differed considerably from the speeches before it.
The Sanhedrin had received the words of the apostles with great
indignation and wanted to kill them. Then Gamaliel spoke,
quelling their agitation by pointing to a kind of natural law that
would render the twelve disciples harmless. When Theudas came
forward he won many supporters, but when he was killed his
arguments came to nothing. When at a later time Judas the
Galilean urged rebellion, the movement he had started had disintegrated as soon as he himself was executed. In this case Jesus

had already died and therefore this movement, started by men, was doomed to failure. There was of course another possibility, namely that the movement was started by God, in which case the Sanhedrin would not be able to prevent it. Probably Luke stressed this possibility more than Gamaliel would have done, trying as he was to soothe an agitated Sanhedrin. In Luke's account, there was a strange phenomenon about the disciples of Jesus: they had not been deprived of power and importance after their Master had been killed.

Gamaliel's speech is vastly superior to the context into which it has been inserted; it cannot however be a reflection of a real event, but is merely a story in a source that goes against all historical probability (see p. XLVII). First, Gamaliel mentioned a man, Theudas by name, who was active at the time of Fadus, the Roman procurator, that is, after A.D. 44, and thus later than the occasion when Gamaliel was supposed to have made his speech. Next he mentioned a man who was supposed to have come forward *after* Theudas, namely Judas the Galilean; this event had happened before Gamaliel's speech, namely at the beginning of the century but not after the time of Theudas. It also presents the difficulty that while Theudas' movement must be supposed to have disintegrated at his death, the same was certainly not the case with Judas the Galilean, who is considered by Josephus to be the man from whom the Zealots were descended. If this is correct, the movement he had created continued to be influential as late as the end of the Jewish rebellion in A.D. 70. Josephus, moreover, considered the Zealots one of the four large parties among the Jews in Palestine (see pp. XLVII–XLVIII).

The account of the imprisonment of the apostles and the report of Gamaliel's speech illustrate for very different reasons—stylistic and historical—the fact that Luke had got hold of some poor sources among all the significant material he was able to collect. Instead of basing a judgment of him only on such mistakes, one ought to value him in accordance with all the invaluable material he has preserved.

PART II

17. THE WIDOWS AND THEIR SUPPORT
(vi 1–7)

VI ¹ In those days, when the number of the disciples was increasing, there arose great dissatisfaction among the Hellenists against the Hebrews that their (own) widows were treated unfairly at the daily distribution. ² Then the Twelve called together the band of disciples and said: "It is not fitting (before God) that we should neglect the word of God to act as stewards. ³ But, brothers, choose seven men from among you who have a good reputation, and who are full of spirit and wisdom, so that we can appoint them to this task. ⁴ We shall then be able to continue devoting ourselves to prayer and the service of the word." ⁵ This pronouncement was applauded by the whole company, after which they chose Stephen, a man full of faith and the Holy Spirit, Philip, Prochorus, Nicanor, Timon, Parmenas, and Nicolaus, a proselyte from Antioch. ⁶ These they set before the apostles, who then offered prayers and placed their hands upon them.

⁷ The word of God prospered, so that the number of the disciples in Jerusalem was very greatly increased, and a large number of priests also accepted the faith.

NOTES

vi 1–6. In this passage we hear for the first time of the problem posed by Christian widows in need. The congregation took care of them, but with the growth of the church difficulties arose. It has been pointed out that there was public Jewish support of the poor. But even if this were true, the church was at that time being persecuted by the Jews, so that the poor who had turned Christian could no longer count on support but rather on persecution on the part of the Jewish authorities. Financial discrimination nearly always appears well in advance of actual physical persecution.

Here (vs. 2) we find the word *the disciples* used for the first time as a name for the Christians. The old name for Jews appears to be Hebrews, which was used about the members of the old synagogues in cities like Rome and Corinth. Hellenists outside the church are mentioned in ix 29 (possibly they are identical with Stephen's opponents in vi 9). Without more definite knowledge of the difference we must stick to the linguistic difference between the two groups. See Appendix VI, on "Hellenists" and "Hebrews."

The appointment (vs. 3) differed from the election of the twelfth apostle (i 21 ff.) in requiring that the men be of *good reputation* and *full of spirit and wisdom;* Stephen is singled out (vs. 5) as being *full of faith and the Holy Spirit.* Afterward this committee arranged for the support of both the Hebrew and the Hellenistic widows.

7. In connection with the general progress made, the many priests, probably low-ranking ones, who joined the church, are mentioned. This is one of the places where the Qumran finds have given rise to theories about the relation of the Essenes to the primitive church. There is however no indication that the priests mentioned belonged to the Qumran community.

COMMENT

The increasing number of members of the church necessitated an expansion of its staff. The congregation gave support to its widows, but tension developed between the two groups, the Hellenists and the Hebrews, because the former thought that widows from their group had been neglected. The twelve apostles, their leaders until then, presented the case to the members of the church. To avoid giving up the service of the word in order to take charge of welfare, the apostles urged the members to choose seven men of good reputation and spiritual endowment to take care of the social services. The congregation approved this plan and chose seven men, who took office with prayers and the laying on of hands. The congregation continued to grow through the addition of many priests.

Attempts have been made to interpret the tension between Hebrews and Hellenists as a tension between Jewish and Gentile Christians or at any rate to see in the Hellenists a kind of preparation for the Gentile mission. This is wrong. Hebrews and Hellenists are groups inside Jewry, to be found also in that section of it belonging to the church. It has not been possible to give a definite explanation of what is behind the two names. A possible explanation has been suggested based on the differences in language and customs between the Aramaic-speaking and the Greek-speaking Jews. But this does not explain the contrast between Jewish Christianity and Gentile Christianity. The church in Jerusalem was a Jewish Christian church with the salvation of Israel as its sole concern. The conflict between the two groups arose from differences over the support given to the widows.

As mentioned above, this tension was resolved by the establishment of a committee made up of members of the congregation, who were to take over the duties of the social services, thereby relieving the apostles who had admitted that they could not cope with both the service of the word and with their task as well. It has been supposed that the seven men with Greek names were all Hellenistic Jews, in this case Greek-speaking Jews who had settled in Jerusalem, and that the congregation had chosen in order to avoid further difficulties. But too much importance should not be attached to the names. At the time, there were many Jews with Greek names—there are two among the twelve apostles. An examination of Jewish tombs excavated in Jerusalem and its vicinity shows a considerable number of Greek names in Jewish families whose other members bear Semitic names. No conclusion about the persons' language and customs can be drawn from their Greek names. Surely, to assume that the primitive church would choose a committee for social services in which only one of the feuding parties was represented would be to underestimate its efficiency in practical matters. Such procedure would probably have given rise to complaints from the Hebrews. There were presumably representatives of both groups among the seven, of which the best-known members, Stephen and Philip, may very well have been Hebrews.

18. STEPHEN'S ACTIVITIES IN JERUSALEM*
(vi 8–15)

VI 8 Full of grace and power, Stephen worked great wonders and signs among the people. 9 And some of those from the synagogue called the Freedmen's (Synagogue), that is, Cyrenians and Alexandrians, and some of them from Cilicia and the province of Asia, came forward and disputed with Stephen. 10 But they could not hold their own against the inspired wisdom with which he spoke. 11 Then they secretly prompted some men to say: "We have heard him speak blasphemous words against Moses and God." 12 Thus they stirred up the people, the elders and the scribes, who therefore came quickly, dragged him with them, and brought him before the Sanhedrin. 13 There they brought forward false witnesses who said: "This man never ceases speaking against [this] holy place and the Law; for we have heard him say that this Jesus of Nazareth will destroy this place, and change the rules Moses gave us." 15 When all who sat in the Sanhedrin looked at him, they saw his face as the face of an angel.

NOTES

vi 8–10. *The Freedmen* is a translation of the Latin *Libertini*, in other words the Jews freed from slavery. From this synagogue, Jews from Cyrene and Alexandria came forward and debated with Stephen; so did other Jews from Cilicia and the province of Asia. Cilicia was Paul's native country and the province of Asia included the western part of Asia Minor.

11–12. They prompted certain people to spread the rumor that Stephen had uttered blasphemies against Moses and God.

13–15. These people presumably the same as in vs. 11 but now

* On Stephen's Samaritan background, see Appendix V.

appearing as court witnesses, spoke falsehoods about Stephen before the
Sanhedrin (cf. the false witnesses in Matt xxvi 59–61; Mark xiv 55–59;
nothing in Luke). In the midst of all these falsehoods, Stephen's face
shone like that of an angel.

COMMENT

The remaining part of chapter vi and all of chapter vii deal
with one of the seven members of the committee on social services.
We learn about Stephen, just as in chapter viii we will learn about
Philip; we learn not about their social service, but about Stephen's
missionary activity among Jews and Philip's work among Samaritans. It might be surprising that those who were supposed to relieve the apostles of work, in order that the latter could devote all
their time to the service of the word, were now themselves occupied in preaching and talking. We are apt to think in too rigid,
categorical terms, but the primitive church saw nothing strange in
members of the committee on social services devoting some of
their time to other Christian work. Stephen's Christian activities
were diverse; he worked miracles and was a superlative speaker
and debater. His opponents could not hold their own against him;
they got some men to testify that they had heard him utter blasphemies against Moses and God, which alarmed the people as
well as the elders and the scribes. Stephen was brought before the
Sanhedrin, where false witnesses were produced who declared that
Stephen continually spoke against the temple and the Law. Like
the false witnesses in Jesus' trial, these witnesses maintained that
he had quoted Jesus as saying that he would destroy the temple
and change the rules that Moses gave them.

Thus the same accusations were brought against Stephen as had
been brought against Jesus and would later be brought against
Paul (see pp. LXXVII–LXXVIII). Naturally many of Jesus' attitudes
toward the temple and the Law reappeared in his first disciples and
left their stamp on the church and on Stephen. It has been asserted by many, but cannot be proved, that there were large
groups among the Christians in Jerusalem who did not share Jesus'
view of the Law and of the religious customs, and did not think
that the temple should be destroyed and rebuilt by him (see p. LXIV).
But Stephen, in following Jesus' opinions, was a good example of
the Jewish Christians in Jerusalem.

19. STEPHEN'S SPEECH
(vii 1–53)

VII ¹ The high priest said: "Is this true?" ² Stephen said: "Brothers and fathers, listen! The God of glory showed himself to our father Abraham while he was in Mesopotamia, and before he had settled in Haran, ³ and he said to him: 'Leave your country and your kin, and go to the country that I will show you.' ⁴ So he left the country of the Chaldeans, and settled in Haran. After the death of his father, God moved him from there to this country where you now live. ⁵ He gave him no land there, not so much as a foot of ground; yet he promised him to give him the country for his own, for himself and for his descendants after him, although he had no child. ⁶ But God spoke thus: 'His descendants shall live as strangers in another country, and men shall make slaves of them, and ill-use them for four hundred years. ⁷ The people they will serve as slaves I shall judge,' said God, 'and afterward they shall go forth and worship me in this place.' ⁸ He gave him the covenant of circumcision; and thus he fathered Isaac, and circumcised him on the eighth day, and Isaac Jacob, and Jacob the twelve patriarchs.

⁹ "The other patriarchs, being envious of Joseph, sold him into Egypt, but God was with him, ¹⁰ and he delivered him from all his afflictions and gave him grace and wisdom in his dealings with Pharaoh king of Egypt, who thereupon appointed him governor of Egypt and of all his household. ¹¹ But famine came upon the whole of Egypt and Canaan, and great hardship, so that our fathers could find nothing to eat. ¹² When Jacob heard that there was grain in Egypt, he sent our fathers there for the first time, ¹³ and during the second journey Joseph made himself known to his brothers, and Joseph's kindred were made known to Pharaoh. ¹⁴ Joseph sent and summoned to him

his father Jacob and all his kindred, seventy-five souls in all.
15 Then Jacob went down to Egypt, and he and our fathers
died (there), 16 and they were moved from there to Sichem
and laid in the tomb Abraham had bought from Hamor's sons
in Sichem for a sum of money.

17 "When now the time approached for the fulfillment of
the promise God had given Abraham, the people increased and
multiplied in Egypt, 18 until there arose another king of Egypt,
who had not known Joseph. 19 He used cunning against our
kindred, and ill-used our fathers, so that they had to expose
their newborn sons in order that they might not live. 20 At that
time Moses was born, and he found favor in the sight of God,
and for three months he was cared for in his father's house.
21 Then when he was exposed, Pharaoh's daughter took him
and brought him up as her own son. 22 Moses was now
educated in all Egyptian wisdom, and he was skilled in planning
and doing.

24 "When he saw one suffer injustice he helped him, and
secured justice for the ill-used man by killing the Egyptian.
25 He thought that his brethren would understand that God
would deliver them by his hand; but they did not understand.
26 Next day he showed himself to [two of] them while they
fought with each other, and he tried to reconcile them with
each other by saying: 'Men, you are brethren, why do you treat
each other unjustly?' 27 But he who had wronged his neighbor
thrust Moses back and said: 'Who has made you a ruler and
judge over us? 28 Will you kill me, as you killed the Egyptian
yesterday?' 29 Then Moses fled because of these words, and he
became an alien resident in the land of Midian, where he
fathered two sons.

30 "When forty years had passed an angel appeared to him
in the flame of a burning thornbush by Mount Sinai. 31 When
Moses saw (it), he wondered at the sight, and as he approached
to look at it, the voice of the Lord was heard: 32 'I am the God
of your fathers, the God of Abraham, Isaac, and Jacob!' Moses
began to tremble, and dared not look. 33 But the Lord said
to him: 'Take off your shoes, for the place on which you stand
is holy ground. 34 I have seen clearly the persecution of my

people in Egypt, and I have heard their groan, and I have come down to deliver them. Now, let me send you to Egypt.'

35 "This Moses, whom they had denied by saying: 'Who has made you a ruler and judge?' God sent as both ruler and deliverer by the hand of the angel who had appeared to him in the thornbush. 36 He led them out by working wonders and signs in the land of Egypt, by the Red Sea, and in the wilderness, for forty years. 37 He is that Moses who said to the children of Israel: 'God will cause a prophet like me to arise before you from among your brethren.' 38 He it is who was in the congregation in the wilderness with that angel who had spoken to him on Mount Sinai, and was with our fathers; and it was he who received living words to give to you. 39 Him our fathers would not obey, but they rejected him and in their hearts turned back toward Egypt, 40 saying to Aaron: 'Make us gods that can go before us, for we do not know what has become of this Moses who led us out of the land of Egypt.' 41 They made a calf in those days, and brought offerings to this idol, and they rejoiced at the works of their hands. 42 But God turned them (away from him), and consigned them to worship the host of heaven, as it is written in the Book of the Prophets:

'Have you brought me sacrifices and (other) offerings
in the forty years in the wilderness, O house of Israel?
43   No, you carried Moloch's tent
and the star of the god Remphan,
the images you made that you might worship them.
Therefore I will remove you beyond Babylon.'

44 "The tent of testimony was with our fathers in the wilderness, as he who spoke to Moses had commanded him to make it, according to the pattern he had seen. 45 This tent was inherited by our fathers under Joshua, and they brought it in with them when they took possession (of the land) from the Gentiles whom God drove back from the face of our fathers. Thus it was till the days of David. 46 He found favor in the sight of God, and asked that he might find a dwelling for the house of Jacob. 47 But it was Solomon who built him a house. 48 But the Most High does not dwell in (houses) built by the hands of men; as the prophet says,

49 'Heaven is my throne,
and the earth my footstool;
what kind of house will you build for me, says the Lord,
or what kind of sanctuary for my rest?
50 Has my hand not created it all?'
51 "You obstinate and uncircumcised in hearts and ears, you always resist the Holy Spirit; as your fathers did, so do you also. 52 Which of the prophets did not your fathers persecute? They killed those who foretold the coming of the Righteous One, and you now living have become his betrayers and murderers, 53 you who received the Law by the mediation of angels—and have not kept it."

NOTES

vii 2–8. In apostolic times the speech of the accused on trial did not defend himself so much as the cause that he supported and represented. Stephen began with the history of Abraham in his rapid survey of Hebrew history. The patriarch Abraham received the call in Mesopotamia and settled in Palestine. When Abraham received the promise he had no children, but after the covenant of circumcision he begot Isaac his son, and circumcised him, from him Jacob and his twelve sons were descended. Stephen approved of circumcision, which could be traced back to the Age of the Patriarchs and could be performed everywhere outside Palestine.

9–16. Thus Stephen covered the history of the Jews from Abraham to Joseph. Joseph's brothers sold him to Egypt, where he, by the help of God, became a governor. A famine in Palestine brought his brothers to Egypt to buy grain, where Joseph made himself known to them and sent for his father and all his kinsfolk to come to him in Egypt (in the LXX and in a Qumran manuscript, Jacob's family is said to have numbered seventy-five; in the Hebrew text, seventy). The family still kept its connection with the tombs at Sichem in Palestine, bought by Jacob (Josh xxiv 32) and not, as Stephen says here, by Abraham, who had acquired the burial cave at Machpelah near Hebron (Gen xxiii 17–20). (Abraham, Isaac, and Jacob were buried at Hebron; Joseph at Sichem.) Joseph, too, had been forced to leave his family and his land to live in a foreign country, but like Abraham he thereby became the one who rescued his family for the future and brought them God's blessing.

17–41. In the history of Moses, Stephen went into more detail. During the reign of a later king of Egypt (Exod i 8, LXX), the people of Israel were reduced to slavery. Moses' history was narrated in accordance with Exod i ff. Moses' intervention in favor of one of his countrymen quarreling with an Egyptian was not understood by the people of Israel. Whereupon Moses left Egypt (according to Exod ii 15, because he was persecuted by Pharaoh) and went to live as a stranger in the land of Midian; there an angel appeared to him in a burning thornbush (here the place is called Sinai, in Exod iii 1 it is called Horeb). The Lord revealed himself to him with the words from Exod iii 6 (the order of vss. 33–34 and vs. 32 is the reverse of Exod iii), and sent him to Egypt (Exod iii 7, 10) to deliver God's people, Israel. In rhetorical style it is said that he, whom the people had denied forty years ago, now became their deliverer, first by working wonders in Egypt (Exod iv ff.), next at the Red Sea (Exod xiv), and in the wilderness for forty years (see for instance Exod xvi–xvii). This was the Moses who predicted that God would send to them a prophet like himself (see Acts iii 22; John i 21, 25, vi 14, vii 40), and who received God's words (the Greek word used here is generally translated as "oracular replies," but in Papias it is used about the content of the gospels, about words as well as acts) and commandments to the people.

42–50. As a punishment for their apostasy, the people were left to idols and afterward their worship of idols led to their being taken into captivity to Babylon. The allusion to the people's disobedience during their wanderings in the wilderness is from Amos v 25–27. Amos reads: "beyond Damascus," i.e. to Assyria; *beyond Babylon* (vs. 43) is only a partial correction of this text; what is meant is, "to Babylon." David wanted to build a permanent sanctuary to take the place of the nomadic *tent of testimony* of the wilderness period; it was not he, however, but Solomon who built the permanent house. This fixed temple built by man was due to a misconception of God and his nature. The quotation in vss. 49–50 is from Isa lxvi 1 f., LXX. It is natural in vs. 46 to read *the house of Jacob* for "the God of Jacob," but then the problem arises of using "house" with two different meanings: the house of Jacob is the people of Israel, while the house that Solomon built is a permanent temple. A "dwelling" is then a tent or a similar temporary sanctuary.

51–53. From the contrast between the nomadic and the settled people of Israel, Stephen turned to the latter, his enemies in Jerusalem. God had spoken to them through Abraham, Joseph, and Moses, but the fathers had not obeyed the Holy Spirit who spoke through them. They had furthermore persecuted the prophets and killed those who had foretold the coming of Jesus, whom they also killed. Our knowledge of the martyrdom of the prophets comes not from the OT but from later tradition. Though the people of Israel had received the Law by the mediation of angels, they had not kept it. Here there is a small but characteristic difference with Paul, who in Gal iii 19 declared that the mediation of the angels was indicative of the inferior value of the Law.

According to Stephen, God had actually—as in Heb i 1—at different times and in various manners spoken to the fathers, but they had been disobedient just as were their descendants who lived at the time of Jesus. After the nomadic Jews of the Diaspora had been described in the figures of Abraham, Joseph, and Moses, their nomadic existence under the powerful hand of God was transformed into a lasting settlement in Palestine with a fixed temple building replacing the easily moved place of worship of the wilderness period. In this, there was a danger of idol worship—the golden calf and Moloch, for instance—and a completely wrong conception of God as dependent on men and the work of their hands.

Stephen was not an enemy of the temple but of a temple that had lost its nomadic character and had ceased to be God's holy place, and had instead become a place for men's self-chosen worship of a God in their own image. We do not know whether in this Stephen was like Jesus, for we know very little about Jesus' opinion of the temple and find it easy to believe that a more detailed tradition about Jesus' attitude toward the temple had disappeared at an early date, because Israel's hostility to the Christians caused the interest in the temple manifested in the primitive church in Acts and in Paul to disappear quickly. Stephen was no precursor of Paul or the mission to the Gentiles. He took a completely different position with his special emphasis on circumcision and the sanctuary of the wilderness period. His criticism of Jewry resembled the castigations of the disobedient people by the prophets or by Jesus. Missionary work among the Gentiles was not within his scope; he was a Jewish Christian from Jerusalem. Stephen had a vision, later fulfilled, of an Israel that in A.D. 70 left Palestine and the temple and went away like Abraham, Joseph, and Moses to foreign lands. Before this emigration, there would be another caused by Israel's unbelief: Jesus and the Gospel would be persecuted in Palestine and the Gospel would be carried to other peoples which were to take up a Jewish inheritance that Israel itself was unwilling to accept.

COMMENT

Stephen's speech begins with the calling of Abraham. He was to leave his country and his family to go to the country that God would show him. When he arrived in the Promised Land, God gave him no share in the land—not so much as an inch of ground—

but he promised that he would give the land to him and his descendants after their exile in Egypt, and gave him the covenant of circumcision. Stephen goes on to tell of Joseph's and Jacob's arrival in Egypt and of how Pharaoh ill-used the people of Israel when the time was approaching for God to give the Promised Land to the people. Moses had to leave his people, who rejected him, and for forty years had to live as a stranger in the land of Midian until God revealed himself in a thornbush and sent him to Egypt to deliver Israel. Not until vs. 45 does Stephen speak of the immigration into Palestine and of Solomon's building of the temple, and he then proves from the Scriptures that the Most High does not dwell in temples (cf. vi 13) built by the hands of men. Even before this he has, by quoting from Amos in vs. 43, indicated their new exile by the words, *I will move you beyond Babylon.* The people's former disobedience and hard-heartedness has repeated itself, now directed against Jesus.

In Stephen's speech, Israel is seen as the people in exile to whom God revealed himself outside Palestine. In the context of Acts, it is important to note that this is the dominant theme of the speech which ends the description of the congregation in Jerusalem. In the following chapters, events occurring outside that city are told. Jerusalem was of course the center of these events, but they begin to take place farther and farther away from the center. We shall return to Jerusalem only when events in Samaria, Caesarea, Antioch, and the Gentile-Christian congregations necessitate such a return. This was the case when the news that Samaria had received the word of God reached the apostles in Jerusalem, and they sent Peter and John to Samaria (viii 14, 25). What was told about the Ethiopian treasurer took place on the road between Jerusalem and Gaza, and might possibly indicate that Philip had been sent from Jerusalem (viii 26). But in Luke's account of this event, the incident has nothing to do with Jerusalem except for the fact that the treasurer had been on a pilgrimage there. The account of Paul's call before Damascus began with his participation in the persecution at Jerusalem (ix 1–2, cf. vss. 13–14), and ended with the account of his arrival in Jerusalem (ix 26–30). Then Peter was in Lydda and Joppa ix 32–43. Peter's visit to the house of Cornelius the Gentile in Caesarea (ch. x) led to an accusation against him upon his return to Jerusalem and a discussion of his behavior (xi 1–18). Then follows the account of the founding of the church in Antioch and of the collection taken by the congregation for their brethren in Judea, which resulted in Paul and Barnabas being chosen to deliver the gift to Jerusalem, whence we return in chapter xii. The controversy over circumcision in Antioch sends Barnabas and Paul to Jerusalem to debate the matter before the Apostolic Council (ch. xv).

From this point on, Jerusalem was kept more in the background of the history of the church. True, the detailed description of events occurring in Jerusalem in chapters xxi–xxvi might seem to argue differently. But for Luke what is significant in these chapters is not so much Jerusalem as Paul—he has now become the center of attention. Indeed, the church in Jerusalem is mentioned only once, in xxi 17 ff. Not even the reason for Paul's journey is acknowledged (xix 21, xx 16)—we have to go to the Pauline letters to find that Paul went up to Jerusalem to take up the collection for the poor (I Cor xvi ff.).

Seen against this background of Jerusalem as the enemy of the church at the beginning of Acts, and the succeeding account dealing mainly with events outside Jerusalem and Judea, Stephen's speech about Israel in exile carries special emphasis in that it forms a transition from the description of the church in Jerusalem to the description of the mission "to the end of the world" (i 8).

20. THE DEATH OF STEPHEN
(vii 54 – viii 1a)

VII 54 When they heard this, they became very angry and gritted their teeth with rage. 55 But, filled with the Holy Spirit, he gazed toward heaven, and saw God's glory and Jesus standing at the right hand of God, 56 and he said: "Behold, I see the heavens opened and the Son of man standing at the right hand of God." 57 But they shrieked aloud and covered their ears, and they all rushed at him. 58 They drove him out of the city and stoned him. The witnesses laid their outer garments at the feet of a young man whose name was Saul. 59 They stoned Stephen, who prayed and said: "Lord Jesus, receive my spirit!" 60 He knelt and cried in a loud voice: "Lord, do not hold them responsible for this sin!" And when he had said this, he fell asleep. VIII 1 And Saul agreed to the murder of Stephen.

Notes

vii 54–56. Verse 56 is the only place in the NT outside the gospels where *Son of man* is used as a title for Jesus. It should be specially noticed that here it is Stephen who uses the title, and not, as in the gospels, Jesus who used it for himself.

57–58. Was this examination before the Sanhedrin and the following stoning a real trial and a legally performed execution? We do not know. The improvised and passionate character of the events as related might suggest that it was illegal, a lynching. Later, James, the Lord's brother, was stoned after having been brought to trial at the instigation of the high priest, but the juridical procedure was found to be illegal and caused the deposition of the high priest (Josephus *Ant.* XX.199–203). Under the provisions of Deut xvii 7, the witnesses start the stoning. Later recorded rules for this kind of execution may have been worked out.

59–viii 1a. The parallels to Stephen in Jesus' passion are found solely in Luke. In a different context Paul recalled his persecution of the church: I Cor xv 9; Gal i 13; cf. i 23; Philip iii 6.

COMMENT

The crowd of assembled Jews is filled with wrath and thoughts of murder, just as it had been with regard to the apostles in v 33. Stephen's eyes turn toward heaven, and his words about seeing the Son of man standing at the right hand of God, serve only to strengthen their hostility. His remark is like a spark that starts an explosion. With loud screams, they rush at Stephen, drag him out of town, and stone him. Once more we hear about the witnesses (cf. vi 11–13) who in this case before stoning the accused removed their outer garments and place them at the feet of a young man by the name of Saul (cf. xxii 20). Thus Paul is introduced for the first time in Acts, but not until xiii 9 is he called Paul. Stephen's death recalls the death of Jesus. He prayed, not to God, however, but to Jesus, to receive his spirit (cf. Luke xxiii 46). Thereupon he knelt and prayed that his enemies might be forgiven (cf. Luke xxiii 34). Paul was pleased with Stephen's death. He had at that time left Gamaliel and had entered the service of the high priest where he would have an opportunity to show his zeal as a persecutor of the Christians, something he never forgot afterward as Christ's apostle.

21. PERSECUTION OF THE WHOLE CHURCH
(viii 1b–3)

VIII 1b On that day there arose a fierce persecution of the church in Jerusalem, so that they were all put to flight throughout the region of Judea and Samaria—except the apostles. 2 Devout men buried Stephen and made a great lament for him. 3 But Saul tried to destroy the church by going into houses and dragging off men and women and throwing them into prison.

NOTES

viii 1b–3. The persecution was confined to Jerusalem. But was any other church in existence at this time? The expansion of the persecution to other cities (cf. xxvi 11) may have been directed against refugees from Jerusalem. What happened in Samaria (viii 4 ff.) and Antioch (xi 19 ff.) may also have happened in other places. The persecution had started the mission among the Jews outside Jerusalem, a mission which the primitive church had not yet begun.

The pious men who took care of the dead Stephen might have been Jews who, like Tobit (Tobit i 12–19, ii 1–9), took care of the unburied dead (cf. Luke xxiii 50–53 par.), but they might also have been pious men who were opposed to the persecution. Or perhaps they were some of Stephen's friends, who remained faithful through all the vicissitudes of life as did the women at the cross of Jesus (Luke xxiii 55–56). Later, we learn that Christians were not only put into prison; they were also put to death by the authorities (Acts xxii 4, xxvi 10–11).

COMMENT

It is hard to explain why the words in vs. 1b have been taken
to mean that this persecution was only concerned with the Hellenists in the church. They all suffered persecution, but the apostles
alone remained behind when all the others fled. We have previously referred to an interpretation of "the promise of the Father" (see pp. 3–4), which might explain the apostles staying
behind. If they were not allowed to leave Jerusalem until this
promise had been fulfilled, and if this unfulfilled promise were
concerned with the conversion of Israel, that would explain why
the apostles alone remained. When Paul visited Jerusalem for the
last time (chs. xxi and xxii f.) and did not meet any of the
twelve apostles, most of them must have been dead. But we know
that Peter was still alive for he was executed in Rome during the
reign of Nero.

22. PHILIP'S MISSION TO SAMARIA
(viii 4–25)

VIII ⁴ Those who had been put to flight now traveled through (the country) preaching the word. ⁵ Philip traveled down to the chief city in Samaria and preached Christ to them (there). ⁶ The crowds listened all together to what Philip said, because they heard and saw the acts he performed, ⁷ for many of those who were possessed by spirits (were healed) when these spirits shrieked with a loud voice and left them, and many who were crippled and paralyzed were cured, ⁸ so that there was great joy in that city. ⁹ But a man named Simon had earlier been in the city and practiced magical arts. He had fascinated the people of Samaria, and asserted that he was some great person, ¹⁰ and all, small and great, had followed him, saying: "He is the so-called great power of God." ¹¹ And they had followed him because he had long awed them with his magic. ¹² But since they had faith in Philip, with his preaching of the kingdom of God and the name of Jesus Christ, they were baptized, both men and women. ¹³ Simon himself also came to believe, and after his baptism he was with Philip continually, and when he now saw great signs and acts of power take place he was overwhelmed.

¹⁴ When the apostles in Jerusalem heard that Samaria had received the word of God, they sent Peter and John to them, ¹⁵ and when these had arrived they prayed for them, that they might receive the gift of the Holy Spirit, ¹⁶ which had not yet come upon any of them; they had been baptized only in the name of the Lord Jesus. ¹⁷ Then they laid their hands upon them, and they received the Holy Spirit.

¹⁸ When Simon saw that the Spirit was granted through the apostles' laying on of hands, he brought them money ¹⁹ and said: "Give me this power also, that all on whom I lay hands

may receive the Holy Spirit." 20 But Peter said to him: "May your silver perish with you, for you have thought to buy this gift of God with money. 21 You have no part, much less right, in this matter, for your heart is not true with God. 22 Turn away from this wickedness of yours, and pray to the Lord that the ambition of your heart may be forgiven, 23 for I can see you are headed for bitterness and the chains of sin." 24 But Simon answered and said: "Pray for me to the Lord, that nothing of what you have said will happen to me."

25 When they now had given witness and spoken the word of the Lord, they returned to Jerusalem, and (on the way) preached the gospel in many of the Samaritan villages.

Notes

viii 4–8. The accounts of Philip are examples of the missionary work performed in the districts of Judea and Samaria by the refugees from Jerusalem. Jesus had forbidden his twelve apostles to preach in any Samaritan town (Matt x 5), but now the mission to the world had been started because of Israel's unbelief and their persecution of the Christians. Beginning with Acts viii, we hear no more about mission work among the Jews in Palestine.

5. If the definite article precedes *city* (vs. 5), the city mentioned becomes the chief city in Samaria.

6–7. As before, the preaching of the word was accompanied by signs and wonders. Cf. Mark xvi 20: "But they went out and preached everywhere, and the Lord worked through them and confirmed the word by the signs accompanying it"; cf. Acts xiv 3.

7. By parenthetically adding *were healed*, it is made clear that it was the spirits that left them and not those who had had the unclean spirits. This grammatical inaccuracy reminds us of the problem connected with the healings of Jesus (e.g. Mark v 6–13). Was the subject the possessed, themselves or the demons?

9–13. According to Acts, Simon was the first magician that the Christian missionaries encountered. He performed magical arts and announced himself to be, in the words of the Samaritans, *the so-called great power of God*. (On the titles of Simon Magus, see Appendix VII.) He was one of the many Gentile healers and preachers who in those days traveled all over the Roman empire. Jesus had been in the neighborhood of Jews who cast out demons, and had talked about them (Mark ix 38–41 par.; Matt xii 27 par.). Since Jesus and the older disciples

performed healings, they might easily be bracketed with these magicians
and exorcists. Paul had to defend himself in a similar way against the
well-known charges which were brought against the apostle by his
opponents (cf. I Thess ii 3 ff.). We shall later encounter healers and
preachers, for instance the Jew Bar-Jesus (xiii 6 ff.) and the many
healers at Ephesus who were known for their magical arts (xix 11–20).
It is worth noticing that Simon was amazed at the wonders performed
by Philip, just as Paul surpassed all the other healers in Ephesus (xix 11).
In situations where special powers were manifested toward people in
need, it was important to delimit fraud and demonic spirits from God's
saving power.

Simon the Magician was mentioned in later sources: by Justin Martyr
who was born in Nablus in Samaria; in the Apocryphal Acts of the
Apostles; and in the pseudo-Clementine writings. In their accounts of
the heresies Irenaeus, Hippolytus, and Epiphanius do not necessarily
have any historical connection with the person we read about in Acts.
All later movements, ecclesiastical as well as heretical, referred to the
figures of the primitive church, the apostles, the seventy-two disciples
who were sent out (Luke x 1 ff.), even such figures as Simon the
Magician, because the primitive period was the period of creation
considered to hold the highest authority for all later generations.

14–17. The strong expression *Samaria had received the word of God*
corresponds to xi 1, "But the apostles and the brethren . . . heard that
Gentiles also had received the word of God," and to the words of the
Jerusalem congregation concerning the baptism of Cornelius, "God then
has granted to the Gentiles also the conversion to life" (xi 18). Cf. xiv
27: "that he had opened a door to faith for the Gentiles," and xv 12, xxi
19. Parallels to these statements are found in the letters of Paul, who,
in his observations on missions (Rom ix–xi), used similar categorical
statements both about the unbelief of the Jews and the fulfillment of the
Gentiles, and about the final salvation of Israel. He speaks in similar
terms of the end of his mission to the eastern part of the Roman
empire (Rom xv 18–24). Jerusalem felt responsible for the new
Christian church in Samaria and sent the apostles Peter and John there.
(This is the last time that John is named in Acts.) The custom of sending
representatives of the Jerusalem church to new Christian communities
was repeated when Barnabas was sent to the church in Antioch (xi 22).
After the Apostolic Council, Judas Barsabbas and Silas were sent with
Barnabas and Paul to Antioch (xv 22), but this was the last delegation
from Jerusalem. No representatives from Jerusalem are mentioned as
being sent to the Gentiles in ch. x or at any later time. Thus Acts also
contradicts the interpretation that Paul's opponents in his congregations
were Jerusalem Christians. The apostles laid their hands on the newly

baptized, whereupon they received the Holy Spirit. While Philip was unable to bestow the Holy Spirit, which other Christians had received with or even before baptism (Acts ii 38, x 44–48), the apostles could do this by the laying on of hands (cf. for Paul xix 6). The limitation of the bestowal of the Holy Spirit to the apostles presupposes a small church within a limited district. Under such circumstances only would the twelve apostles be sufficient to bestow such a fundamental gift. Therefore the limitation may have been a rule going back to the early days of the church, but the missions to the Gentiles had already made it unworkable. Even if there were other apostles—and possibly a number of them—who performed this work (apart from the twelve apostles who devoted themselves exclusively to missions among the Jews), the Holy Spirit was too important to be a prerogative of the apostles.

The laying on of hands was frequently used in the primitive church, as it is today, in various contexts: the apostles prayed and laid their hands on the Seven (vi 6); here it is used for the bestowal of the Holy Spirit (viii 17–19); Ananias healed Paul (ix 12, 17; in the last passage he also bestowed the Holy Spirit); the Antioch prophets let Barnabas and Paul travel after the laying on of hands (xiii 3, but this is probably what in xiv 26 is explained in the following manner: "[Antioch] where they had been commended to the grace of God for the work they had [now] completed." Besides the above-mentioned passage (xix 6) about Paul's bestowal of the Holy Spirit, xxviii 8 can be cited. Paul laid his hands on the father of Publius and healed him.

18–25. Simon, who by virtue of his earlier life closely observed all wondrous faculties and powers, was struck by the apostles' ability to make the baptized prophesy and to speak in tongues by the laying on of hands. If he could learn to do this, at whatever cost, the world would be open to him. Despite his faith and hope, Simon the Magician held a completely materialistic view of the Holy Spirit and the gift of being able to bestow it on others. From these verses the word "simony" derives, which really should mean: the attainment of an ecclesiastical office through a payment of money, as in an early use in the *Apostolic Constitutions* (VIII.xlvii.29), but which has assumed a far more comprehensive meaning, especially in Cardinal Humbert's *Three Books Against the Simonians* (11th century). If comparisons are made between Simon's treatment and the death penalty given to Ananias and Sapphira (Acts v 1 ff.), and the delivery to Satan of a member of the congregation (I Cor v 1 ff.), Simon's treatment must be said to be characterized by clemency—whether this was due to his quick repentance or to the possibility that "simony" was not judged as strictly by the primitive church as in the Middle Ages.

COMMENT

The action on the part of the Jews, which was intended to stop the life of the church, proved to be helpful to the Gospel. Philip, one of the seven, preached to the people in the chief city of Samaria and they were responsive and rejoiced in the signs he performed. Philip met a magician named Simon, whose supporters had been baptized, and after he also gained the faith, he observed and wondered at the signs and powerful deeds performed through Philip.

When rumors reached Jerusalem that Samaria had received the word of God, the apostles Peter and John were sent there and through the laying on of hands, conveyed the Holy Spirit to the Christians in Samaria. Simon became enthusiastic over this gift of God to the apostles and wanted to buy it from them, but Peter reprimanded him, pointing to the difference that exists between this heathen attitude and the possession of a heart true toward God.

23. PHILIP AND THE ETHIOPIAN TREASURER
(viii 26–40)

VIII 26 Now an angel of the Lord spoke to Philip and said: "Get up and go south along the way that leads from Jerusalem down to Gaza." (This is the desert road.) 27 After he had started on his journey he met an Ethiopian eunuch, who was an official at the court of the Ethiopian queen, Candace, and the head of her treasury. He had traveled up to Jerusalem to worship, 28 and was now on his way back and sat in his chariot reading the prophet Isaiah. 29 And the Spirit said to Philip: "Go and get near this chariot!" 30 When Philip ran over to it he heard him reading the prophet Isaiah, and he said: "Do you really understand what you are reading?" 31 He answered: "How could I do that, when there is no one to guide me?" Then he invited Philip to come up and sit by him. 32 The passage he was reading was this:

"He was led like a sheep to the slaughter,
and as a lamb is dumb before the man who shears it
so he opens not his mouth.
33   By his humiliation, his conviction was quashed.
Who will be able to tell of the span of his life?
For his life is taken away from the earth."

34 The eunuch spoke and asked Philip: "Tell me, of whom does the prophet say this? Of himself, or of another?" 35 Philip spoke, and starting with the Scriptural text he brought him the gospel of Jesus. 36 As they traveled along the road they came to some water, and the eunuch said: "Look, there is water, what can prevent my being baptized?" 38 And he gave orders that the chariot should stop, and both of them, Philip and the eunuch, went down into the water, and Philip baptized him. 39 But when they had come up out of the water, the Spirit of

the Lord seized Philip. The eunuch did not see him again,
but he continued on his way joyfully. 40 But Philip was then
found on the way to Azotus, and he traveled about preaching
the gospel in all the towns until he came to Caesarea.

NOTES

viii 26–29. This narrative is a good example of Luke's faithfulness to
his sources. Just as in the preceding narrative and in many other texts, he
has not effaced its characteristic features by maintaining a definite
theological view. In this account, Philip's divine guide is at one time the
angel of the Lord and at another the *Spirit*. No mention is made of
where he started (see p. XLI). The road going from Jerusalem to Gaza
led to the coastal plain along the Mediterranean, where the main caravan
road to the south went toward Egypt. If it was the town that was
deserted, this may refer to the older town of Gaza, destroyed by
Alexander the Great; if it was the road, it might mean the continuation
beyond Gaza, but when Philip obeyed the angel he caught sight of the
Ethiopian, and the goal of his mission was clear. The Ethiopians were
Nubians living between Aswan and Khartoum in Upper Egypt and the
Sudan; they were not, as has later been assumed, identical with the
Abyssinians. *Candace* is not a personal name but a title like "Pharaoh."
It was used about the sovereign queen. An Ethiopian on a pilgrimage to
Jerusalem must supposedly have been a god-fearing Gentile. But if so,
why did they make so much of the god-fearing Gentile Cornelius in ch.
x?

30–35. After the custom of the time, the Ethiopian was reading
aloud. (Augustine, we remember, wondered that Ambrose read silently
—*Confessions* VI.3.) The first line of the quotation (vs. 32) can be
translated by *like a sheep to the slaughter* whereby the comparison
with the Servant (or Jesus) does not occur till the third line. The primitive
church did not feel the same inclination as later generations of Christians
to apply this text to Jesus, but this was done in Philip's answer, when the
Ethiopian asked the question which has been steadily repeated right
up to our own time: Does the prophet in this passage speak of himself
or of another? In Philip's answer this text, and probably the whole
context, was explained as expressing the Gospel about Jesus.

36–38. The terseness of the narrative may well make it appear that the
baptism was briefer than it actually was. *What can prevent my being
baptized?* represents the early baptismal words, with which we are again
confronted in Acts x 47, xi 17. In the Neutral text, the baptism took
place on the initiative of Philip, without any assistance from the
Ethiopian (cf. vs. 38). The Western text has added vs. 37 reading: "And

Philip said to him, 'If you believe with all your heart, thou may.' And he answered and said, 'I believe that Jesus Christ is the Son of God.'" Thus the person asking for baptism made a confession. Verse 37 has been omitted as it is not found in the best mss.

39–40. What happened to Philip recalls the story of Elijah, even in its choice of words (e.g. *the eunuch did not see him again,* cf. II Kings ii 12).

COMMENT

This narrative takes us into an Old Testament atmosphere by recalling the account of Elijah. The Spirit was like a tremendous wind. The angel of God led Philip to the deserted road between Jerusalem and Gaza, where a proselyte was returning from a pilgrimage to Jerusalem. Sitting in his chariot, he was reading the prophet Isaiah, and when the Spirit had brought Philip up to the chariot, the Ethiopian asked him to explain Isa liii 7 f. to him. This gave Philip an opportunity to speak of Jesus, the suffering Servant of the Lord. Following Philip's explanation, the Ethiopian's baptism took place in just as surprising a hurry as that of the prison guard in Philippi (xvi 25 ff.); Cornelius' (ch. x) and Paul's baptism (ix 18; cf. xxii 16) could also be mentioned in this connection. Just as in the Old Testament, Philip was removed in a wondrous way and the Ethiopian joyfully continued his long journey. Similarly, Philip suddenly finds himself in the town of Azotus, whence he starts on a missionary journey through the neighboring towns until he comes to Caesarea, where we meet him again during Paul's visit (cf. xxi 8 ff.).

24. PAUL'S CALL
(ix 1–19a)

IX 1 But Saul, whose heart was still set on threats and murder toward the Lord's disciples, went to the high priest 2 and asked him for letters to the synagogues in Damascus, so that if he found any who belonged to "the way," whether men or women, he might bring them to Jerusalem as prisoners. 3 When on his journey he drew near to Damascus, he was suddenly surrounded with a blaze of light from heaven, 4 and falling down he heard a voice say to him: "Saul, Saul, why do you persecute me?" 5 He said: "Who are you, Lord?" He (answered): "I am Jesus, whom you persecute. 6 But get up and go into the city, and you will there be told what you are to do." 7 The men who were traveling with him stood dumbfounded, for although indeed they heard the voice, they saw no one. 8 Saul got up from the ground, but when he opened his eyes he could not see. So they led him by the hand and brought him into Damascus. 9 He was blind for three days, and he neither ate nor drank.

10 In Damascus there was a disciple named Ananias, and the Lord said to him in a vision: "Ananias." He answered: "Here I am, Lord." 11 The Lord (said) to him: "Get up and go to the street called Straight, and seek out in the house of Judas a man from Tarsus named Saul; for he is praying, 12 and he has seen [in a vision] a man called Ananias coming in and laying his hands upon him, in order that he might see again." 13 But Ananias answered: "Lord, I have heard of this man from many, of how much evil he has done in Jerusalem to your saints, 14 and here he has authority from the high priests to arrest all who call on your name." 15 But the Lord said to him: "Go, for this man is my chosen agent to carry my name before Gentiles and kings and Israelites, 16 and I will show him all he

is to suffer for my name's sake." 17 Ananias went there and came into the house, and he laid his hands upon him and said: "Brother Saul, the Lord has sent me—Jesus, who revealed himself to you on the way you came—that you may see once more and be filled with the Holy Spirit." 18 At once there fell as it were scales from his eyes, so that he could see again, and he arose and was baptized. 19 After he had eaten, he recovered his strength.

NOTES

ix 1–2. *the way* is a name for Christianity in Acts cf. xix 9, 23, xxii 4, xxiv 14, 22). It has been questioned whether the high priest had jurisdiction over the Jews outside Palestine, but not enough is known about the matter to reject Luke's account of it.

3–6. The revelation was sudden; Christ revealed himself to Paul in a blaze of heavenly light. As always happened at revelations, man was overwhelmed by the heavenly reality and fell to the ground. Christ identified himself with his church; it was he whom Paul persecuted by persecuting the church. These words are the same in the three accounts of the revelation in Acts. Whereas the account in xxvi 4–18 does not name Ananias but has Christ himself give a detailed explanation of the call, in xxii 3–16 and here, it is Ananias who transmits Christ's further instructions about the call (cf. also xxii 17–21). In these texts, therefore, Christ sent Paul to Damascus to acquire a deeper understanding of his revelation.

7–9. The other members of the caravan had heard the voice but had not seen anyone. This is not the case in xxii 9, where they see the light (cf. xxvi 13) but do not hear the voice. These points of disagreement show that Paul alone got the message; the others were unable to understand what had happened.

10–14. It has been assumed that the Jerusalem congregation emphasized Ananias in order to show Paul's dependency on men (Gal i 12), but as stated, Ananias only transmitted Christ's direct revelation: he did not replace Christ. The attitude of the Jerusalem congregation was not so hostile toward Paul (Gal i 22–24) as to give rise to such a tradition. The rejection of Paul's dependency on men in Galatians was aimed only at his opponents in Jerusalem (Gal i 1, 12–24, ii 1–21). Nobody has ever accused Paul of being dependent on anyone in Damascus. It has been pointed out that we get two completely different pictures of Ananias: one here, the other in xxii 12–16. Here he is obviously a Christian, in xxii 12 he is described as a pious Jew and speaks mainly in Jewish phrases. The fact that Paul prayed must be taken as an example of the seriousness with which he had embraced Christianity. The touching naïveté with which Ananias seeks to convince Christ that his information about Paul is incorrect and then listens to him and is guided by him, testifies to a piety praying without fear and obeying implicitly.

15–16. Here the words explaining the call follow. With the expression *my chosen agent* compare I Thess ii 4. With an allusion to Jer i 10 (LXX), Paul's task is described as bringing the name of Christ to Gentiles, kings, and the sons of Israel. In xxvi 17, there is a weak parallel to the prediction of Paul's suffering for the sake of Christ, but the word in the present passage points forward to Paul's trial in Jerusalem.

17–19a. Luke does not mention (vs. 19a) that Paul received the Holy Spirit. Such repetitions were not necessary.

COMMENT

The calling of Paul is related three times in Acts—here, xxii 3–16, and xxvi 4–18. If one compares these reports with each other and with Paul's own, much briefer presentation in Gal i 13–17, similarities and differences are to be observed. The deviations are most pronounced with regard to the course of external events, while as far as the aim of the narrative is concerned, there is more agreement. Christ's revelation of himself to Paul is without precedent. Paul was an unbeliever, a zealous Pharisee, ardently occupied with the traditions of the fathers and a fanatic persecutor of the Christians who, on his own initiative, extended the persecution to cities outside Jerusalem. He was journeying to Damascus for this purpose when Christ revealed himself to him. In all four accounts, Paul's call was related in the same way as the call of the Old Testament characters in the history of salvation. Like Paul's, their call had no story leading up to it and came from God as a claim that could not be refused. But there is no Old Testament parallel to Paul's being called while an unbeliever and a persecutor. Paul was called to something greater or more glorious than any of the Old Testament prophets and servants were. The texts behind Luke's and Paul's accounts are above all the passages of the Servant of the Lord in Isaiah (xlii 6–7, xlix 1–6) and of Jeremiah's call (Jer i 4 ff.), but strangely enough the same texts are not used in the different accounts.

Unlike the other two accounts in Acts the present passage is

not part of a speech (nor part of a polemic as in Gal i 13 ff.),
but appears as part of the historical account. That is why the
narrative of Paul's Jewish past was omitted. His Damascus experience was the first revelation of Christ outside Palestine and it
abolished the monopoly of the Gospel hitherto enjoyed by the people of Israel in Palestine. Jesus ordered Paul to go to Damascus
where he would be informed about what he should do. When he
got up from the ground, he was blind and had to be led into
the city. Here a Christian named Ananias had a revelation of
Christ, who sent him to Paul to inform him about the extent of
his new service and of the sufferings he must endure for the
sake of the name, and to cure his blindness, baptize him, and
bestow the Holy Spirit upon him.

25. PAUL IN DAMASCUS AND JERUSALEM
(ix 19b–30)

IX 19b He spent some time with the disciples in Damascus, 20 and began preaching openly in the synagogues that Jesus was the Son of God. 21 All who heard it were greatly astonished and said: "Is not this the one who in Jerusalem sought to destroy those who invoked this name, and who came here in order to take them to the chief priests as prisoners?" 22 Yet Saul gained more in power, reducing to silence Jews living in Damascus by proving that this man was indeed the Messiah.

23 After some time the Jews plotted to kill him, 24 but their plot became known to Saul. They even kept watch at the city gates day and night to kill him; 25 but the disciples took him by night and lowered him over the city wall in a basket.

26 When he had reached Jerusalem he tried to join the disciples, but everyone feared him, for they did not believe that he was a disciple. 27 But Barnabas took charge (of him) and brought him to the apostles, and he explained to them how he had seen the Lord on the way, how the Lord had spoken to him, and how he had boldly preached the name of Jesus in Damascus. 28 Saul came and went among them in Jerusalem, boldly preaching the name of the Lord. 29 He talked and disputed with the Hellenists, but they tried to kill him. 30 When the brethren heard of this, they took him to Caesarea and sent him away to Tarsus.

NOTES

ix 19b–22. *some time.* The indications of time here and in vs. 23 are vague so that they can agree with the assumption of a longer period of time, but it seems more natural to assume that Luke was imagining that the events related here had happened in rapid succession. Paul, who had barely been healed and was still recovering his strength, threw himself with all his usual energy into preaching about Christ to the Jews in their synagogues. In his preaching he asserted that Jesus was *the Son of God* (vs. 20), that he was *the Messiah* (vs. 22) [which probably was taken to be the same thing], and proved it (vs. 22), we must suppose, by OT texts (cf. xiii 16–41, xvii 1–3, 10–11).

23–25. As on other occasions (xiv 4–6; xxiii 12–22) there were in the opponents' camp, people who sympathized with the apostle and gave away the plans of those who would have killed him. The reading "his disciples" is better attested but it is sensible to read *the disciples,* i.e. the Christians of that town. If one wants to bring the present narrative about the flight from Damascus into agreement with II Cor xi 32–33, where it was not the Jews but King Aretas' ethnarch who attempted to seize Paul, one can consider the Jews the instigators of the persecution and the ethnarch the executive authority. But there are many problems concerning this Nabataean official or chief as Damascus did not belong to the Nabataean kingdom. As Paul does not mention the Jews and as his account of his own life is usually preferred to that of Acts, there is every reason to believe him when he said that it was the ethnarch and not the Jews who had on that occasion persecuted him, but it is impossible to explain what exactly occurred.

26. As in Damascus, the people of Jerusalem were astonished by the conversion of the persecutor, but here, where he had been an active persecutor, it was harder to forget and to accept the man.

27. Barnabas (cf. NOTE on iv 36) helped Paul to get in touch with the apostles and this was the beginning of the relationship between the two men (cf. xi 25–30, xii 25, xiii 1–15, 39). What has been told about Paul, has been thought to be in Barnabas' words but there is nothing against viewing it as Paul's own account.

28–30. The Hellenists attempted to kill him, possibly just as in vi 10–11 concerning Stephen, because they were unable to stand up to him.

COMMENT

Shortly after his call, Paul preached in the synagogues in Damascus, where he astonished all the people and refuted the Jews. They decided to kill him, but learning about their plan Paul fled to Jerusalem. Paul aroused the same astonishment in the church there as in Damascus; was it really likely that the persecutor had become a Christian? They feared that his new confession was nothing but a ruse under which he might get a better hold on the church and prepare more effectively for its destruction. Barnabas was the one who managed to get Paul in touch with the apostles, and in Jerusalem, Paul also began to preach and to dispute, especially with the Hellenists. But here also the missionary activity led to persecution and as the Christian brethren in Damascus had had Paul led into safety, so the disciples in Jerusalem helped Paul to get away to Tarsus.

The description in Acts of Paul's stay in Jerusalem does not agree with his own account of his first visit to Jerusalem after his call outside Damascus in Gal i 18–20. The source followed by Luke reckoned with a connection between Paul and the whole apostolic circle and with a stay lasting for some time. What was related in Acts was a natural conclusion based on the fact that Paul had been in Jerusalem. This can also be seen from the fact that Paul's Judaistic opponents in the Galatian congregations had reasoned in exactly the same way, yet with a stronger polemical sting (this is seen in such passages as Gal i 11–12). The true story is probably told in Gal i 18–20. The visit had been of a private nature and had only led to contacts with the two leaders, Peter and James, the brother of the Lord. It is understandable that the tradition about Paul could easily have transferred well-known details about him from one city to another: Paul's arrival provoked strife, strife led to persecution, the congregation helped Paul to escape. For he was a man who by virtue of his personality always made a deep impression and acquired devoted friends and implacable enemies.

Although Luke had belonged to the group of Paul's disciples and fellow workers, there is no reason to believe that Luke must have known all that Paul knew. The apostle had scarcely been interested in autobiography. True, his call had served as a paradigm of the Gospel, but Luke can hardly have spent evenings listening to Paul's reminiscences.

It has been supposed that the present narrative, ix 26–30, was intended to show that Paul had been duly recognized as a Christian missionary by the Twelve. This assumption represents a late survival of the thought of the Tübingen School and is hardly acceptable from the point of view of primitive Christian thought. If it was Christ who had called Paul, the verdict of mankind could not have been relevant.

26. PETER'S PASTORAL VISIT TO LYDDA AND JOPPA
(ix 31–43)

IX 31 The church throughout the whole of Judea, Galilee, and Samaria was now at peace and it was strengthened; it walked in the fear of the Lord and became rich in the strength of the Holy Spirit.

32 Peter during his travels in all regions also visited the saints living in Lydda, 33 where he found a man named Aeneas, who had been bedridden with paralysis for eight years. 34 Peter said to him: "Aeneas, Jesus Christ heals you! Rise and make your bed!" At once he got up. 35 All who lived in Lydda and the plain of Sharon saw him and they turned to the Lord.

36 In Joppa there was a woman disciple named Tabitha (which in translation is Dorcas). She was full of good deeds and gave many alms. 37 But it so happened that at that time she fell sick and died; and when they had washed her, they laid her in an upper room. 38 Since Lydda is near Joppa, the disciples, who had heard that Peter was there, sent two men to him with this request: "Do not delay in coming to us." 39 Peter rose and went with them, and when he had arrived they led him up to the upper room. All the widows came to meet him, and weeping showed the tunics and mantles which Dorcas had made while she was with them. 40 But Peter sent them all outside and knelt and prayed; then he turned to the dead body and said: "Tabitha, rise up!" She opened her eyes, and when she saw Peter she sat up. 41 He stretched out his hand to her, helped her to her feet, then called the saints and the widows and set her (before them) alive. 42 It became known throughout Joppa, so that many believed in the Lord. 43 Peter stayed a long time in Joppa with a tanner named Simon.

NOTES

ix 31. This is the only place in Acts where the church in Galilee (cf. NOTE on i 8) is mentioned. From this circumstance, one can draw various conclusions: Galilee had not received Jesus and the disciples had therefore gone to Jerusalem to work; or the mission had already been come to an end there (cf. Jesus' grief over the towns of Galilee, Matt xi 20–24 par.); or the mission in Galilee had progressed steadily without any special problems, and the future of the church would not be decided there. The last seems to be the most obvious explanation.

32–35. Lydda was situated inland, southeast of the Mediterranean port of Joppa. Aeneas is not said to be a member of the church. In his healing word, Peter stressed that it was Christ who acted (cf. iii 12–16). *Make your bed* is understood by many to mean "make your dining couch ready," that is, for a meal. In either case an impossible act was demanded of the sick man; but through his will, or his belief, it became possible and his action was a sign of his having been healed.

36–42. In nearby Joppa, there was a Christian woman named Tabitha, rendered in Greek by *Dorcas,* i.e. "gazelle."

38. Generally messengers went in pairs as indicated in the NT especially by Luke (two not named in Luke vii 19, x 1 par., xix 29 par.; Acts x 7— Peter and John in Luke xxii 8 par.; Acts viii 14—Barnabas and Paul in Acts xiii 1–xv 35—Paul and Silas, and Barnabas and Mark in Acts xv 36–40—Timothy and Erastus in Acts xix 22). It was not directly stated that they would like the apostle to restore the dead woman to life.

In the primitive church, widows were needy women, who received support (Acts vi 1–6; James i 27), and this is also the case here. Later "widow" was used as the name for a church office (I Tim v 9). If the word was used in the latter sense, the widows served as nurses or professional mourners. Peter made all of them leave the room (cf. Jesus who in Jairus' house sent the crowd away, Mark v 21–43 par.). The dead woman first opened her eyes and then sat up (as did the widow's son in Nain, Luke vii 15). Peter helped Dorcas to get up and, calling in the Christians, among them the widows, presented her to them (cf. i 3: Jesus had presented himself to the apostles).

43. This verse forms a transition to the following narrative. It is characteristic of Luke in Acts that he gives an accurate address: Simon the tanner's house by the sea. We saw above (ix 11) that Paul lived in Judas' house in the street called Straight in Damascus. We shall afterward learn that he stayed in the house of Lydia, a woman from Thyatira, in Philippi (xvi 14 f.), with Jason in Thessalonica (xvii 5–7), with Aquila and Priscilla in Corinth (xviii 2–3), in Caesarea with Philip the evangelist

(xxi 8), in Jerusalem with Mnason (xxi 16). In addition, his stay with Publius on Malta (xxviii 7) could be mentioned. This type of information, is given far more frequently than the names of the places where Paul preached—it is, however, mentioned that in Corinth Paul preached in the house of Justus beside the synagogue (xviii 17) and in Ephesus at the school of Tyrannus (xix 9)—or the places in Jerusalem where the disciples met, and shows the author's penchant for accurate information on what would appear to be unimportant matters.

COMMENT

While the preceding and the following passages deal with decisive events, Paul's call and Peter's baptism of the first Gentile, this short passage forms a pause in the account of the great climaxes. The church was now at peace and Peter found time to visit the congregations in Lydda and Joppa where two wonders are related. Just as wonders had their place as an accompaniment to the first preaching of the word (cf. NOTE on viii 4–8), so the same wonders acquired a missionary effect in the daily life of the church. All in Lydda and on the plain of Sharon who saw the healed Aeneas were converted to the Lord. The news of Dorcas raised from the dead caused many in Joppa to believe in the Lord.

27. THE BAPTISM OF CORNELIUS
(x 1–48)

X 1 In Caesarea there was a man named Cornelius, a centurion of the Italian cohort. 2 He was devout, and he and all his household were god-fearing; he made generous contributions to the people, and was committed to continual prayer. 3 About the ninth hour of the day he saw clearly in a vision an angel of God enter and say to him: "Cornelius!" 4 He gazed at him in fear and said: "What is it, Lord?" The angel answered him: "Your prayers and your generosity have reached heaven and have been heard by God. 5 Therefore send men to Joppa and let them bring one called Simon, surnamed Peter, 6 who is staying as a guest of a certain Simon, a tanner, whose house is by the sea." 7 When the angel who spoke to him had departed, he called two of his house slaves and a devout soldier from among his men, 8 and he explained the matter to them and sent them to Joppa.

9 Next day, while they were on their way and approaching the city, Peter went up on the roof to pray at the sixth hour. 10 He became hungry and wished to eat. While (the food) was being prepared, he fell into a state of ecstasy 11 and saw the heavens opened, and something that looked like a great cloth descended and was lowered to the earth by the four corners. 12 In it were all four-footed beasts, reptiles of the earth, and birds of the air. 13 A voice came to him: "Get up, Peter, kill and eat!" 14 But Peter replied: "By no means, Lord, for I have never yet eaten anything ritually impure and unclean." 15 A voice (came) to him for the second time: "What God has declared ritually pure, you shall not call impure." 16 This happened a third time, and it was then taken up to heaven.

17 While Peter was uncertain what the vision could mean, the men sent by Cornelius had inquired their way to Simon's house

and at this very moment stood at the gate 18 and called, and asked whether Simon surnamed Peter was staying there as a guest. 19 While Peter pondered the vision, the Spirit said: "Behold, two men are seeking you; 20 get up and go down and accompany them without hesitation, for I have sent them." 21 Peter went down to the men and said: "I am he for whom you are looking. For what purpose have you come here?" 22 They replied: "The centurion Cornelius, who is a just and god-fearing man, of good repute throughout the Jewish people, has been commanded by a holy angel to have you brought to his house, and to listen to what you have to say." Then Peter asked them to come in and received them as his guests.

23 The next day he left and went with them, and some of the brethren from Joppa traveled with him. 24 On the following day he came to Caesarea, and Cornelius was waiting for them and before this had called together his kindred and closest friends. 25 When Peter was about to enter, Cornelius came to meet him, fell down at his feet, and greeted him as one divine. 26 But Peter made him rise, saying: "Get up, I too am only human." 27 Talking with Cornelius he entered, found many gathered, 28 and said to them: "You know that it is against the Law for a Jew to associate with a Gentile, or enter his house; but God commanded me (through a vision) not to call any man ritually impure. 29 Therefore I came without objection when I was sent for. I now wish to know why you have sent for me."

30 Cornelius said: "Four days ago, at this very ninth hour, while I was praying in my house, a man stood before me in a shining robe 31 and said: 'Cornelius, your prayer has been heard and your alms have been remembered by God. 32 Therefore send word to Joppa and have Simon surnamed Peter brought here; he is staying as a guest in the house of Simon the tanner, by the sea.' 33 At once I sent word to you, and it is good of you to come. Therefore we are now all assembled in the sight of God to hear all that you have been commanded by the Lord."

34 Peter then spoke thus: "Truly I see that God is not biased in his judgment of mankind, 35 but that in every nation he who fears him and deals justly is accepted by him. 36 It is this

message he sent to the Israelites when he proclaimed peace through Jesus Christ, who is the Lord of all. 37 You know what has happened throughout Palestine, from Galilee onward—after John had preached baptism— 38 about Jesus of Nazareth, that God anointed him with the Holy Spirit and power, and that he traveled through (the country) doing good and healing all who were in the devil's power, for God was with him. 39 We are witnesses to all that he did, both throughout the land of the Jews and in Jerusalem; whom they killed by crucifying him. 40 God raised him on the third day and let him appear visible, 41 not to the whole people, but to those witnesses who had beforehand been chosen by God, to us, who ate and drank with him after his resurrection. 42 He commanded us to preach to the people and to witness that he is the one whom God has appointed to be judge of the living and the dead. 43 All the prophets witness to him that all who believe in him receive forgiveness of their sins by virtue of his name."

44 While Peter was still speaking these words, the Holy Spirit came upon all who heard his preaching. 45 The believers who belonged to the circumcision party, who had traveled with Peter, were surprised that the gift of the Holy Spirit had been poured out upon Gentiles also; 46 for they heard them speaking in tongues and praising God. Then Peter said: 47 "Can anyone deny these people water that they may be baptized? For they have received the Holy Spirit as have we." 48 And he commanded that they should be baptized in the name of Jesus Christ. Then they asked him to remain some days.

NOTES

x 1. Caesarea (by the sea) was the Roman capital of Palestine. It was the residence of the Roman procurator (cf. xxiii 23–24 et passim), and it had a considerable Roman garrison. Cornelius was an officer in command of one hundred men, in Latin a centurion; a Roman army cohort numbered four to six hundred men. We know that an Italian cohort at a later time had its home base in Syria; the time of the event in the narrative, however, must have been earlier than A.D. 41 when Agrippa became king of all Palestine, and if the Italian cohort had been moved to the East at a fairly early date, the soldiers and this officer could easily have been of Syrian origin.

2. The Roman officer's positive attitude toward the Jews recalls Luke's description of the centurion from Capernaum (Luke vii 1–10). Such likenesses must, however, not be used for identification or for the establishment of literary categories. A Roman centurion might be like this and some of them indeed were. Prayers and alms are characteristic features of Jewish piety (cf. Matt vi 1 ff.; Acts ix 36); *Devout* probably indicates that he was one of the Gentiles who participated in the service at the synagogue (cf. NOTE on xiii 43).

3. The ninth hour is one of the hours of prayer, cf. NOTE on iii 1.

4–6. Peter is mentioned to Cornelius as a person unknown to him. He is called *Simon surnamed Peter* just as in x 18, 32, xi 13. The reason for his coming is not mentioned here but in vss. 22 and 33.

7–8. The messengers are two of the centurion's slaves (who according to vs. 2 held the same religious belief as their master) and a pious soldier. They reach Joppa (about thirty miles away) the following day at the sixth hour (vs. 9), i.e. at noon.

9–16. Just as Paul's revelation was followed by a revelation to Ananias (ch. ix), so the angel's message to Cornelius is followed by this revelation to Peter. Since in Cornelius' house Peter states that God has shown him that he shall not consider any man ritually unclean (vs. 28; the same expression occurs in Peter's exclamation during his vision about food in vs. 14; also in xi 8), it seems natural to take the context here as dealing with ritually clean and unclean men, with Jews and Gentiles. According to the view that the Cornelius narrative is a traditional story extensively adapted (see pp. XLI–XLII) we may be led to assume that this interpretation cannot be the original one. From Gal ii 11 ff., we know about Peter's irresolute attitude in the matter of sharing common meals with Gentile Christians, who were considered by the Jews to be Gentiles. The Cornelius event may precede the meeting in Jerusalem (in Gal ii 1 ff.) and therefore may be placed between chs. xii and xv in Acts (see p. XXXIII).

17–23a. Perhaps Peter's hospitality toward the messengers may already be taken as an indication of his new attitude toward the Gentiles. Two messengers are mentioned, either because Luke always referred to two messengers (see p. 8), or because only the slaves were messengers, the soldier accompanying them being a kind of escort; but according to xi 11 there were three.

23b–33. Some members of the church in Joppa traveled with Peter to Caesarea; according to xi 12, there were six and they were expressly stated to be Jewish Christians (x 45). When receiving Peter, Cornelius prostrated himself before him as before a divine being, but the apostle stopped him. Cornelius' pagan heritage was shown here as in xiv 11–13.

The first words Peter spoke in Cornelius' house referred to his present action as being against all Jewish custom.

30. This second report of Cornelius' experience is related in a slightly different way: the angel is mentioned only as *a man . . . in a shining robe*. The elaborate indication of time at the beginning of vs. 30 is best interpreted that it was four days since Cornelius had his vision.

31. *Your prayer has been heard.* Cf. the angel's word to Zechariah in Luke i 13.

34–43. Peter's speech at Cornelius' house presents even in its linguistic form many difficulties. The individual sentences come out without much coherence. The translation aims at giving the most likely meaning of the whole passage, without being able to provide satisfactory solution to all the problems posed by the text. It is possible that Luke has taken over sources without adapting them, thus giving us a glimpse of the previous history of the narrative and an impression of the adaptations of the Cornelius story. The difficulties may also be explained by the fact that later copyists found it hard to understand the pronouncements, found side by side in the text, giving Israel preference over the Gentiles and the Gentiles' direct access to the Gospel.

Peter's speech opens with what he had learned, according to vs. 28b, from the revelation in Joppa. But it is now in a more carefully worked out form: God did not allow his judgment to depend on a man's being a Jew or a Gentile but in all nations he who feared him and dealt justly would be accepted by him. Justice (see vs. 35) must be here considered to be the quality which Cornelius had shown in his prayers and giving of alms. Verses 36–38 reveal the lack of grammatical coherence: in vs. 36 both in the opening and the concluding parts of the sentence, again in vs. 37 in connection with the construction beginning with "that" which occurs several times (i 1, 22; cf. Luke xxiv 47), and again in vs. 38 in regard to "Jesus of Nazareth." While "Judea" has hitherto been used about the province of Judea in southern Palestine, it is here (vs. 37) used in its other possible meaning of the land of the Jews, i.e. all Palestine. Jesus' victory over the powers of evil constitutes an important factor in primitive Christianity's faith and life (cf. Col ii; see also p. 44). In vs. 41 the apostles are called witnesses (just as before in i 8, 22, ii 32, iii 15, v 32, xiii 31; Paul, too, is called a witness in xxii 15, xxvi 16). In vs. 39 they witness of Jesus' ministry on earth, and in vs. 41 they witness his resurrection. As in i 4, the apostolic witnesses' sharing of food and drink with the risen Christ is stressed. As reported in vs. 42 the words of Jesus (i 8) apply to Israel alone: the witnesses were to preach to the people. This is an historically correct account of Jewish Christianity's theory of missions. In its present context, *witnesses* has a strange effect and contributes to making the verse somewhat vague. Christ has been appointed to be the judge of the living and the dead. In Paul's speech in the Areopagus, this appointment of the risen Christ as judge on the Last Day was also a call to repentance (xvii 31). It is sometimes exceedingly difficult to find the OT texts that NT authors refer to in making such summary statements, but in this case it is possible to point to the OT passages in Rom x 11: "No one who believes in him will be disappointed" (from Isa xxviii 16), and x 13 "For everyone who calls upon the name of the Lord will be saved" (from Joel iii 5; cf. Deut xxx 14, in Rom x 8-9).

44-48. The talking in other languages is described in terms similar to those in ii 11; that it happens just as it did on the day of Pentecost is stressed in vs. 47, and later in xi 15: "the Holy Spirit fell on them as it did upon us also in the beginning." This was the unique character of the event. No wonder the brethren from Joppa were dismayed; now, Gentiles (and no longer only Jews—cf. ii 1-13 and NOTE) had been heard speaking in tongues and had received the Holy Spirit. And since the Holy Spirit was bestowed upon believers only it was an irrefutable sign of God's acceptance of the Gentiles. In *deny* (vs. 47), we also have a primitive baptismal formula which we have already had in viii 36 (see NOTE) and shall meet again in xi 17.

COMMENT

Peter was invited to a house in Caesarea which belonged to a Gentile, and going there, he baptized all the Gentiles present. This, the first baptism of Gentiles mentioned in Acts (see, however, NOTE on viii 37), was performed only after many difficulties had been overcome. An angel appearing to Cornelius ordered him to send for Peter in Joppa. As the messengers were approaching Joppa, Peter had a vision which abolished the difference between what was clean and what was unclean. When the Spirit ordered him to go with the messengers, Peter went with them willingly and entered Cornelius' house. He said there in his sermon that the Gospel was intended for the children of Israel (vs. 36) and for the people (vs. 42), but that in every nation, he who feared God and dealt justly would be acceptable to him (vs. 35) and that everybody who believed in Christ would by virtue of his name receive forgiveness for his sins (vs. 43). Then the Holy Spirit came upon the Gentiles, and they spoke in tongues and Peter allowed them to be baptized. The angel's command to Cornelius, the revelation to Peter, the Spirit's command to him and the outpouring of the Holy Spirit upon the Gentiles in Cornelius' house—all were necessary for the baptism of the first Gentiles.

Some scholars take the position that the story of Cornelius has been adapted by Luke, and no doubt that is true. Luke has treated the narrative as one dealing with an event of fundamental importance. It has therefore been given an important place as a story about the first mission to the Gentiles, and in the structure of Acts, it anticipates the Apostolic Council, where missions to the Gentiles are approved by the Jerusalem congregation. This position has in turn led to a thorough sifting of the material which Luke had at his disposal. At first, the many repetitions are isolated and seen as emphasizing the importance of what is told. Then, stripped of these repetitions, an original Cornelius story, a simple legend about the baptism of a Gentile somewhat like the story of Philip and the Ethiopian treasurer (viii 26 ff.), is arrived at. But it is impossible to reach so simple a legend—one will always have, even omitting certain details, in the end an account of the baptism of a Gentile at the specific command of heaven. Luke was not the first to adapt the story. It recalls the gospel accounts of Jesus' meetings with Gentiles; the best parallel is the story of the Canaanite woman (see p. LXV) in either Matt xv 21–28; or Mark vii 24–30. In Matthew, the big question discussed was whether the Gentiles should be won over to God's kingdom at all ("It is not right to take the children's bread and throw it to the dogs"), or whether Jesus should gather only the children of Israel; Mark's version, with the words "Let the children first be fed" preceding the quoted word of Jesus, showed a later development, taking it for granted that the Gentiles should also receive the Gospel, but not until it had been preached to Israel (cf. Acts iii 26, xiii 46; Rom i 16, ii 9). Just as Jesus had been sent only to the lost sheep of Israel's house (Matt xv 24), so Peter too had only been ordered to preach to Israel, but in the Cornelius narrative, the Holy Spirit commanded him to go to a Gentile's house and baptize the Gentiles assembled there.

Just as through the adaptation of the narrative of the Canaanite woman (and of that of the centurion in Capernaum, Matt viii 5–13 par.) Jesus had become involved in the church's discussion of missions to the Gentiles, so through an adaptation of the narrative about his baptism of a single Gentile and his family and friends Peter has been made the first missionary to the Gentiles. Thereby the close connection and agreement between the primitive church and Paul over the mission to the Gentiles is confirmed by Luke (Acts xv 12–35) just as it is by Paul (Gal ii 7 ff.), and the latter's picture of the early history of the church has certainly not been embellished.

As in Jesus' case, the exception has been turned into the decisive event that determines the future. This had doubtless been done before Luke.

28. PETER'S DEFENSE OF HIS RELATIONS WITH CORNELIUS
(xi 1–18)

XI ¹ But the apostles and brethren living in Judea heard that the Gentiles also had received the word of God. ² When Peter then came up to Jerusalem, those of the circumcision party attacked him ³ and said: "You have entered the houses of uncircumcised men and you have eaten with them." ⁴ Then Peter began to describe to them what had happened: ⁵ "I was in the city of Joppa praying, and in a state of ecstasy I saw a vision: something that looked like a great cloth descended, and the cloth was lowered from heaven by the four corners, and it came to me. ⁶ I gazed into it and looked at it more closely, and I then saw four-footed beasts of the earth, wild beasts, reptiles, and birds of the air. ⁷ I also heard a voice saying to me: 'Get up, Peter, kill and eat!' ⁸ But I answered: 'By no means, Lord, for nothing ritually impure has ever yet passed my lips.' ⁹ A voice from heaven was heard a second time: 'That which God has declared clean, you must not call ritually impure.' ¹⁰ This happened a third time, then all was drawn up to heaven again. ¹¹ And at that very moment three men stood by the house where we were, sent to me from Caesarea. ¹² And the Spirit said to me that I was to go with them, without discrimination (between Jews and Gentiles). With me came these six men also, and we went into the man's house. ¹³ He told us that he had seen the angel standing in his house and saying: 'Send word to Joppa, and let Simon surnamed Peter be brought. ¹⁴ He shall speak words to you by which you and all your household shall be saved.' ¹⁵ But when I began to speak the Holy Spirit came upon them as he did upon us also in the beginning. ¹⁶ Then I remembered the words of the Lord, which were: 'John indeed baptized with water, but you shall be baptized with the Holy Spirit.' 17 Now when God gave them the same gift as had been given us after they had come to believe in the Lord Jesus Christ, who then was I to stand in the way of God?" 18 When they had heard this they ceased (their attack), and they began to praise God, and said: "God then has granted to the Gentiles also conversion to life."

NOTES

xi 1–3. The Jews are explicitly called *those of the circumcision party* in contrast to *the uncircumcised* as the Gentiles were called. The Jewish Christian church in Jerusalem was just as dismayed as the brethren from Joppa (in x 45).

4–17. Peter's answer is a repetition of the events in the preceding chapter, told in a different order and again with slight variation. It begins in Joppa with the revelation he had received at noon: the cloth that was approaching him (vs. 5) and the wild beasts (vs. 6). As was often the case the words spoken are almost identical with those in ch. x. It is interesting to note that Cornelius' name and his piety are not mentioned. Verse 14 is an expansion of the angel's words in vs. 13, where he was just called *the angel*—although only the reader had heard about him before; Peter's audience had not (cf. x 22, 33). On the other hand Peter's introductory words in Cornelius' house and his speech are omitted. Only after he began to speak is it stated (vs. 15) that the Holy Spirit came upon the Gentiles present. It is not said that this happened in the form of speaking in other languages, but Peter refers to the similarity between this event and what "we" had experienced in the beginning. In vs. 17 Peter continues his argument, corresponding to x 47, with the inclusion of the primitive Christian baptismal formula. The reception of the Holy Spirit was dependent on faith both for the Jews at the beginning and for the Gentiles in Caesarea.

18. The final formula *the conversion to life* is a variant of *the word of God* in vs. 1.

COMMENT

Although the Jerusalem church did not take the initiative for new advances, when something happened, it did hear of it, and came to a decision and, if necessary, took a hand in the further course. Now they heard that the Gentiles had received the word of God. These words may cause surprise to us because they do not fit into modern theories about missions, but within primitive Christianity they carried their full weight. On this point, Luke was in agreement with Paul, when he related (Gal ii 9) that Peter was an apostle to the circumcised, while he himself was an apostle to the Gentiles. When in Rom x 14–21 Paul spoke about the apostles sent to Israel and their mission, he alluded to their complete failure in quoting from Isaiah: "Lord, who has believed what he has heard from us?" and from Ps xix: "Their voices have gone all over the earth, and their words to the ends of the world." While by the first quotation, Paul showed that these apostles sent to Israel had not been able to convert unbelieving Israel, by the second quotation, he confirmed that these apostles to the Jews had now finished their work. Although they had not been literally everywhere or preached the Gospel to every single Jew, they had brought their preaching to all of Israel to an end. Those sections of the chosen people to whom they had preached stood for the whole Jewish nation.

In Rom xv 17–24, we hear about the mission among the Gentiles. Paul had finished most of this work, for he had been active from Jerusalem to Illyria and no longer had tasks to perform within this area. In other words Paul had finished in the East and now intended to visit the church in Rome in order to use it as a missionary base for work in Spain.

The problem we find inherent in other theories about the apostles' mission to Israel is: Had they then finished with all of Israel? And with regard to Paul's remarks in Rom xv: Had Paul at that time finished in the East? Even if we count the churches founded by Paul and others and double that number by adding those we assume to have been founded by other, unnamed missionaries called by Christ, we still arrive at only a modest number of churches with relatively small memberships. When, nevertheless, Paul maintained that he was finished in the East, it must be because he did not think of the individual Gentiles and their personal attitude toward the Gospel, but thought that it was the Gentile nations that were to hear the Gospel and accept or reject it. The cities where the apostles had preached and where churches had been founded had thereby committed themselves to Christ on behalf of their nation. In other words, in so far as the East was concerned, there had been a representative acceptance of the Gospel by the individual nations, and this was why the apostle had no longer any "room" in these regions and had to go westward to preach to Spaniards, Gauls, and Britons.

This Pauline view, which may be suitably named "representative universalism," represented a Semitic outlook. A part could take the place of the whole. Where a part had accepted the Gospel, then the whole, that is the nation concerned, had accepted it, and where a part had rejected it, the nation as a whole had rejected it. Here in the opening and closing verses of this section of Acts, we encounter the same way of thinking: the Gentiles had received *the word of God* (*the conversion to life*), although all we have learned directly is that Cornelius and his family and some close friends had been baptized.

On Peter's return to Jerusalem he was called to account. The community did not complain of his baptizing these Gentiles without demanding their circumcision and observance of the law of Moses, but charged him with having entered the house of Gentiles and having eaten with them (vs. 3). Peter then recounted the instruction God had given him through a revelation and all that had happened which had made him enter a Gentile house and eat with the people there. Peter's account convinced the members of the Jerusalem congregation (vs. 18), and their positive attitude to the case had a lasting effect (see ch. xv). This is not to say, however, that the demands for circumcision and obedience to the law of Moses were not in the foreground in primitive Christianity.

PART III

29. THE MISSION TO THE GENTILES BEGINS IN ANTIOCH
(xi 19–26)

XI ¹⁹ Those who had been put to flight by the persecution
that had arisen because of Stephen traveled through (the country) as far as Phoenicia, Cyprus, and Antioch, and they preached
the word only to Jews. ²⁰ But there were some of them, men
of Cyprus and Cyrene, who came to Antioch and spoke to the
Greeks also, preaching Jesus as the Lord. ²¹ The hand of the
Lord was with them, so that a large number believed and turned
to the Lord. ²² The news of this came to the ears of the church
in Jerusalem, and they sent Barnabas to Antioch. ²³ When he
had come and seen God's gracious work, he was glad, and he
exhorted all to remain true to the Lord with all their heart and
will; ²⁴ for he was a good man, and filled with the Holy Spirit
and with faith. And a great crowd was brought to the Lord.
²⁵ He went to Tarsus to seek out Saul, ²⁶ and when he had
found him, he brought him to Antioch. And it happened that
they were together in the church for a whole year and taught
a great crowd. It was in Antioch that the disciples were first
called Christians.

NOTES

xi 19–21. Hitherto the events reported in Acts have happened in
Palestine and Jerusalem; with these refugees we make our way into
the great world. Antioch was the third largest city of the Roman empire,
capital of the province of Syria, and home of a large colony of Jews.
Obviously these refugees would preach only to Jews (vs. 19) and we are
told this only because of the subsequent turn in events. It has been
unduly stressed that the disciples who first preached to the Gentiles
were natives of Cyrene and Cyprus and thus were what in Jerusalem
were called Hellenists. More widely traveled than their Aramaic-speaking

brethren, it was their knowledge of the Greek language which enabled them to preach the Gospel to the Greek-speaking inhabitants of these regions. But as in the case of so many other things that have proved to be decisive in world history, no real explanation exists for this new development.

22–26. When the church in Jerusalem heard rumors that the Gospel had been brought to Antioch, they sent Barnabas there to find out what had happened. If his experience (told very quietly in contrast to the detailed, emphatic way in which Peter's meeting with Cornelius was described) occurred shortly after Stephen's death, when, according to viii 1, all but the apostles were forced to flee Jerusalem then Barnabas' journey to Antioch would hardly have started from Jerusalem, but from quite another place, possibly Cyprus. Barnabas approved of the new work in Antioch and joined the mission in order to strengthen it. As the new congregation continued growing, he sought out Paul to help him with the work. According to ix 30, Paul had gone to his native city of Tarsus; just as Acts (ix 19–20) described Paul as a missionary in Damascus soon after Christ had revealed himself to him, so one must imagine his stay in Tarsus as missionary work anticipating his work later. The collaboration of Barnabas and Paul so increased the number of Christians in Antioch that throughout the city they became distinguished from the Jews and were called Christians after their Master. The term was formed by adding to the name "Christ" the ending "-ians," a way of identifying an adherent (cf., "Herodians," Mark 6, xii 13 par.). The naming showed that Christ, really the Messiah, was understood to be a proper name, which can also be seen from the Pauline letters.

COMMENT

This section deals with the beginning of the mission to the Gentiles in Antioch, which was an offshoot of the persecution of the church in Jerusalem after Stephen's death. Christians fleeing from Jerusalem had carried the Gospel farther away than Samaria and the coastal plain where Philip had preached (viii 4 ff. and viii 40). Peter's visit to the churches in Lydda and Joppa and his call to seek out Cornelius related in chapters ix and x did not occur until after the persecution had ceased (cf. ix 31). We are, in this and the following two sections, returning to the time immediately after the outbreak of the persecution and will concentrate on events in Antioch until the time of King Agrippa's death (A.D. 44).

Probably because of Luke's usual faithfulness to his sources, the following narrative deals with matters preceding Cornelius' baptism. Thus literary dependence, not chronological order, makes Peter's baptism of Gentiles take precedence over the missionary activities in Antioch. Just as Peter became a fugitive from the persecution of King Agrippa (ch. xii) and presumably did not return to Jerusalem until the peaceful period following the king's death, so the fugitives from Jerusalem, who had originally come from Cyprus and Cyrene, presumably returned also (ix 31). In Antioch a church came into being which may possibly have been of a mixed character with both Jewish Christian and Gentile Christian members. It was at this place that Jewish Christians from Judea later demanded that Gentile Christians should be circumcised if they wanted to be saved (xv 1). Again it was here, according to Paul (Gal ii 11–13), that during Peter's visit, the Jewish Christians after the arrival of "some from James" withdrew from the common meals with the Gentile Christians. It is however open to doubt whether the congregation in Antioch was a mixed congregation, for the Jewish Christians mentioned in Galatians may have included apostles and missionaries, but not ordinary Jewish Christians. This must remain an open question.

When compared with this account about the beginning of the mission to the Gentiles in Antioch, the narrative about Cornelius seems, from an historical point of view, to be left hanging in mid-air as a detached fragment. Its importance within the framework of Acts is obvious (see p. 96), but despite this, the Cornelius story had no continuation and was of no effect within the historical series of events. Afterward, as well as before, Peter remained an apostle to the Jews; of course Cornelius and all his household had been baptized, but to which congregation were they admitted? Was a Gentile Christian congregation founded in Caesarea? And to whom did Cornelius preach and whom did he win over to Christ? All this would seem to indicate that the Cornelius story was a detached account which had continued to be discussed and retold within that part of the church not concerned with missions to the Gentiles.

As was so often the case in the history of both the primitive and the later church, it was not the recognized leaders of the organized church who started the mission to the Gentiles in Antioch. It was neither expected nor prepared, just as had happened when the risen Christ appeared to the persecutor Paul on the caravan road outside Damascus. In the present case, it was the strong compulsory effect of the persecution that made the Christians from Jerusalem go as far away as Antioch. There something new and hitherto unknown came into existence, namely the preaching of the Gospel to non-Jews. Luke went on immediately with his account of the great effect of this venture, with effects just as revolutionary as those which followed the preaching of the Gospel to the Jews. Paul told a different story and, as in so many other cases, his was the true one.

It must be admitted that the actual moment when the message about the new mission work became known to the Jerusalem congregation might have followed the Cornelius episode and Peter's negotiation with the congregation, so that the dispatch of Barnabas could be understood as a positive evaluation of the occurrence. But such juxtaposition must be our own construction. Luke had not hinted anything of the kind and his account of Barnabas' activities in Antioch could very well indicate that he was so successful because he himself interpreted his task and with outstanding ability fulfilled it without depending on Jerusalem's opinion at the time. The situation was rather that the most important event in the history of the church was brought about by unknown Christians, who through persecution were faced with an emergency.

Thus two different traditions, one about Cornelius and the other about Antioch, each with an independent existence, were brought together by Luke in his account of the Apostolic Council (ch. xv). This meeting of the Council reached the crucial decision that became the scene of the church's approval of missions to the Gentiles without demanding circumcision and obedience to the law of Moses. No longer was it necessary to become a Jew in order to become a Christian.

30. A GENERAL FAMINE AND A COLLECTION FOR ITS VICTIMS
(xi 27–30)

XI 27 In those days prophets came from Jerusalem to Antioch, 28 and one of them, named Agabus, came forward and predicted by the Spirit that there would be a great famine throughout the whole world; it happened in the reign of Claudius. 29 Every one of the disciples decided to send what each could afford to the brethren living in Judea. 30 This they did by sending (what had been collected) to the elders (in Jerusalem) in the care of Barnabas and Saul.

NOTES

xi 27. In primitive Christianity, *prophets* were spiritually gifted preachers who, starting from the OT and Jesus' life and words, combined the actual present of the church with approaching tribulations and final salvation. John the Baptist is called prophet in Matt xiv 5, xxi 26 par.; Luke i 76; Jesus, in Matt xxi 11, 46; Luke vii 16, 39, ix 8, 19 par., xiii 33, xxiv 19; John iv 19, vi 14, vii 40, 52, ix 17; Acts iii 22, 23 (Deut xviii 15, 18); cf. vii 37. Acts frequently refers to preachers and teachers as prophets: Barnabas, Simeon and their companions in Antioch (xiii 1); Silas and Judas from Jerusalem (xv 32); and Agabus, who appears here and again in Caesarea (xxi 10) where he joins Philip the evangelist all of whose four daughters are prophetesses (xxi 9). All attest to the strong prophetic character of Christianity.

28. The Western text inserts before *one of them* "there was much rejoicing; and when we were gathered together"—the first example of a "we" passage (see Introduction, pp. XLII–XLIII).

a great famine throughout the whole world. No empire-wide famine is known in the reign of Claudius (A.D. 41–54), but famines did occur in various parts of the empire. One in Palestine in A.D. 46–48 was so severe that the country was in dire need. To prophesy a world-wide famine would turn the thoughts of the Antioch Christians to the already suffering Jerusalem church, as the collection (vss. 29–30) suggests. Perhaps the phrase *decided to send what help each could afford* indicates that the collection had been going on for some time, as was the case with the later collection, also for Jerusalem (see NOTE following), vide I Cor xvi: "On the first (day) of every week each of you is to put aside and store up whatever he gains. . . ."

what had been collected. We know, though not from Acts, of another collection for Jerusalem, a large one in the Pauline churches during Paul's third missionary journey (I Cor xvi 1–4; II Cor viii–ix; Rom xv 25–33). Both collections have been variously interpreted. In Gal ii 9–10, it is stated that when Paul and Barnabas met James, Peter, and John in Jerusalem, the meeting ended in a separation of the apostolate to the Jews from the apostolate to the Gentiles, the only link remaining between them being that the apostle to the Gentiles must not forget the support of the poor. On the basis of this statement it has been assumed that this important agreement was concerned with a church tax like the Jews' tax for the upkeep of the Jerusalem temple. But obviously on the occasion mentioned here in chapter xi, it was not a question of a required tax but of a gift to which the brethren of Antioch were making voluntary contributions. To arrive at the other interpretation, a very definite assumption must be read into the text. Exactly the same can be said to hold with regard to the Pauline collection.

30. *elders.* A term used of those who held office in the primitive church. Acts records elders in the congregation in Jerusalem—appearing together with the Twelve (xv 2, 4, 6, 22, 23, xvi 4) or by themselves (xi 30, xxi 18)—and in the Asia Minor congregations (xiv 23, xx 17).

COMMENT

When Barnabas' and Paul's collaboration in Antioch had lasted for more than a year, events occurred which made Luke change the scene of his narrative. A prophet, Agabus, predicted a great famine all over the world; Luke added that this famine occurred during the reign of Claudius (A.D. 41–54). This prophecy turned the Antioch Christians' thoughts toward the congregations in Judea of which the congregation of Jerusalem was the most important. A collection was taken and the money sent to the elders in Jerusalem by Barnabas and Paul.

31. KING AGRIPPA I PERSECUTES THE CHURCH
AND DIES
(xii 1–25)

XII 1 At that time King Herod took violent action against some members of the church. 2 He executed James the brother of John by the sword. 3 When he saw that this pleased the Jews, he went on to arrest Peter also; it was during the days of unleavened bread. 4 When he had seized him he put him in prison, and charged four details of four soldiers each to guard him, for he intended to bring him to trial before the people after Passover. 5 Peter was now under guard in prison, but prayers were constantly made to God for him by the church.

6 When the time came for Herod to bring him to trial, Peter slept on the preceding night between two soldiers, bound with two chains, and sentries at the door guarded the prison. 7 Suddenly an angel* of the Lord stood there, light shone in the cell, and the angel touched Peter on the side, woke him, and said, "Get up quickly!" And the chains fell off his hands. 8 Then the angel said to him, "Get dressed and put on your sandals!" He did so. After this the angel said to him, "Put on your cloak and follow me!" 9 He went out and followed him. He did not know that what the angel did was actually happening, but thought it was a vision. 10 But they passed the first guard, and the second, and came to the iron gate that led to the city; this opened for them of its own accord, and they went out and passed through one street, when all at once the angel left him. 11 When Peter came to himself, he said: "Now I really know that the Lord has sent his angel and released me from the

* N.B. It is by no means clear here, or in much of the rest of the NT, whether "angel" is a heavenly figure or a human messenger. This passage is certainly more intelligible if the Greek is rendered "messenger."—W.F.A. and C.S.M.

hand of Herod and from all that the Jewish people had anticipated."

12 After he had realized this, he went to the house belonging to Mary, the mother of John surnamed Mark, where many had gathered and were praying. 13 When he knocked at the gateway door, a maid named Rhoda came to open it, 14 and she recognized Peter's voice. In her joy she did not open the gate but ran in and announced that Peter was standing outside. 15 They said to her, "You are mad!" But she insisted that it was so. But they still said: "It is his messenger." 16 However, Peter went on knocking; so they opened the door, saw him, and were overcome with awe. 17 But he gestured with his hand that they were to be quiet, and then began to explain to them how the Lord had brought him out of the prison. Then he said to them: "Tell James and the brethren!" departed, and went to another place.

18 When day had come, there was no little commotion among the soldiers over what had become of Peter. 19 When Herod had searched for him and not found him, he examined the guards, commanded them to be removed, and he went down from Judea to Caesarea and remained there.

20 Herod was furiously angry with the inhabitants of Tyre and Sidon; but they came to him jointly, and after they had won the support of Blastus, the king's chamberlain, they sought an accord, for their country got its supplies from the king's country. 21 On an appointed day Herod put on a royal robe, ascended his throne, and made a speech to them. 22 And the people shouted, "It is the voice of a god, and not of a man!" 23 Immediately an angel of the Lord struck him down because he did not give God the glory, and he was eaten up by worms and died.

24 But the word of the Lord increased and spread. 25 Barnabas and Saul returned from Jerusalem when they had completed their ministry, and they took with them John, surnamed Mark.

NOTES

xii 1. *At that time* indicates that the sending of the delegation with the gifts (xi 30) came after the events related in ch. xi.

2. In recent research scholars have assumed that the account of James' death found here was identical with the assertion that Papias of Hierapolis (ca. A.D. 100) had stated that the brothers James and John were killed by the Jews (fragment in *Philippus Sidetes,* ed. by C. de Boor, 1888, p. 170). Most quotations ascribed to Papias are not very reliable; thus there seems to be no reason for preferring this statement to Luke's account and Clement's (ca. 150–215) narrative (in the seventh book of *Hypotyposeis,* Eus. *Hist. eccl.* II.ix.1–3) of James' imprisonment and death; neither Luke nor Clement speak of the death of John. We have already discussed (see NOTE on ix 23–25) the divergent accounts of Paul's persecution in Damascus: whether it was at the hands of the Syrian king's ethnarch, as Paul says in II Cor xi 32–33, or at the hands of the Jews, as Luke says in Acts ix 23. When we are able to keep these two traditions apart, why should the Luke and Clement accounts— that one of the brothers, James, was beheaded by King Herod—be forced into agreement with the Papias ascription—that the apostolic brothers, James and John, were executed by the Jews? Clement, loc. cit., tells how the jailer, under the impact of James' testimony, confesses himself a Christian, and, Clement continues, "thus they were both beheaded together." Is this passage the source of the incorrect tradition in the quotation from Papias?

3–5. The people's enmity toward the Christians was surprising after Luke's previous account of their sympathetic attitude (ii 47, iv 21, v 13, 26). While Jesus, whom they had been afraid to arrest during the festival (or in the festival assembly) (Matt xxvi 5 par.), had been sentenced and executed during the Passover festival, Peter's sentence and execution were postponed until the end of the festival. Passover is described as *the days of unleavened bread* (vs. 3; cf. Luke xxii), i.e. the week of the Passover festival which began with the killing of the paschal lamb.

4. The twelve hours of the night were divided into four three-hour watches and for each watch there were four guards on duty.

6–10. Peter slept, submitting himself to his fate. Throughout his liberation, initiated and carried out at every stage by the angel, Peter was as passive as one in a dream.

10. No explanation is offered concerning the passive attitude of the soldiers or the opening and closing of the iron door as the angel led Peter away.

11–12. Not until he was outside in the city, did Peter recover (in x 17 the Western text has a reading with the same meaning) and realize what had happened. The house which served as a meeting place for the Christians was fairly large and had an entrance gate with locked doors (cf. NOTE on i 13).

13–14. The story of Peter waiting at the door for Rhoda and the others in the house to open it is related with great skill and a simplicity that is psychologically convincing. Luke is capable of telling a good story. It may seem strange that during a persecution, a female slave should go out to open the gate in the middle of the night, but even under unusual conditions ordinary habits might prevail.

15–16. Probably an instance of the not uncommon belief that the moment a man dies his guardian angel appears. In this case, it would have been a sign that the Christians' prayer (cf. vs. 5) had not been granted, but that Herod had had the apostle executed in prison.

17. The salutation to James is generally thought to be an indication that from now on he was to be the leader of the Jerusalem congregation after Peter's departure. This is a modern conclusion, based on quite primitive material. The expression that he went to *another place* might originally have been a deliberate attempt to avoid mentioning Peter's whereabouts, later it was probably a statement based on ignorance. Antioch or Rome have been suggested, but many other cities could be mentioned with the same lack of certainty. He probably came back as soon as Agrippa had died and a Roman procurator had become the ruler of Palestine.

18–19. Peter's disappearance had grim consequences. At Herod's command, the guards were led out and executed. According to Roman custom the guard was responsible with his life for his prisoner. This explains the scene in Philippi where the prison guard, seeing the doors to the prison wide-open, drew his sword and was about to commit suicide when he was stopped by Peter (xvi 27). It also explains why, when Paul's ship runs aground off Malta, the soldiers wanted to kill the prisoners before they had any opportunity to get ashore and escape (xxvii 42 f.). Agrippa probably left Jerusalem after the Passover festival in order to resume his affairs in Caesarea, where the conflict with the Phoenician cities was to be ended.

20–23. Herod died immediately after his persecution of the church. Thus everybody could draw their own conclusions as was in fact done in both Jewish and Gentile circles. Judas had suffered a terrible death not long after his betrayal of Jesus (i 16–20). Josephus too has told of Herod's death and assumed that it came as a divine punishment, because the king allowed the crowd to hail him as a god (Josephus *Ant.* XIX.viii.2). The two accounts are in agreement with regard to essential points: Agrippa, magnificently attired, died suddenly after a few flattering acclamations addressing him as a god. According to Josephus, he was present at a festival in honor of the Emperor. Some scholars have wanted to identify this as the Vicennalia in March A.D. 44. The dating of the event by Acts within the year does not differ much from this. Other great sinners had died from an illness where worms had attacked the ailing man while he was still alive: Herod the Great (Josephus *Jewish War* I.xxxiii.5), Antiochus Epiphanes (II Macc ix 9), and Judas according to Papias (see NOTE on i 18).

24–25. Just as the events in chapter xii were prepared for by the collection in Antioch, and the journey of Barnabas and Paul to Jerusalem with the gift (xi 30), thus turning the reader's attention back to that city and its church, so the remarks about their return journey to Antioch together with Mark, prepares the way for the missionary journey itself, of which an account is given in chapters xiii–xiv.

COMMENT

The Jews persecuted their Christian countrymen whenever it was possible. As they had killed Jesus, so they stoned Stephen to death and in the following extensive persecution of the church, they had tried to discipline the disciples by imprisonment and death. But, just as later the Romans started persecutions and allowed them to wane, so did the Jewish people and their leaders. Thus, as already noted, Luke's remark in ix 31 that the church in the whole of Palestine was at peace, indicated a pause. But now in chapter xii a new persecution began, aimed above all at the leaders of the congregation: the apostle James, the son of Zebedee, who was beheaded, and Peter, who was put in prison pending execution after the Passover. Peter was freed by an angel who, unseen by the guards, led him out into the city. After a brief stay at the house belonging to Mary, Mark's mother, a meeting place for the congregation, Peter left Jerusalem.

King Herod Agrippa I was a grandson of Herod the Great. Caligula had bestowed on him Philip's territory of Trachonitis, Batanea, and Gaulanitis as early as A.D. 37, and after banishing Herod Antipas, had given him Galilee and Perea in A.D. 40. After Caligula's death, Claudius gave him Judea and Samaria in A.D. 41, and, as King Herod Agrippa I (A.D. 41–44), he thus united all Palestine under his rule. He had had a checkered career. Educated with the imperial family in Rome, he led a dissolute life in his youth, incurred a huge debt and begged support from Antipas his brother-in-law, had been in prison, and had considered suicide. Now raised by imperial favor to the dignity of a king, the former prodigal became a capable ruler.

For political reasons, he favored the Pharisees, who compared their position under him to that prevailing under Queen Alexandra (76–67 B.C.). It was in order to please his Jewish subjects that he had taken action against the church. To the Jews his brief rule was a time they were long to recall joyfully. To his Roman masters, however, he was less satisfactory. He was suspected of having allied himself with other kings of the Near East—his settlement with Tyre and Sidon, made a few days before his death, may have been a move in this political game. His sudden death in A.D. 44 freed Rome from many worries. Whereas previously only Judea and Samaria had (at one time) come under direct Roman rule, now the whole of Palestine was placed under a procurator.

32. PAUL AND BARNABAS ON CYPRUS
(xiii 1–12)

XIII 1 There were in the church at Antioch some prophets
and teachers, namely Barnabas, Simeon called Niger, Lucius
from Cyrene, Manaen, who had been brought up with Herod
the tetrarch, and Saul. 2 While they were worshiping the Lord
and fasting, the Holy Spirit said: "Set apart Barnabas and Saul
for me for the work to which I have called them." 3 They
fasted and prayed, and they laid their hands upon them and
sent them away. 4 Those who had thus been sent forth by the
Holy Spirit traveled down to Seleucia, and from there they
sailed for Cyprus. 5 When they came to Salamis, they preached
the word of God in the Jewish synagogues; and John was also
with them as their assistant. 6 When they had traveled through
the whole island as far as Paphos, they met a Jew who was a
magician and charlatan; his name was Bariesou, 7 and he was
with the proconsul Sergius Paulus, an intelligent man, who summoned Barnabas and Saul and was very eager to hear the word
of God. 8* But the magician Elymas—for so his name may be
translated—resisted them and tried to prevent the proconsul
from believing. 9 But Saul, also called Paul, filled with the Holy

* The text here is apparently in a state of some disorder, and there seems
little hope of any solution at the present time. The Peshitta offers us "a
magician Bar-Shuma, whose name is in translation Elumos." The word
shuma is not otherwise known in Syriac, while the Greek *elumos* is said to
have the following meanings: case, quiver; a kind of flute; a kind of grain,
millet. The suggestion that the word is a Semitism, akin to the Arabic *'alîm*,
wise man, may be discounted. It is hard to think of any reason which would
satisfactorily explain why a Jew living in Cyprus, at the court of a Roman
consular governor, should be called by an obscure Arabic word, which was
not to be attested for many centuries. Some Western textual evidence exists
for reading *hetoimos*, "ready," "worthy," or "equal," and there is known
to us from Josephus (*Ant.* XX.vii.2) a Cypriot sorcerer called Atomos,
whom Felix is said to have used in his attempts to procure Drusilla, the
wife of Azizus. But this is considerably later in time than the Acts text.
—W.F.A. and C.S.M.

Spirit, looking at him 10 said: "You who are full of all deceit and all evil, you child of the devil, you enemy of all that is righteous, will you not cease to twist the straight paths of the Lord? 11 Listen then: the hand of the Lord is upon you, so that you will become blind, and will not see the sun for a time." Then dimness of vision and darkness at once fell upon him, so that he groped about him and looked for someone to guide him. 12 When the proconsul saw what had happened he believed, being deeply impressed by the teaching about the Lord.

NOTES

xiii 1–3. The Holy Spirit sent Barnabas and Paul, as its agents. The emissaries started their journey from Antioch, their missionary base, but the spiritual authority and the conduct of the mission rested with those who had received the call, not the Antioch church. Prophets and teachers are mentioned together in Rom xii 6 f.; I Cor xii 28 f.; Eph iv 11. It is worth noting that among the prophets and the teachers were *Lucius from Cyrene,* who for no good reason was identified by the primitive church with Luke himself, and *Manaen,* who may well have been educated with *the tetrarch* Herod Antipas (Matt. xiv 1; Luke iii 19, ix 7), or at least had acquired a title that indicated as much though it had lost its meaning. "Manaen," too, can mean "son of consolation," the meaning ascribed to Barnabas' name in iv 36. "Tetrarch" was used about a dependent prince of a rank lower than that of king.

4. *Seleucia* was the seaport and some sixteen miles to the west of Antioch, an artificial harbor on an otherwise straight coast line; the quays of this port have to a certain extent been preserved and lasted until our time. After B.C. 22 *Cyprus* was a province of the Roman senate, its governors titular proconsuls (really propraetors).

5. *Salamis* was the most important town on Cyprus. Only a small part of its extensive ruins, buried under a forest, has been excavated. It had a large Jewish population, so there were several synagogues.

Mark was not an apostle but a servant to Barnabas and Paul.

6. From Salamis on the east coast the apostles went westward across the island to *Paphos* the official capital and residence of the proconsul. In his entourage, there was a Jew who performed magical arts. The Jews were known for this at the time and the magic papyri extant show Jewish elements. This Jew could be called a *charlatan,* precisely because he was a Jew who pretended to be a religious prophet, but did not live righteously before God.

7–8. *Sergius Paulus,* who supposedly held his office between A.D. 40

and 50, showed his good sense by taking an interest in the Christian preaching, but Bariesou, whose position was threatened by this new interest, attempted to prevent the Roman from cultivating it. For the problem of the magician's name see editors' footnote on p. 117.

9–11. Hitherto the apostle has been called Saul, but from now on his name is Paul. The change of name at this place calls for an explanation. Just as with vss. 6–8, it has been assumed that a new source may have been started which used "Paul" as the name of the apostle. Another assumption would be that the proconsul Sergius Paulus had adopted Saul and gave him his own name. But a Hellenistic Jew would in any case have had two names already and often two that were as much alike as Saul and Paul. A Roman citizen would be even more likely to have had two names, a name and a surname, and here the surname was Paul. One returns to why Luke ascribed the new name to him just then at Cyprus. An obvious but seldom given explanation is that he knew that Paul himself had changed his name at this time and had begun using his surname. The reason may have been that as his travels into the Greek world were beginning, this would be a natural thing to do.

Fixing his eyes on the Jewish magician, Paul pronounced a curse which was to produce a temporary blindness in the Jewish magician. Just as the Christians, filled with the Holy Spirit, were able to do good (cf. iii 4), so they could also strike the guilty with punishment. This we have seen in Peter's punishment of Ananias and Sapphira (v 7 ff.). In the case of the hostile magician, who as a son of the Devil attempted to prevent the proconsul from hearing the word of God, it was a punishment due to a man who was impenitent. Compare this temporary blindness with Zechariah's loss of speech (Luke i 20).

12. Many scholars doubt that Sergius Paulus accepted the Christian faith, for it is nowhere said that he was baptized. But this does not take the briefness of the account into consideration. With neither the proconsul nor the reader of Acts did God's punishment of Bariesou leave any room for doubt about the results of unbelief.

COMMENT

There were prophets and teachers in the church in Antioch. At a service preceded by fasting, the Holy Spirit demanded that Barnabas and Paul be set apart for the work to which they had already been called. So they sailed from Seleucia to Salamis and across the island to Paphos, where they were invited to converse with Sergius Paulus the proconsul, but were annoyed by a religious protégé of his, the magician Bariesou. Paul overcame him by striking him with temporary blindness.

33. PAUL'S SPEECH IN PISIDIAN ANTIOCH
(xiii 13–41)

XIII   13 After Paul and his company had set sail from Paphos they came to Perga in Pamphylia; but John left them and returned to Jerusalem. 14 The others traveled through (the country) from Perga, and came to Pisidian Antioch, and on the sabbath day they went to the synagogue and sat down. 15 After the reading from the Law and the Prophets, the heads of the synagogue sent them a message saying: "Brothers, if you have an exhortation to the people, speak out." 16 And Paul stood up, gestured with his hand, and said:

"Israelites, and you who fear God, listen to me! 17 The God of this people Israel chose our fathers, and he raised up the people (from their low estate) during their sojourn in the land of Egypt, and with his mighty power brought them out. 18 For about forty years he took care of Israel in the wilderness. 19 Then he destroyed seven nations in the land of Canaan, and gave their land to the people for an inheritance 20 about four hundred and fifty years. Then he gave them judges until the prophet Samuel. 21 They then asked for a king, and God gave them Saul the son of Kish, a man of the tribe of Benjamin, for forty years. 22 When he had removed him, he raised David as their king and gave him this testimony: 'I have found David son of Jesse a man after my own heart; he will do all my will.' 23 From his posterity God has raised up Israel's promised savior, Jesus, 24 before whose coming John had preached the baptism of repentance to the whole people of Israel. 25 And when John was nearing the end of his course, he said: 'I am not the one you take me to be, but after me will come one whose sandals I am not worthy to untie.'

26 "Brothers, descendants of Abraham, and those of you who fear God, it is to us that the word of this salvation has been sent. 27 For those who live in Jerusalem and their leaders did

not know this (Jesus), and they caused the words of the prophets, which are read aloud every sabbath, to be proved true by condemning him. 28 Though they found no fault that merited death, they asked Pilate that he might be executed. 29 And when they had fulfilled all that was written about him, he was taken down from the cross and laid in a tomb. 30 But God raised him from the dead, 31 and for many days he appeared to those who had come with him from Galilee to Jerusalem, those who are (now) witnesses to the people about him. 32 And we tell you of the promise made to the fathers, 33 that God has fulfilled it in us their children by raising Jesus, as it is written in the second psalm:

'You are my son,
    today I have brought you into the world.'
34 As to his raising him from the dead, so that he shall not later return to corruption, he has spoken like this:

'For you I will fulfill the holy and solemn pledges to David.'
35 Therefore it is also said in another (psalm):

'You will not allow your holy one to see corruption.'
36 For David, after he had served the will of God in his own generation, fell asleep and was laid with his fathers and saw corruption. 37 But he whom God raised did not see corruption. 38-39 Therefore be it known to you, brothers, that through him forgiveness of sins is preached to you, and that through him everyone who believes is vindicated in respect of everything for which there was no remission under the law of Moses. 40 Take care that what is spoken of in the Prophets does not happen to you:

41   'Behold, you scoffers, be astonished and perish,
      for I perform a mighty act in your days,
      an act you would not believe if anyone were to tell you
      of it.'"

NOTES

xiii 13. *Perga* was a town situated near the river Cestius *in Pamphylia*, Asia Minor. Arriving by water, one could probably get quite close to the town or could land at the seaport of Attalia (mentioned in xiv 25) and travel overland to Perga. Pamphylia had been an independent province A.D. 25 to 43 when, together with Lycia, it became an imperial province. A little later it was added to the province of Galatia and still later reunited with Lycia.

No explanation was offered for Mark's departure, but Paul's attitude in xv 38 showed that he had considered Mark's action a desertion from missionary work. Paul was a hard worker with a strong sense of duty, who demanded a great deal of others as he did of himself (cf. I Cor iv 9–13; xv 30–39; II Cor xi 23–33). In this respect he never showed any forbearance.

14. The journey might have been guided by the Holy Spirit, but no statement about this was made. The Jewish colonies in the cities of the interior were considered a decisive factor in deciding where to go. It has been further supposed that later the Galatian congregations were to be found in these cities (the so-called South-Galatian theory) and that therefore, in Gal iv 13, Paul was referring to this journey from Perga in the malaria-infested coastal district to Pisidian Antioch about 3600 feet above sea level. This may be possible but is not certain. *Pisidian Antioch* (there were so many cities with the name Antioch—called after princes named Antiochus of the royal Seleucid family in "Syria" which after the death of Alexander the Great devolved upon one of his generals—that an explanatory name was needed) was situated not in, but near, Pisidia. It belonged to the province of Galatia and was a Roman colony. The sabbath day here mentioned seems to have been a sabbath at the beginning of Paul's visit, as his special message did not seem to be known by the leader of the synagogue.

15. It often happened that a guest was asked to speak. The service in the synagogue included reading of the Law and of the Prophets, and the reading was followed by a sermon if anyone present were able to undertake it. The account of Jesus in the synagogue at Nazareth shows us such a service with a guest speaker (Luke iv 16 ff.).

16. We know nothing about the text on which Paul was to deliver his sermon. While according to Luke iv 20 Jesus sat down to speak, Paul rose (cf. Philo, *On the Special Laws* II.62). Those addressed by Paul as *you who fear God* might have been the god-fearing Gentiles who attended the services at the synagogue. Another possibility would be that they were the same persons whom he addressed as *Israelites*.

18–21. For *took care of* may be read "endured." In a way similar to ch. vii, the various epochs are mentioned with indication of their chronology (forty years in the wilderness, the first period in Canaan about four hundred and fifty years, Saul's kingdom for forty years, vs. 21). The *seven nations* were mentioned in Deut vii 1; Josh iii 10, xxiv 11 (Exod xxiii 23 f.; Deut xx 17 mention only six). The Neutral text counted the four hundred and fifty years as the period from the patriarchs to the immigration into Palestine, whereas the Western text used that figure for the period after the immigration, namely the age of the judges.

23. Here there is a transition to the account about Jesus as the Savior.

24–25. John the Baptist's preaching *repentance and baptism to the whole people of Israel* came before Jesus. Toward the end of his life, John the Baptist testified to Jesus as being far greater than himself (cf. Luke iii 15–17, John i 19 ff.). The audience was expected to know about John the Baptist and Jesus, but Paul had something new to relate about Jesus.

26. With a new address to his audience, Paul started another section of his sermon, on Jesus' death and resurrection. As at the beginning in vs. 16, he addresses both the Jews and the god-fearing Gentiles: The gospel of salvation in Christ concerns both. Does this explain why the Gentiles appeared in vss. 44 ff.?

27–28. The people and the leaders in Jerusalem had acted out of ignorance, just as was said in iii 17–18. In this passage it is the Jews who realized that Jesus was innocent, in Acts iii 13 (cf. NOTE), it was Pilate.

29. Here too, the text deviates from the gospels, where Joseph of Arimathea, a member of the Sanhedrin not guilty of Jesus' death, supervises the taking down of his body from the cross and its burial (Luke xxiii 50–53 par.).

he was taken down. A passive construction is used instead of the active "they took him down" for the agent might be the Romans, the Jews, or the disciples. Jesus' being laid in a tomb demonstrated the reality of death.

30–31. *for many days,* is a variation on the "forty days" mentioned in i 3. Paul would hardly have mentioned revelations to the Galilean disciples without mentioning his own revelation of Christ (cf. I Cor xv 5–8). The author is at times apt to forget that it was Paul who was speaking.

32–35. The "we" used here does not refer to the Jewish Christian apostles but to the apostles to the Gentiles, who address themselves both to the people of Israel and to the Gentiles; here in the synagogue they speak of the OT promises of the flesh as well as of the spirit— possibly the promises given to the patriarchs mentioned in vs. 17, but more probably those spoken to the OT ancestors (e.g. Ps ii 7, xvi 10; Isa lv 3) had now been fulfilled through the resurrection of Jesus.

36–37. The promises spoken to David referred not to him but to Jesus; cf. Acts ii 29–31.

38–41. Through Jesus, the forgiveness of sins was preached and everyone who believed in him would be acquitted of all that he could not be remitted from under the law of Moses. This was not, as has so often been assumed, Pauline theology but already Jewish-Christian dogma, as can be seen from Acts xv 10–11; Gal ii 15–16. (See NOTE on xv 7–11.)

The quotation is from the LXX version of the twelve minor prophets, Hab i 5.

COMMENT

From Paphos, Paul and his companions crossed to Perga, where Mark left them and returned to Jerusalem. The others went inland to Pisidian Antioch where in the synagogue Paul delivered a speech, rendered here in great detail, which attracted great attention. Many points of Paul's speech call to mind the speeches made by others. The account of the early history of Israel in certain points resembles Stephen's speech (vii 2 ff.). The Messiah's suffering, death, and resurrection are related in terms that come close to Peter's speeches earlier (xiii 27–31 = iii 13–15) (xiii 31 = i 3) (xiii 34–37 = ii 24–32).

Paul's speech deals with God's election and mankind's acceptance or rejection of his salvation. God elected the people of Israel and delivered them from Egypt and in his grace, he gave them judges and kings. He deposed Saul and raised David as a man who would do God's will. The Messiah whom the Jews in Palestine had rejected was of David's stock. But he is nevertheless God's Messiah by virtue of his resurrection and he bestows righteousness by faith. The listeners should take care not to deny God.

34. THE ISSUE OF THE MISSIONARY WORK IN
PISIDIAN ANTIOCH
(xiii 42–52)

XIII 42 When Paul and Barnabas were about to leave, the people earnestly asked that they might be told of this matter on the following sabbath. 43 When the synagogue congregation had been sent away, many Jews and god-fearing proselytes followed Paul and Barnabas, who spoke to them and tried to persuade them to hold fast to God's grace. 44 On the next sabbath almost the whole city had gathered to hear the word of God. 45 But when the Jews saw the crowds, they were filled with jealousy, and they blasphemously contradicted what was said by Paul. 46 Paul and Barnabas spoke boldly and said: "It was necessary that the word of God should be spoken to you first. Since you reject it and do not consider yourselves worthy of eternal life, listen then: we shall turn to the Gentiles. 47 For the Lord has commanded us thus:

'I have set you as a light for the Gentiles,
  that you may be a means of salvation to the ends of the
    earth.'"

48 When the Gentiles heard this they rejoiced and glorified the word of the Lord; and as many as were destined for eternal life believed. 49 The word of the Lord spread throughout the whole region. 50 However, the Jews stirred up the god-fearing women of high rank and the men of standing in the city, and they began a persecution of Paul and Barnabas, and drove them away from their territory. 51 But they shook the dust from their feet against them and went to Iconium; 52 and the disciples were full of joy and of the Holy Spirit.

NOTES

xiii 42–43. The juxtaposition of *proselytes* and *god-fearing* is surprising. "Proselytes" signify Gentiles who had undertaken to keep the law of Moses and had been admitted to Judaism by circumcision and proselyte baptism; "god-fearing" is used about Gentiles who had been attracted by the Jewish religion and who were allowed to participate in the service at the synagogue. It is, however, disputable whether "god-fearing" is actually a technical term for a strictly limited group of Gentiles in connection with Judaism.

44–45. The next sabbath not only the members of the synagogue but the whole city had assembled to hear the word of God. This did not suit the Jews. They accepted proselytes and admitted a few god-fearing Gentiles, but did not engage in missionary work (see p. LXII) and certainly did not want Gentiles to receive that which was promised to Israel alone. Therefore they responded with feelings of jealousy. This reaction —an important factor in closing Jewish hearts to the Gospel and in changing their early interest in Christianity into burning hate and sanguinary persecution—Paul regarded not only as something negative but also as something positive. As he explains in Rom ix–xi, the Jews' rejection of the Gospel is God's decision which would remain in force for some time, and jealousy is the means whereby God converts Israel's unbelief to faith. Were these ideas completely unknown to Luke? The Jews' jealousy manifested itself directly in their contradiction of what Paul preached and their blaspheming of the Christ about whom he spoke.

46. This speech by Paul and Barnabas showed the procedure used both by the Jewish Christian primitive church and by Paul and other missionaries to the Gentiles.

47. This quotation reveals a single aspect of the OT basis of Paul's thoughts about his call. He is set "as a light for the Gentiles . . . to be a means of salvation to the ends of the earth" (Isa xlix 6). As an apostle to the Gentiles, he is destined to prepare the Gentile world for the conversion to Christ.

48–49. For the addition *as many as were destined for eternal life*, compare ii 39.

50–52. The large number of unbelieving and hostile Jews use their connections in high circles to stir up hostility, which drove the two apostles away from their domain. The apostles responded with the action known from the speeches in the gospels: they left the city and shook off the dust from their feet and thus their listeners both in the town and in the country were held to their reactions to the sermon on God's king-

dom (Matt x 14 par.; Luke x 11). Thus they will stand before the judge
with the same attitude that they have adopted toward the Gospel, and
Sodom and Gomorrah will face a more tolerable fate on that day (of
judgment) than these cities (Matt x 15 par., xi 20–24 par.).

COMMENT

The congregation asked Paul to speak to them on the following
sabbath day, but when all the inhabitants of the town with its
large number of Gentiles assembled to listen, the Jews began to
protest against the apostles preaching the Gospel. The latter maintained that they had, as was their duty, first addressed themselves
to the Jews but since the Jews refused to receive their words, they
would now turn to the Gentiles. This pleased the Gentiles, but the
Jews started a persecution which drove the apostles from Pisidian
Antioch and took them to Iconium.

35. PAUL AND BARNABAS IN ICONIUM
(xiv 1–7)

XIV 1 In Iconium also it happened that they went into the synagogue of the Jews, and spoke in such a way that a great number, both Jews and Greeks, believed. 2 But those Jews who had not received the gospel began to stir up the Gentiles and arouse bad feeling against the brethren. 3 They remained there some time preaching boldly, since the Lord confirmed the preaching of his grace by allowing signs and wonders to be done by their hands. 4 But the people of the city were divided, so that some supported the Jews, and others the apostles. 5 When an agitation began on the part of the Gentiles and the Jews and their leaders to maltreat and stone them, 6 they fled, when they heard this, down to the cities of Lycaonia—Lystra and Derbe—and the surrounding country, 7 and there they preached the gospel.

NOTES

xiv Iconium, in contrast to Lystra and Derbe, is still a town, the present-day Konia, in Turkey. Here the reponse was greater than in the previous towns: a large number, both Jews and Greeks, believed. However, as vss. 2 and 4–5 show, the unbelieving Jews still held the upper hand and carried the crowd in the city along with them. Nevertheless the apostles spent a long time in Iconium and their preaching was accompanied by signs and wonders. With regard to vs. 6: *they fled . . . down to the cities of Lycaonia—Lystra and Derbe* etc., William Ramsay (*The Bearing of Recent Discovery on the Trustworthiness of the New Testament,* 2d ed. [London, 1915], Ch. 3, pp. 39 f. and Ch. 4) has pointed out that Iconium was here regarded not as a city situated in Lycaonia, to which Lystra and Derbe belonged, but as a city belonging to Phrygia, and ancient testimonies prove Luke to be right in this geographic division (see p. LVI).

The Western text (p. LXXXVI) has attempted to explain the strange pause in the persecution of the apostles between vss. 2 and 5 by the addition of "but the Lord quickly gave peace" at the end of vs. 2 and of "for the second time" in vs. 5.

COMMENT

It is difficult to give an accurate description of Paul's procedure as a pioneer missionary. In chapters xiii–xiv and xvi–xvii he is seen several times starting work in a city, which he is not allowed to finish. Not until he reaches Corinth (ch. xviii) and Ephesus (ch. xix) is he able to stay for a longer time in one city and its surrounding area. Before Corinth his work in a single place followed the same pattern. He would start in the synagogue with the Jews. There a division of the Jews and the god-fearing Gentiles would occur and sooner or later he would be persecuted. This persecution would even be carried from one city to the next; Paul's journeys to new cities did not pass unnoticed by his enemies; they would follow him and destroy any new possibilities for missionary work in the same way as they had persecuted him in their native towns. Dogged by such persecution his missionary work in any one locality was too short-lived, one might think, to put down roots and endure. But we have letters from Paul to the Thessalonians and the Philippians showing that these two congregations, both cases in point, survived in spite of the unfavorable circumstances at the time of their foundation, and indeed, in the case of the latter, flourished for many years.

Thus the dramatic pace does not seem to have been due to the apostle, although his restless energy appeared capable of coping with the difficult circumstances. He had time, although he had "all the world for his parish," and he was not rushed despite the fact that the mission to the Gentiles had as its future goal Israel's conversion and the second coming of Christ.

36. PAUL AND BARNABAS IN LYSTRA
(xiv 8–20)

XIV   8 In Lystra there sat a man whose feet were paralyzed; a cripple from his mother's womb, he had never been able to walk. 9 He listened while Paul was speaking; Paul gazed at him, and when he perceived that the man had faith to be cured, 10 he said in a loud voice: "Stand upright on your feet!" And he leaped up and walked about. 11 When the crowds saw what Paul had done, they raised their voices and said in Lycaonian: "The gods have taken human form and come down to us"; 12 so they called Barnabas Zeus, and Paul Hermes, because he was the spokesman. 13 The priest of the temple of Zeus outside the city brought bulls and garlands to the gates, and wanted to join with the crowds in offering sacrifice. 14 But when the apostles Barnabas and Paul realized this, they tore their clothes and rushed into the crowd shouting: 15 "Men, why are you doing this? We also are human beings, with the same nature as you, and we preach to you that you should turn away from these vanities to the living God, who made heaven, earth, the sea, and all that is in them. 16 In past ages he allowed all nations to walk in their own ways. 17 Yet he did not remain without witness to himself, but did good by giving you rain from heaven and fruitful seasons, filling your hearts with joy at the harvest." 18 Even with these words they hardly restrained the crowds from sacrificing to them. 19 But Jews came from Antioch and Iconium who won the crowds over, and they stoned Paul and dragged him out of the city, believing him to be dead. 20 As the disciples stood round him, he got up and went into the city. The next day he left, together with Barnabas, and went to Derbe.

NOTES

xiv 8–10. Similarities between this healing of a cripple and Peter's healing of the lame beggar at the temple in Jerusalem (iii 1 ff.) have been
pointed out and attempts have been made to demonstrate the author's
deliberate tendency to let Peter and Paul appear in parallel situations (cf.
v 17–42, pp. 46–47). In both accounts the lame man has been a cripple
from birth; the healer gazes at the cripple and the cripple jumps up in
living proof of the miracle. It is hard to see how such a healing could
have been reported in two different ways, if both cases presented the
same kind of disablement. An account of a miraculous healing is rather
stereotyped wherever found, because the miraculous cannot be described in any way other than by stressing the seriousness and long duration of the ailment, the meeting between the healer and the sufferer
together with the healer's words and actions, and finally the healing,
always revealing an element of surprise and excitement, which is proved
by the former invalid's sudden ability to do all that he had never been
able to do before. Thus there is no reason to believe that the author had
wanted to relate a healing performed by Paul as a parallel to a previously
reported healing performed by Peter. The two accounts do differ in that
Paul perceived that the cripple had gained faith, so he could be healed.
This often-repeated theme was not missing in ch. iii, but it was found in
Peter's speech only in vs. 16 and not in the account of the healing where
it might have been expected in vss. 6–8. On the other hand, here in
Lystra, no mention is made of the theme that the healed man praised God.

11–14. In Lystra Paul was confronted with a bilingual population
(see p. XXVII). They were able to hear and understand the Gospel
preached in Greek, but when they were under the influence of the divine,
they would speak in their native tongue. Some scholars have attempted to
find a reference to this episode in Paul's words in Gal iv 14, that the first
time he came to the Galatians, they received him as an angel of God.
This juxtaposition must, however, be rejected as improbable. A parallel
case can be seen in the reaction of the Maltese to Paul's ability to stay
alive, although bitten by a serpent: they kept repeating that he was a
god (xxviii 6). In the gospels, Jesus' miraculous healing or other powerful
deeds made the individual or the crowd give expression to the unique
quality present in the healer in a Jewish manner: in Luke v 8, Peter
said to Jesus: "Leave me, Master, for I am a sinful man"; Luke vii 16:
"A great prophet has appeared among us!" and "God has visited his
people"; cf. Matt xiv 33 (after the walking on the sea): "and . . . they
fell down before him and said, 'You are certainly God's son.'" In this
bilingual situation, the gods about whom they had spoken in Lycaonian
might well have been rendered in Greek by Zeus and Hermes, but they

probably had Lycaonian names and were not thought of in quite the same way as the two Greek gods. As we have no knowledge of these local deities, we are not even allowed to imagine Barnabas as a mature man with a fine head of hair and a big beard, and Paul as a younger, agile figure. (Zeus who was worshiped in the temple outside the city was likewise a Lycaonian god, who was identified with the Zeus of the Greeks.) In the past, it was a common practice to identify local deities with the Greek and Roman gods who had already been mutually identified. In this way it was possible to reduce the confusing multiplicity of polytheism. That such identifications might also have political importance is for instance seen in Baalbek (in Lebanon), where from the second to the third century A.D., Roman emperors, with great enthusiasm and generous grants of money, had raised temples to three Syrian deities who were worshiped here under the Roman names of Jupiter, Venus, and Mercury. In this Lycaonian confusion, the apostles were for a long time unable to get any explanation and it was not until they saw the consequences of the misunderstanding, that they could attempt to prevent the sacrifices to them.

The sacrificial animals were usually decorated with garlands.

The gates might be the gates of the city, where a cripple, like his counterpart at the temple in Jerusalem, would be allowed to sit and beg, but this is by no means certain.

The apostles tore their clothes as a sign of their horror and attempted to make themselves comprehensible to the enthusiastic Lycaonians by addressing them in Greek.

15–18. In contrast to all earlier speeches in Acts which had Jewish audiences, they were here addressing Gentiles. Christian missionaries speaking to Jews can reckon with certain important ideas about God being held in common (although on some points they do deviate); but here the apostles must attempt to make their listeners relinquish their idols and worship God, the creator of the world (described with the use of Exod xx 11) and its sustainer. The same topic is likewise treated in the Areopagus speech in ch. xvii, and in both speeches it is pointed out that God had certainly allowed the Gentiles to follow their own ways (cf. xvii 30) but had not left them without testimony of himself. While the speech here has parallels to the first part of the Areopagus speech (xvii 23–29), nothing corresponds to xvii 30–31. According to that passage, the earlier period is over and it is now imperative to repent before the judgment of the world. This sermon excluded all possibility of the apostles being gods; they were just messengers of the living God whom the audience ought to worship.

19–20. The healing of the cripple may very well have happened at the beginning of their missionary activity in Lystra. At any rate no attempt has been made to date the subsequent end of their stay in the city.

When the disciples found Paul and surrounded him, he miraculously got up and was able to walk back to the city.

The central part of present-day Turkey, the setting of the first missionary journey, consists of the plateau by Iconium and the mountains around Pisidian Antioch. At that time it must have been much more heavily populated than it is now; its many cities were probably close to one another and the well-developed network of roads that served commerce and industry was now to hasten the spreading of the Gospel.

COMMENT

In Lystra, the healing of a cripple made the inhabitants think that Barnabas and Paul were the gods Zeus and Hermes, who had descended to them. The apostles had great difficulty in preventing them from sacrificing to them. Paul was the one who addressed the crowd, and in a speech which had points in common with his Areopagus address in chapter xvii he urged the listeners to desert their idols and referred to God's testimony of his goodness to the Gentiles, manifested in his creation and sustenance of them. This testimony on the part of God was given earlier when God had allowed all Gentiles to follow their own ways.

Here in Lystra where the Gentiles had received the apostles, Jews from Pisidian Antioch and Iconium followed them and stirred up the always fickle mob to stone Paul. Although he survived, this event put an end to his stay in Lystra.

37. THE END OF PAUL'S FIRST MISSIONARY JOURNEY
(xiv 21–28)

XIV 21 They preached the gospel in that city, and when they had persuaded many to become disciples they returned to Lystra, to Iconium, and to Antioch. 22 They strengthened the hearts of the disciples, exhorting them to remain firm in the faith, saying, "It is only through many trials that we may enter into the kingdom of God." 23 Then they appointed elders for them in each church, and after prayer and fasting, they commended them to the Lord in whom they had come to believe.

24 They traveled through Pisidia and came to Pamphylia. 25 When they had preached the word in Perga, they came down to Attalia, 26 and from there set sail for Antioch, where they had been commended to the grace of God for the work they had now completed. 27 When they had arrived and had gathered the congregation, they told of all that God had done through them, and how he had opened a door to faith for the Gentiles. 28 They then remained for some time with the disciples.

NOTES

xiv 21–23. The account of the missionary activity of Paul and Barnabas in Derbe is very brief, stating only that the apostles converted many to the faith. It should be noticed that they were not persecuted and that there is no mention of Jews in Derbe. In the other cities also persecution appeared to have spent its force, so that they were able to return to Lystra, Iconium, and Pisidian Antioch.

An implied "and said" introduces a direct address in which it is stated that they must suffer those hardships and persecutions which had already been predicted by Jesus, before they would be able to enter the kingdom of God (cf. I Thess iii 3). The title, *elders*, is found for the first time in the Pastoral Epistles (1 Tim v 17, 19; Tit i 5). It is difficult to see why this circumstance must make us doubt Luke's account of "elders" in Jerusalem (xi 30) and in Asia Minor. The service held before their departure is similar to the one held in Antioch before Paul and Barnabas were sent out on their mission (xiii 3); they pray and fast and commit them to the Lord.

24–26. Their return through Asia Minor continued in reverse order. From Pisidian Antioch they journeyed through Pamphylia to Perga, where the apostles preached, which they were not mentioned as having done on their way up (in xiii 13–14). From there they traveled to Attalia, and took ship from there to Antioch.

27–28. On their return to Antioch, the two apostles gave an account of the acts God had performed through them. This feature, repeated in xv 12 and xxi 19, shows how the material contained in Acts, often dealing with events that occurred in remote places to which only the apostles could testify, became the common property of the churches in Antioch and Jerusalem.

COMMENT

After ending their first missionary journey in Derbe, the two apostles returned to the cities they had visited earlier. Here they tried to strengthen the congregations and to prepare them for what they had already experienced, namely, that the road to the kingdom of God led through persecutions and tribulations. These Gentile Christians would come to suffer as many hardships as the Jewish Christians had before them. To head the churches, "elders" were installed, chosen by the apostles from the disciples. The account of this mission on their return to Antioch was likewise brought to an end with a strong formula: "God has opened a door to faith for the Gentiles" (cf. viii 14; xi 1, 18).

38. PRELIMINARIES TO THE APOSTOLIC COUNCIL
(xv 1–5)

XV 1 Some men came down from Judea and told the brethren: "If you do not have yourselves circumcised according to Mosaic law, you cannot be saved." 2 After not a little dissension and controversy had arisen between Paul and Barnabas and these men, it was decided that Paul and Barnabas and some of the brethren should go up to see the apostles and the elders in Jerusalem about this dispute. 3 When they had been sent on their way by the church, they traveled through Phoenicia and Samaria and told of the conversion of the Gentiles, and they caused great joy among all the brethren. 4 When they came to Jerusalem, they were received by the church, the apostles, and the elders, and then they told all that God had done through them. 5 But some of those of the Pharisee party who had become believers came forward and said: "The Gentiles must be circumcised and exhorted to keep the Mosaic law."

NOTES

xv 1–2. *it was decided* (i.e. they decided) is ambiguous. The Western text has understood this to mean that the brethren from Judea decided that the leaders from Antioch should go up to Jerusalem and there be held responsible for their mission (cf. p. LXXXVI). It seems better with the Neutral text to take the verse as meaning that it was the congregation in Antioch that made the decision. Among *some of the brethren*, they may of course have thought of Titus (Gal ii 1, 3). James the Lord's brother was not an apostle (also not an apostle according to Gal i 19), but belonged to the elders.

3–5. This is the first time we hear of Christian congregations in Phoenicia (see, however, xi 19). In vs. 5, *the Gentiles* has been substituted for "they," which was introduced with a surprising abruptness, and

must be understood to refer to the Gentile Christians in general. It is
unlikely that it should refer to the other emissaries from Antioch and
that Titus (Gal ii 1, 3) should be among them so there should here be an
attempt at harmonizing the texts of Acts and Galatians.

COMMENT

As related in xi 1–18, after Peter's account of his baptism
of Cornelius and some other Gentiles in Caesarea, there was satis-
faction in Jerusalem over this as well as gratitude that God had
also given conversion to life to the Gentiles. This description of
a positive attitude to missions to the Gentiles was now interrupted
by an account of a visit by Jewish Christians from Judea to the
Gentile Christians in Antioch. During their stay in Antioch these
Jewish Christians taught the Gentile Christians that they could not
be saved unless they were circumcised according to the Mosaic
law. The unexpected demand was the cause of a serious controversy between Paul and Barnabas and these disciples from Judea.
It has never been explained why both parties did not join in
traveling to Jerusalem to have their controversy adjudicated there.
At this point the brethren from Judea vanish from the picture.
There is every indication that it was the Christians of Antioch
who managed to make Jerusalem adopt their cause and denounce
the Judean brethren, as will be shown in the following pages.

One special point is worthy of notice, namely the conviction
in the church of Antioch that it was only necessary to make the
journey to Jerusalem in order to find the apostles at home and to
put any matter whatsoever before them and the elders. There is
certainly a wide gap between this view and the Pauline conception
of an apostle (see p. LXII f.). The apostles are here conceived as an
authority always residing and available in Jerusalem.

The emissaries from Antioch traveled through Phoenicia and
Samaria and gratified the disciples there with their account of the
conversion of the Gentiles, and the same happened in Jerusalem
where they were received by the church, the apostles, and the elders.
The brethren from Judea visiting Antioch were not the only ones
to make demands of the Gentile Christians. Some former Pharisees
in the church in Jerusalem made the same demands with regard
to circumcision of the Gentiles and their obedience to the law of
Moses at their admission to the Christian church.

39. THE NEGOTIATIONS AT THE APOSTOLIC
COUNCIL
(xv 6–21)

XV   6 The apostles and the elders met to consider this matter.
7 After much debate, Peter stood up and said to them:
"Brothers, you know that from the first days God made the
decision among you, that from my lips the Gentiles should
hear the preaching of the gospel and so believe. 8 God, who
knows the heart, confirmed this by giving them the Holy Spirit,
as he did to us also. 9 He has made no difference in any
respect between us and them and has purified their hearts by
faith. 10 Why then do you try God by laying upon the shoulders
of the disciples a yoke which neither our fathers nor we have
had the strength to bear? 11 We believe, however, that we shall
be saved by the grace of the Lord Jesus, just as they will."

12 Then the gathering fell silent and listened to Barnabas
and Paul, who told of all the signs and wonders God had
worked through them among the Gentiles. 13 After they had
become silent, James spoke: "Brothers, listen to me! 14 Simeon
has told how God first provided for the Gentiles, to take out
of them a people for his name. 15 And with this the words in
the Book of the Prophets agree, as it is written:
16 'After this I will return,
       and I will rebuild the fallen tabernacle of David,
       and I will rebuild its ruins,
       and I will raise it again,
17   so that the people who are left may seek the Lord,
       and all the Gentiles over whom my name has been called,
       says the Lord, who does this, 18 known from of old.'
19 Therefore I hold that we should not make difficulties for those
of the Gentiles who turn to God, 20 but should write to them
that they are to abstain from idol worship, from sexual im-

purity, from what has been strangled, and from blood. 21 For from the earliest times Moses has had in every city those who preach him, for his law is read aloud in the synagogues every sabbath."

NOTES

xv 6. Attempts to harmonizing the descriptions in Acts xv and Gal ii 1 ff. (see p. LXVIII) show how difficult it is to understand the text of Acts. Thus it has been supposed that the meeting here in vss. 6 ff. was the meeting that Paul had privately with the leaders (Gal ii 2). If so *the gathering* in vs. 12 would only consist of the apostles and the elders, but the mention of the whole church in vss. 22 and 23 (cf. vs. 4) would seem to indicate that obviously members of the congregation were present at the above-mentioned meeting and had taken part in the discussion (cf. vs. 7). There does not seem to be more than one meeting in Acts xv.

7–11. Peter's speech together with James' in vs. 13 ff. were the decisive contributions to the meeting.

in the early days sounds surprising, as if it were a very long time ago. The faith of Gentiles is stressed several times in the gospels, for instance, that of the centurion in Capernaum (Matt viii 10 par.; cf. John iv 50, 53) and of the Canaanite woman (Matt xv 28). Similarities in wording between the present speech and the Cornelius narrative in chs. x–xi, include "purify" (x 15, xi 9, xv 9), "make no difference" (xi 12, xv 9), and "as he did to us also" (x 47, xv 8, 9, 11). Taking everything into consideration, it would, according to Peter's opinion at that time, only try God if one were to disregard his clearly stated will and demand the circumcision of the Gentile Christians. To the Jews, the Law was not a heavy burden; it had been given by God to his chosen people so that they might follow it and acquire merit. Peter here thus gave expression to a Jewish Christian view of the Law, following Jesus' own interpretation of it (see p. LXIV). Many scholars have unhesitatingly denied that Peter could have said what Luke reported. They maintain that Luke presented his own view using Peter as his mouthpiece. One should think twice before making such an assumption. Peter's argument is repeated in Gal ii 14 ff. (see p. LXVIII), where Paul presented the views of Peter and of Jewish Christianity—views which were at variance with the conduct of Peter and the other Jewish Christians in the church of Antioch (Gal ii 11–13). To be sure Paul spoke in the first person plural, but as we know that he was speaking on behalf of the Jewish Christians, and that he himself had not had the experiences which he here attributes to the Jewish Christians, his words could only express the conviction of Peter and the Jewish Christians from Jerusalem. We know this from Philip iii 4 ff., where Paul explains that his meeting with Christ was decisive for his understanding the Law. It is the other way round with Peter and Jewish Christianity, according to the words of the apostle in Gal ii 15–16: "We ourselves are Jews by birth, not sinners of Gentile origin; but we know that a man is not justified by the works of the Law but only by faith in Christ Jesus—so we believed in Christ Jesus, in order to be justified by this faith and not by the works of the Law—for by doing the works of the Law, no one can be justified." On this point, Peter's speech in Acts xv agrees with Peter's and the Jewish Christians' statements in Paul's rendering (Gal ii 14 ff.). It is the grace of Jesus and not the Law that brings salvation.

12. The silence that followed might indicate the impression made by Peter's speech, but it more likely indicated that it was now possible (cf. vs. 13) for the missionaries to the Gentiles to tell about God's action, which like his bestowing of the Holy Spirit (vs. 8), demonstrated that, according to God's will, the Gentiles should receive the Gospel as Gentiles. There is no need to supply the details of this narrative for they have already been given in the preceding chs. of Acts.

13–21. The speech of James led directly to the settlement of the matter. James used the form *Symeon* (also found in II Pet i 1) instead of the usual Simon. It may seem strange that James should quote Amos ix 11–12 from the LXX and that his interpretation should depend on the peculiarities of the Greek text. This indicates that the words of James have been thoroughly reworked. According to the speech, Amos predicted that God would rebuild the ruined dwelling of David. God first took pity on the Jewish people, and once he had won them over, to reach out to the Gentiles and convert them. This attitude toward missions also explains vs. 21 which has seemed incomprehensible to most people. Since the road to the conversion of the Gentiles was by way of the Jews and their synagogues in the various cities, it was both reasonable and right to show consideration for the Jews by keeping the rules mentioned in vss. 19–20—thus making co-existence possible. It was not by chance that two of the rules in the so-called Apostolic Decree were concerned with food for, as mentioned earlier (see p. LXVI), the common meals were very important to primitive Christianity. Precisely because the Law could not and was not to be kept, the one essential was to make it possible for Jews and Gentiles (that is, for Jewish Christians and Gentile Christians) to meet at the common table (Gal ii 11 ff.; Acts xi 3 ff.). The decree was aimed precisely at this; it did not offer any solution to the question of the Gentile Christians' obedience to the law of Moses. Four things were forbidden, of which two were directly related to eating: (*a*) first, idol worship; (*b*) secondly, sexual impurity; (*c*) thirdly, strangulation as concerned with food. The animal must have been butchered in such a way that all the blood had been drained from it; (d) the fourth rule reiterated the Jewish prohibition against eating meat from which the blood had not been drained.

At a later time, the provisions of the Apostolic Decree were modified so as to conform with later demands of the church: thus, according to the Western text, James suggests that Gentile Christians "abstain from idolatry, from fornication, and from bloodshed and from doing to others what they would not like done to themselves."

COMMENT

After the introduction to the Apostolic Council, we hear Peter and James. After Peter's speech and before James', we hear that Barnabas and Paul told of what God had done through them on their mission. Yet Luke's simple account does show that everything must have been very complicated. Not only does what follows show that the negotiations started with the apostles and the elders assembling to consider this matter, but also that the whole congregation, the apostles, and the elders, all had a part in the decision arrived at in the council meeting (vs. 22 f.). After Peter's speech the crowd was silent—its attitude must be supposed to have been voiced earlier. The content of the two speeches is, however, more convincing than these very fragmentary references to the external course of the meeting.

Peter's speech pointed back to his mission to Cornelius and to the fact that God had made no distinction between Gentiles and Jews. Neither earlier generations of Jews nor Peter's own generation had been able to fulfill the Law. Why then should this yoke be laid upon the necks of the converted Gentiles? The Law cannot save Jews or Gentiles, but the grace of the Lord Jesus can save both.

In his speech James also referred to Peter's mission to Cornelius. Quoting a text from Scripture, he referred to the mission to the Gentiles as a consequence of the mission to the Jews (see p. LXIX). It was of course not necessary to demand that Gentile Christians obey the law of Moses. However, since the Gospel was first preached to the Jews, their synagogues, in every city, served as meeting places for the church. The Gentile Christians, who had to live alongside these Jewish Christians must accept a few rules, and these were to be written down and sent to them.

40. THE END OF THE APOSTOLIC COUNCIL
AND ITS EFFECT
(xv 22–33)

XV 22 Then the apostles, the elders, and the whole church decided to choose representatives and send them to Antioch together with Paul and Barnabas, namely Judas surnamed Barsabbas, and Silas, men who occupied leading positions among the brethren. 23 They wrote in their own hand: "The apostles and the elders, (your) brothers, send greetings to the brethren in Antioch, Syria, and Cilicia who were Gentiles. 24 Since we have heard that some of us have troubled you and brought confusion to your minds through statements which are not authorized by us, 25 we have agreed to choose men and send them to you with Barnabas and Paul, who are dear to our hearts, 26 and who have risked their lives for the sake of our Lord Jesus Christ's name. 27 We have therefore sent Judas and Silas, who will tell you the same thing by word of mouth. 28 For the Holy Spirit and we have decided not to lay upon you any burden other than the following, which is necessary: 29 to abstain from meat that has been offered to idols, from blood, from what has been strangled, and from sexual impurity. If you abstain from these you will be doing right. Farewell!"

30 After they had taken their leave, they went down to Antioch, gathered the congregation, and delivered the letter. 31 They read it and were happy at the comfort (it contained). 32 Both Judas and Silas, who were also prophets, in the same way gave support and strength to the brethren by their preaching. 33 After spending some time there they parted from the brethren on the best of terms and returned to those who had sent them.

Notes

xv 22–29. The chosen men were Judas Barsabbas, probably a relative of Joseph Barsabbas (see Note on i 23), and Silas, who Paul chooses as his companion on his second missionary journey (xv 40 ff.). In the Pauline letters, Silas was called Silvanus (II Cor i 19; I Thess i 1; II Thess i 1; also mentioned in I Pet v 12).

they wrote in their own hand does not mean that the people in question had penned the letter, but that they were messengers who carried the letter to the recipients. The letter confirmed that the brethren from Judea, who had caused the whole controversy, had held no mandate from Jerusalem. Such was not the case with the two disciples, Judas and Silas, who were sent out to confirm the content of the letter; the letter writers emphasized that Barnabas and Paul were men loved and highly respected by the Jerusalem church. The letter ended with the rules of the Apostolic Decree and heavily stressed their being decreed by the Holy Spirit and the Jerusalem church.

30–33. The question as to whether Gentile Christians should be circumcised had been answered with a clear no. The letter delighted the Antioch church and the two Jerusalem emissaries understood quite well, being prophets, how to comfort (cf. I Cor xiv 3) and strengthen its members.

vs. 34 is missing in the Neutral text. It reports Silas' determination to stay on in Antioch and Judas' departure by himself for Jerusalem. The Western text addition is an attempt to explain vs. 40 where Paul takes Silas as a traveling companion, when according to vs. 33 he had gone back to Jerusalem with Judas. Unless one insists on the events occurring immediately one after the other, there is always a possibility that some time had elapsed between the selection of Silas and the beginning of Paul's second journey.

Comment

The proposal made by James was adopted and the Apostolic Decree was now, through Paul and Barnabas and two representatives of the Jerusalem church, Judas and Silas, transmitted to the Gentile Christians in Antioch, Syria, and Cilicia by word of mouth and by letter. The decision delighted the church in Antioch and the Jerusalem emissaries were of great help to it.

PART IV

41. THE BEGINNING OF PAUL'S SECOND MISSIONARY JOURNEY
(xv 35–41)

XV 35 But Paul and Barnabas stayed in Antioch, and with many others taught and preached the word of the Lord. 36 After some time Paul said to Barnabas: "Let us return and see how the brethren are getting along in all those cities where we preached the word of the Lord." 37 Barnabas wished to take John (named Mark) with them also; 38 but Paul held that they should not take with them the one who had left them in Pamphylia and had not gone with them to the ministry. 39 Bitterness arose, so they separated, and Barnabas took Mark with him and set sail for Cyprus. 40 But Paul chose Silas and set off, after he had been committed by the brethren to the grace of God, 41 traveled through Syria and Cilicia, and strengthened the churches.

NOTES

xv 35–38. According to Col iv 10, Mark was Barnabas' cousin. The disagreement over him has been associated with the controversy provoked by Peter in Antioch (Gal ii 11 ff.), where to the great annoyance of Paul, Barnabas followed Peter and withdrew from the fellowship, together with other Jewish Christians. This tendency to look for and to discover everywhere a theological difference, where there is in fact every indication that it is a matter of ordinary human attitudes and thoughts, is to be rejected. We have preferred to regard the difficulty in ch. vi 1–6 as a matter of food and to view the problem here as a matter of morale in the work and of the duty to do what one has promised.

39–41. It has been noted that the Antioch church considered Paul's missionary journey as the essential one, whereas Barnabas' journey is not celebrated in the same way by a solemn leave-taking (cf. xiii 3, xiv 26).

COMMENT

Paul and Barnabas were in Antioch once more and for the last
time. Paul made plans for a journey which was to take them to
the churches founded on their first journey. Barnabas wanted to
take John surnamed Mark with them, but Paul was definitely
against this because Mark had failed to go with them to the mission
field. This dispute led to a separation; Barnabas went to Cyprus
with Mark; Paul went to the churches in Asia Minor with Silas.

A COMPARISON OF GAL ii 1–10 AND ACTS xv

The two accounts of a meeting in Jerusalem between the leaders
of the Jerusalem church and the two representatives of the mission
to the Gentiles, Paul and Barnabas, differ with regard both to form
and content.

As to form, the description in Acts is a piece of historical writing
which may or may not have covered the actual events. Its close
connection with the Cornelius narrative in x–xi and the careful treatment and central position accorded to both this and the Cornelius
account in Acts would indicate that they were of special importance
to Luke. Here, in the description of Peter's visit to Cornelius in Caesarea and in the account of the final authorization of similar missions
to the Gentiles, thus effectively ending all opposition, one sees the earliest stages of the transition to the Gentile mission.

Paul's description in Galatians of a meeting in Jerusalem is part
of his polemic against the Judaizers' opinions and arguments which
he wanted to refute in order to bring the Galatians back to their
original relation to him and to the Christian message. That it was
controversial was demonstrated in ii 1 ff. as well as in chapter i by
the fact that in general the apostle was repudiating false views.
The most frequently used word is "not." Positive sentences emphasizing the important agreement confirmed between the church
of Jerusalem and the Gentile mission do not occur until ii 7.

As to contents, Paul and Acts are surprisingly at one in their
view of the close agreement between Jewish and Gentile Christianity; but apart from this important point, there are many discrepancies between the two accounts. Their existence prompts us to

ask whether Luke was describing the same meeting as Paul or whether, on the basis of only partly reliable sources, he had reconstructed a meeting which should have been identical with that described by Paul but was not, because he combined details incompatible with Paul's description together with more reliable characteristics.

In a consideration of the value of the two descriptions it must be immediately noted that Paul described a meeting at which he himself was present, whereas Luke has built up his account on the basis of oral and written sources.

According to Paul, a revelation caused the meeting (Gal ii 1–2). It was God who had commanded Paul to go to Jerusalem. In Acts, it was caused by the arrival in Antioch of brethren from Judea who claimed that Gentile Christians should be circumcised or they would not be saved. When Paul and Barnabas challenged the visitors' opinion on this point and a serious controversy arose, the Antioch church decided that the two missionaries, accompanied by some of their number, should take up the matter with the apostles and the elders in Jerusalem.

According to Gal ii 1, 3, Titus was present at the meeting along with Paul and Barnabas. Paul submitted for approval "to them," but especially to "those of repute," the Gospel that he had preached to the Gentiles in order that he might not have traveled or be traveling in vain (Gal ii 2). On the basis of Acts xv 2, this statement has often been explained in such a way as to cover the mission to the Gentiles and to show that Paul admitted his dependency on Jerusalem, a dependency he denied in Galatians. This is an unlikely interpretation and in a controversial context the words must have another meaning. If one considers the expression "traveled in vain," one notices that in most cases in Paul (I Cor ix 15, xv 10, 14; II Cor vi 1; Philip ii 16; I Thess ii 1, iii 5), the words "in vain" are used about his apostolate. In Philip ii 16, the full expression "traveled in vain" occurs and is used in an eschatological context in which the Philippians were urged to cling to the word of life, so that in the day of Christ the apostle may be proud that he had not 'neither have traveled in vain nor have labored in vain.' Paul was undoubtedly also speaking in Gal ii 2, about his call and God's judgment on his performance of it. In what sense could the apostle, upon a command given by God in a revelation, have been eager to seek out the Jerusalem church and its leaders in order to avoid God's condemnation of his performance of his apostolate? Obviously these words present more possibilities than the theory mentioned before which was based solely on the wish to harmonize Paul's account with that of Acts xv. It is obvious too that in a polemical context, Paul would not have made an admission which could have been interpreted by his opponents as a confirmation of their claim concerning his dependency on the Jerusalem leaders. According to Galatians, the time of the meeting in Jerusalem must have fallen between Barnabas' and Paul's combined activities in Antioch (Acts xi 25 ff.) and their return to this church after their first missionary journey (Acts xiv 28). The natural time would be before the first missionary journey, when Paul had started his preaching to Gentiles (Gal ii 2) but had not yet set out on his journey to his new field of activity. At that time the mission to the Gentiles was still in the making; it had not yet lost its character of being "to the Greeks also" (Acts xi 20). The question now before them was: should the mission advance into those regions of the Roman empire where Jews constituted only scattered colonies in a Gentile world? That this, and *not* the demands in Acts xv concerning circumcision and obedience to the law of Moses, was the matter presented to the meeting is shown by the agreement reached by the two parties, according to Gal ii 7–10. The mission to the Jews and the mission to the Gentiles divided the world between them into two missionary fields, one of the circumcised or the Jews, the other of the Gentiles. As will be seen this religious division was, however, also a geographical one. Besides Palestine, the regions reserved for the Jewish mission were Syria, Mesopotamia, and Egypt, whose missionary history we do not know. The Roman empire from Syria to its Western confines became Paul's mission field. This geographical division was also a religious one. This was obvious in the case of Peter, a Jew who preached only to Jews. In the case of Paul, the religious nature of the division was less obvious. He knew that the conversion of the Jews would not cause the salvation of the Gentiles; on the contrary, the Gentiles' reception of the Gospel might lead to the salvation of all Israel (Rom xi). But because the salvation of the Jews was—to him and to Jewish Christians—the great goal of all missions, he had first preached to the Jews in the Gentile cities he visited. When the Jews in their unbelief turned to persecute him and his newly converted Christians, Paul left the synagogue and preached to the Gentiles, until the Jews' persecution drove him away. This picture of his missionary acitivities found in Acts is confirmed in his letters, where he mentioned both his missionary practice with regard to the Jews (I Cor ix 20), and his persecution at the hands of the Jews (II Cor xi 25). In another text (I Thess ii 16), Paul says of the Jews, "they try to keep us from speaking to the Gentiles that they may be saved," again providing a picture of the persecution by the Jews, which corresponds to that found in Acts and which might well be taken to refer to Paul's later experiences in Thessalonica, Berea, and Corinth (as they are known from Acts xvii 5, 13, xviii 4–6).

The details given in Gal ii 2–7 hark back to Paul's controversial situation. When the apostle says that even in Jerusalem circumcision was not forced on Titus (vs. 3), Paul could here state an historical fact, namely that Titus was indeed circumcised, and at the same time reject the wrong conclusion, that of the Judaizers, that it had happened at the demand of the Jerusalem church. In other words, Titus was circumcised, but voluntarily. Of course, as one reads the whole letter to the Galatians, one cannot conceive of Paul's giving his approval to the circumcision of a Gentile. It is surprising that other scholars, who take the meeting, as related by Paul, to be identical with the Apostolic Council of Acts xv, should claim that Titus was actually circumcised at the very time when Paul opposed the circumcision of Gentiles and when the meeting ended with a general acceptance of Paul's view.

Another explanation for this episode may be found in the Judaizers' demand that during his visit Titus should undergo circumcision and Paul's denying that Titus had been circumcised. A third possibility exists, namely that in this controversial situation Paul drew the logical conclusion from his opponents' point of view: had the Judaizers been right in their conception of the Jerusalem church's attitude toward the circumcision of Gentiles, then Titus should have been compelled to undergo circumcision immediately; nothing of the sort happened because the position of the Jerusalem church and its leaders differed quite considerably from the Judaizers' conception of it.

The same holds for vss. 4–5. The false brethren who had slipped in and who "wanted to bring us into bondage (to the Law)" could only have sneaked into the Gentile Christian churches in Paul's mission field "in order to spy upon the freedom we enjoy." They cannot be the Pharisees of Acts xv 5, but perhaps are the visiting brethren from Judea (xv 1). This account is thus not concerned with Paul's conduct at the Jerusalem meeting but with his total rejection of the Judaizers' demands whenever or wherever he confronted them in the Gentile Christian churches. Possibly Paul was here refuting a charge made by his opponents, who maintained that he had not always refused their demands. Paul, they claimed, while in Jerusalem, and like the leaders there, had both preached the Gospel and demanded circumcision and obedience to the law of Moses. But, they continued, when he was sent out among the Gentiles, he had gone his own way, and had dropped these requirements in order "to please men" (i 10), asking only that they believe the Gospel. Thus, they concluded, the apostle had not consistently followed any fixed line. The Galatian Judaizers believed that firmness would be found only in Jerusalem, where they thought Christianity would be combined with Judaism in the same distorted fashion as in their own Judaizing circles. It is possible, though unlikely, that Paul himself followed up their charges, for he wrote: "I yielded to their demand for the moment" (according to a variant reading of ii 5).

From vs. 6 on Paul returns to the meeting with "the men of repute" and he reflects their positive attitude toward his apostolate and preaching. These men did not require Paul to add anything to his Gospel—as had been the expectation of his opponents. Paul was thus able to say that the men of repute had understood that he had a call and ministry to the Gentiles, just as Peter had to the circumcised. Fully recognizing that the grace of God had been bestowed on Paul, they entered upon a brotherly agreement with him and Barnabas, sending them to do missionary work among the Gentiles, while they themselves remained among the circumcised. This division was not a hard and fast separation, but a distinction based on the different calls of the two apostles, a distinction which was to unite what in practice had been divided. Both parties recognized each other and the validity of the missionary work in both fields and beyond that the only thing to be remembered was that the mission to the Gentiles should care for the poor in Jerusalem.

This last recommendation has been thought to contradict Paul's words that those of repute did not add anything, but if Acts xi 29–30 precedes the meeting, this is no new decree, but the decision that something already in existence should not be discontinued. It is, however, more important to note that the reference to those of repute not adding anything was uttered in a polemical situation, and Paul intended it to refer to nothing else but the specific

Judaistic demands. For the same reason it would be wrong to say that the Apostolic Decree could not have been passed at the meeting because in that case something would have been added. Thus it is possible that many decrees could have been added without contradicting these words of Paul, because these words should be taken in a very particular sense in this context.

In addition, it is correct to doubt—and this for many reasons—that Paul would have given his consent to the Apostolic Decree, which required the Gentiles, after all, to obey the law of Moses, although in a greatly modified version. From I Cor viii–x, we know that Paul did not insist on a strict observance of the Apostolic Decree by the church in Corinth. It seems highly improbable that despite his efforts to take everybody into consideration (I Cor ix 19–23), the apostle should have agreed to such a decree and then not have kept it. The other request, that of not forgetting the poor in Jerusalem, he always kept, and indeed risked his life to bring the gift to Jerusalem despite many warnings of danger (cf. Rom xv 30–31). The local nature of the Apostolic Decree, which can be explained on the basis of those to whom it was addressed (xv 23), would presumably indicate that these rules had been imposed on mixed congregations in predominantly Jewish districts, but it cannot prove that Paul had agreed to a compromise—an unlikely thing in itself, and which, in fact, he did not keep.

It has usually been assumed that Gal ii and Acts xv describe the same meeting and that the two reports can be made to agree. Generally this is done by accepting Luke's account as basically reliable, and interpreting Paul's words in its light, severely criticizing any deviation from it. In this case as well as in others, one must warn against attempts at harmonizing the texts. Agreement with regard to external characteristics should not be stressed when decisive differences can be found, especially on essential points. Of course both accounts testify to the good relationship between Jewish Christianity and the mission to the Gentiles, but whereas Acts xv gives an account of a meeting held to deal with the demand for circumcision, Paul's meeting was primarily concerned with his call and led to the significant mutual recognition of the two missions. In this respect the meeting became the fruitful basis for expansion in the apostolic age.

Therefore Luke and Paul cannot be describing the same meeting. Most likely, Luke gathered material for the speeches, material which in their context sounded convincing, although they contained some surprising details, but so far as information concerning the goal, cause, and results of the meeting goes, we may have to assume that his material must have come from sources that were either unreliable or referred to another meeting. If the Apostolic Decree is considered an historical document, it came into being in order to make the coexistence of Jewish and Gentile Christians possible in mixed congregations. Although Paul went on preaching to the Jews, his congregations were on the whole not mixed congregations, for there were very few Jews among the Gentiles. In other words Acts xv, as well as Acts x, contains good source material which had been used to support the views of Jewish Christianity; however, for this very reason this material cannot be assumed to be an authentic account of a meeting of which Paul gave a true account.

42. PAUL'S VISIT TO THE CHURCHES FROM THE FIRST JOURNEY
(xvi 1–5)

XVI 1 Paul also came to Derbe and to Lystra. There was a disciple there named Timothy, the son of a Jewish woman who had become a Christian, but his father was a Greek. 2 He was well spoken of among the brethren in Lystra and Iconium. 3 Paul wished him to travel with him, and he circumcised him out of consideration for the Jews living in those regions; for they all knew that his father was a Greek. 4 As they now traveled through the cities, they delivered to them the decrees agreed upon by the apostles and the elders in Jerusalem, for their observance. 5 The churches were strengthened more and more in the faith, and they (the disciples) increased in number daily.

NOTES

xvi 1–3. This text may give rise to the belief that Timothy was from either Derbe or Lystra. In xx 4, he is called an inhabitant of Derbe. According to II Tim i 5, his mother was Eunice and his grandmother Lois; both were Christians who had formerly been Jews. As a Jewess, Eunice could not according to the Mosaic law have contracted a legal marriage with a Gentile. Therefore her children must have been considered illegitimate; since such children followed their mother's nationality, they were thus Jews. For this reason Timothy was not a Gentile whom Paul had circumcised but a Jew. It should be noticed that Paul had Timothy circumcised out of consideration for the Jews of the region, because the apostle wanted the young man to accompany him on his journey. Obviously a man who was going to be a missionary to the Jews and was himself a Jew must be particularly careful at that time (see p. XLIII)—and the journey mentioned in vs. 3 had been planned not to go beyond Asia Minor (cf. xv 36) when the event took place. The remark *all knew that his father was a Greek* must thus mean that Timothy was uncircumcised.

4–5. Although according to the letter from Jerusalem (xv 23) the Apostolic Decree had been sent only to the brethren in Antioch, Syria, and Cilicia, it is here stated that Paul and Silas gave it to the Christians in the province of Galatia as well. Luke concludes this section by again stating that the churches were strengthened in the faith and that their number increased day by day (ii 41, 47, iv 4, v 14, vi 7, ix 35, 42). This may well have been due both to the decree of the Apostolic Council and to Paul's return to the churches he had founded earlier.

COMMENT

Paul now returned to the churches that he and Barnabas had founded in the interior of Asia Minor on the first journey. Besides Silas, he was now accompanied by Timothy, whom he had circumcised. On this journey, he delivered the Apostolic Decree to the churches, which were strengthened in the faith and the number of the disciples continued to increase.

43. THE VISION OF THE MACEDONIAN
(xvi 6–10)

XVI   6 They traveled through Phrygia and the Galatian country, having been prevented by the Holy Spirit from speaking the word in the province of Asia. 7 When they were then going toward Mysia, they attempted to travel to Bithynia, and the spirit of Jesus would not permit it; 8 so when they had traveled through Mysia, they came down to Troas. 9 During the night a vision came to Paul: a Macedonian appeared and begged him, "Come over to Macedonia and help us!" 10 When he had seen the vision we hastened to go at once to Macedonia, concluding that God had summoned us to preach the gospel to them.

NOTES

xvi 6–7. Without any clear indication, the subject is changed from the churches to Paul and his companions. They traveled west and northwest of Iconium which itself was situated in Phrygia (cf. NOTE on xiv 6). And through the Galatian country—a vague name for the regions to the north of the Lycaonian cities mentioned in the previous section. Paul did become active there until his third journey (cf. xix 1–20, xx 18–21). On their way north to Mysia, Paul and his companions wanted to travel to the northeast, to Bithynia, but were once more prevented by the Spirit, here called the *spirit of Jesus*. They turned west instead through Mysia and reached the coast of Asia Minor at Troas. According to what has been related, the Spirit's activity at this time is a purely negative one, controlling the disciples attempts to find the road which God wanted them to follow, but not as yet directing them to a specific area. Still, God was the director of the apostle and of his mission. No human beings were—God alone, to whom all must submit, must be praised or blamed for the mission. Even the Roman authorities were expected to submit during Paul's trial.

8–10. In Troas, this depressing situation gave way to a positive command: to sail for Macedonia. It is needless to speculate whether the Macedonian would be identified by his special dress, or whether crossing over from Asia to Europe would be considered an experience of particular interest. In vs. 10 we are confronted for the first time in our text (see NOTE on xi 28) with the word "we," which Luke uses when referring to Paul, Silas, Timothy, and himself.

COMMENT

Paul was often led by visions (xviii 9–10, xxii 17–21, xxiii 11, xxvii 21–26), but at the beginning of his second journey he was in a state of great uncertainty. He had planned to preach the Gospel both in the western and in the northern part of Asia Minor, but he was prevented from doing so by the Holy Spirit, although he was not told what to do. It was not before he had reached Troas on the Aegean that he received positive direction. In a revelation, a Macedonian urged him to cross over to Macedonia and help the people there. Thus Christianity entered Europe.

XVI 11 When we had sailed from Troas, we set our course straight for Samothrace, the day after for Neapolis, 12 and from there for Philippi, which is "first city" of that part of Macedonia, and a colony. We then spent some days in this city. 13 On the sabbath we went outside the city gate and along the river, where we thought people used to pray, and we sat down and talked to the women who had assembled. 14 A woman named Lydia, a seller of purple from the city of Thyatira, a god-fearing woman, listened. The Lord opened her heart to what was said by Paul. 15 When she had been baptized together with her household, she invited us, saying, "Since you have acknowledged me as a believer in the Lord, come to my house and stay there." And she persuaded us to do so.

16 It happened, as we were on our way to the place of prayer, that a servant-girl who was a medium met us. Her divinations were very profitable to her owners. 17 She followed Paul and us, and kept calling out: "These men are the servants of the Most High God, and they preach the way of salvation to you." 18 She did this for many days. Then Paul lost patience, turned round, and said to the spirit: "In the name of Jesus Christ I command you to leave her!" And it left her at once.

19 When her owners discovered that their expectation of profit had left them, they seized Paul and Silas and dragged them to the market place before the authorities. 20 When they brought them before the praetors, they said: "These men, who are Jews, are causing disturbances in our city, 21 and they preach customs which it is not legal for us Romans either to accept or to observe." 22 The crowd also rose against them, the praetors stripped their clothes off them and gave orders that they should be beaten. 23 When they had beaten them many

times they put them in prison, and gave the jailer orders to guard them carefully. 24 Having received such an order, he put them in the closest guard and locked their feet in the stocks.

25 However, at midnight Paul and Silas were praying and singing hymns of praise to God, and the prisoners were listening to them, 26 when suddenly there was such a violent earthquake that the foundations of the prison were shaken, and immediately all the doors were opened and the chains of all the prisoners were loosed. 27 The jailer woke up, and when he saw that the doors of the prison had been opened, he drew his sword, being about to kill himself, believing that the prisoners had escaped. 28 But Paul shouted in a loud voice: "Do yourself no harm, for we are all here." 29 Then he called for light, ran in, and fell trembling at the feet of Paul and Silas. 30 He led them out and said: "Sirs, what shall I do to be saved?" 31 They said: "Believe in the Lord Jesus, and you and your household will be saved." 32 Then they began to speak the word of God to him and to all that were in his house. 33 He took them with him in the middle of the night, bathed their wounds, and he and all his were at once baptized. 34 He took them to his home, and setting a meal before them, he began to rejoice with all his household at having believed in God.

35 When day had come the praetors sent their lictors, with the message: "Release those men!" 36 The jailer reported these words to Paul: "The praetors have sent word that you are to be released. So go out now and leave in peace." 37 But Paul said to them: "They have, without trial, publicly beaten us, who are Roman citizens, and put us in prison. Do they now want to release us secretly? No, on the contrary, they must themselves come and lead us out." 38 So the lictors reported these words to the praetors, who were alarmed when they heard that they were Roman citizens. 39 They came and apologized to them, conducted them out, and asked them to leave the city. 40 When they had come out of the prison they went to (the home of) Lydia, where they saw the brethren, encouraged them, and then departed.

NOTES

xvi 11. We have in this passage—as later in chs. xx–xxi—a first-hand account of the disciples' voyage from Troas to the island of Samothrace and, the next day, Neapolis (the modern Kavalla) in Macedonia. From there they went inland to Philippi, the city named for the father of Alexander the Great. After Antony and Octavian (later Augustus) had defeated Brutus and Cassius, in a battle nearby (42 B.C.), the city was enlarged to receive colonists from Italy. The title *first city* does not mean capital city (Thessalonica was the provincial capital), but was an honorary title given to a city of importance and only rarely to a *colony*. Generally speaking, when a province was conquered, it was divided into parts or districts. Originally a colony was a Roman city populated by Roman citizens forming a garrison in conquered territories. Afterward colonies became places where Roman veterans were settled. They had a definitely Roman form of administration and were under Roman laws. Many other cities mentioned in Acts were colonies, among those mentioned earlier: Pisidian Antioch, Lystra, and Troas. When Philippi is labeled a Roman city, this was presumably because it had an unmistakable Roman character.

12–13. *some days* must be understood as the days before the *sabbath day*.

along the river. A Jewish synagogue will be found to be near running water. *where . . . people used to pray* is probably synonymous with a synagogue.

14–15. Lydia was from the city of Thyatira in Lydia in the province of Asia. It is possible that her name derived from this. A god-fearing Gentile, her family is mentioned as the first to be baptized and it was at her house that Paul and his companions stayed (cf. vs. 40).

16–23. Like those possessed by demons in the gospels (Mark iii 11, v 7 par.; Luke iv 41), the soothsayer spoke the truth about those she met. Her words showed her to be a Gentile. The Romans were tolerant with regard to Judaism (see p. LII), but did not permit Jews to turn Romans into proselytes. Although vs. 17 contains the last "we" form until xx 6, there is no reason to assume that the "we" source ends just at vs. 17 (see p. XLII). It is interesting that Paul was not included in the "we" in this passage nor in xxi 18.

24–34. The jailer, having received special orders to guard these dangerous prisoners carefully, placed them in the innermost cell and chained them in the stocks. At midnight they were singing hymns of praise to God (cf. II Cor vi 10: "sorrowful, yet always rejoicing"). The jailer drew his sword (vs. 27) because by Roman custom he was responsible for the prisoners with his life (cf. NOTES on xii 19 and xxvii 42).

"light" (vs. 29) is a plural but has been translated as a singular in order to leave the way open for several possibilities: lamps, torches, etc. The earthquake and its effects had convinced the jailer that the dangerous prisoners placed under his care were in reality men with a message from above. As the inhabitants of Lystra had previously (see NOTE on xiv 11–13), he realized that he was confronted with men of unique significance. With the same dramatic speed as we encountered in the account of the Ethiopian treasurer (see NOTE on viii 26–38), the jailer and everybody in his household were baptized the very same night.

35–40. The praetors in Philippi were, like high Roman officials elsewhere, surrounded by lictors. Since Silas and Paul were Roman citizens they were not to be given corporal punishment (see NOTE on xxii 25–29). They had, however, without a trial, been publicly whipped and thrown into prison (cf. "but though we had already suffered and were shamefully treated, as you know, at Philippi"—I Thess ii 2).

COMMENT

From here onward, Acts' description of the visits to the different cities becomes far more precise. Events taking place in Philippi, Athens, Corinth, and Ephesus are given special attention. In the present section on Philippi we hear of individuals such as Lydia, a seller of purple, the Gentile slave girl with a gift of prophecy, and the jailer. It should be noticed that the Jews were not of much importance in this city, nor did they start a persecution of the apostle.

On a sabbath day, on their way to the synagogue, Paul and his companions meet a slave girl, a soothsayer. Paul cures her, which means that she can no longer prophesy, and is now of no value to her owners. Because of this financial loss, they drag Paul and Silas to the market place and to the city officials (the praetors) charging them as troublemakers, Jews who were trying to introduce customs unlawful to the Philippians, who were Romans. This accusation causes the crowd to congregate; the praetors have the accused stripped, flogged, and thrown into prison. A miraculous earthquake leads to the conversion of the jailer and to his baptism but does not influence the fate of the missionaries. The authorities regret their rash actions of the day before and want to release Paul and Silas. Paul replies that he will not agree to being secretly released.

The magistrates themselves must come and conduct them outside, because he and Silas—both Roman citizens—had, without a trial, been publicly whipped and thrown into prison. When the praetors hear this they are alarmed and come and lead them outside, asking them to leave the city. Paul and Silas go back to Lydia, encourage the brethren, and depart.

45. PAUL IN THESSALONICA
(xvii 1–9)

XVII 1 Now Paul and Silas traveled by way of Amphipolis and Apollonia and came to Thessalonica, where the Jews had a synagogue. 2 Paul went there, as was his custom, and for three sabbaths he conversed with them on the Scriptures, 3 expounding and explaining that the Messiah was bound to suffer and rise from the dead, and saying: "He is the Messiah, this Jesus of whom I tell you." 4 Some of them were convinced and joined Paul and Silas, together with a large number of the god-fearing Greeks and not a few prominent women.

5 But the Jews were jealous, took with them some worthless persons from among the idlers in the market place, and gathering a crowd, threw the city into an uproar. Attacking Jason's house, they sought to bring Paul and Silas before the municipal assembly. 6 When they did not find them, they dragged Jason and some of the brethren to the politarchs, shouting: "These men who stir up trouble in our part of the world have come here also. 7 Jason has received them as guests, and they are all acting against the decrees of Caesar, saying that another, one Jesus, is king." 8 Thus they stirred up the crowd, and the politarchs also when they heard it. 9 When they had taken security from Jason and the rest, they released them.

Notes

xvii 1–3. Thessalonica was originally the capital of the second division of Macedonia; the proconsul resided there. It is unlikely that the stay in Thessalonica lasted only three weeks. For one thing a congregation was founded which was forced to continue on its own and managed to survive; for another we learn from Philip iv 16 that during Paul's second missionary journey, the church in Philippi had a couple of times sent money for the support of Paul while he was staying in Thessalonica.

Although the distance between Thessalonica and Philippi is not great, this circumstance as well as the one first mentioned would indicate that his stay had been of more than three weeks' duration. With *he conversed with them on the Scriptures* compare I Cor xv 3–4.

4–9. The position of Jews in a predominantly Gentile city was not so strong that they could act as persecutors. Under such circumstances, an excited crowd might turn on the Jews themselves. Instead the Jews made these disturbances appear as uneasiness among the local inhabitants, whom some strangers had provoked to justified anger by acting against the Emperor's decrees and by stating that another, the hitherto unknown Jesus, ought to replace the Emperor. These charges had nothing to do with the conflict between Israel and Christ.

Politarch is chiefly, but not exclusively, a Macedonian title given non-Roman city officials. The Macedonian cities seem to have had several politarchs, the number varying according to their size. Thus Thessalonica had five during the reign of Augustus; later the number was extended to six.

The charges brought against Paul in Thessalonica, like others made in the following years, will provide the basis for the trial of the apostle in Jerusalem (cf. also xxviii 21–22).

COMMENT

After their banishment from Philippi, Paul and his companions traveled through Amphipolis and Apollonia to Thessalonica. True to his custom, Paul turned first to the Jews, preaching in their synagogue on three sabbath days. According to the Old Testament prophecies, Paul explained, the Messiah was to suffer and rise from the dead; and he added, Jesus, who died and rose again, is the Messiah. The apostle's sermon won over only a few Jews but many god-fearing Greeks and several women of high-standing. This aroused jealousy in a majority of the Jews, so that, assisted by hired loafers, they stirred up disturbances in the city. After looking in vain for Paul and Silas in Jason's house, they dragged Jason and some of the Christians before the magistrates, charging them with having received as guests the two missionaries who stirred up trouble everywhere in the world and who now had come to Thessalonica for the same purpose. The missionaries were accused of having transgressed against the Emperor's decree by maintaining that Jesus was the true emperor. Their accusations impressed the crowd and its politarchs, and the latter let Jason and the Christians out on bail.

46. PAUL IN BEREA
(xvii 10–15)

XVII 10 The brethren immediately sent both Paul and Silas away by night to Berea; and when they had arrived, they went to the Jewish synagogue. 11 The Jews there were more courteous than those in Thessalonica, and some of them received the word with great interest, and every day examined the Scriptures to see whether it was true. 12 Many of them and some of the most respected Gentile women and men believed. 13 But when the Jews in Thessalonica learned that the word of God was preached by Paul in Berea as well, they came there too and stirred up a riot among the crowds. 14 Then the brethren sent Paul away at once, to go right down to the sea, while Silas and Timothy stayed there. 15 Those who took Paul went with him to Athens, and returned with a message to Silas and Timothy that they were to come as soon as possible.

NOTES

xvii 10–13. Paul and Silas were sent westward to Berea, by the brethren in Thessalonica, and their promising missionary work was interrupted only by the arrival of Jews from Thessalonica. From Acts xx 4, we know that one of the Berean converts—Sopater the son of Pyrrhus—is listed as one of the representatives of the churches chosen to accompany Paul on his journey to Jerusalem with the collection. His presence indicates that in spite of the interruption a vigorous congregation had been founded in Berea.

14–15. The description of Paul's flight from Berea is given in the words *down to the sea* and *to Athens,* which may mean that the brethren accompanied him down to the Aegean coast and put him on board a ship bound for Athens. But as it is stated that they "went with him to Athens," the words "down to the sea" may possibly refer to an overland journey all the way to Athens. For the subsequent journeys of Silas and Timothy and reunion with Paul (see NOTE on xviii 5).

COMMENT

In Berea Paul and Silas had a better reception than in the other cities. Glad and grateful listeners, the Jews in Berea came to believe in Christ. But just as Jews from Pisidian Antioch and Iconium had come to Lystra and incited the inhabitants there to persecute Paul (xiv 19), so in this case Jews from Thessalonica came to Berea and started a persecution there. Paul was the one in danger and the brethren sent him off probably by sea to Athens. Silas and Timothy were to follow him.

47. PAUL IN ATHENS
(xvii 16–21)

XVII 16 While Paul waited for them in Athens, he became filled with indignation when he saw how idolatrous the city was. 17 He argued with the Jews and god-fearing people in the synagogue, and daily in the market place with those who happened to be there. 18 Some Epicurean and some Stoic philosophers confronted him, and some said: "What exactly is this phrase merchant trying to say?" Others: "He appears to be a preacher of foreign deities"—for he preached the gospel of Jesus and the resurrection. 19 They took hold of him and took him to the Areopagus, and said: "May we know what this new teaching is that you commend? 20 For what we have heard from you seems strange to us; we now wish to know what it means." 21 (All the Athenians and the foreigners living there had no time for anything but telling and listening to the latest novelty.)

NOTES

xvii 16–17. These verses give a lively description of Athens. In the agora, or "market place," Athenians gathered to report and listen to the latest news, or when so inclined, to hear the arguments of Stoic and Epicurean philosophers. Nearby was the Areopagus, the hill where the Council of the same name had its meeting place and—at other times—a quiet place where, without being disturbed, speakers could present their ideas to everyone interested. The life in the agora and on the Areopagus was typical of this city which both in antiquity and in later ages has been considered the center of Greek culture.

16. Another characteristic of Athens was that it was full of idols, a fact noted by other visitors, though expressed in other words. The site of the agora, now between the railway to Piraeus and the Areopagus, has been excavated by American archaeologists, but one still has to imagine how overloaded with statues and altars it was at the time of Paul.

17. Generally Paul preached first to the Jews and afterward to the

god-fearing Gentiles, but here he argued with both groups simultaneously.

18. Paul's discussions recall those of Socrates. In this way he came into contact with Stoic and Epicurean philosophers. Even after Athens had become a mere shadow of itself, it still continued to be the city of the philosophers, for it had not been forgotten that the whole post-Socratic philosophy had started there.

The Stoic philosophers aimed at living according to "nature," i.e. in agreement with that reason which pervaded the world; in Paul's day this school was of great importance and counted among its adherents such famous men as Seneca, Epictetus, and Marcus Aurelius. With them and their contemporaries, philosophy assumed a religious tone and became of importance to the existing religions.

Like Epicurus, the founder of their school, the Epicureans have always been regarded as men who elevated the principle of pleasure above all others, but Epicurus himself did make a distinction between higher and lower pleasures, and in practice the Epicureans might at times resemble the Stoics.

Some of his listeners took Paul to be a mere phrasemonger while others thought of him as one who introduced new gods. Possibly the parenthetic close following *foreign deities* was intended to show that they understood Jesus to be a god and Resurrection (*Anastasis*) a goddess.

The Areopagus was at that time the Supreme Council of Athens. See NOTE on vs. 16–17.

19–21. Curiosity about his teaching, not an accusation made against him, brought Paul and his audience to the Areopagus. Luke's interest in the episode seems nevertheless to be centered on the fact that the Areopagus was a court and that thus in Athens, as nearly everywhere else, Paul had appeared before the court (see p. LXXVII) and had not been sentenced. The Athenians' concern for what was new might also hold good for Paul's audiences in many other cities, but such curiosity was, time and again, considered characteristically Athenian.

COMMENT

Alone in Athens, Paul looked at the city without any enthusiasm for its historical and art treasures. He saw and judged everything as an apostle of Jesus Christ. (In the nineteenth century, John Henry Newman, later Cardinal, traveled in Italy in the same way, showing no interest in antiquity, concerned only with early Christianity.) The apostle spoke both to the Jews in the synagogue and among the Gentiles in the city. Stoic and Epicurean philosophers argued with him, and, eager to know more about the new doctrine, brought him to the Areopagus. Thus all Athenians acted; they wanted to know and to discuss the latest news.

48. PAUL'S SPEECH IN ATHENS
(xvii 22–34)

XVII 22 Paul stood in the middle of the Areopagus and said:
"Athenians, I find that you are rather given to religious obser-
vances in the worship of your gods. 23 For as I was walking
around looking at your shrines, I came upon an altar on which
was written: 'To an unknown god.' The one whom you thus
honor unwittingly is he whom I am preaching to you. 24 The
God who made the world and all that is in it, and who is Lord
of heaven and earth, does not dwell in temples made by hands.
25 Nor can he be served by human hands, as if he needed
anything, since he gives life and breath and everything to all
mankind. 26 He made out of one every nation, to live on the
whole surface of the earth, after having fixed times and bound-
aries for their dwellings, 27 that they should seek God, that they
might feel their way toward him and find him. Indeed he is not
far from any of us, 28 for

'By him we live, move, and exist,'
as some of your poets also have expressed it:
'For we also are his offspring.'
29 Since we are God's offspring, we ought not to believe that
the Godhead is the same as gold, silver, or stone shaped by
human art and thought. 30 After having borne with these
ignorant past ages, God now proclaims that all men everywhere
must repent. 31 For he has appointed a day when he will judge
the world justly by a man whom he has ordained to do so,
and whom he has accredited by raising him from the dead."

32 But when they heard of the resurrection of the dead, some
mocked. Others said: "We will hear you speak about this on
another occasion." 33 So Paul left them. 34 Some men joined
him and believed, among whom was Dionysius, who was a
member of the Court of Areopagus, and also a woman called
Damaris, together with others.

Notes

xvii 22–23. The altar "to an Unknown God" has not been found in Athens, but altars to unknown gods have been unearthed in other cities. In polytheistic religions such altars may have been erected to allay the fear that some gods might be forgotten. As shown by the reception of his preaching (vs. 18), the God whom Paul proclaimed was unknown to the Athenians and the "Unknown God" whom they already worship but do not know becomes in Luke's presentation Paul's God. What follows reveals that God was unknown only because the Athenians had not wanted to know him. So Paul was not introducing foreign gods, but God who was both known, as this altar shows, and yet unknown.

24–27. In his proclamation of the true God, Paul presents him as the Creator and the Ruler of the universe in words reminiscent of Isa xlii 5 (cf. Notes on Acts iv 23–28, xiv 15–18). No one has the right to talk of gods, for there is only one God who has created all nations from the first man and has fixed their dwelling both in time and space for one purpose only, that they seek and perhaps find God. Thus if God is to be found, man must himself do the finding (and, Paul adds, this obviously has not happened yet).

28–29. *as some of your poets also have expressed it.* The quotation comes from Aratus (*Phaenomena,* line 5). The words "For by him we live, move, and exist" are a modification of the fourth line of a quatrain ascribed to Epimenides by Diogenes Laertius (*Lives of Philosophers* i.112). The quatrain's second line is quoted by Paul in Tit i 12. Epimenides was one of the Seven Sages of Greece (probably in the sixth century B.C.).

30–31. In the NT God's forbearance is often stressed as the means of man's salvation. In xiv 16, we heard that in past generations God had allowed the Gentiles to walk in their own ways. In Rom iii 25, Paul mentions that God had in his forbearance overlooked former sins. In many other texts, (e.g. Rom ix–xi) we find the same lenience and forbearance which shows that God concentrates all his efforts on salvation.

But it appears from our present text (vss. 30–31) that, as mankind had not found God through the creation, God had changed his plan of salvation and decided to let the course of this world end with a day of judgment which will then be reason enough for all men to repent. God does not want the sinner's death but his conversion. And the one who is to be at one and the same time both Judge and Savior is the man whom he has raised from the dead. Once more the resurrection has been made the central point.

32–34. This speech was interrupted by shouts from the audience. The idea of a resurrection of the dead was foreign to Greek thought, as can be seen also in I Cor xv. The individual soul might well be immortal, but Greeks were unwilling to think of a resurrection of the body. The exact nature of the congregation Paul founded in Athens suffers from lack of information; unlike the converts from the synagogue, Athenian church members did not belong to distinct groups, but were individual persons who are not always identified by name.

Scholars have wanted to connect Paul's "failure" in Athens, the disappointing response to his "philosophical" sermon, with the apostle's subsequent vigorous rejection of "excellency of speech or of wisdom" (I Cor ii 1 KJV), pointing out that the decision to know nothing "except Jesus Christ and him crucified" among the Corinthians (cf. I Cor ii 1–5) was a result of the above-mentioned failure. But as we have already stated (and according to Acts xvii) Paul did not fail in Athens. It is also out of the question to think of Paul trying his hand at a philosophical sermon in Athens and afterward claiming that there was so decided a difference between the Gospel and the wisdom of the world as would render useless any philosophical sermon.

COMMENT

Paul's Areopagus speech has been the object of many examinations and bold hypotheses. In recent years much has been written about its Jewish and Greek elements. No studies are more revealing, however, than those that relate the speech to Paul and his letters. It is important at the outset to realize that though we have none of Paul's sermons, they must have differed in form at least from his letters.

This speech begins with a reference to an altar to an unknown god, which Paul had found in Athens and which showed the Athenians' great solicitude for the worship of the gods. This served as an introduction to his own sermon, as something of interest to his audience, because he was preaching precisely about this unknown god and was able to give a profounder exposition of what they had only guessed at. The God he preached about was the Creator of the world, who did not need temples or sacrifices as did the gods of Athens, but who had from the beginning of the world so arranged men's life on earth that they should seek and, if possible, find God. This thought is expressed also in Rom i 19–23, where Paul states that God is indeed known through his creation.

But the Gentiles, he adds, had not wanted to honor or give thanks to their creator and sustainer. Instead of attaining God through the creation, they had preferred to worship it by fashioning for themselves gods in human or animal form. If a transference of this mode of thought to a missionary sermon could be imagined, we should come very close to the Areopagus speech.

In both Romans and Acts we see that man has not taken advantage of the opportunity given him by God: he has not walked toward him or found him. In Acts, it is mentioned that the audience had not availed itself of what God held up as a way and a goal. But instead of pronouncing God's judgment on those who, in thus arrogantly refusing him and preferring polytheism, had fallen deeper into iniquity (cf. Rom i 24–32), Paul, in the first part of the Areopagus speech (Acts xvii 22–29), describes God as the bestower of all good gifts, as one very near to man who would gladly allow himself to be found.

Offense has been taken at some of the expressions in vss. 27–28, on the presumption that they are pantheistic propositions. But "by him we live, move, and exist" states the reasons for God's closeness to mankind and is a variant of the end of vs. 25: "giving life and breath and everything to all mankind." If the end of vs. 28 is translated by "For of him we are also kindred," it might sound as if gods and men had combined in the production of mankind, whereas the translation chosen here: "For we also are his offspring" stresses that human beings are the creatures of God, owing everything to him.

Paul emphasized that being the offspring of God, man ought not to think so little of him as to worship material objects artistically formed instead of the eternal creator and sustainer, who wants to benefit mankind. But now the time to seek and find God in his creation has come to an end; this road has proved impracticable. Still wanting to save mankind, God has now chosen a new way of proclaiming to all men that they must repent. Though the world is soon to be judged, it will be preceded by a summons to repentance proclaimed all over the earth. God has appointed a day of judgment, ordained a man (Jesus Christ) to act on his behalf and has confirmed him as judge by raising him from the dead.

Paul might well have delivered such a missionary sermon. It has an excellent introduction, its doctrine is a reworking of thoughts in Romans transformed into missionary impulse, and it deals, in the main, with Christ and the mission to the world. Nothing in the text indicates that this speech was rejected by the listeners. They reacted in different ways; but we cannot know how many were mocking at and how many were affected by Paul's preaching. The sketch that follows, the formation of a congregation in Athens, says nothing about the results of his missionary work in the synagogue. The idea that Paul met with failure in Athens because of his sermon of a somewhat philosophical nature may be considered a myth invented by scholars, without any foundation in the texts.

49. PAUL IN CORINTH
(xviii 1–17)

XVIII 1 After this Paul left Athens and came to Corinth. 2 (There) he met a Jew named Aquila, whose family was from Pontus, lately come from Italy with his wife Priscilla, for Claudius had issued a decree that all Jews were to leave Rome. So he went to them, 3 and as Paul and Aquila were of the same craft, he stayed with them and they worked at their trade as tentmakers. 4 Every sabbath he held discussions in the synagogue, and tried to convince both Jews and Greeks.

5 When both Silas and Timothy came down from Macedonia, Paul was absorbed in preaching the word, testifying to the Jews that Jesus was the Messiah. 6 When they blasphemously rebuffed (him), he shook his garments and said to them: "Your blood shall be upon your own heads! I am without blame, and from now on I shall go to the Gentiles." 7 He went away and came to a house belonging to a man named Titius Justus, a god-fearing man, whose house stood beside the synagogue. 8 Crispus, the leader of the synagogue, and all his household believed in the Lord. Many Corinthians who heard believed and were baptized. 9 The Lord said to Paul in a vision at night: "Do not be afraid, but speak and do not be silent! 10 I am with you, so that no one shall make any attempt upon you to do you harm, for there are many people who will follow me in this city." 11 Then he stayed there a year and a half and taught the word of God among them.

12 While Gallio was proconsul of Achaia, all the Jews rose against Paul, and they brought him before the court of justice, 13 saying: "This man persuades people to worship God against the Law." 14 When Paul was about to speak, Gallio said to the Jews: "If this were a case of some crime or an evil act, you Jews, I would deal with your complaint as reason would demand.

15 Since, however, it is a dispute concerning teaching, persons, and your law, you must deal with it yourselves; I will not be judge in these matters." 16 And he drove them away from the court. 17 Then they all seized Sosthenes, the leader of the synagogue, and beat him before the court, but Gallio took no notice.

NOTES

xviii 1–3. Corinth was the capital of the province of Achaia. Of its two harbors, nearly four miles apart, one, Cenchreae, faced the Aegean Sea and the East, the other, Lechaeum, the Adriatic Sea and the West; smaller ships were hauled across the isthmus (Nero attempted in A.D. 67 to canal it—in vain) to avoid the difficult run to the south around the Peloponnese. The city had a highly mixed population; but despite a few Jewish conversions, the later Christian congregation in the city did not seem to indicate a significant number of Jewish members.

Aquila may very well have been a man of Pontus by family, and yet never have been there himself. We will meet him again in Ephesus and Rome. *Priscilla,* his wife, was called Prisca by Paul (Rom xvi 3; I Cor xvi 19; cf. 2 Tim iv 19); Luke uses the familiar, Paul, the formal name. The couple had left Rome because of the Emperor Claudius' banishment of the Jews in Rome (ca. A.D. 49). The sources do not clearly state the purpose of this persecution, but in all likelihood it was neither severe nor of long duration. If, as has been suggested, Aquila and Priscilla had become Christians in Rome, one may pause over a remark—granted, a vague one—of Suetonius on Claudius' persecution. The Jews, he said, were indulging in constant riots "at the instigation of Chrestus" (*Life of Claudius* XXV.4). One may suppose that Christianity had been introduced in Rome early, possibly by Jewish pilgrims on their return from religious festivals in Jerusalem. Unfortunately no more is known about this.

4. *Jews and Greeks.* In connection with the synagogue (Was there really only one in Corinth?) this phrase must be taken as referring to Jews and god-fearing Gentiles.

5. *Silas and Timothy* had remained in Berea, when Paul fled to Athens (xvii 14), and we are now told that they joined Paul in Corinth. But their joining him was more complicated than Luke's account would indicate; he either knew nothing about the details or thought it unnecessary to go into them. Evidently Timothy had come to Paul in Athens, for, according to I Thess ii 17–iii 5, Paul—now long absent from Thessalonica and apprehensive about the fate of the congregation

there, sent Timothy in his stead to determine how the faith had fared
in Thessalonica, under difficult circumstances. From this journey Timothy
returned with good news, to which I Thess iii 6 ff. testified. As for
Silas' movements at this time, there is no information available. Citing I
Thess iii 1, some scholars have inferred that Silas was with Paul when
Timothy was sent out, but this would mean interpreting Paul's use of the
plural, which he frequently used about himself, far too literally. Of
course, if the "we" of the verse cited *is* editorial, Timothy may not have
joined Paul in Athens; he may have gone, still at Paul's request, direct
from Berea to Thessalonica. Another element is involved, too: Would
Timothy have had time to travel from Macedonia to Athens and back
again?

While Paul's account undoubtedly gives a far more accurate description than Acts of what his fellow workers were doing, there is no
reason to criticize Luke, who did include what he considered the essential points in his account. Paul's account, too, included only what was
of importance and concern to him and was far from exhaustive.

The change in Paul's missionary work upon the arrival of his fellow
workers in Corinth might be taken to mean that they had gifts with
them from the poor but always generous Macedonians (II Cor xi 8 f.;
Philip iv 15), which made it possible for the apostle to stop working at
his craft and concentrate all his efforts on preaching.

6. *Your blood shall be upon your own heads.* Paul concludes his
words with a characteristically Jewish phrase (cf. Matt xxvii 25), thus
placing all responsibility for the Jews' rejection of the Gospel on themselves; free from blame himself, he would now go to the Gentiles
(xiii 46, xxviii 28). The apostle's words can also be interpreted in a
way that does not condemn the listeners as in xiii 51 (see NOTE)
but indicated that he was "innocent" in relation to them, i.e. relieved
of his obligations to them (cf. xx 26–27).

7–8. And with these words he left the synagogue and turned to the
house of a god-fearing Gentile, Titius Justus, a house which stood near
the synagogue—both a suitable and dangerous location. Not all Jews
had rejected the Gospel and among them was Crispus, the leader of the
synagogue (Is he the Crispus mentioned in I Cor i 14?).

9–11. Encouraged by the vision, Paul was active in Corinth for
eighteen months; this period may date either from the separation of
the church from the synagogue or further back to the time of his
arrival.

12–13. *While Gallio was proconsul of Achaia.* Gallio was a brother
of the philosopher Seneca (ca. 3 B.C.–A.D. 65). His activity as proconsul
in Achaia can be dated approximately by means of an inscription in
Delphi showing that he held office A.D. 51–52. As the office could only
be held for one year or at the most two, Gallio may have been
proconsul in 50–51 or in 52–53. This dating is important to Paul's

chronology because it shows that his stay in Corinth must have occurred between A.D. 50–52. If the uprising is assumed to have been at the beginning of Gallio's proconsulate, it may be supposed that the Jews wanted to exploit the inexperience of their new governor. Instead of stirring up trouble in the city, the Jews of Corinth chose to rid themselves of the Christian apostle by bringing him to trial in court and having him sentenced.

This man persuades . . . the Law. The charge they brought was ambiguous, because the Law might be both Roman law (cf. xvi 21, xvii 7) and Jewish law (see p. LXXII). When the charge is made, it is not Paul, who as the accused was supposed to answer it, but Gallio himself who speaks up in order to reject the case.

14–15. The proconsul, having listened to the charges, defined his task as a Roman judge, clarifying the two meanings of the law.

16–17. Gallio's attitude was clear and reflected the Romans' view that the relation between Christians and Jews was an internal Jewish affair (see p. LXXI). In the excavated agora of ancient Corinth, one can still see Gallio's judgment seat, which for a long time was supposed to have been built into a chapel erected in memory of the event. Finally, it can be said about Gallio that Luke's sympathetic view of this man (who shortly after Seneca's fall in the reign of Nero, ca. A.D. 65) was obliged to commit suicide is most fitting even in a text composed before that time (cf. p. LXXX).

COMMENT

After his stay in Athens, the apostle worked in Corinth. Claudius' persecution of the Jews in Rome had caused a Jewish couple, Aquila and Priscilla, to move to Corinth. Paul, getting a job with Aquila, moved in with them and they became fellow workers. By the time Silas and Timothy arrived from Macedonia, Paul was completely absorbed in his missionary work, especially among the Jews. But just as in other places the Jews turned against him and mocked him, so he shook off the dust from his garments and addressed his preaching to the Gentiles. Then many Corinthians came to believe, and likewise a few Jews. Christ revealed himself to Paul in a vision urging him to continue his preaching in Corinth.

After eighteen months, the Jews gathered forces against Paul. They brought him before the court and accused him of persuading people to worship God against the Law. Paul was given no opportunity to answer this charge, for Gallio himself immediately ended the case, stating that it was the duty of his court to deal only

with criminal cases; when, as here, it was a case concerning doctrines, persons, and Jewish law then it became an internal Jewish
affair belonging under the jurisdiction of the Jewish community itself. Gallio therefore refused to have anything to do with the case.
Nor would he listen further to Jewish pleas but had the Jewish
spokesmen removed from the court. The scene ended with a vivid
little incident: "they all seized Sosthenes . . . and beat him before
the court, and Gallio took no notice." Was it the dissatisfied Jews
who gave vent to their resentment against Paul by beating their
leader who had not been able to win their case for them? Or did
other Corinthians take it out on the Jewish representative?

50. PAUL IN CORINTH, EPHESUS, AND JERUSALEM
(xviii 18–23)

XVIII 18 Paul stayed there some time longer, and then took leave of the brethren and sailed for Syria with Priscilla and Aquila. Before this he had had his hair cut short in Cenchreae, for he had taken a Nazirite vow. 19 When they had come to Ephesus he left them there, but he himself went into the synagogue and debated with the Jews. 20 But when they asked him to stay there longer, he refused, 21 and took his leave, with the words: "I shall return to you, if God wills," and then set sail from Ephesus.

22 When he had landed at Caesarea, he went up to greet the church, and then went down to Antioch. 23 After spending some time there he set out, journeying from place to place through the Galatian country and Phrygia and strengthening all the disciples.

NOTES

xviii 18. Possibly the emphasis on the fact that Paul had continued his stay in Corinth for some time was meant to prove that no lawsuit was initiated to put an end to his activity in that city.

It is grammatically possible that it was not Paul but Aquila who had had his hair cut short in Cenchreae, but on the other hand Aquila could have had his hair cut all his life without its being recorded in Acts. It was the faithful Jew, the apostle Paul, who was mentioned because he continued to keep the Jewish customs. A cutting of the hair was only mentioned because it is part of the conclusion to a Nazirite vow (Num vi 1–21; cf. Acts xxi 23–26).

Ruins of parts of the harbor at Cenchreae, Corinth's Aegean seaport partly submerged, have been preserved. In Rom xvi 1, Phoebe of Cenchreae is mentioned.

19–23. When Paul left Aquila and Priscilla in Ephesus, it is natural to assume that he did this in preparation for his future work in that city. His own answer to the request of the Ephesian Jews—that he should stay longer—did not contradict such an assumption. It only showed that he stood firm on his decision to continue his voyage to Syria. The addition *if God wills* showed only the speaker's piety; it indicated neither that his coming was uncertain from a subjective point of view, nor that his journey to Jerusalem was of the same dramatic and perilous nature as his next journey (xx 1 ff.). There may have been other reasons for Paul's refusal of the Jews' request, which might seem to have indicated that they were ready to receive the Gospel. If the church that he visited from Caesarea was the Jerusalem church this might provide a reasonable argument for Paul's delay in coming to Ephesus, although unfortunately we do not know anything about the purpose of this visit to Jerusalem. The mention of Paul's journey through Asia Minor takes us into known territory (cf. xvi 6 ff.). This does not seem to have been a missionary journey but rather a journey of inspection of the Christian churches in order to strengthen the disciples. In xvi 6, the Holy Spirit prevented Paul from preaching in the province of Asia, but this time using the same roads, he succeeds in arriving at Ephesus, and in performing an important task in the city and in the province.

COMMENT

The Jews' attempt to have Paul sentenced does not succeed, and he continues his activities in Corinth. He does not leave Corinth until later, and after concluding a Nazirite vow in Cenchreae, he sails toward Syria. Arriving en route at Ephesus, he prepared for his future stay in this city by leaving Aquila and Priscilla behind and by visiting the synagogue. Faced with the Jews' request to stay in the city for some time, he remains firm in his resolve to continue his voyage to Syria, but he promises them that "if God wills" he will return to them. The goal of his journey was Caesarea in Palestine though in all likelihood it actually was the Jerusalem church— but nothing is said at this point about the purpose of this visit. Then Paul goes to Antioch in Syria, and after a stay there of some duration, he goes westward into Asia Minor and visits the Galatian country and Phrygia, ending his journey, as we shall soon hear (xix 1), in Ephesus. The stay in Caesarea (Jerusalem) and Antioch marks the end of Paul's second missionary journey and the beginning of his third.

51. EVENTS IN EPHESUS BEFORE PAUL'S ARRIVAL
(xviii 24–28)

XVIII ²⁴ There came to Ephesus a Jew named Apollos, whose family was from Alexandria. He was a learned man, and well read in the Scriptures. ²⁵ He had been instructed in the way of the Lord, and with an ardent spirit he spoke and taught accurately concerning Jesus. However, the only baptism he knew was that of John. ²⁶ So he began to speak boldly in the synagogue, but when Priscilla and Aquila heard him they took an interest in him and explained God's way to him more exactly. ²⁷ As he wished to go to Achaia, the brethren encouraged him and wrote to the disciples to make him welcome. When he had arrived there his gift of graciousness made him of great help to those who had believed, ²⁸ for he energetically refuted the Jews point by point, publicly proving with the aid of the Scriptures that Jesus was the Messiah.

NOTES

xviii 24–26. There has been a general tendency to misunderstand Apollos. Since it is here stated that his family was from Alexandria, he is immediately assumed to have been a pupil of Philo the Jewish philosopher, and to have been instructed in allegorical interpretation. But just as with respect to xviii 2, it was maintained that Aquila, whose family was from Pontus, possibly might himself never have been in Pontus, so Apollos may well have grown up and been educated in places other than the city where his family had originally resided. But even if he himself really did come from Alexandria, his connection with Hellenistic Jewish philosophy and its interpretation of the OT would be open to question. He may have become well versed in the Scriptures in many other ways. A decisive argument against a connection with Philo can be found in the statement that he knew only the baptism of John the Baptist. It is unlikely that a disciple of John the Baptist would be able to derive much from Philo's philosophy and exegesis.

The picture of Apollos' Christian faith and preaching is highly important because it reveals dogmatic points of view that seem strangely at odds with later Christian views. In the transition from Judaism to Christianity it must have been quite possible to find such surprising combinations. To Luke such points of view were important as testifying to a connection between Judaism and Christianity. On the one hand Apollos had been taught *in the way of the Lord,* so he had had some instruction in Christianity, even if inadequate. His teaching *concerning Jesus* was certainly accurate; it would appear that he might very well have been called a "disciple," as Luke called the twelve whom Paul met in Ephesus (xix 1), and who, like them, had known of no baptism but John's. From this it can probably be assumed that Apollos like the twelve did not know of the Holy Spirit (xix 2).

with an ardent spirit. Translated thus here; others have taken these words to mean that he spoke and taught, and was moved by the Holy Spirit; but if this interpretation were possible, then a lack of knowledge on Apollos' part about the Holy Spirit would be unlikely.

Naturally Priscilla and Aquila therefore took it upon themselves to teach him more of the way. When they had succeeded in this task, they and, we must suppose, the other Ephesian disciples were ready to send a letter recommending Apollos to the church of Corinth (cf. II Cor iii 1–3). While at Ephesus, Apollos had preached in the synagogue; in Corinth he was active in the church.

27–28. Paul told about Apollos' Corinth stay in I Cor i 10 ff. Some groups within the congregation claimed that different Christian leaders had been their teachers, one mentioning Apollos. But there were no factions as such inside the church of Corinth, as had previously and wrongly been assumed, and former attempts at interpreting Paul's polemics in the early chs. of the letter as aimed at the individual groups (thus in i 12 ff. Apollos and his group) have now in general been abandoned. Paul's way of speaking of Apollos shows his thoroughly positive attitude toward his fellow worker. In I Cor iii 4 ff., he referred to himself and Apollos as Christian preachers—for he and Apollos were the only persons, among those mentioned in i 12, who had been active in Corinth. And in xvi 12, it was Paul who had implored Apollos to come to Corinth even though he did not want to come until a later date. Apollos may perhaps at that time have been in Ephesus, whence Paul wrote. He must at any rate have been not too far from the place where Paul stayed. No more is heard about Apollos in Acts.

COMMENT

Although Paul was still traveling a long way from Ephesus, this important city has already become the focal point of the account. A Jew by the name of Apollos arrives there; his family comes from Alexandria and he himself is a learned man, well versed in the Scriptures. He has already received instruction in the way of the Lord, and what he says about Jesus is correct, but he knows only the baptism of John the Baptist. He preaches in the synagogue to the best of his ability and the missionaries, Priscilla and Aquila, help him to understand the Gospel further. Like so many others in Acts, Apollos likewise was an itinerant teacher and preacher; his desire to leave Ephesus to do missionary work in Achaia had won the support of the brethren (in Ephesus), who wrote a letter of recommendation for him to the church in Corinth. Here Apollos assumed great importance within the church.

PART V

52. CHRISTIANS BAPTIZED WITH JOHN'S BAPTISM
(xix 1–7)

XIX ¹ It happened that while Apollos was staying in Corinth, Paul, having traveled through the hills inland, came to Ephesus, where he met some disciples. ² He said to them: "Did you receive the Holy Spirit when you believed?" They replied: "No, we have not even heard that there is a Holy Spirit." ³ Then he asked: "How were you baptized, then?" They replied: "With John's baptism." ⁴ Paul said: "John baptized with a baptism of repentance, at the same time saying to the people that they were to believe in him who was to come after him, that is, Jesus." ⁵ When they heard (this), they were baptized in the name of the Lord Jesus. ⁶ When Paul laid his hands on them, the Holy Spirit came upon them, so that they spoke with tongues and prophesied. ⁷ All together there were about twelve men.

NOTES

xix 1–7. *disciples* here is used for Christians, not for disciples of John the Baptist or others. Paul's question to the twelve men calls forth a statement of fundamental importance. It is undoubtedly phrased so as to lead to the essential point in the discussion between Paul and those disciples.

baptism of John. The Fourth Gospel presents John the Baptist as the forerunner of Jesus—an identification made by the Baptist himself (John i 15–36, iii 26–36; cf. v 33–36). Very little is known about the influence of John the Baptist after his death, in Palestine or the rest of the Jewish world. The Mandaeans' relation to John the Baptist could be taken as proof of the continued existence of a tradition concerning him if it could be maintained that the John the Baptist of the Mandaean texts were a portrayal independent of the New Testament tradition and not, as it is in general, a dependent one. The present passage is sufficient to prove that he was at least not forgotten, Acts and especially John show indirectly that his relation to Jesus is still in need of clarification (cf. also Matt xi 2–19 par.).

COMMENT

The narrative about Apollos, a Jew who knew only John's baptism, was naturally followed by a description of the twelve disciples who, baptized with John's baptism, knew nothing about the Holy Spirit. During Paul's absence, Priscilla and Aquila had helped Apollos to a deeper understanding of Christianity. In this case, it is Paul who, on his return from a journey through the hilly interior of Asia Minor, teaches the twelve Ephesians. To anyone who has followed in the steps of the apostle from Antioch to Ephesus, it would seem unnecessary to doubt this interpretation. It is Phrygia and the Galatian land, which are mentioned here but with a change in wording characteristic of Luke.

In Ephesus as well as in other places where no thorough missionary work had yet been performed, one found, as Paul did, people affected by Christianity and called disciples but who revealed severe shortcomings with regard to their understanding of Christian doctrine. Paul's question about the Holy Spirit makes their deficiencies plain: they have never even heard of such a Spirit, for their baptism had been John's. Paul then explains John's vocation: his was a baptism of repentance accompanied by his proclamation of the coming Jesus (see xiii 24 f.). Now that this expectation has been fulfilled, his anticipatory baptism is superseded, and Jesus' baptism is now in its place. After hearing this, the twelve Ephesians have themselves baptized with the baptism of Jesus; Paul lays his hands on them, whereupon they receive the Holy Spirit, speak many tongues, and prophesy.

53. PAUL'S PREACHING IN EPHESUS AND HIS DEFEAT OF THE MAGICIANS
(xix 8–20)

XIX 8 Then Paul went to the synagogue, and for three months he spoke boldly, conversing and trying to explain what the kingdom of God was. 9 But since some were hardened and would not believe, while speaking evil of "the way" to the crowd, he left them and took away the disciples, and every day he debated in the school of Tyrannus. 10 This continued for two years, so that all who lived in the province of Asia, both Jews and Greeks, heard the word of the Lord.

11 God also wrought unusually powerful deeds by the hands of Paul, 12 so that they even took scarves or garments from his body to the sick, and their diseases vanished, and the evil spirits left them. 13 Some of the wandering Jewish exorcists also tried invoking the name of the Lord Jesus over those who had evil spirits, saying: "I conjure you by that Jesus Paul preaches." 14 There were seven "sons" of some Jewish high priest or other, named Sceva, who did this. 15 But the evil spirit answered and said to them: "Jesus I know, and Paul I have heard of; but you, who are you?" 16 Then the man who had the evil spirit leaped at them, overpowered them, and gained the advantage over them, so that they fled out of the house naked and wounded. 17 This became known to everyone, Jews and Greeks, living in Ephesus, so that fear fell upon them all, and the name of the Lord Jesus was praised. 18 Many of those who believed came to confess and tell of their use of magical spells. 19 Many of those who had practiced magic collected their books and burned them in the sight of everybody. Their value was estimated and found to be fifty thousand silver drachmas. 20 In the strength of the Lord the word prospered and gained power.

NOTES

xix 8–10. *school of Tyrannus.* As in Corinth (xviii 7), the apostle found a suitable meeting place for the now homeless Christian congregation. Thus two years passed which, together with the three months in the synagogue (vs. 8) and "for a time" mentioned in vs. 22, might approximate the "three years" of xx 31.

All who lived in the province of Asia . . . heard the word of the Lord. This phrase does not mean as much as the expression used previously, that they had "received the word of God," and it has not been used about any other missionary work in a single city. A comparison with the description of Paul's work in Corinth shows the difference.

Except for the following account of the silversmiths' demonstration against the apostle (vss. 23–40), we have no material to illustrate the results of the mission other than the names of three churches in the province of Asia, namely, Colossae, Laodicea, and Hierapolis (Col iv 13). As all three were in the same region, there is reason for thinking that during Paul's stay in Ephesus churches were founded in other places.

It was while Paul was in Ephesus that he had great trouble with the church in Corinth. His first "lost letter" (inferred from I Cor v 9–11 and a fragment of which may be preserved in II Cor vi 14–vii 1) and our First Corinthians were followed by a brief visit to the congregation (inferred from II Cor xiii 1 ff.). Paul then wrote the "severe letter" in which he demanded the submission of the congregation (inferred from II Cor ii 4, 9 and vii 8)—a letter which has been lost though a fragment of it may be preserved in II Cor x–xiii. When the congregation yielded, Second Corinthians followed, in which the past was discussed, the collection for Jerusalem resumed, and the apostle's visit to Corinth in the near future anticipated. Luke does not speak of the persecutions by the Jews Paul suffered in Ephesus (see NOTE on xx 19). Our knowledge of their severity depends once more on Paul's own letters (I Cor xv 32; II Cor i 8–11).

11–12. Just as God provided that Paul should preach unhindered, so he also allowed Paul to perform unusually powerful works.

13–17. Jewish exorcists who knew of Paul's miracles tried to imitate him by intoning the name of Jesus over those possessed by demons (cf. Mark ix 38 par.) saying as precisely as possible: "the Jesus about whom Paul preaches."

some Jewish high priest . . . named Sceva. We know of no such person. The name Sceva is itself not Jewish. As we have seen (NOTE on iv 5–6), many priests of high rank were given the title without ever having officiated as high priest. The exorcists might very well have claimed descent from such a high-ranking family without any right to it; nor were they necessarily brothers.

they fled . . . naked and wounded. He who tries to conquer evil spirits is in danger; he must confront evil itself and either win or lose. The name and power of Jesus brought light into the darkness of human misery and called forth simultaneously terror and praise.

18–20. Ephesus was known as the city of the magicians. Just as it was natural for Paul to speak with philosophers in Athens, so it was equally natural for him to meet magicians in Ephesus. Nor was it strange that among the newly converted Christians there should be many who as pagans used magical arts. Where Christ was, there was no room for magic, and now they not only confessed to their sinful use of demonic names and powers, but they burned their magic books in an act of faith.

COMMENT

In Ephesus Paul resumed the mission with the synagogue begun on his passage from Corinth to Syria (xviii 19–21) which had been carried on in his absence by the Christians (xviii 26). For three months the apostle preached and disputed boldly about the kingdom of God, but then, as elsewhere in other cities, the Jews became stubborn and mocked "the way." He therefore left the synagogue and for two years held forth in the school of Tyrannus, with the result that all who lived in the province of Asia, both Jews and Greeks, heard about Jesus Christ.

Together as usual with the preaching of the word were acts. Worked through Paul, they were even called extraordinary. Their repute led people to remove small pieces of clothing that had been in contact with Paul and to use them to perform miracles. In their conjurings Jewish exorcists tried to reproduce the name of Jesus, in the same way as heathen magicians tried to imitate the Ineffable Name, as we know from Greek magical papyri. Although they used Jesus' name with bad results, the name became known, and was both feared and praised. Among the recently converted Christians likewise, there were people who had formerly used magical arts; they now came to confess their sins and burn their magical books.

In Palestine as well as elsewhere, primitive Christianity was confronted by and in danger of being confused with the legerdemain of magicians and exorcists. If the Christians wanted to follow their Lord and Master, they were obliged to make the distinction clear. Magicians, Gentile and Jewish, shared with Jesus and his disciples one great compassion: both were concerned with the endless misery of the world and its incurable diseases, the sufferings physical or mental in nature that ruined lives and the unflagging will of the afflicted to conquer their distress. Many of the sick had already been to physicians and had not been cured. But they and their relatives did not give up hope. Their need was so great that they resorted to all possible means and consulted exorcists who knew the secret and terrifying names—and some, indeed, were cured.

How great this need was may be realized from the gospels' numerous accounts of the crowds that flocked together around Jesus bringing with them the sick and suffering (Matt iv 23–25 par.). In individual scenes, we see four relatives or companions arrive carrying a paralytic who later rises up and goes home (Matt ix 1–8 par.), or the hopeless sufferers themselves call out to him— the blind who are given sight (Matt ix 27–31), the untouchable lepers who are cleansed (Luke xvii 11–19), or a demoniac who is restored to sound mind (Mark v 13 par.). And the disciples continued the task Jesus had begun. Thus the preaching of the Gospel became a great spiritual movement accompanied by won-drous healings and powerful deeds. Just as hopeless sufferers reached for Jesus' clothes in order to be healed by the power emanating from him (the suffering woman, Matt ix 20–22 par.), so in Ephesus clothing Paul had worn was taken to the sufferers, and illnesses were cured and demons exorcised.

Of course, one may assume that such miracles cannot occur, but it cannot be doubted that they were of decisive importance to primitive Christianity. We shall not be able to understand the latter unless we take the accounts of these healings seriously.

54. THE DEMONSTRATION OF THE SILVERSMITHS
(xix 21–40)

XIX 21 After these events, Paul made up his mind to travel to Jerusalem by way of Macedonia and Achaia, and said: "After I have been there, I must visit Rome also." 22 He sent two of his helpers, namely Timothy and Erastus, to Macedonia while he himself stayed for a time in the province of Asia.

23 At this time there arose a considerable stir because of "the way." 24 For a man named Demetrius, a silversmith, brought a good deal of business to craftsmen by the manufacture of silver shrines of Artemis. 25 He called together these craftsmen and the workmen who were engaged in this business, and said: "You know, fellow craftsmen, that we earn a good living by this work, 26 but you see and hear tell that not only in Ephesus but almost throughout the whole province of Asia this Paul has led a great many people astray, persuading them that handmade objects are not gods. 27 There is danger, not only that this craft of ours will be discredited, but also that the shrine of the great goddess Artemis will be despised, so that she who is honored by the Asian province and the whole world may even be deposed from her place of high honor."

28 When they heard (this) and were filled with rage, they shouted: "Great is Artemis of the Ephesians!" 29 The city was filled with confusion, so that all rushed to the theater, dragging the Macedonians Gaius and Aristarchus, who were Paul's traveling companions, with them. 30 When Paul wanted to go to the assembly the disciples would not allow him, 31 and some of the Asiarchs, who were his friends, sent word to him asking him not to go to the theater. 32 Now, some shouted one thing, some another, for it was a very confused assembly, and most of them did not know why they were gathered. 33 Members of the crowd explained the matter to Alexander when the

Jews pushed him forward, and Alexander made a gesture with his hand and tried to offer a plea before the assembly. 34 But when they realized that he was a Jew, they all shouted out together for nearly two hours: "Great is Artemis of the Ephesians!"

35 Then the city scribe succeeded in quieting the crowd and said: "Ephesians, who is here who does not know that the city of the Ephesians is the guardian of the great Artemis and the image that fell from heaven? 36 Since this is indisputable, then, you should remain calm and do nothing rash. 37 You have brought these people (here) though they have neither desecrated the temple nor blasphemed our goddess. 38 If Demetrius and his craftsmen have a case against anyone, there are court sittings and there are proconsuls. Let them bring actions against each other (there). 39 But if you seek something else, it can be settled at the lawful people's assembly. 40 We are even in danger of being accused of rioting because of what—for no reason—has taken place today, and we shall not be able to account for this crowd." When he had said this he dismissed the assembly.

NOTES

xix 21–22. Luke's information in this passage is confirmed by Rom xv 23–26. As previously mentioned, messengers usually traveled in pairs (see NOTE on ix 36–42). Paul planned to travel through Macedonia and Achaia, but sent two fellow workers no farther than Macedonia. At this time, the controversy between Paul and the church of Corinth was not ended; his letter of reconciliation was written after his departure from Ephesus. The journey to Macedonia could have been undertaken in order to complete the collection for Jerusalem. Erastus might, but need not, be identified with the Corinthian official of the same name mentioned in Rom xvi 23 (cf. II Tim iv 20).

23–28. The description of the silversmiths' demonstration against Paul cannot be an account of one of the serious persecutions mentioned by Paul in I Cor xv 32 and II Cor i 8–11 (see NOTE on Acts xx 19). Since only miniature temples made of terra cotta have been found, and none of silver, Luke's account has been doubted on this point. As a substantive which literally means "builder of temples" was used as a title for the guardians of Artemis' temple in Ephesus, Luke may possibly have misinterpreted Demetrius' title as "guardian of the temple" (an inscription from Ephesus dating from the middle of the first century A.D. mentions a "temple builder" Demetrius). This Demetrius is more likely to have made silver statuettes of Artemis than temples. If this is correct, it does not appreciably change the content of the narrative. Neither Demetrius nor the city scribe later exaggerated the importance of Artemis and her temple in Ephesus. The earlier temple had been considered one of the Seven Wonders of the World and the contemporary temple was famous everywhere.

29–31. With growing agitation the silversmiths rushed the theater (which seated about twenty-five thousand people and survives to the present day). They carried along with them two of Paul's fellow workers, the Macedonians Gaius and Aristarchus. In xx 4, Aristarchus is referred to as a Thessalonian and Gaius a Thessalonian or a native of Derbe. There may also have been more than one Gaius, and an Aristarchus is mentioned as Paul's fellow prisoner in xxvii 2 (cf. Col iv 10; Philem 24). It might seem as if the surging crowd had swept bystanders along into the theater (such as Alexander and other Jews, vs. 33), but the city scribe's words about the crowd that had brought *people* (*here*) *though they* [Paul's helpers] *have neither desecrated the temple nor blasphemed against our goddess* suggest that it was a deliberate action directed against people known as Christians. There is no indication that anyone was harmed. While this was happening to his two fellow workers, it must have been difficult to keep Paul at home in the house. It should be remembered that his many opponents in the city were one of his reasons for remaining there (I Cor xvi 9). Friends managed to keep him from making straight for the agitated crowd: these were not only his disciples but other friends, *Asiarchs*, the highest ranking priests, present and past, of the imperial cult of emperor worship in the cities of the province of Asia. These cities had formed a union whose essential charge was to secure the actual performance of the official Roman worship. Only the most prominent, wealthy, and aristocratic men of the province were made Asiarchs. It is worth noting not only that Paul had such friends but also that they conducted themselves at such a decisive time as men whose friendship took precedence over religious differences.

32. After the lengthy chorus of speeches, the angry rebellion seemed to have reached its peak. There was no definite trend, but various groups, with different slogans, swelled the ranks of the already confused assembly; many asked why they were here in the theater.

33–34. These verses come as a surprise and appear to be a fragment out of a completely different context. If one were to explain this "fragment" in connection with this narrative, the Jews, Paul's opponents, must have been part of the crowd that desired to maintain the Artemis cult against Paul's aggressive activity. Alexander, one of their number, might in this case have wanted to defend Jewry and to show that it was not party to Paul's attack on the goddess of the city. But whether because of enmity toward the Jews or because of a suspicion that they, like Paul and his followers, were involved in the affair, Alexander was not allowed to speak. The shouting drowned out everything but did nothing to change the uncertainty of the crowd or prevent its dispersal.

35–40. *image that fell from heaven.* Not mentioned in any other source. As well as this one in Ephesus, others were found elsewhere. They were generally meteorites which, unlike the pagan idols Paul inveighed against as made by human hands (vs. 26), were altogether of heavenly origin.

The city scribe listed the places where they would have had a right to present their case. The theater, now occupied by the crowd, was the place where the lawful people's assembly would have met. But the ways and means chosen exposed the city to an accusation of rioting.

The Roman empire ensured peace and order in its cities and among its citizens. The city scribe pointed out that their riotous conduct could cause the loss of their existing privileges of self-government, and thus was able to make the crowd to disperse.

COMMENT

Paul's missionary activity in Ephesus was characterized not only by his victory over the magicians, but also by a decline in the worship of pagan gods so marked that a craft depending on such worship felt itself victimized financially and rose in protest against the apostle's activity. The description of the silversmiths' demonstration follows a statement to the effect that Paul intended to end his stay in Ephesus in order to go by way of Macedonia and Achaia to Jerusalem and afterward to Rome, and to prepare for this journey, two fellow workers were sent to Macedonia. Demetrius, a man well known inside his trade, assembled both craftsmen and workers engaged in the manufacture of small silver Artemis shrines. Up to now, this had been a good business, but in the city as well as in the whole of the province of Asia Paul had "seduced," as they phrased it, many to the belief that what was made by human hands could not be a god. Thus their source of livelihood was endangered, and what was worse, the universal veneration and recognition surrounding the goddess was being undermined. Incited by these words, the silversmiths shouted: "Great is Artemis of the Ephesians!" The agitation spread in the city, and the theater was filled with demonstrators and others who happened to have been carried along with the crowd, among whom were Gaius and Aristarchus, Paul's traveling companions. Both the disciples and some Asiarchs friendly to Paul had made the undaunted debater desist from going to the theater. A certain Jew named Alexander tried to address the crowd but only succeeded in provoking renewed shouting, this time for fully two hours. In this embarrassing situation, it was the city scribe who managed to pour oil on troubled waters and to send the crowd home. In a well-turned speech, he recalled the secure position that the city and the goddess enjoy. There was no reason to bring these men to the theater when they had made no attempt either to desecrate the temple or to offend the goddess. If Demetrius and his craftsmen had a case against anybody, there were court days and proconsuls before whom they could appear and as a last resort there would be the lawful people's assembly. They had from the start managed this affair badly by inexcusably causing a disturbance in the city.

It is no wonder that this account of Paul's great influence in Ephesus and the province of Asia has been questioned by several scholars who consider this scene to be without basis in reality. It is, however, not historically improbable that the apostle could have had such great influence in the city and its vicinity. We have evidence of a similar local expansion of Christianity a half century later. This evidence is distinguished by its source: the Roman governor of Bithynia, Pliny the Younger. In a well-known letter to the emperor Trajan (Epistle X.96, ca. A.D. 112), Pliny speaks of measures to contain Christianity in his province. For, he wrote toward the end of the letter, he had found pagan temples almost deserted, their services fallen out of use, buyers for the meat of the sacrificial animals hard to find . . .

In both the Lucan and Plinian cases, the spread of Christianity and a concomitant decline of pagan worship cannot have been of long duration. Had they been, other sources would confirm them, however scant our knowledge of primitive church history. It is quite possible that in both cases Christianity was experiencing an upsurge that carried many people along with it yet soon spent itself. A wave once it has crested falls into a trough.

55. THE BEGINNING OF PAUL'S SLOW JOURNEY
TO ROME
(xx 1–16)

XX 1 After this uproar had died down, Paul sent for the disciples and, having encouraged them, said good-by and set off for Macedonia. 2 When he had traveled through those regions and had energetically preached and exhorted them (the disciples), he came to Greece. 3 There he stayed three months, intending then to sail for Syria. But when a plot against him was formed among the Jews, he decided to return by way of Macedonia. 4 With him went Sopater, son of Pyrrhus, from Berea; of the Thessalonians, Aristarchus and Secundus; Gaius of Derbe, and Timothy, Tychicus and Trophimus of the Asian province. 5 These went ahead and waited for us at Troas; 6 but we set sail from Philippi after the days of unleavened bread, and joined the others in Troas after five days, and there we stayed for a week.

7 On the first day of the week, when we were assembled to break bread, Paul spoke to them, and because he was resuming his journey next day, he went on talking until midnight. 8 There were many lamps in the upper room where we were assembled. 9 A young man named Eutychus was sitting in the window; he became very drowsy because Paul went on talking so long; and, overcome by sleep, he fell from the third story and was picked up as dead. 10 But Paul went down and threw himself upon him, and when he had put his arms around him he said: "Do not be alarmed, for life is in him." 11 He went upstairs again, broke bread and ate, and talked for a further time, until dawn, and then he left. 12 The boy was brought (up) alive, and this was a great comfort to them.

13 We went ahead on board the ship, and sailed for Assos, where we were to take Paul on board; for this was what he had

decided, wishing himself to go by land. 14 When he had joined us at Assos we took him on board, and so came to Mitylene. 15 We sailed on from there, and the following day were opposite Chios, and next day approached Samos, and the day after that we came to Miletus. 16 Paul had decided to sail past Ephesus, so that he might not be delayed in the province of Asia; for he was in a hurry to be in Jerusalem, if possible, on the day of Pentecost.

NOTES

xx 1–3. It was during the journey in *those regions,* i.e. Macedonia, that Titus joined Paul (II Cor vii 5–16), and that Paul wrote II Corinthians.

Greece. The word "Hellas," seldom used in the NT, probably meant Achaia and thus also Corinth. The letter to the Romans was composed during Paul's stay there. Second Corinthians viii 18–23 and ix 3–5 (cf. Rom xv 25–28) show that Paul had finished the collection for Jerusalem and had assembled representatives of the churches participating in it, so that after a stay of three months he was ready to start his journey to Jerusalem. While the Neutral text sees the Jewish conspiracy as the reason for Paul's decision to travel overland instead of sailing to Syria, in the Western text the conspiracy causes him to leave Greece, but his itinerary is determined by the Holy Spirit.

4–5. Paul's traveling companions are mentioned; Sopater from Berea and Aristarchus (cf. xix 29, xxvii 2) and Secundus from Thessalonica, thus three being from Macedonia. The author of the "we" source also comes from there (see p. XLII).

Such an extension of the traveling suite was exceptional, as all those who were to go with Paul to Jerusalem had been together with the apostle in Corinth and been ready to sail straight from there to Palestine. Gaius was from Derbe and Timothy from the same district (xvi 1), that is from the Galatian churches, and Tychicus and Trophimus were from the province of Asia.

Although we have relatively good information about the collection from the Pauline letters (I Corinthians, II Corinthians, Romans), it is not quite clear which churches participated in the collection. In I Cor xvi 1–5, the Corinthians were requested to collect money in the same way as the Galatians had done. In Rom xv 25–33, where the account of the collection ends, Paul informs the Roman church that Macedonia and Achaia have completed their collections. The crisis in the Galatian churches, which caused Paul to write them a letter, may well have prevented a continuation of the collection there, but the mention of Gaius and Timothy suggests that they had a part in it. In agreement with I Cor xvi 1–5, Paul boasts about the people of Corinth (Achaia) who have been ready with their collection since "last year" (II Cor ix 2), and the Macedonians who, though extremely poor, were yet able to take part in it because of their zeal and prayers (II Cor viii 1–5).

The brethren mentioned in II Cor viii 18–24 were representatives of the churches participating in the collection which were probably situated east or south of Macedonia, either in Derbe and Lystra or in Ephesus and its vicinity, where Paul had started his journey. They might then have been either Gaius and Timothy or Tychicus and Trophimus from Ephesus, who were referred to in II Corinthians, or even quite different persons. Titus, whose name we might have expected after the reference to him in II Cor, is nowhere mentioned in Acts. It should be noted that the words "us" and "we" in xx 5 f. may include several unnamed persons. In other words, there may have been representatives of Achaia and Corinth though none are named. In these places the collection had likewise been beset by difficulties between the congregation and the apostle, but II Cor states that the congregation had asked for peace and had once more started to make collections. The new difficulties, mentioned in II Cor, with the Jewish Christian apostles who had recently arrived might have hindered a collection but this is not very likely.

6–16. *after the days of unleavened bread.* Paul with some of his companions celebrated Passover in Philippi, possibly mentioned merely as an indication of the passage of time. By sailing from Corinth to Palestine on a ship with Jewish pilgrims, Paul would probably have reached Jerusalem in time for the Passover celebration, but getting wind, no doubt, of a plot to kill him once on board ship, he chose the slower roundabout route via Macedonia. Thus the festival that he was now aiming to attend was the day of Pentecost, fifty days after Passover (vs. 16). The sea route from Philippi followed the western coast of Asia Minor and the ships called at only a few places on the way.

Troas was a Hellenistic city not far from the old Troy.

Eutychus was killed by his fall and was raised from the dead by Paul, but the miracle was told in such a quiet manner that it is not surprising that others made little of it. Paul's conduct toward the dead boy is slightly reminiscent of Elijah's (I Kings xvii 21–22) and Elisha's (II Kings iv 34–35).

COMMENT

After the uproar in Ephesus had died down, Paul decided to begin the journey planned in xix 21 by going to Macedonia and Greece. It has generally been assumed, and rightly so, that he was in Greece the winter of A.D. 56–57 ending his three-month stay in Corinth. The journey from Ephesus and through Macedonia would then be the journey mentioned in II Cor ii 12–13; vii 5–6.

Afterward Paul traveled by land—the same way he had come— on account of a Jewish conspiracy against his life. After celebrating Passover in Philippi, Paul did his utmost to reach Jerusalem for Pentecost. A detailed description is given of the various stages and day-by-day progress of the voyage down the coast of Asia Minor to Miletus. Special care is lavished on the visit to Troas, where presumably Paul raised Eutychus from the dead. Ephesus, however, is bypassed; Paul could not risk the possibility of being delayed there, though he knew that he would never see the congregation there again (see next Section).

Paul had this time an unusually large number of traveling companions—at least eight men—which presumably indicates that the churches contributing to the collection had also sent their representatives to Jerusalem.

We have the apostle's own view of his journey in Rom xv 23–32. The statements there are not at variance with Luke's remarks in this passage, except for the fact that Luke does neither mention the collection—thus offering no explanation for Paul's visit to Jerusalem—nor indicate the purpose behind Paul's visit to Rome.

56. PAUL'S FAREWELL ADDRESS AT MILETUS
(xx 17–38)

XX 17 From Miletus he sent word to Ephesus, and had the elders of the church brought to him. 18 When they had come to him, he said to them: "You know what my way of life has been among you always, from the first day I came into the province of Asia, 19 serving the Lord in all humility, with tears and trials which I suffered from the persecutions of the Jews. 20 I did not shrink from preaching to you and telling you of all that is good, publicly and privately, 21 bearing witness both to Jews and to Greeks that they should turn to God in repentance and believe in our Lord Jesus. 22 And now, listen carefully: compelled by the Spirit I am about to travel to Jerusalem, without knowing what will happen to me there, 23 except this, that in every city the Holy Spirit bears witness to me and says that chains and tribulations await me. 24 Yet I consider my life not worth mentioning, if only I may complete my allotted span and the ministry I received from the Lord Jesus, that is, of bearing witness to the gospel of God's grace. 25 Now listen closely to what I say: I know that you will not see my face again, you among whom I traveled preaching the kingdom. 26 Therefore I declare to you this day that I am free from any man's blood,* 27 for I did not shrink from preaching to you the whole will of God. 28 Look to yourselves and to the whole flock, of which the Holy Spirit has made you overseers, to guard the church of God, which he won for himself by the blood of his own (Son). 29 I know that after my departure savage wolves will force their way in among you, and they will not spare the flock. 30 Even among you men will arise who will distort the truth in order to win over the disciples. 31 Be on your guard

* The expression "I am free from any man's blood" *may* be a very early modification of an original "I am not responsible for any man's sin." In the oral Greek form, an haplography between the words for *sin* and *blood* is easily understandable, i.e., *haimatos, hamartias*—W.F.A. and C.S.M.

therefore, remembering that for three years I never ceased, night or day, to warn each one of you with tears. 32 Now I commit you to the Lord and to the word of his grace, which is able to build up and grant the reward of inheritance to all who are sanctified. 33 Of no one have I asked silver, gold, or clothing. 34 You know yourselves that these hands have earned what was needful for me and for those who were with me. 35 I have shown you in every way that one ought to work like this, and so help those who have not the necessary strength, and that you should remember the words of the Lord Jesus, 'It is more blessed to give than to receive.'"

36 And when he had said this, he knelt down with them all and prayed. 37 But they all broke into weeping. They embraced Paul and kissed him, 38 distressed most of all by his saying that they would not see his face again. They went with him to the ship.

NOTES

xx 17–18. Paul looks back upon his stay in Ephesus (*Asia*, vs. 18) and his conscientious fulfillment of his apostolic calling there. We also find such retrospective accounts of his relations with one of his churches in I Thess and II Cor. The elders of Ephesus, to whom he addresses himself, are in the speech called "overseers" (vs. 28) which points to an earlier more casual use of official title.

19–21. *persecutions of the Jews*. Not mentioned in Acts xix which, however, does mention that Paul left the synagogue and was forced to carry on his discussions in the school of Tyrannus because of their obduracy (xix 9). It is also stated that Demetrius stirred up trouble because the silversmiths were suffering losses on account of the Christian movement that was passing over Ephesus (xix 23–41; cf. vs. 10).

Besides Paul's speech, other texts testify to the fact that in Ephesus Paul was exposed to persecutions of the most serious kind, which cannot be identified with the disturbance started by the silversmiths. In I Cor xv 32, Paul says: "What do I gain if, humanly speaking, I fought with beasts at Ephesus?" And in II Cor i 6–11, Paul tells about "our distress" in the province of Asia where he (or they) had given up hope of escaping death, but had been saved by God from this deadly peril. We can here take Paul's words in the address as a reference to one or both of these deadly perils. It is probable that the persecutors were the Jews, although we have previously seen that Luke was capable of ascribing persecutions to them which were not necessarily their work (see Note on ix 23–25).

22–25. In this passage Paul turns from the past to the immediate circumstances confronting him. His present journey was undertaken at the command of the Holy Spirit. Paul's other journeys had likewise been directed from above, for instance by negative instructions (cf. xvi 6–7). Under such orders Paul now faces an uncertain future. In xxi 4, the disciples, through the Holy Spirit, urge him not to go to Jerusalem, and in xxi 10–14 the prophet Agabus announces that the apostle will be bound by the Jews and handed over to the Gentiles. There is reason to believe that in this speech Paul is referring to similar messages received from the Holy Spirit in the cities where he had already visited the congregations. But in this respect Paul remains firm in his obedience to the Holy Spirit. He does not consider his own life of any value, but only wants to be able to complete his course and the ministry he received from the Lord Jesus (cf. II Tim iv 7). The apostle's readiness to risk his life in the service of God is mentioned in Acts xv 26, xxi 13; Philip i 20–26, ii 17; I Thess ii 8.

26–31. As one who is taking his leave on his way to imprisonment and death, he testifies that he is free from any man's blood, cf. Testament of Levi x 2, xiv 2. In connection with vs. 27, it may be remembered that according to Gal i 10 (cf. ii 6), the Judaizers assumed that to please the Gentiles Paul had neglected to preach the whole of the Gospel, omitting the part that dealt with circumcision and obedience to the law of Moses.

The Holy Spirit has made the elders "overseers" in the church of God, which God won for himself by the blood of his own (Son).

Paul foretells that two things will happen after his death: from without savage wolves will bring bloody persecution upon the congregation (cf. Deut xxxi 29; Testament of Joseph xx 1), and within there will be apostasy leading to false doctrines (cf. Jubilees vii 26–27). The expected Antichrist had precisely these two aspects: he was the world power that persecuted and the false prophet that tempted (the church) to apostasy (Rev xiii has both aspects, II Thess ii 3–13 only the latter). Therefore the elders must be vigilant and remember the example of the apostle's pastoral work.

32–38. With such a future in mind, in which the apostle will no longer be able to intervene personally in favor of his churches, he commits the Ephesian congregation to Christ. He once more reminds them of his conduct while with them. He had worked for his own support in Ephesus —and that of his companions—and had thereby been an example: one who was not a burden to others, but who was able to help the weak in accordance with Jesus' saying: "It is more blessed to give than to receive." This saying is not found in the canonical gospels and must be termed an *agraphon*, i.e. a saying of Jesus recorded outside the four gospels.

COMMENT

When the ship called at Miletus, Paul had the opportunity of sending for the elders from Ephesus and addressing them. His speech is an example of a farewell address, a definite form both within and outside the Bible. Farewell speeches occur in the Old Testament (e.g. Joshua's in Josh xxiv 1–24; Samuel's in I Sam xii; and Moses' in Deuteronomy xxix–xxx), and they are even more frequently found in the Old Testament Apocrypha and Pseudepigrapha (e.g. IV Ezra xiv 18 ff.; I Enoch xci 1–19; Jubilees vii; the Testaments of the Twelve Patriarchs; and the Assumption of Moses). In the New Testament, farewell speeches are found in II Pet i, ii; II Tim iv 6–22; Luke xxii 21–38; and John xiii–xvii.

After the elders of Ephesus gathered around him, Paul began his farewell speech by stressing his blameless course of life in the province of Asia. Now the Holy Spirit was guiding him toward Jerusalem, where prison and tribulations awaited him. He knew that he would not see them again. He emphasized that he was guiltless with regard to them, for he had not withheld anything which he had been commissioned to preach. Now the elders from Ephesus must watch over the church which after his death would be attacked from the outside by dangerous wolves that would not spare the flock, and from among themselves dangerous heretics would arise. They should then think of the example he had set during his three-year stay in Ephesus. He committed them to the Lord and reminded them of how he had worked with his hands to provide the necessities of life for himself and his companions.

In summing up, it can be said that Paul's farewell address has these four characteristic features: (a) before he traveled farther on his way to death, he gathers the elders from Ephesus so that in this, his last address, he might give them definite instructions; (b) he addresses those whom he was about to leave behind; (c) he presents himself as an example in his relation to the church and also in his financial independence; and (d) he predicts the persecutions that the congregation would have to endure, and the false teachers that would appear after his death.

The numerous parallels to the Pauline letters in this address were mentioned in the NOTES.

57. FROM MILETUS TO CAESAREA
(xxi 1–14)

XXI ¹ When we had torn ourselves away from them and set sail, we came straight ahead to Cos, the next day to Rhodes, and from there to Patara. ² When we had found a ship bound for Phoenicia we went aboard and set out. ³ We sighted Cyprus, and leaving it on the left sailed toward Syria and touched at Tyre; for there the ship was to unload its cargo. ⁴ We found the disciples and stayed there for a week. Through the Spirit they told Paul not to travel on to Jerusalem. ⁵ When we had completed our days there, we went out and set off, all of them with their womenfolk and children going with us out of the city. We knelt down on the shore and prayed, ⁶ then said good-by to one another, and we went aboard the ship while they returned to their own homes.

⁷ We then came from Tyre to Ptolemais, and so concluded the voyage. We greeted the brethren and stayed one day with them. ⁸ Next day we set out and came to Caesarea, and entered the house of Philip the evangelist, one of the seven, and stayed with him. ⁹ He had four daughters, who were virgins and ecstatics. ¹⁰ During our long stay a man came down from Judea, an ecstatic named Agabus; ¹¹ and coming to us he took Paul's belt, bound his own feet and hands, and said: "This is what the Holy Spirit says: 'So shall the Jews in Jerusalem bind the man to whom this belt belongs and hand him over into the hands of Gentiles.'" ¹² When we heard this, we and the people living there begged him not to go up to Jerusalem. ¹³ But Paul answered: "What are you doing, with your weeping and your attempts to make me faint-hearted? I am ready not only to be bound, but also to die in Jerusalem for the name of the Lord Jesus." ¹⁴ Since he refused to be dissuaded, we ceased and said: "The Lord's will be done."

Notes

xxi 1–6. Paul's voyage continued from Miletus without stop until in Patara he and his traveling companions changed over to a ship bound for Phoenicia, with Tyre as its first port of call. During his visit there, Paul got in touch with the local congregation which urged him not to go up to Jerusalem because of the Holy Spirit's prediction that his life would be imperiled there. When the ship had unloaded her cargo, Paul went on board again after taking a solemn leave of the congregation.

7–9. The voyage continued to Ptolemais, the present-day Acre; its importance to shipping in our day has been taken over by Haifa. After a day's stay with the congregation there Paul went—by ship or by land —to Caesarea (see Note on x 1 f.). The apostle stayed with Philip the evangelist—it is impossible to determine the exact meaning of this title —who had four virgin daughters known for their prophecies. No mention is made in vss. 10 ff. of the fact that Philip and Agabus have been mentioned before (viii 4–40 and xi 27–30 respectively).

10–14. *Judea* appears to refer to the mountainous country of Judea, possibly Jerusalem (see Note on x 37). Agabus performed a prophetic act (e.g. Isa xx 2 ff.; Jer xiii 1–11), but his prophecy was not fulfilled in a literal sense. The Jews neither bound Paul nor handed him over to the Gentiles; they did, however, attempt to lynch him in the temple, and the Romans, in order to protect him, put him in prison (xxi 27–30). The present formulation (vs. 11) may well have been an attempt to make Paul's trial seem more like Jesus' (Matt xvii 22, xx 19) (cf. p. LXXVII).

Comment

From Miletus Paul went on to Caesarea by way of Tyre. In both these cities the Holy Spirit spoke to Paul and predicted that his life would be in danger in Jerusalem; he must not "travel on to Jerusalem" (vs. 4), where the Jews shall bind him and "hand him over into the hands of the Gentiles," as the prophet Agabus said in Caesarea (vs. 11). Paul did not allow himself to be influenced, but was ready to go on to the end in the service of the Lord.

58. PAUL IN THE CHURCH OF JERUSALEM
(xxi 15–26)

XXI 15 After this we got ready and traveled up to Jerusalem, 16 some of the disciples from Caesarea also going with us, so that they might take us to someone with whom we might stay as guests, Mnason, a Cypriot and a disciple from the early days.

17 When we came to Jerusalem the brethren received us joyfully. 18 On the following day Paul went with us to James, and all the elders assembled. 19 When Paul had greeted them, he recounted in detail what God had done among the Gentiles through his ministry. 20 When they heard it they praised God and then said to him: "You see, brother, how many tens of thousands have believed among the Jews. But they are all devoted to the Law. 21 They have been told this of you: that you teach all the Jews living among the Gentiles to renounce Moses, telling them that they are not to circumcise their children or live according to the customs. 22 What now? They will certainly hear that you have come. 23 Do then as we advise: There are here with us four men who are under a Nazirite vow. 24 Take them with you, and purify yourself together with them, and pay for them to have their heads shaved, and all will then understand that what they had heard about you was not true, but that you maintain the Law and observe it yourself also. 25 As for those Gentiles who have believed, we have written, having reached a decision, that they are to avoid meat that has been offered to idols, blood, what has been strangled, and sexual impurity." 26 Then Paul took the men with him, purified himself with them on the following day, and went into the temple, giving notice of the end of the days of purification when each man's offering would be brought.

59. PAUL ARRESTED BY THE ROMANS
(xxi 27–40)

XXI 27 But when the seven days were nearly ended, the Asian Jews caught sight of Paul in the temple, and they stirred up the whole crowd, and laid hands upon him, 28 shouting: "Come and help, Israelites! Here is the man who teaches all men everywhere against the people, the Law, and this place; moreover he has brought Greeks into the temple and defiled this holy place." 29 For they had earlier seen Trophimus of Ephesus with him outside in the city, and they thought that Paul had brought him into the temple. 30 So the whole city was roused, and a crowd gathered. They seized Paul and dragged him out of the temple, and at once the doors were shut. 31 While they tried to kill him, a report was made to the tribune of the cohort: "The whole of Jerusalem is in an uproar." 32 He ran down to them at once with soldiers and centurions, and when they saw the tribune and the soldiers, they stopped beating Paul. 33 When the tribune arrived, he seized him and gave orders that he should be bound with two chains. He inquired who he might be, and what he had done. 34 But some in the crowd shouted one thing, some another, and since he could gain no clear information because of the uproar, he gave orders that Paul should be taken up to the barracks. 35 When he was near the steps things got so far out of hand that the soldiers had to carry him because of the violence of the crowd. 36 For the mob was following and shouting: "Away with him!"

37 Just as Paul was about to be led into the barracks, he said to the tribune: "Am I allowed to say something to you?" He said: "Do you speak Greek? 38 Then you are not the Egyptian who some time ago stirred up trouble and led the four thousand extremists out into the desert?" 39 Paul said: "I am a Jew from Tarsus, citizen of a considerable city in Cilicia; I beg you,

let me speak to the people." [40] When he had given permission, Paul came forward on the steps and gestured with his hand to the people. When a deep silence had fallen, he began to speak in Hebrew and said:

NOTES

xxi 27–29. The attack on Paul resulted from the expected hostility mentioned by him in Rom xv 31 and feared by James at Paul's arrival (xxi 20–22), and when it did occur, it was once more Jews and not Jewish Christians who sought his life. While the Court of the Gentiles was open to everybody, to bring Gentiles into the temple was a crime punishable by death and any Gentile found there paid with his life. In order to warn everybody against entering the inner courts notices were posted enjoining the prohibition with special mention of the penalty. If these Jews had heard anything of Paul's ideas about the collection for Jerusalem and "the Gentiles" (i.e. the Gentile Christians) who in the last days were to bring gifts to Jerusalem as foretold by the prophets (cf. Isa ii 2 ff., lx 5 f.; Micah iv 1 ff.), it is natural to suppose that they had understood that the Gentile church would bring the collection to the congregation in Jerusalem, that it would be literally a procession of Gentiles going up to the temple to deliver the money collected.

30–32. There is every indication that the episode did not develop very quickly. The news had spread into the city; the temple authorities had had time to remove the man from their area and the Roman military headquarters had been alerted.

If there were several centurions it may mean that each of them led a hundred men—in other words, a considerable force to stop the disturbance. A tribune commanded a cohort of four to six hundred men (see NOTE on x 1) and here he was the commander in Jerusalem, having under him a cohort fortified by, *inter alia,* cavalry.

33–38. The clamor for Paul's death recalls the people's clamor against Jesus (Luke xxiii 18; John xix 15). It was repeated against Paul in xxii 28. The tribune had hoped to seize a very different person, an Egyptian who had stirred up trouble and had led four thousand Sicarians out into the desert. This Egyptian in Josephus (*Jewish War* II.xiii.3), is a charlatan, who gaining about 30,000 followers, marched them from the desert to the Mount of Olives, where Felix the procurator awaited them. Most were killed or captured, but the Egyptian himself escaped. Josephus does not refer to the Egyptian as a Sicarian, but mentions him after them. The Sicarians were an extremist group within the Zealot party actively working for deliverance from the Roman yoke, among other means by assassinations—from which they got their name (Lat. *sica* means dagger).

39. *Citizen of a considerable city* is a common expression for one's native city; Josephus uses a similar expression of his family in the opening words of his autobiography.

Despite his bodily injuries Paul was able to make a speech and his purpose seems to have been to soothe the crowd; at the beginning he succeeds in this, and at the same time in defending himself against the charges which were the cause of the disturbance.

COMMENT

When the week for the purification was nearly over, the storm broke in the temple. The opposition against Paul flares up and an attempt to kill him is made by Jews from the province of Asia, who knowing Paul by sight, had recognized him in the city in the company of a Gentile Christian, Trophimus of Ephesus (cf. xx 4). When they saw Paul in the temple they supposed that Trophimus was still with him. These Jews seize Paul shouting accusations against him, accusations which in essence covered the charges to be made at the trial that follows: this man has preached everywhere in the world against the (Jewish) people, the Law, and the temple; he has taken Gentiles into the temple, thereby desecrating it. This outcry throws the whole of Jerusalem into a commotion, and Paul, dragged out of the temple, is now attacked by an agitated mob about to lynch him. The Romans, always on the alert, having followed the events in the temple and in the city, now intervene and rescue him. The Roman soldiers arrest him; and bound by chains Paul is led, and in the end carried, up the steps to the fortress of Antonia, the furious crowd pressing against him. Here Paul asks the tribune for permission to address the crowd, which is granted.

60. PAUL'S SPEECH FROM THE STEPS OF THE FORTRESS
(xxii 1–21)

XXII ¹ "Brethren and fathers, listen to my defense to you now." ² When they heard that he spoke to them in Hebrew, they calmed down still more. He said: ³ "I am a Jew, born in Tarsus in Cilicia, but brought up in this city, carefully instructed in the law of the fathers at the feet of Gamaliel, and I was zealous for God, as all of you are today. ⁴ I persecuted this 'way,' often to the death, by binding both men and women and delivering them to prisons, ⁵ as the high priest also—and the whole presbytery—can witness on my behalf. I was given letters by them, and went to the brethren in Damascus to bring those also who were there to Jerusalem as prisoners for punishment.

⁶ "But it happened, as I was on my journey and approaching Damascus, that about noon a bright light suddenly shone round me from heaven. ⁷ I fell on the ground, and I heard a voice say to me: 'Saul, Saul, why do you persecute me?' ⁸ I answered: 'Who are you, Lord?' He said to me: 'I am Jesus of Nazareth, whom you persecute.' ⁹ But those who were with me indeed saw the light, but did not hear the voice of the one who spoke to me. ¹⁰ I said: 'What shall I do, Lord?' The Lord said to me: 'Get up and go on to Damascus, and there you will be told about all it has been decided you are to do.' ¹¹ As now I could not see because of the brightness of this light, I came to Damascus, led by the hand by those who were with me. ¹² But a man called Ananias, a devout man according to the Law, and of good reputation among all the Jews living there, ¹³ came and stood by me and said to me: 'Brother Saul, open your eyes!' And I looked up at him at that same moment. ¹⁴ He said: 'The God of our fathers chose you to learn his will, to see the Righteous One, and to hear a voice from his lips; ¹⁵ for you are to be

his witness to all mankind of what you have seen and heard.
16 And now, why do you hesitate? Get up and be baptized,
and your sins will thus be washed away in calling upon his
name.'

17 "It happened, when I had returned to Jerusalem and was
praying in the temple, that I fell into a state of ecstasy, 18 and
I saw the Lord. He said to me: 'Make haste, and leave Jerusalem
at once, for they will not accept your testimony about me.'
19 I said: 'Lord, here of all places they know that I imprisoned those who believed in you, or beat them in the
synagogues. 20 When the blood of your martyr Stephen was
shed, I too was there and agreed to it, and I looked after the
clothes of those who killed him.' 21 But he said to me: 'Depart,
for I will send you far away to the Gentiles.'"

NOTES

xxii 1–2. This speech is the second of the three accounts of Paul's
call. As usual Luke varies his presentation so that this version deviates
clearly from the version in either ch. ix or ch. xxvi. One is surprised at
Paul's use of *brethren and fathers* in addressing the people when one observes that he uses only "brethren" in addressing the members of the Sanhedrin (xxiii). As he spoke in Hebrew, and not as had been expected, in
Greek, which would have been natural in this international city, the
people in front of him became even more quiet.

3. Here the apostle spoke of his Jewish past (on Paul's education,
see Appendix VIII), his birth in Tarsus, his childhood in Jerusalem, his
studies with Gamaliel and his zeal much like that displayed by his
listeners with regard to himself on this day.

4–5. In the next episode of his Jewish past, he describes himself as
a persecutor. He refers to his activities in Jerusalem and calls the high
priest and the Sanhedrin as witnesses to this (cf. ix 1–2), stressing the
special initiative he had shown in extending the persecution to Damascus.

6–16. In his description of his call we notice the strong light at noon
in vs. 6, recalling Deut xxviii 28–29. In vs. 9 his companions saw
the light but did not hear the voice that spoke to him; this is also the
best interpretation of xxvi 13–14. In ix 7 the companions hear the voice
but see no one.

An account is given of Ananias' coming to Paul in Damascus, as in
ch. ix, but the description of him here is that of a Jew highly respected
by all the Jews who said that it was *the God of our fathers* who

had revealed himself to him. Paul emphasizes Ananias' devotion according to the Law and does not give us any information about Jesus and the Gentiles. Afterward when the storm had broken we realize why this is so. The speaker had steered a cautious and skillful course, but at his first forthright words about his mission, the crowd in front of the steps rise against him.

17–21. At the end of this passage we first hear about the Gentiles. When Paul returned to Jerusalem (presumably under the same conditions as in ix 26–30), he fell into an ecstasy while praying in the temple and saw *the Lord* (*Jesus* is mentioned by name only in vs. 8), who ordered him to leave Jerusalem in great haste, because its inhabitants were not willing to receive Paul's testimony about him. Here we find a sequence familiar in Acts: Paul preaches to the Jews, they are not willing to receive his testimony, and so Paul turns to the Gentiles. Paul's answers to Jesus (vss. 19–20) were also of current interest in the present situation. He thought that since he had once been of the same mind as his listeners and had taken an active part in the persecution of the church at the time of Stephen's death, they would surely listen to him. But Jesus simply ordered him to leave and go to the Gentiles.

COMMENT

The ill-treated apostle is able to address the crowd at this unusual outdoor meeting. As in xxvi 4–18 (cf. ix 1–19a), his topic was his apostolic call. He handles the speech with great caution as is evident, for instance, in the description of Ananias. Paul succeeds for a time in keeping his audience quiet, but when he mentions that in the temple the Lord sent him to the Gentiles in distant lands, the uproar begins once more.

61. PAUL AND THE ROMAN TRIBUNE
(xxii 22–29)

XXII 22 They listened to him as far as this assertion, then they raised their voices and said: "Away with such a man from the earth! For it is not right that he should live." 23 As they shouted, threw aside their clothes, and hurled dust into the air, 24 the tribune ordered that he be taken into the barracks, adding that he was to be questioned under the lash so as to find out why they shouted against him in this way. 25 But when they began to tie him up to be flogged, Paul said to the centurion who was standing (there): "Are you allowed to flog a man who is a Roman citizen, and without trial at that?" 26 When the centurion heard (this), he went to the tribune, reported (it), and said: "What is this you are doing? This man is a Roman citizen." 27 The tribune went over to Paul and said: "Tell me, are you a Roman citizen?" He said: "Yes." 28 The tribune exclaimed: "I bought this citizenship for a large sum of money!" Paul said: "But I am a citizen by birth." 29 Then those who were about to question him at once drew back from him. The tribune also was afraid when he realized that Paul was a Roman citizen—and that he had put him in chains.

NOTES

xxii 22–23. Paul's last words (vs. 21) seemed to the Jews to indicate that Jerusalem was not the center of their religion, and that the distant and unclean world of the Gentiles was worth more than Israel and the temple. The crowd started shouting again, demanding the death of the apostle, waving garments and throwing dust into the air, all expressive of their total rejection of Paul (see NOTE on xiii 51).

24–26. So the tribune returns to his original command: Paul is to be taken into the fortress. Moreover, he orders that the necessary information about the prisoner and his crime, which they have not been able to ascertain so far (cf. xxi 33–34), should now be obtained from the prisoner himself by an interrogation which, as was customary with slaves and strangers, is an examination under torture. But when the soldiers strap the apostle firmly to prepare for the scourging, we are again suddenly confronted with the Paul whom we remember from the morning in Philippi, when he, calling attention to the fact that he and Silas had been whipped without a trial and thrown into prison although they were Roman citizens, demands that they be properly conducted from the prison by the authorities (xvi 35–40). The centurion on duty passes Paul's protest on to the tribune.

27–29. It is difficult to state what the rights of a Roman citizen were, especially when these rights were not on paper but had to be applied to daily life in more or less distant parts of the Empire. What seemed to be most important in this connection was that a Roman citizen could not be chained or whipped so long as he had not been sentenced. At any rate, the tribune was overwhelmed by the information about Paul's citizenship. He naïvely confesses that he himself had obtained his citizenship by paying a large sum of money. This purchase of citizenship had become possible during the reign of Claudius thanks to Messalina, Claudius' wife; by their time a large number of freedmen were minor officials of the State. The tribune's frankness calls forth the discouraging answer from Paul that he Paul had inherited his citizenship, as if he thereby held a much higher rank among Roman citizens. Various assumptions have been made as to how Paul's father had become a Roman citizen, and these have been somewhat complicated by confusing them with Jerome's quite unreliable account of Paul's birth at Gischala in Palestine. Nothing definite has been established. The last verse reveals the tribune's terror when he suddenly realizes that his prisoner is a Roman citizen whom he had put in chains and had barely avoided flogging.

COMMENT

The word "Gentiles" once more starts the uproar which had ceased during Paul's speech. The tribune has his prisoner taken into the fortress and orders him to be questioned under the lash, in order to learn why the crowd made such an outcry against him. Paul tells the centurion about his Roman citizenship and the latter warns the tribune. A conversation follows between Paul and the tribune, concerning Roman citizenship. But the tribune is horrified to learn that his prisoner is a Roman citizen whom he has unwittingly put in chains.

62. PAUL'S EXAMINATION BEFORE THE SANHEDRIN
(xxii 30 – xxiii 10)

XXII 30 The next day he let him out, and as he wished to find out exactly why he was being accused by the Jews, he gave orders that the chief priests and the whole Sanhedrin should assemble. He led Paul down and set him before them. **XXIII** 1 Paul looked steadily at the Sanhedrin, and said: "Brethren, I have lived before God with a completely clear conscience to this very day." 2 But the high priest Ananias commanded those who stood by him to strike him on the mouth. 3 Then Paul said to him: "God will strike you, you whited wall. You sit in judgment on me according to the Law, and contrary to the Law you order that I shall be struck." 4 Those who stood there said: "Do you insult God's high priest?" 5 Then Paul said: "I did not know that he was a high priest, brethren; for it is written: 'You shall not speak insultingly to a ruler of your people.'"

6 Since Paul knew that one of the parties consisted of Sadducees and the other of Pharisees, he called out to the Sanhedrin: "Brethren, I am a Pharisee, son of Pharisees; I am being tried because of the hope and the resurrection of the dead." 7 As he said this, dissension arose between the Pharisees and the Sadducees, so that the assembly was divided. 8 For the Sadducees say that there is no resurrection, nor any angel or spirit, while the Pharisees accept them. 9 A loud outcry arose, and some of the scribes of the Pharisee party rose, fought hotly, and said: "We find no evil in this man; and what if a spirit spoke to him, or an angel . . ." 10 There being great dissension, the tribune feared that Paul would be torn to pieces by them. He commanded the detachment to move down and rescue him from among them and take him to the barracks.

NOTES

xxii 30. The Roman authorities would not normally send a Roman citizen, who had been in peril of his life in the temple, to appear before the Sanhedrin. The meeting must have been called at the initiative of the Sanhedrin.

xxiii 1–5. *Ananias,* a son of Nebedaeus, was high priest from A.D. 48–58 during the reigns of the emperors Claudius and Nero.
commanded those who stood by him to strike him on the mouth. Cf. John xviii 22 f., where one of those who stood beside Jesus struck him (see p. LXXVIII). In both cases the reason for the blow was indignation at the prisoner's conduct before the high priest. Paul's words concerning the high priest's transgression of the Law are echoed in the trial of James the Lord's brother (Josephus *Ant.* XX.199–203): James was tried for a transgression of the Law, but during the case the high priest violated the Law and was dismissed at the request of the Jews.
you whited wall may as in Matt xxiii 27 point up the difference between the fine outer appearance and the unattractive interior, thus expressing the same sense as the next sentence: that he who should judge according to the Law was violating the Law in ordering the prisoner be struck.

6–10. Confronted with this assembly of Sadducees and Pharisees, Paul claims that he is a Pharisee, born and bred, and that his case concerns the hope of the Messiah and the resurrection of the dead (cf. xxiv 15, xxvi 6, xxviii 20). The Sadducees, who did not believe in a resurrection nor in the existence of angels or spirits, turned against Paul, while the Pharisees, who did believe and were willing to grant that a spirit or an angel had spoken to him, found no evil in him. This exchange shows that Paul had spoken of his call near Damascus, where according to his account the risen Messiah (Jesus Christ) had spoken to him. The meeting takes such a tumultuous turn that the tribune orders his soldiers to take the apostle back to the safety of the fortress of Antonia. There is apparently no difference between the conduct of the mob and that of the Sanhedrin whenever this man appeared.

COMMENT

In an attempt to throw light on Paul's situation, the tribune lets him out of prison and allows him to appear before the Sanhedrin, assembled in council. Uncertainty arises here, as it will later also (xxv 9), about the legality of this meeting, which seems to have

such a decisive influence on Paul's case. However, in this context
the importance of the Jewish authority and its competence to judge
Paul's case is quite limited. Paul states frankly that he is innocent.

The high priest Ananias then orders the servants to strike him
on the mouth. Paul answers with a curse. When asked how he
dared curse the high priest, he answered, "I did not know that he
was a high priest." As Paul can hardly have been ignorant of
Ananias' office, his utterance must be ironical: one would not expect a high priest to so transgress the Law. Such irony would easily
occur to a Pharisee when confronted by a Sadducean high priest,
so different were their interpretations of the Law. But like a good
Pharisee, Paul is able to phrase his real regret at flaunting authority
in correct Pharisaic form with a reference to Exod xxii 28.

One may doubt that Paul could have conducted himself as described here, since in Philip iii 5 ff., he spoke of his Pharisaic
youth as a thing of the past. Most scholars are also so strictly
imbued with the idea of a later Pharisaism that they are unable to
conceive of the movement as it was when many questions were
still unsettled and Christianity had not yet separated from Judaism.
Paul considered himself a Jew, an Israelite, for whom all God's
promises to the chosen people had been fulfilled, and whose first
task was to so convince all Jews. His confessing that he was a
Pharisee must be regarded in a similar way. What he had learned
at home and from his Pharisaic teachers in Jerusalem, namely, the
hope of the coming of the Messiah and of the resurrection of the
dead, was still of central importance to him. Standing before the
Jewish court he was anxious to win over to the Gospel, or to
which at all events he wanted to bear witness, Paul confessed what
was to him at the heart of Pharisaism. It is unreasonable to suppose that Paul intended this as a stratagem to end the meeting
in confusion, thus preventing the Jews from carrying out their plans.
However, even if this had not been his intention, it was what happened. The members of the assembly disagree so violently that they
nearly come to blows.

As the meeting ends in chaos, the tribune has his prisoner
brought to safety.

63. PAUL TAKEN INTO SAFETY IN CAESAREA
(xxiii 11–35)

XXIII 11 The following night the Lord stood beside Paul and
said: "Be of good courage, for as you have borne witness to the
facts about me in Jerusalem, so will you bear witness in Rome
also."

12 When day had come, the Jews formed a conspiracy, and
bound themselves under pain of a curse neither to eat nor drink
until they had had Paul killed. 13 There were more than forty
who made this plot. 14 They went to the chief priests and the
elders, and said: "We have solemnly, under pain of a curse,
pledged ourselves not to eat or drink until we have had Paul
killed. 15 You are therefore now—together with the Sanhedrin—
to request the tribune to bring him down to you, as though you
intend to end his case by a more thorough examination. However, we will be ready to kill him before he gets there."

16 When Paul's nephew heard of the ambush, he came and
went into the barracks and told Paul of it. 17 Paul summoned
one of the centurions, and said: "Take this young man before
the tribune, for he has something to tell him." 18 So he took
him with him and brought him to the tribune, saying: "The
prisoner Paul summoned me and asked me to bring this young
man to you, as he has something to say to you." 19 The
tribune took him by the hand, led him aside, and asked:
"What is it you have to tell me?" 20 He said: "The Jews have
decided to request you to bring Paul down to the Sanhedrin
tomorrow, as if to make a more thorough examination about
him. 21 But do not agree, for more than forty men among them
are lying in wait for him, and they have pledged themselves
under pain of a curse neither to eat nor drink until they have
killed him. Now they are ready and waiting (only) for you to
agree." 22 Then the tribune let the young man go, after warning

him not to tell anyone that "you have come to me with information about this."

23 And he summoned two of his centurions and said: "Two hundred soldiers—and seventy horsemen and two hundred lightly armed troops—are to be ready to go to Caesarea at the third hour of the night." 24 He added that they were to provide mounts for Paul to ride, and bring him safely to Felix the governor. 25 He wrote a letter to this effect:

26 "Claudius Lysias greets the honorable Governor Felix! 27 This man, who had been seized by the Jews and was about to be killed by them, was rescued by me, when I had arrived with the detachment, after I had learned that he was a Roman citizen. 28 As I wished to discover the reason why they accused him, I took him down to their Sanhedrin, 29 and I found him to be accused concerning disputes in their law, but not on any charge that might lead to a death sentence or chains. 30 Since I have been informed that there is a plot against the man, I am sending him to you at once, and I have also given his accusers orders to make their accusation to you."

31 As they had been ordered, the soldiers took Paul with them, brought him during the night to Antipatris, 32 and the next day letting the horsemen travel on with him, they returned to the barracks. 33 The horsemen came to Caesarea, delivered the letter to the governor, and set Paul before him. 34 When he had read it and had asked what province he came from, and had been told that he was from Cilicia, 35 he said: "I will question you when your accusers also have arrived"; he commanded that he should be kept under guard in Herod's palace.

NOTES

xxiii 11. The Lord's message in the vision during the night can be understood in two ways. It may be the promise that Paul was to go to Rome and preach there, just as earlier (ix 28–29) he had preached in Jerusalem. The context, however, points in another direction, and the words about Jerusalem probably refer to his present stay and the testimony he has just given to the authorities; the promise then is that the apostle would *in the same way* testify to the authorities in Rome.

12–22. *the Jews*. This expression is used here and in John (cf. e.g. v 15–18, vii 1, 11, 13) as a name for the enemies of Jesus or of Paul. These men had pledged themselves under oath to kill Paul. When the legal path did not take them to their goal, hatred of the apostle made them resort to assassination. For the execution of their plot they needed the assistance of the Sanhedrin because only a new examination would take the apostle outside the safety of Roman military territory. As far as can be seen, the Sanhedrin did not have time to consider this request before the situation had changed completely. Having heard of the plot, the son of a sister of Paul's revealed it to him; this information being immediately passed on to the tribune, and the nephew sworn to silence, preparations were set in motion to remove Paul from prison under heavy military escort that night.

Nothing is known about Paul's family and its attitude toward him after his Damascus experience. His Pharisaic family may well have broken off all connection with him. It is interesting to note that the apostle on his flight from Jerusalem (ix 29–30) went to his native town of Tarsus where had his family broken with him trouble might have arisen. In the same way it could be said of his nephew that he must be a Jew since he had heard about the conspiracy but he was nevertheless ready—at the risk of his life—to try to foil the plot to murder his uncle.

23–30. Instead of a convoy of prisoners, there was a nocturnal military sortie of considerable size serving as camouflage for the real purpose. None of the forty assassins spying in the streets supected the units that were leaving; no one looked for the apostle wearing a cloak and a helmet on an extra mount. Two detachments of infantry and one of cavalry with extra mounts set out toward the northwest. Nobody knows exactly what the *dexiolabi* (spearmen) making up one of the infantry detachments were; the cavalry was presumably to make the whole trip to Caesarea, and the infantry, prepared to subdue street fighting, was to ensure that the prisoner and his escort got out of Jerusalem and its suburbs, where the conspirators watched.

31–33. It has been doubted that the infantry could march from Jerusalem to Antipatris in one night, but the location of this town is uncertain. Their goal was Caesarea, where Felix the procurator resided. There a letter accounting for his forceful action of the tribune was to be delivered. The content of this letter cannot be said to be contrary to the facts as they are known to us. Only a few remarks are necessary here: the tribune had not rescued Paul after having learned that he was a Roman citizen, but the verbal form used may very well indicate that he heard of Paul's citizenship after he had liberated him. The last sentence of the letter, to the effect that the tribune had ordered the apostle's accusers to present their case to Felix in Caesarea, tells something which did not occur until after the letter was written, and after information about Paul's successful transfer was available.

34–35. When Paul was handed over to Felix in Caesarea, the governor asked the usual questions about his hometown and the province in the empire to which he belonged (cf. Luke xxiii 6–9). Once more the apostle's address is given: he is under guard in Herod's palace, now the residence of the procurator.

COMMENT

While in prison Paul was encouraged by the Lord, who revealed himself to him and told him that he would get to Rome and testify there as he had already done in Jerusalem. Events now occur that make the commander in Jerusalem send his prisoner to Caesarea, to his superior Felix the procurator. Whether or not the Sanhedrin had arranged the examination of Paul (see NOTE on xxii 30), it had failed to achieve its purpose; an entirely new attack is aimed at the apostle in which more than forty men pledge not to eat or drink until they have killed him. The conspirators seek the help of the Sanhedrin: the latter is to request a new examination of Paul, who, on his way to the meeting, would be stabbed to death (cf. xxv 2–3). If there was here a definite agreement between the assassins and the Sanhedrin, the latter was acting as Paul's enemy on this occasion. Had it already done so at his examination, and was it then due to Paul's conduct that the council disagreed so violently as to cause its original intention to fail? A son of Paul's sister, hearing about the plot, reports it to Paul and the tribune, who takes measures to have Paul taken to safety during the night. With a large escort drawn from different branches of the Jerusalem garrison, he is taken away from the scene where his life was endangered. With the prisoner, whom the escort hands over to Felix the procurator in Caesarea, goes a letter from the tribune, who like earlier and later Roman officials maintained that Paul had been accused by the Jews only with regard to certain disputed points concerning the law of Moses, and had done nothing deserving prison or death under Roman law.

64. PAUL WITH FELIX
(xxiv 1–27)

XXIV 1 Five days later the high priest Ananias came down there with some elders and an advocate called Tertullus, and laid their accusations against Paul before the governor. 2–3 When he had been summoned, Tertullus started his case by saying: "We acknowledge in every way and in all places with great gratitude that we enjoy great peace under your rule, and that reforms have been made among this people by your planning, most noble Felix. 4 But not to weary you too long, I ask you in your kindness to listen to us for a short time. 5 We found this man a pestilence, and one who stirred up trouble among all the Jews around the world, being a leader of the Nazarene sect. 6ᵃ He even tried to desecrate the temple, but we seized him. 8ᵇ By making inquiries into all these matters, you will be able to obtain information from him about the charges we make against him." 9 The Jews also accused him and said it was so.

10 Then, when the governor had nodded to him to speak, Paul answered: "Knowing that you have for many years been a judge over this people, I set forth my case with confidence. 11 You can obtain confirmation that it is not more than twelve days since I went to Jerusalem to worship. 12 They did not find me in the temple arguing with anyone, or causing a mob to collect, neither in the synagogues nor in the city. 13 Indeed, they have no proof whatever to give you of the charges they are now bringing against me. 14 But this I admit to you, that in accordance with that "way"—which they call sectarian—so I worship the God of my fathers, believing all that is written in the Law and the Prophets, 15 trusting in God, as do also these men here, that there will be a resurrection both for the righteous

and for the unrighteous. 16 Therefore I strive always to have a clear conscience toward God and man.

17 "After many years I came here to give alms to my people and to make offerings. 18 In doing so, they found me in the temple after I had purified myself, but not surrounded by a crowd, nor in the midst of a disturbance. 19 It was only some Jews from the province of Asia, who ought to be here and to accuse me, if they have anything against me. 20 Otherwise these men can say themselves whether they discovered any crime when I was before the Sanhedrin, 21 except in connection with the statement which I shouted when I stood among them, which was only: 'Because of the resurrection of the dead I am on trial before you today!'"

22 Then Felix announced the deferment of the case, as he had a fairly detailed knowledge of everything concerning "the way," and he said: "When the tribune Lysias comes down here I will conclude your case." 23 He gave the centurion orders that Paul was to be kept under guard, though with some freedom, and that none of his friends should be prevented from attending to his wants.

24 Some days later Felix arrived, together with his wife Drusilla, who was a Jewess. He had Paul brought, and heard him speak of the faith in Christ Jesus. 25 But when he spoke of righteousness, temperance, and (God's) judgment to come, Felix was conscience-smitten and exclaimed: "You may go for the time being! When I have more time, I will call you." 26 At the same time he hoped that Paul would give him money, so he had him summoned very often, and talked with him. 27 But when two years had passed, Felix was succeeded by Porcius Festus, and as Felix wished to do the Jews a favor, he left Paul in prison.

Notes

xiv 1–6a. After Paul's removal from Jerusalem, the accusers were told that they would have to bring their case to Caesarea (cf. xxiii 30). The high priest Ananias and some elders were accompanied by the legal consultant to the Sanhedrin, Tertullus, who sometimes spoke as a

Jew, and sometimes as a Gentile. After flattering Felix, he maintains that Paul was responsible for the disturbances that occurred all over the empire, pointed to his leading position within the Christian sect, and finally to his attempt at profaning the temple in Jerusalem. If, as we have seen, the tribune is open to blame because in his letter to Felix he makes his knowledge of Paul's Roman citizenship the basis for rescuing him, how much blacker is the case against Tertullus' who claims that the Jews had arrested Paul, when in truth there was no arrest but a tumultuous attempt at lynching, from which the Romans rescue Paul.

6a–9. The Western text adds the words which appear in the text of the KJV and in the footnote of the RSV at vss. 6b–8a, missing in our text: "and we would have judged him according to our law. But the tribune Lysias came and with great violence took him out of our hands, commanding his accusers to come before you." This text gives effective support to an understanding of the tactics afterward used by the Jews with respect to Festus, namely, that what was important to them was to have Paul extradited to their jurisdiction (see NOTE on xxv 1–3, 9). But for this reason, this text may well have come into existence after reflection upon the text and its possibilities.

10–23. Paul's flattering words to Felix with their emphasis on his many years of service as a judge in Palestine furnish one of those indications of time which may be used for chronological calculation only with proper caution. The twelve days mentioned by Paul probably indicate the time after his arrival in Jerusalem. During this period he had done nothing to confirm the charges made by his adversaries. In contrast to xxiii 6, the hope in vs. 15 is solely the hope of a general resurrection of the dead, both of the righteous and of the unrighteous. In other texts in the NT the resurrection of the righteous is clearly distinguished from that of the unrighteous, and before this comes the millennium (Rev xx 1–15; I Cor xv 23–24; I Thess iv 13–18). The resurrection (and the judgment) are motives for a clear conscience (vs. 16; xvii 30–31; cf. in the Pauline letters, among other passages, Philip ii 14–16). Apart from his supposed brief visit in xviii 22, Paul had not according to Acts been in Jerusalem since the Apostolic Council (ch. xv). The "many years" in this passage is not well-suited to detailed chronological calculations, but it stresses the improbability of the accusation with regard to Jerusalem. A pilgrimage undertaken by a Jew living outside Palestine would naturally include alms and offerings in the temple. A reference has been found in these words to the collection among the Gentile Christians for the poor in the congregation of Jerusalem (see NOTE on xx 4).

some Jews from the province of Asia. Paul's remark about these men who had caused the uproar against him in the first place (xxi 27–29) points to valuable witnesses whom the Jewish authorities for unknown reasons had not produced. After the accuser and the accused had addressed the court, Felix postponed the case because according to Luke he now had accurate information about the Christians. The official reason given was that the tribune from Jerusalem must first be heard.

24–27. Antonius Felix was a brother of Pallas, one of Claudius' freedmen, who served as a kind of minister. Felix was procurator in Palestine from A.D. 52 to ca. 60. Tacitus has characterized him as one who "exercised the power of a king with the mind of a slave" (*Annals,* XII.54). It is therefore difficult to doubt that Luke is correct in assuming that he wanted to get money from Paul. Here once more the collection appears as the only wealth that the poor apostle and tent maker possessed. The assertion that Felix left Paul behind him as a prisoner in order to please the Jews likewise becomes probable. At this time Felix was the husband of Drusilla, a Jewish princess, daughter of Agrippa I and thus a sister of Agrippa II and the princess Bernice.

COMMENT

This chapter marks an intermezzo. The events in Jerusalem were followed in Caesarea, by the court meeting before Felix the procurator; at this meeting, a decision in the case was postponed for an indefinite period of time. The Sanhedrin or at any rate its Sadducean leaders headed by the high priest, appeared in public as Paul's accusers in Caesarea. This showed a marked development from the apparently accidental attack on Paul's life in the temple, and his examination before the Sanhedrin in Jerusalem. Now in Caesarea the highest Jewish authority appears as Paul's adversary and accuser. The charge was that Paul had stirred up trouble among the Jews around the world, that he was a leader of the Nazarene sect, and that he had even tried to desecrate the temple. Paul's reply shows that the accusations had been intended to separate Judaism in general from the Christians of whom Paul was assumed to be the leader. But no mention is made of the mission to the Gentiles. The case was a purely Jewish affair: the question was, Did the apostle belong with Judaism or not? Paul demonstrates that the charge brought against him was false. He had been in Jerusalem for only twelve days and had not conducted himself in the temple and elsewhere in such a manner as to stir up trouble. The purpose of his journey to Jerusalem after a sojourn of many years in other countries had been to give alms to his people and to make offerings, and it was while doing this that Jews from the province of Asia had caused riots against him.

The only point Paul is willing to grant is that he served the God of his fathers in accordance with the Christian "way," which his accusers wrongly termed a sect. This service consisted in believing all that was written in the Old Testament and in hoping for a general resurrection—so did all Jews believe and hope (except his adversaries the Sadducees). The one thing his opponents were able to hold against him was the statement he made before the Sanhedrin (xxiii 6) claiming that his case concerned the resurrection of the dead. Behind these details can be seen the Jewish accusers' attempt to separate Paul and the Jewish Christians from the Jewish religion, and the apostle's struggle to maintain that he and his fellow believers formed a genuine part of Judaism. As was the case at the meeting of the Sanhedrin (xxiii 1 ff.), his trial developed into a showdown with regard to a problem of decisive importance to the Christians, namely, whether they were part of Israel (see p. LXXXI). A negative decision on this point would have subjected the new movement to constant persecution, no longer by the Jews but by the Romans, a persecution which did occur from the time of Nero to the reign of Constantine (see p. LXXXII). But the primitive church struggled to remain within Israel, where it was at home, and believed itself to be the true Israel and the community of the new covenant, deeply rooted in the Israel of the flesh and the community of the old covenant. Paul's trial, with its probably negative outcome which legally decreed that Christianity was not Judaism, has proved decisive though this was not evident during primitive Christianity (see p. LXXXIII).

As time went on the postponement of the case appeared increasingly strange. In conversations with Paul, Felix obtained additional information about Christianity, although he found some of its doctrines personally frightening. He hoped to get money from Paul, but two years passed and Felix was replaced by Porcius Festus. Because of the Jews' attitude toward him, Felix had found himself in a very difficult situation and left Paul a prisoner in Caesarea.

65. PAUL BEFORE FESTUS
(xxv 1–12)

XXV 1 Three days after Festus had arrived in his province, he went from Caesarea up to Jerusalem. 2 The chief priests and Jewish leaders began to make charges against Paul before him. They begged him 3 that as a favor to them—and to injure Paul—he would have him brought to Jerusalem. They would then lie in wait to kill him on the way. 4 Festus answered that Paul was under guard in Caesarea, but he himself would soon be leaving. 5 "Those of you who are competent," he said, "can then go with me there, and if the man is found to have done anything wrong, they can charge him."

6 When he had spent some eight to ten days with them, he went down to Caesarea. The next day he sat in the tribunal and commanded that Paul be brought in. 7 When he had appeared, the Jews who had come down from Jerusalem gathered round him and made many serious charges, of which they could give no proof. 8 Paul declared in his defense: "I have committed no offense either against the Jewish law or the temple, or Caesar." 9 As Festus wished to do the Jews a favor, he asked Paul, "Are you willing to go up to Jerusalem and there stand your trial before me concerning these matters?" 10 Paul said: "I hereby appeal to the court of Caesar; that is where I should be tried. I have committed no offense against the Jews, as you very well know. 11 If now I have committed an offense and done something deserving the death sentence, I will not try to escape death. Since, however, none of the charges they make against me is true, no one can hand me over to them; I appeal to Caesar." 12 Then Festus, when he had conferred with his council, answered: "You have appealed to Caesar; before Caesar you shall go."

NOTES

xxv 1–3. Festus gave the impression of being an energetic man, who investigated the facts (vss. 16 and 17) and took immediate action according to his own conviction. It is therefore strange that after Paul's appeal he had to confess that he did not understand the case at all and was at a loss as to how to formulate his report on this case to the emperor (vss. 26–27). The case which had been shelved by Felix, was immediately laid before Festus by the highest Jewish authorities in Jerusalem, who wanted it tried there. They mentioned that it would be a favor to them if this could be done. They did not, however, seem to have any hope of winning the case as they planned to have Paul murdered during his stay in Jerusalem.

4–7. Festus answered that he would soon be back in Caesarea and that those among the Jews who were competent in the Law could accompany him and present any charges there. The day after his return to Caesarea he sat in the court; Paul was brought before him and the Jewish accusers laid many serious charges against him, but as Luke added, without being able to prove them. As will be seen later, this was also Festus' opinion.

7–8. Paul's answer to the charges centered on his denial of having committed any offense against the Jews or against the temple. Either could also have been a crime against the emperor (see NOTE on xviii 16), this being the third point made by Paul.

Could it be mere chance that the emperor was mentioned just before Paul made his appeal to the court of Caesar?

9–12. Like his predecessor Felix, who had kept Paul in prison to favor the Jews, Festus for the same reason asked whether Paul would be willing to stand trial in Jerusalem. Some scholars have thought that Festus' proposal meant that the Sanhedrin and not Festus himself would judge the case. This would certainly give a particular significance to Festus' words that the Romans never extradited a prisoner as a favor (vs. 16). But as shown in the Introduction (see p. LXXVI) Festus is not likely to have proposed this. Paul answered Festus' questions by appealing to the court of Caesar, which was his right as a Roman citizen. He even took the liberty of telling Festus that he had committed no offense against the Jews as the procurator well knew. Had he committed a capital crime, he would not try to avoid the death penalty; but since none of the Jews' accusations were true, he could not in all justice be delivered into their hands; this was why he appealed to Caesar.

COMMENT

After the dramatic events related in chapters xxi–xxiii, everything had come to a halt under Felix (ch. xxiv). Paul, the restless missionary, whose life had centered on his call as apostle to the Gentiles, always on journeys or fully occupied in the cities where new churches were to be founded, was now kept inactive for two years. All his expectations about obtaining "the fullness of the Gentiles" (Rom xi 25), which was to provide the occasion for the salvation of the whole of Israel, could not be fulfilled, because he, who had been called, was now in prison. It is difficult to imagine the sufferings Paul must have endured during this period of imprisonment.

Now with Felix recalled to Rome and succeeded by Festus, the Jews had their chance. They thought they might cajole the new procurator before he was firmly in control and fully aware of the circumstances. Later, between the death of Festus and the succession of Albinus, the high priest succeeded in having James the Lord's brother, and some other Christians executed after a highly dubious trial (see NOTE on xxiii 3). The Jews attempted to have Paul tried in Jerusalem, where, just as had been planned two years before, he could be assassinated. Paul escaped this danger and by his appeal to the emperor managed to leave the prison in Palestine and reach Rome, where he might either be acquitted or sentenced to death (see p. LXXVI). At any rate he would not be rotting in a Palestinian prison as under Felix or be released only to be assassinated outside the prison. For two years no progress had been made with regard to his case, and it had now been brought back by Festus to the same stage as when the tribune had to send him away from Jerusalem in secrecy to save his life. The speed with which Festus acts on the initiative of the Jews, even before he has had a proper opportunity to make a study of the special problems in connection with this case, testifies to his being a poor protector of a prisoner accused by the Jews. In vs. 3, Luke speaks in plain terms about the tendency among the Palestinian Jews to resort to the assassination of adversaries who cannot be legally executed.

66. KING AGRIPPA'S VISIT TO FESTUS
(xxv 13–27)

XXV 13 After some time King Agrippa and Bernice came to Caesarea and visited Festus. 14 When they had spent some days there, Festus laid Paul's case before the king and said: "There is a man whom Felix left prisoner, 15 and the chief priests and Jewish leaders brought charges against him when I came to Jerusalem, asking that he might be sentenced. 16 I answered them that it was not customary for Romans to hand over any person before the accused had stood face to face with his accusers and had had an opportunity to defend himself against the charge. 17 When they had come down here together, I did not delay, but sat in the tribunal the next day, and commanded the man to be brought before me. 18 When the accusers stood there, they made no charge against him of the kind of crimes I had expected, 19 but they had some disputes with him about their religion, and about a certain Jesus, who was dead, but whom Paul asserted to be alive. 20 As I was at a loss how to investigate these matters, I asked if he would go to Jerusalem and there stand his trial concerning these matters. 21 But when Paul demanded to be kept in custody until the verdict could be pronounced by the Emperor, I gave orders that he should be kept in custody until I could send him on to Caesar." 22 Agrippa then (said) to Festus: "I too would like to hear this man." He answered: "Tomorrow you shall hear him."

23 Next day therefore Agrippa and Bernice came with pomp and ceremony, and went into the audience chamber with tribunes and leading men from the city. When Festus had given the order, Paul was brought in. 24 Festus said: "King Agrippa, and all of you who are present with us, you see this man, concerning whom the whole Jewish crowd came to me in Jerusalem and here also, crying that he ought not to live any

longer. 25 However, it became clear to me that he had done nothing that deserved the death sentence, and when this man appealed to the Emperor I decided to send (him on). 26 I am not in a position to make out a definite charge against him to my lord, and for this reason I brought him before you, and especially before you, King Agrippa, so that I may have something to write when the preliminary inquiry has been held. 27 For it seems to me pointless to send a prisoner on without at the same time stating the charge against him."

NOTES

xxv 13–22. After Herod the Great's rule (37–4 B.C.) in Palestine had ended, the kingdom was divided among his sons and when it was necessary to depose Archelaus, his region, Judea and Samaria, had been placed under a Roman procurator. Agrippa I, grandson of Herod the Great (A.D. 41–44), once more united his grandfather's kingdom but after his death this came to an end. Agrippa II was a son of Agrippa I (see p. 115) and a brother of the princesses Bernice and Drusilla (cf. NOTE on xxiv 24). As a result of his father's policy of alliances with other Oriental princes, Palestine was, at his death, placed under a Roman procurator. When Agrippa II became king, he reigned over Chalcis in Syria, until in A.D. 53 he acquired his uncle Philip's possessions to the northeast of the lake of Tiberias along with a few districts outside Palestine. His sister Bernice had been married to her uncle, Herod of Chalcis, but afterward lived at her brother's court.

Festus (procurator A.D. 60–62) mentioned Paul's case to Agrippa, who was rightly called an expert in Jewish affairs. Festus added his fine statement about the rights of an accused man among the Romans with which he was supposed to have answered the Jews when they demanded that Paul be sentenced. These words would have sounded more convincing, if in vs. 9 he had not gone a long way to meet the wishes of the Jews. Festus' report of his words and acts recalls the letter of Claudius Lysias, in which Paul's Roman citizenship was probably made the basis of his release (xxiii 27), and Tertullus' words about the arrest of Paul by the Jews (xxiv 6). These reports are throughout a slightly improved version of the actual events which succeed in making all concerned appear entirely blameless. Moreover, Festus stressed his quick handling of the case, which seems praiseworthy, but which had only helped to further the plans of the Jews. To the surprise of the procurator the Jews did not accuse Paul of crimes said to have been committed by him, but only of opinions in which

Paul deviated from those held by other Jews. They had in particular disagreed about a man, by the name of Jesus, supposed to be dead, but claimed by Paul to be alive. In this difficult situation Festus had wanted the court to sit in Jerusalem, but Paul had then appealed to the court of Caesar. Just as in his time his great-uncle Herod Antipas had long desired to see Jesus (Luke xxiii 8), so here Agrippa II testified that he had wished for a long time to hear Paul.

23–27. This happened the next day, in a large assembly with the king and princess in the company of the procurator surrounded by high officials. In his opening address, Festus stressed the to him inexplicable difference of opinion between Paul and the Jews who were anxious to have him executed. Festus himself had been unable to find Paul guilty of anything that might carry a death sentence. Like Claudius Lysias (xxiii 29), and earlier, Gallio in Corinth (xvii 14–15), he had no charge against the prisoner, but he was obliged to write a report to the emperor which must go with the prisoner to Rome; the meeting that had been called here should serve this purpose, and on this occasion Agrippa with his superior knowledge of the Jews and their customs would assume special importance.

COMMENT

King Agrippa II and his sister, the princess Bernice, arrived to pay their respects to the new procurator Festus. During their visit Festus placed before the king the difficult case against Paul, who had been charged by the Jewish authorities with religious antagonistic views and not for any crimes. When the procurator had proposed that he should stand trial in Jerusalem, Paul had appealed to Caesar's court. As Agrippa showed interest in the case, Festus arranged a confrontation between the king and the prisoner for the next day. This meeting, which was conducted with great ceremony and attended by a large group of distinguished people, was opened by Festus with an explanation of what was going to happen. The prisoner whom the Jews had accused and for whom they requested the death sentence was not guilty of any offense that carried such a penalty. The trial in Palestine was closed by the prisoner's appeal to the emperor, but as Festus did not know what to say in the report to the emperor, this public meeting had been arranged to provide him with the information that he lacked.

67. PAUL'S SPEECH BEFORE AGRIPPA
(xxvi 1–23)

XXVI 1 Then Agrippa said to Paul: "You are permitted to speak on your own behalf." Then Paul gestured with his hand and made a speech in his defense:

2 "I consider myself most fortunate in defending myself before you today, King Agrippa, concerning all the charges made against me by the Jews, 3 because you are a great expert in all the customs and controversies of the Jews; therefore I ask you to listen to me patiently. 4 As to my way of life, which was spent from my earliest years among my own people and in Jerusalem, 5 all the Jews have known for a long time—if they will admit it—that as a Pharisee I have lived in accordance with the strictest sect within our religion. 6 Now I am on trial because I hope for the promise made to our fathers by God, 7 and which our twelve tribes hoped to share, worshiping (God) as they did constantly night and day. For the sake of this hope I am accused by the Jews, O king. 8 Why is it considered incredible among you that God should raise the dead?

9 "I also was sure that I ought to do many things against the name of Jesus of Nazareth, 10 and I did so in Jerusalem; I shut up many of the saints in prison—with authority from the chief priests—and when they were killed I cast my vote in favor. 11 Round about in all the synagogues I tried—often by threat of punishment—to force them to blaspheme, and in raging fury against them I persecuted them as far as and even into foreign cities. 12 When in the course of this I was on my way to Damascus with authority and permission from the chief priests, 13 I saw on my journey, O king, in the middle of the day, a light from heaven shine round me and those who were traveling with me, with a blaze brighter than that of the sun. 14 When we had all fallen to the ground I heard a voice say to

me in Hebrew: 'Saul, Saul, why do you persecute me? It hurts you when you kick against the goads.' 15 I said: 'Who are you, Lord?' The Lord said: 'I am Jesus whom you persecute. 16 But get up and stand on your feet, for this is why I have revealed myself to you: to appoint you an interpreter and witness both of what you know and what will be revealed to you. 17 I will rescue you from the people and from the Gentiles to whom I am sending you 18 to open their eyes, so that they may turn from darkness to light, and from the power of Satan to God, so that they may receive forgiveness of sins and a place among those who are sanctified by faith in me.'

19 "Therefore, King Agrippa, I did not disobey the heavenly vision, 20 but I preached, first to those in Damascus and in Jerusalem, and then to the people throughout the whole of Judea and to the Gentiles, that they should repent and turn to God, and do works fitting for repentance. 21 Because of these things the Jews seized me in the temple and tried to kill me. 22 God having helped me, I have to this very day been a witness both to great and to small, and I say nothing but what both the prophets and Moses have spoken of as something that was to come: 23 that the Messiah must suffer, that being the first to rise from the dead, he would bring light both to our people and to the nations."

NOTES

xxvi 1–3. Agrippa conducted the meeting and gave Paul permission to speak; the whole of the ensuing speech was therefore formally addressed to the king (cf. vss. 2–3, 7, 13, 19; cf. vss. 26–29). As was the case when confronting Felix (xxiv 10), Paul here addressed himself to Agrippa with an introduction intended to induce a friendly hearing of what was about to be said. Still more than Felix, let alone Festus, Agrippa was an expert with regard to the circumstances of the Jews. In the speech the Jews are mentioned without the use of the definite article, just as in xxv 10, in accordance with the common practice in Attic court addresses that opponents were mentioned without an article.

4–5. As in xxii 3 (and Gal i 14), Paul began by describing his youth, with which, he said, the Jews were well acquainted. He took it for granted that the Jews knew of his past (see p. 216). It seems obvious that in his missionary preaching Paul used the account of his call as a paradigm of God's mercy to sinners (see p. 82). Here in Acts the three accounts given of Paul's life seem to demonstrate that it was the heavenly powers, the God of Israel, and the risen Jesus that had started the mission to the Gentiles by their call of the apostle.

among my people may mean the people of Cilicia in contrast to Jerusalem but may also mean Judea.

6–8. Paul's trial represents a continuation of the Pharisaic point of view held during his youth. He has been accused of believing in God's promises to the patriarchs, promises which the people of Israel rehearsed in their worship and hoped to share in the future. In xxiii 6, Paul had said that he was standing trial because he hoped in the resurrection of the dead; and before Festus in xxiv 21, he had stated that, in his examination before the Sanhedrin, he had cried that it was also for the resurrection of the dead that he was on trial.

The sentence following in vs. 8 might seem to show that the hope mentioned here was concerned with the resurrection of the dead, but vs. 23 shows that Christ was the first who had risen from the dead. It might be supposed that it is Luke's usual desire for variation that has caused the different ways of using the term "the hope." At any rate xxvi 8, 23 show that the Messiah and the resurrection of the dead were linked together. It seemed strange to Paul that it should be the Jews who were charging him with that hope, and it was incomprehensible to him that Jews would not believe that God should be able to raise the dead. To disbelieve in the resurrection of Christ was to Paul to disbelieve in the resurrection of the dead (I Cor xv 12 ff.). It has been suggested that vs. 8 be placed after vs. 22 so that the sentence in vs. 23 runs parallel to the clause in vs. 8, governed by the interrogative sentence.

9–11. Paul returns to the description of his youth, now mentioning his persecution of the Christians (cf. ix 1–2, xxii 4–5; Gal i 13). It was his firm resolve to persecute the name of Jesus, and he did so first in Jerusalem, where he put many Christians in prison, and was pleased when they were sentenced to death. It is doubtful that the Jews had obtained permission from the Romans to execute Christians, but Paul's story demonstrates that illegal executions by assassination might occur. In the synagogues Paul tried, often by force, to make the disciples of Jesus blaspheme against this name (i.e. to deny Christ), and he had extended his violent persecution to the cities outside Palestine.

12–18. While engaged in these efforts, he was on his way to Damascus, authorized by the high priest to carry out persecutions there. Then he saw a light stronger than the sun, and falling to the ground, heard a voice addressing him in Hebrew. The words here are the same as those in ix 4–5 and xxii 7–8. At this point, there is an extension of the otherwise identical remarks, for to the first of these words has been added, *It hurts you when you kick against the goad*. This is supposed to have been a Semitic proverb, but it has been found only in Greek, where it may be read in writers as diverse as Pindar and Libanius. At one time, Euripides' tragedy, *The Bacchae*, was suggested as a source of quotation here and elsewhere in Acts, but the sentence is a very common Greek proverb which means: "from now on it will be difficult for you to kick against the goad," or in other words: "the call of Christ will from now on constrain you."

This account deviates from the other two accounts in Acts in not mentioning Ananias. Instead of sending Paul into Damascus to have the message of his call supplemented by this Christian brother, Jesus himself immediately spoke of the meaning of his call. The wording here in xxvi 12–18 comes closest to that of Paul's own account in Gal i 15–16. Paul was to be Christ's servant and to bear witness to what he had seen and to what he would see later. Jesus promised to rescue him from Israel and from the Gentiles to whom he was now sending him in order to turn them away from the power of Satan to God, so that they would be able to receive forgiveness of sins and a place among the holy. For this account of Paul's call, use has here been made of both Jer i 7–8 and Isa xlii 6–7 (cf. lxi 1 [LXX]) and other parts of the same OT texts concerning calling have been used in the three other accounts of this event.

19–23. Thereafter Paul's whole life was directed in accordance with this heavenly command. He had obediently preached the Gospel in Damascus and Jerusalem (ix 19–30) and afterward all over Palestine (xv 3; cf. ix 30, which may be doubtful when compared to Gal i 22–24) and to the Gentiles (Acts xi ff.). His activities had caused the Jews to seize him and attempt to kill him, but despite such adversaries Paul had been preserved by the help of God (cf. vs. 17) until now in order to bear witness to the prophecies of Moses and the prophets.

In order to understand Festus' interruption in vs. 24, in the next section, it will be necessary to insert vs. 8 between vs. 22 and vs. 23, allowing the speech to end with proofs from the Scriptures intended to deny that it would be incredible, that God could not do what he had done. Festus cuts short this stream of Bible quotations with his remark.

COMMENT

Paul's speech before King Agrippa marks a climax during his trial in Palestine, but Festus' introductory words show that he was thinking of his report on the case. At the same time Agrippa had an opportunity to see and hear his prominent prisoner, and could assist the procurator on the basis of his knowledge of the Jews.

The speech led from Paul's Pharisaic youth to his trial, where Jews were accusing him for believing what the Jews themselves believed. The strict piety of his youth and his participation in persecutions of the Christians form an introduction to a description of his call near Damascus.

This story is told here for the third time in Acts, and despite a number of variations it is still the same story with the same inner meaning. God had called his adversary to become Christ's apostle. By the grace of God, he has become what he is now, and it is the God of Israel who has made him the apostle to the Gentiles. Their obvious objection to his preaching about the Messiah and the resurrection of the dead caused him, toward the end of his speech, to produce Old Testament textual proofs for the faith of his youth and his manhood. Once again we have in Acts a speech that is not brought to its formal conclusion, but where everything that needs saying has been said.

68. FESTUS AND AGRIPPA STATE THEIR OPINION OF PAUL'S CASE
(xxvi 24–32)

XXVI ²⁴ When Paul finished his defense, Festus said in a loud voice: "You are mad, Paul! Your great learning makes you mad." ²⁵ But Paul said: "I am not mad, most noble Festus. On the contrary, the statements I make are the sober truth. ²⁶ The king is familiar with these things, and to him I speak openly. Nothing will convince me that any of this has escaped his attention, not being a hole-and-corner affair. ²⁷ Do you believe in the prophets, King Agrippa? I know that you do." ²⁸ Agrippa (said) to Paul: "In a little while you will persuade me to turn Christian." ²⁹ Paul replied: "I would to God that, whether in small or in great matters, not only you, but also all those listening to me today, might become such as I am, apart from these chains."

³⁰ Then the king rose, with the governor and Bernice and those sitting with them. ³¹ They withdrew and spoke together and said: "This man has done nothing deserving the death sentence or chains." ³² Agrippa said to Festus: "This man could have been released if he had not appealed to Caesar."

NOTES

xxvi 24–25. An unexpected parallel to Festus' exclamation and Paul's answer exists in one of the papyri with the misleading title of The Acts of the Alexandrian Martyrs. The scene is laid at a trial where the emperor says to Appianus: "I generally manage to bring to their senses those who are raging and who have lost all feelings of shame." And Appianus replies: "By your genius, I am neither raging, nor have I lost all feelings of shame." In this papyrus (*Acta Appiani*, P. Yale Inv. 1536, col. IV, lines 9–15), the two speakers are at cross purposes and use strong expressions. Festus, however, is described not as an unwilling and unjust judge, but rather as an ignorant man, who in dealing with complex Jewish affairs makes a hasty decision, which later proves wrong. This ignorance is revealed in his judgment of Paul. The Romans were not able to dismiss these Jewish and Christian matters, vital as they were to this trial and important as they were politically.

26–29. Turning away from his interrupter, Paul addressed the chairman of the meeting with masterly courtesy. What Festus could not understand would all be clear to the king. He knew what had occurred in Palestine during the past thirty years and Paul assumed that he believed in the sayings of the prophets, with which Paul was in agreement. Agrippa courteously evaded answering by means of an extravagant assurance that he had come very close to persuading him to become a Christian. A prince who was friendly to the Jews but with a position among educated Greeks and Romans had to get out of a difficult situation by a noncommittal reply. In answering Agrippa, Paul had the last word. He wishes that all those present might join him in his fortunate position as a servant of Christ—but not in chains.

30–32. At such a meeting, it is often of the greatest importance to know what was said afterward, and this Luke tells us. Claudius Lysias' words from xxiii 29 concerning the innocence of the prisoner are repeated, but just as elsewhere in Acts, the conclusion also points toward death.

COMMENT

It was not Agrippa, who was conducting the meeting, but Festus who interrupted Paul by saying that the latter, with his peculiar opinions and his long quotations from the Scriptures, had shown a confused mind that bordered on sheer madness. Paul protested against this and appealed to Agrippa who, as far as he knew, had to be aware of the facts he referred to in his speech. With respect to the proofs from Scripture, Paul felt sure that Agrippa believed in the message of the prophets. Of course the king had an expert knowledge of Judaism but he was not a believing Jew, and for this reason he did no more than point to the fact that little more seemed necessary to make him a Christian. Faced with this rodomontade, Paul gives wholehearted expression to his wish that all present in the hall would gain the faith he himself held, but not in chains. Then the many dignitaries depart in a solemn procession. Finally remarks are exchanged between Festus and Agrippa; they agree that Paul has done nothing deserving imprisonment or a death sentence. To this Agrippa adds, "this man could have been released if he had not appealed to Caesar." This last sentence might sound like a guarantee of his acquittal in Rome. But in reality it voiced a possibility wasted. The prisoner could still have been released, but his own voluntary action would result in a continuation of his case in Rome, and how likely would he be to succeed there?

69. THE VOYAGE TO ROME
(xxvii 1–44)

XXVII 1 When it had been decided that we were to set sail for Italy, Paul, together with some other prisoners, was handed over to a centurion named Julius, of the Augustan Cohort. 2 We therefore went aboard a ship from Adramyttium which was bound for places in the province of Asia, and set sail; Aristarchus, a Macedonian from Thessalonica, being with us. 3 On the following day we put in at Sidon, and Julius, who treated Paul with kindness, allowed him to go to his friends (there), to be cared for by them. 4 When we had set sail again, we kept under the lee of Cyprus because the winds were contrary, 5 and having thus traversed the waters along Cilicia and Pamphylia we landed at Myra in Lycia. 6 Having found an Alexandrian ship there, bound for Italy, the centurion put us on board. 7 After sailing slowly for many days, and with great difficulty getting as far as Cnidus, we sailed in the lee of Crete off Salmone, because the wind would not allow us to make headway. 8 Having sailed past it (the town) with great difficulty, we came to a place called Fair Havens, near which was a town called Lasea.

9 Since much time had passed, and the voyage was already dangerous because even the Fast was already over, Paul warned them: 10 "Men, I see that this voyage will mean hardship and great loss, not only of the cargo and the ship, but also of lives." 11 But the centurion listened to the master and the owner rather than to what Paul said. 12 Since the port was not suitable for wintering, the majority decided that they should set sail in order, if possible, to reach Phoenix, a port in Crete open to the southwest and northwest, and winter there.

13 When a light south wind arose, they thought that their hope was fulfilled, and they weighed anchor and sailed past Crete, hugging the coast. 14 Not long after, a storm-wind called

"Euroclydon" struck us from there, 15 and, since the ship was swept along and could not be turned up against the wind, we gave way and let ourselves drift. 16 Then running under the lee of a small island called Cauda, we got hold of the ship's boat with great difficulty. 17 When they had hauled it aboard, they took protective measures by undergirding the ship, and fearing that they would be driven down into the Greater Syrtis, they let down the drag anchor, and thus let themselves drift. 18 As we were hard pressed by the storm, they started to jettison the cargo next day, 19 and on the third day threw the ship's gear overboard with their own hands. 20 But when neither sun nor stars had appeared for many days, and a violent storm raged, any hope that we would be saved was abandoned.

21 As little had been eaten, Paul stood in their midst and said: "Men, you should have been guided by me, and not have sailed from Crete and suffered this hardship and loss. 22 Now I urge you to keep up your courage, for none of you will lose your lives; only the ship will be lost. 23 For last night there appeared to me an angel of the God to whom I belong and whom I worship, 24 saying: 'Fear not, Paul! You must appear before Caesar, and see: God has granted you as a favor the lives of all those who sail with you.' 25 Keep up your courage, therefore, men, for I have faith in God that it will be as I have been told. 26 But we must be driven ashore on some island."

27 When the fourteenth night had come, and we were drifting in the Adriatic, the sailors felt about midnight that they were approaching land. 28 So they took a sounding and found twenty fathoms. When they had sailed a little farther and sounded again, they found fifteen fathoms. 29 Fearing that we should run aground somewhere on the rocks, they dropped four anchors from the stern, and prayed that dawn would come. 30 When the sailors tried to escape from the ship, and had already lowered the ship's boat into the water, as though they were going to drop anchors from the bow, 31 Paul said to the centurion and the soldiers: "Unless these men stay on the ship you cannot be saved." 32 Then the soldiers cut the ropes of the boat and let it drift away.

33 As dawn began to break Paul urged them all to take some

food, and said: "Today is the fourteenth day that you have waited continuously without food, without nourishment of any kind. 34 I therefore urge you to eat; it will strengthen you; for none of you shall lose a hair of his head." 35 When he had said this and had taken some bread, he thanked God in the sight of all, broke it, and began to eat. 36 Then they all took courage and ate. 37 We were two hundred and seventy-six souls in all on board the ship. 38 When they had eaten their fill, they lightened the ship by throwing the cargo of wheat into the sea.

39 When day came they could not recognize the land, but they observed a bay with a beach, and resolved to ground the ship there, if they could. 40 They cast off the anchors and let them fall in the sea, at the same time unlashing the steering oars; then hoisting the foresail to the wind, they made for the beach. 41 But they struck a place where two currents met and ran the ship aground, and while the bow bored itself in and stuck immovably fast, the stern began to break up under the force of the waves. 42 Then the soldiers decided to kill the prisoners, so that none would swim ashore and escape; 43 but the centurion, who wished to save Paul, prevented them from carrying out their purpose. He ordered that those who could swim should be the first to jump overboard and swim ashore, 44 and (then) the others, some on planks, others on wreckage from the ship. And so all came safely ashore.

NOTES

xxvii 1-3. Paul's voyage to Rome is undertaken in a convoy with other prisoners under the command of a humane centurion (he belonged to cohort Augusta, stationed in Syria in the first century A.D.). The voyage is divided into stages determined by the availability of ships able to carry the convoy in the right direction. The first ship, from Adramyttium on the western coast of Asia Minor, is bound for ports in the province of Asia.

Aristarchus . . . from Thessalonica, who was with the convoy, is mentioned during the demonstration of the Ephesian silversmiths (xix 29), then as a participant in the journey to Jerusalem with the collection (xx 4). He sends greetings in Col iv 10, where he is called by Paul "my fellow prisoner" and in Philem 24 where he is termed Paul's fellow worker. The Aristarchus mentioned in Acts may well be the same person.

From xxvii 1 to xxviii 16, the "we" form is once more used in the account. The ship puts in at Sidon, where the centurion Julius demonstrates his friendly feelings toward Paul by allowing him to visit his friends (presumably Christians) so that they are given an opportunity to care for him.

4–5. The voyage from Sidon appears to have taken the ship to the east of Cyprus and along the southern coast of Asia Minor from Cilicia past Pamphylia to Myra.

6–8. At Myra they board an Alexandrian ship bound for Italy, but the progress is very slow—among the islands off the southwestern coast of Asia Minor and along the southern coast of Crete; they finally arrive at the harbor of Kaloi Limenes near the city of Lasea.

9–11. The voyage had started late in the year, the winds were contrary and now the time arrives when the Fast in connection with the Day of Atonement is celebrated (the tenth of Tishri, i.e. in September or October) when it is dangerous to be at sea. It is already past the sailing season, and time to find a place to lie up for the winter and await the coming of spring. Paul utters a warning against the risks that a continuation of the voyage would entail. There is no possibility of reaching Italy before winter sets in. Not only the ship and her cargo but also the people on board might be lost in such an attempt. The centurion, however, obeys the captain and the owner rather than Paul.

12–20. As the harbor they reach is not suitable for wintering, the majority vote to go on in order to reach Phoenix—farther to the west on Crete—and to winter there. When a light breeze rises, they weigh anchor and sail on along the southern coast of Crete. But a northeasterly wind, called *"Euroclydon"* strikes from Crete and drives the ship out into the open sea. Then, they find themselves in a storm and they are obliged to let themselves drift. When running under the lee of a small island named Cauda, they succeed in securing the ship's boat and the hull of the ship is strengthened with ropes. For fear of drifting into the big graveyard of ships on the shoals of Syrtis Major west of Cyrene, a drag anchor is let down to act as a brake. The next day various pieces of cargo are jettisoned to lighten the ship, and on the third day parts of the rigging sacrificed. Day by day the hope of survival grows dimmer. The storm continues, no sun or stars appear and as the position of the ship is unknown, hope of surviving the storm is abandoned.

21–26. During all this time nobody has eaten. Stepping forward, Paul reminds them that they ought to have followed his advice and stayed on Crete. As shown in the Introduction (see p. xxxv) this remark is highly characteristic of the apostle. Now he assures them that nobody on board would be lost, only the ship itself. He knows this from an angel

sent by the God he serves, who during the past night had told him not to
be afraid, for he would appear before Caesar's court; moreover, God had
granted him the rescue of all on board. The order of importance indicated in the angel's words is noteworthy: Paul's task before the emperor
was God's foremost aim, the saving of two hundred and seventy-six human lives was secondary. Nothing is said about the effect of his speech;
it does not seem to have convinced those who were without hope.

27–29. In the course of the fourteenth night, when the ship is adrift
in the Adriatic, the crew has the impression that they are approaching
land. When soundings are taken, the depth is at first found to be twenty
fathoms and then fifteen, and anchors are let down to prevent the ship
running aground in the dark on an unknown and possibly perilous coast.

30–32. The sailors try to get ashore by the ship's boat which they
have launched under the pretext of letting down more anchors. Before
they are able to get in it, Paul tells the centurion that it is necessary
that the sailors stay on board if the others are to be rescued, and the
soldiers cut the ropes that hold the boat so that it drifts away empty.
It is of interest to note that the heavenly prophecy and aid were so matter of fact: the sailors were to stay on board and everyone was to eat
before leaving the ship in an attempt to reach the shore.

33–36. At dawn Paul makes those on board eat after their long fast
of about two weeks. Paul himself sets a good example by saying grace
and then beginning to eat. This brings a change of atmosphere and all
of them begin to eat. They are thus strengthened and all are able to
help with the rescue. This comes very close to Paul's logic in Philip
ii 12–13.

37–41. After they have eaten, the ship is lightened by throwing the
cargo of wheat into the sea. (A ship from Alexandria on her way to
Italy would quite naturally be loaded with wheat.) It might seem from
vss. 18–19, that all the cargo had already been thrown overboard but
perhaps they had not been able to get at the major cargo of wheat until
the storm had subsided a little and they had a chance to open the main
hatches. When dawn arrives, nobody recognizes the coast, but they see a
suitable place to run the ship aground. They cut the anchor ropes drop-
ping the anchor into the sea, and at the same time unlash the rudder in
order to be able to steer the ship, hoist the foresail to the wind so as to
make steering possible, and make for the beach. But they do not get
ashore there for the ship runs aground on a sandbar with its bow firmly
wedged in the sand, while the waves begin to batter the stern.

42–44. The soldiers, knowing that they are answerable with their
own lives for the lives of the prisoners (cf. xii 18–19, xvi 27), want to
kill them to prevent them from escaping on land, but they are thwarted

from carrying out their plan by the centurion who wants to save Paul. He commands everyone to jump overboard, first those who can swim, then the others who, by drifting in with the flotsam from the wreck, manage to reach the shore.

COMMENT

In the Bible world very little sea-faring is recorded. Jesus and his apostles crossed Lake Gennesaret and the prophet Jonah was exposed to a storm, in which the Lord overtook him when he deserted from his mission to Nineveh. Among the predictions about the world to come, it is said in Rev xxi 1: "the sea is no more." But when Paul has to go to Rome he sails, and Luke gives a vivid description of the voyage. Here we are confronted with stormy weather and great danger, a stranded ship and a treacherous shore. We already know that the apostle is accustomed to the sea. "I have been shipwrecked three times," "danger at rivers," "a night and a day I have been at sea," "danger at sea," these are details that we can pick out of an enumeration of the apostle's sufferings in II Cor xi 23 ff. In the past, man's relation to the sea differed from that of later times. The ships crept along, hugging the coasts and did not willingly take to the open sea. When Virgil sailed, Horace was beside himself with anxiety, and in a song not unknown to school children (*Carm*. I, III), he besought the ship to bring the great man safely ashore.

Paul's experience differed entirely from that of Jonah, for in his case the storm was not caused by his presence—on the contrary, when Jonah had been thrown overboard, the ship was out of danger, while in Paul's case it was he whom God wished to bring to Rome. Perhaps the perils at sea of Paul and his fellow passengers were due to a last effort on the part of the always energetic but often thoughtless Festus, who had despatched the convoy of prisoners immediately although it was late in the year and sailings ought to have ceased.

Because of the prevailing winds, the route to Rome from Syria and Egypt first went to the east and north, and then followed the southern coast of Asia Minor, the islands lying off it and the long breakwater of Crete, and then out to open sea in the direction of Italy. As winter was rapidly approaching, it was important to lie up for the winter in Crete, but an attempt to reach a better harbor than Kaloi Limenes took them into storm and danger on the open sea. Not until two weeks later did their situation improve; the ship ran aground on Malta, and all those on board got safely ashore.

In the meantime the ship's crew, the soldiers guarding the convoy of prisoners, and the passengers, all had parts to play, with those of the captain, the owner, the centurion, and Paul, being particularly important.

70. PAUL TRAVELS FROM MALTA TO ROME
(xxviii 1–16)

XXVIII 1 When we had escaped, we learned that the island was called Malta. 2 The inhabitants there showed us uncommon kindness; for they lit a fire and looked after us all, because it began to rain and was cold. 3 When Paul had collected a bundle of brushwood and put it on the fire, a viper came out because of the heat, and it fastened on his hand. 4 When the natives saw the creature hanging from his hand, they said to one another: "This man is no doubt a murderer, whom justice would not allow to live, even though he had been saved from the sea." 5 But Paul merely shook the creature off into the fire and was not harmed. 6 They however expected him to swell, or suddenly fall down dead. When they had waited a long time and had observed that nothing happened to him, they changed their minds and said he was a god.

7 Near this place the chief magistrate of the island, whose name was Publius, had some estates, and receiving us as his guests for three days, he treated us kindly. 8 It happened that Publius' father was ill in bed with fever and dysentery; Paul went to him and prayed, laid his hands upon him, and cured him. 9 When this had happened, the rest of those on the island who were ill came too and were cured. 10 They honored us with many tokens of esteem, and when we were to set sail, they gave us what was needed for the voyage.

11 Three months later we set sail on an Alexandrian ship that had wintered in the island; its figurehead was the Sign of the Twins. 12 We put in at Syracuse and stayed there three days. 13 Then we sailed on and came to Rhegium. After one day the south wind rose, and the next day we came to Puteoli; 14 there we met some brethren and were asked to stay a week with them; and thus we came to Rome. 15 The brethren there,

hearing our story, came to meet us at the Appian Forum and
the Three Taverns. When Paul saw them, he thanked God and
was encouraged. 16 When we had arrived in Rome, Paul was
permitted to lodge privately with the soldier who guarded him.

NOTES

xxviii 1–2. The island on which the shipwrecked voyagers land is Malta,
where the inhabitants, unusually friendly toward them, light a fire for
them because of the rain and the cold.

3–6. Paul, always indefatigable, is not to be found among those sitting round the fire, but among those who tend it. When he is collecting
brushwood, a poisonous viper fastens on his hand. The inhabitants think
that he is near death and decide that this prisoner must have committed
murder since Dike, the goddess of Justice, has attacked him even though
he has succeeded in avoiding death by drowning. As a result of his
snake bite, they expect his hand to swell up and then him to suddenly
fall dead. But when nothing happens, they change their minds and
decide that he must be a god. Here Jesus' words are fulfilled, that his
disciples "will take snakes in their hands, and if they drink poison, it
will not hurt them" (Mark xvi 18). The Maltese awe of Paul reminds
one of the Lycaonians' attempt to bring sacrifices to Barnabas and Paul
as gods (xiv 11–13).

7–10. The chief magistrate of the island, whose exact title is used by
Luke, resides near where they have run aground. He is named Publius
and he receives "us" in his house for three days; this may be taken to
mean either Paul and some others or all the shipwrecked people. During
this time, Paul healed the father of Publius, whereupon other ailing
people came flocking to him and were cured. Paul was much honored
for these healings, and at their departure, he is provided with everything
he needs for the journey.

11–16. Because the voyage had started at such a late date, the
wintering in Malta lasts only three months. The shipwrecked party is
able to sail for Italy on an Alexandrian ship bearing the figurehead of
the Dioscuri. The twins, Castor and Pollux, come to the aid of sailors.
They touch first at Syracuse in Sicily and stay there three days. From
there they sail to Rhegium where the difficult navigation through the
Strait of Messina begins. Then a day later, when a southerly wind rises,
they go at full speed to Puteoli, situated in the volcanic landscape north
of Naples. There are Christians here with whom Paul and his companions are allowed to stay a week. The last stage of the journey is made
overland to Rome. Here the Christians have heard of Paul's coming and
congregate to meet him as far outside Rome as Forum Appii and Tres

Tabernae. To do him honor, they lead him into the city in which he is to die, and seeing them, Paul takes courage and praises God. In Rome he is allowed to live in private lodgings with only one soldier who acts as his guard.

COMMENT

The stay on Malta turned out to be a period of peace, following the perils and hardships of the voyage. A friendly population gave them a generous reception, and there was a possibility of healing sufferers. On landing, Paul happened to demonstrate his special powers to the inhabitants which made them believe that he was a god. When winter had passed, the convoy of prisoners sailed from Malta to Puteoli, and from there they went on to Rome by land. There the apostle was received by the Christians and was imprisoned, but not—strictly speaking—confined.

71. PAUL AND THE JEWS IN ROME
(xxviii 17–28)

XXVIII ¹⁷ Three days later Paul invited the leaders of the Jews. When they had come, he said to them: "Brethren, although I had committed no deed against the people or the customs of our fathers, I was handed over to the Romans as a prisoner from Jerusalem. ¹⁸ When they had examined me, they were going to release me because I had done nothing that deserved the death sentence. ¹⁹ When the Jews objected, I felt forced to appeal to Caesar—not that I have any charge to make against my own people. ²⁰ This then is the reason I have invited you, to see you and speak with you, because it is for the sake of the hope of Israel that I am in chains." ²¹ But they said to him: "We have received no letter from Judea about you, nor have any of the brethren come and reported or spoken ill of you. ²² But we ought to hear from you what your opinions are, for as regards this sect, we know that it is spoken against everywhere."

²³ Having fixed a day with him, they came to his lodgings in still greater numbers, and he explained the matter to them from morning until evening, bearing witness to the kingdom of God, and trying—both through the Law of Moses and through the Prophets—to convince them about Jesus. ²⁴ Some were convinced by what was said, but others disbelieved. ²⁵ They parted without agreement, after Paul had made one statement: "Rightly did the Holy Spirit say to your fathers through the prophet Isaiah:

²⁶ 'Go to this people and say:
  You shall indeed hear, but never understand,
  you shall indeed see, but never grasp.
²⁷ For the heart of this people grew dull,
  and their ears were hard of hearing,

and they have closed their eyes,
lest they should see with their eyes,
and hear with their ears,
and understand with their heart, and turn
for me to heal them.'

28 Be it known to you that this salvation of God has been sent
out to the Gentiles; they will listen."

NOTES

xxviii 17–20. Only three days after his arrival Paul invites the leaders of the Jews in Rome to his lodgings, and explains to them the peculiar situation in which he finds himself, namely, that he, who could
wish himself accursed and cut off from Christ for the sake of his Jewish
countrymen (Rom ix 3), has now apparently become the enemy of the
Jews. As he had done before his judges in Palestine (xxiv 20–21, xxv 8,
10), he stresses here that he has not committed any crime against the
Jews.

handed over to the Romans. Strangely enough he uses the expression
Agabus used (xxi 11), before his arrival in Jerusalem, and Tertullus used
later (xxiv 6–7), but which does not correspond to the actual account of
the Jews' attack and the Romans' arrest of the apostle (xxi 27–34): that he
has been brought from Jerusalem and surrendered to the Romans as a
prisoner. Paul rightly points to the fact that the Romans would have
liked to release him since they had not found him guilty of any crime
(xxiii 29, xxv 18, xxvi 31). But since the Jews would not agree to this, he
was forced to appeal to Caesar's court (xxv 9–12). The true motive
force behind all these events was Israel's hope of the Messiah and the
resurrection of the dead which had caused him to preach the Gospel all
over the world and to gather the collection and take it to Jerusalem.
For these reasons he is now in chains.

21–22. The leading Roman Jews answer that they had had no letter
about Paul from Judea and none of their coreligionists had come and
spoken ill of him. This statement is entirely convincing, as Paul's ship
must have been among the first that arrived in Italy after the winter,
and representatives of the Jewish authorities in Jerusalem could not have
arrived, nor could a letter about the case. It should not be forgotten
that Paul's case prior to his appeal to the Emperor had been a local
Palestinian affair. Only after that would Jerusalem be interested in trying to influence the outcome of the case in Rome. It is more difficult to
understand their final remark about the Christians as a sect of which
they had no direct knowledge but only knew that it existed and that it
met with opposition everywhere. For it is generally assumed that Chris-

tianity had come to Rome at an early date. In this city Christianity had not yet been influenced by Paul and the mission to the Gentiles; Claudius' persecution was due to a controversy between Jewish Christians and other Jews (see NOTE on xviii 2). Luke's remarks here are not generally considered to be reliable. But it is possible that they are, and if so, this would suggest that Suetonius' remark did not refer to Jesus Christ but to an unknown Chrestus, and that the Epistle to the Romans was written to a Gentile Christian congregation in Rome (which it certainly was), and in addition that this Gentile Christian congregation was the first Christian church in Rome. The picture of Christianity in Rome should like so many other NT assumptions, be reconsidered and possibly revised.

23–24. The lively beginning leads to another meeting between Paul and the Jews with an even larger attendance, and for a whole day the apostle bears witness to the kingdom of God, trying through Moses and the prophets to convince them that Jesus is the Messiah of God.

25–28. The meeting ends in a disagreement between those who were convinced and those who were not. Paul's last words indicate that the latter constituted the great majority. The words, quoted from Isa vi 9–10, had already been spoken by Jesus in the same sense in the synoptic gospels (Matt xiii 14–15; Mark iv 12; Luke viii 10) and by John the evangelist in his final characterization of Jesus' ministry (John xii 40). After this speech about Israel, Paul states that he would go to the Gentiles. Israel's unbelief became the cause of his preaching the Gospel to the Gentiles. From Rom ix–xi, we know that this is not the end of the matter. Paul knew that the Gentiles reception of the Gospel in its turn would cause God to save all Israel. Verse 29, which originated in the Western text and was then admitted to the Neutral text, has here been omitted. It is given in the KJV text and here in the RSV footnote: "And when he had said these words, the Jews departed, holding much dispute among themselves."

COMMENT

Paul's sojourn in Rome started, as did all his missionary activities, with his working for the salvation of the Jews but when they rejected the Gospel, he declared, quoting Isa vi 9–10 to them, that he would now go to the Gentiles. As Luke, in the first book of the two-part work, Luke iv 16–30, started with Jesus' preaching to the Jews who rejected his sermon and began instead to persecute him, so here the two-part work comes to an end with Paul's sermon to the Jews in Rome and their unbelieving rejection of the Gospel.

72. PAUL'S TWO-YEAR IMPRISONMENT
(xxviii 30–31)

XXVIII ³⁰ Paul then stayed in his own hired lodgings for a period of two whole years, and he received all those who came to him. ³¹ So he preached the kingdom of God, and taught about the Lord Jesus Christ, publicly and without hindrance.

COMMENTS

For two years Paul remained a prisoner in his rented lodgings in Rome. He was free to receive everybody and to preach to them about the kingdom of God and Jesus Christ, nor was he prevented from doing this in public.

This curious end to the account of a ministry of rare dramatic quality confronts every reader with the question: What happened then? There is no convincing explanation of why Luke did not continue his account. Was it approaching a conclusion with the death of the apostle, or would it have continued with his once more being at liberty to preach all over the world? Only one plausible explanation can be found: Luke knew no more than he has recounted here, because his two-part work, Luke-Acts, was written at that very stage of the story, and had as its object a defense of Christianity and of Paul in this particular situation.

APPENDICES

FOREWORD TO APPENDICES

When Johannes Munck passed away in February 1965, I undertook the task of preparing the English text for publication, with the aid of Dr. C. S. Mann of London and Baltimore. We found it advisable to write a series of appendices on problems not discussed in detail by the author. Actually, our appendices crystallized around preliminary material generously placed at our disposal by Professor Abram Spiro of Wayne State University (Detroit) for inclusion in the volume. All the material in the appendices has been carefully checked by both Dr. Mann and me.

We are convinced that the content of the first chapters of Acts accurately reflects a tradition earlier than originally thought by any of the contributors to this volume.

We now know that apostolic Christianity was ecumenical in the strict etymological sense of the term, with Pharisees, Essenes, Baptists, and Samaritans included among its adherents. All these sects were then widely scattered over the civilized world (*oikoumenē*). On one vital point all were united—their firm belief in the Risen Lord.

For the archaeological and chronological background of Acts see the Bibliography.

W. F. Albright

I. LUKE'S ETHNIC BACKGROUND

1. THE CHRISTIAN TRADITION

The oldest patristic reference to Luke's origin seems to be found in the Old Gospel Prologue to Luke, which states: "Luke was a native of Syrian Antioch, by profession a physician, who became a disciple of (the) apostles." The first five words run: *Estin ho Loukās Antiocheus Syros,* literally, "This Luke was an Antiochene, a Syrian." Since there were at least twenty-four different Antiochs, a number of which were still flourishing towns in Roman times, this is tantamount to saying, "he was a native of Antioch in Syria." Several Greek scholars whom I have consulted agree that this must be the sense of the expression. The Old Gospel Prologue to Luke was dated by D. de Bruyne (1928) in the late second century A.D., but R. G. Heard, *Journal of Theological Studies,* N.S. 6 (1955), 1 ff., dates it much more plausibly in the third or early fourth century A.D. It is, in any case, the oldest concise statement on the subject, since Eusebius is vague, saying in his *Ecclesiastical History* III.iv.6, that Luke was of Antiochene extraction (Gr. *to men genos ōn tōn ap' Antiocheia*). Obviously this statement is no more specific about his ethnic origin than the gospel Prologue. There is nothing to indicate whether he was of Jewish or non-Jewish origin. The later tradition of the Eastern church states emphatically that he was Jewish; Epiphanius says that he was one of the Seventy Disciples; later Byzantine tradition makes Luke the companion of Cleophas on the road to Emmaus.

2. THE NAME

Greek *Loukās* is unquestionably derived from one of the numerous Latin names beginning with *Luc-* (*Lucius, Lucianus, Lucanus, Lucullus,* etc.). Latin names borne by Jews at that time were nearly always a sign of their origin as freedmen (chiefly descendants of Jews who had been sold into Italian slavery during

the Roman wars in Palestine in the first century B.C. and had taken
their owner's name, which they kept after being freed for more
profitable service to their patrons than was possible for slaves to
render). The two most likely sources of his name are *Lucius* or
Lucanus. *Lucanus* is probably better, since it is explicitly given as
a name of Luke in two Old Latin manuscripts of the gospel.
This is a gentilic either from Luca in northern Etruria or Lu-
cania in southeastern Italy. Though there are genuinely Greek
abbreviated names ending in *-as,* parallels of Semitic origin like
Silās and *Barnabas* for the common Aramaic shortened names
She'īlā, Shīlā and *Barnabū* are more common. The former is
often found in inscriptions, but it is also the normal writing of the
name *Silās* in both the Syriac and the Palestinian Aramaic versions of the New Testament. For our purposes it is just as irrelevant that Silas may have been called "Silvanus" as it is that
Paul had the Jewish name "Saul."

The name *Barnabas* comes from *Bar-Nabū,* a common pagan
Aramaic name of this period, which also appears in the shortened
forms *Barnai* and *Barnaios*. It is highly probable that the Greek
genitive *Barnabă* is a late hypercorrection and that the original
form was *Barnabās*. This itself is again an obvious hypercorrection
of *Barnabū,* taken erroneously to be a genitive on the analogy of
tamiās, genitive *tamiū* (*tamíou*). For the pagan name, cf. Apollos,
an abbreviation of some such name as Apollodorus.

3. References to Luke in the New Testament

From the references in the Pauline epistles and Acts we know
that Luke was a much-traveled man, a physician interested in many
things (including legal matters), and not a member of the circumcision party. Henry J. Cadbury demonstrated long ago that the
references to medical matters in Luke and Acts by themselves
could have been written by almost any reasonably educated man
who was interested in the life around him. But some of his followers have unfortunately jumped to the quite erroneous conclusion that Cadbury had proved that our author was *not* a physician. This is, of course, utter nonsense. When the internal
evidence is weighed against the explicit statement in Col iv 14 that
Luke *was* a physician, we have two prima facie lines of evidence
confirming one another and placing the burden of proof squarely

on the shoulders of those who separate this Luke from the author
of Acts and the Gospel, and insist that the latter was not a physician.

The inference that Luke was not himself circumcised has often
been drawn from Col iv 10–11 and 14, "they (who are) of (the)
circumcision" (*hoi ek peritomēs*). This is quite wrong; Dr. Leona
Running has called my attention to the fact that we do not have
merely a variant text or expression omitting the article, but that
hoi ek peritomēs without the article designates the party which
considered circumcision as a necessary prerequisite for salvation.
It actually occurs in over half a dozen passages, with only a single
poorly attested variant inserting the article. She also points out
that some grammarians have spoken of the "qualitative" force of
the use of a Greek noun without article. The term in question is
rather ambivalent, so it may be preferable to call it a syntactic
device to give adjectival meaning to a construction containing an
anarthrous noun (without article). In this case, *hoi ek peritomēs*
would mean "those belonging to the circumcision party." Most of
these passages, especially Acts x 45 and xi 2, refer to those Jewish
Christians who held that circumcision was necessary for Gentiles,
and this is obviously the meaning of the phrase in Col iv 10 f.
and Titus i 10. Usually Paul is very charitable toward people with
this point of view, but in Titus i 10 he explodes, obviously because of the extraordinary ideas and practices which sometimes
accompanied the approach in question.

4. LUKE'S JEWISH INTERESTS

One of the most remarkable features of Luke's research into
the beginnings of Christianity is his extraordinary interest in the
background of John the Baptist, which occupies most of the long
first chapter of his Gospel. Paul Winter has demonstrated in a
series of articles, beginning in 1955 (*Bulletin of the John Rylands
Library,* 37 [1954–55], 328–47), that there was a close relation
between these hymns and hymns from the intertestamental period
preserved in the Apocrypha and Pseudepigrapha, including especially the hymns in I Maccabees, the "Psalms of Solomon," etc.,
from the last century B.C. He has shown conclusively that the type
of composition of the Magnificat and Benedictus is characteristic
of the last two or three centuries of the Second Temple, and that

they contain the same kind of mosaic of Old Testament materials and related matter which we find in these hymns. The hymns can all be translated back into perfect Hebrew poetry of the second or first century B.C., a fact which alone proves that Luke was following very good tradition. Since this initial publication of Winter much more material has come to light, including similar late hymns and poetic compositions from the caves at Qumran.

It has also been established by W. L. Brownlee, Jean Daniélou, and others that the account of John the Baptist given by Luke can be harmonized exceedingly well with the obvious inference from Luke i 80 that John the Baptist had been attached from childhood to an Essene community in the desert. It has been noticed by others since shortly after the discovery of the Dead Sea Scrolls that all the references to John the Baptist in the New Testament could be explained very readily as evidence for his Essene origin, either because he accepted Essene beliefs and practices or because he reacted strongly against them. It may well be that Luke had been under the influence of baptist sectarians in his early life, just as was true of Apollos (Acts xviii 25). This would certainly help to explain his broadmindedness with regard to other "Jewish" sectarians such as the Samaritans. That he was interested in Jewish matters beyond what might be expected of a converted pagan is also obvious from his references to Pharisees and Sadducees in Acts and the Gospel.

W. F. Albright

II. "EYEWITNESSES" IN LUKE

In view of the fact that Luke-Acts is a two-part work, and in view also of the claims which Luke makes in the preface to his Gospel, it is of some moment to examine precisely what may be meant by his use of the term which the majority of our versions translate by "eyewitnesses." In this connection, a work by Krister Stendahl (*The School of St. Matthew,* Uppsala, 1954) has hardly received the attention that it merits.

Stendahl's important study arose partly from an interest in, and a desire to find a satisfactory explanation for, the differences in hermeneutic method displayed by Paul on the one hand, and by the gospels on the other. Paul's method (which may with justice be called post-Hillel) has far more in common with the interpretative methods which were later to be embodied in the Mishnah— a method which is concerned with the precise meaning of words and phrases in the Old Testament and the tradition. The four gospels belong to a wholly dissimilar world of interpretation, far more at home with broad themes, with "fulfillment," rather than with precise verbal meanings (though it would be quite erroneous to assume a total *lack* of interest in precision). For the material in the gospels, we now have ample parallels in interpretative method in the Dead Sea Scrolls, and the thought world of the Essene community can be contrasted with that of the Mishnah, or of Paul.

Stendahl's approach to interpretative problems also had part-origin in dissatisfaction with the assumptions and presuppositions of the Dibelius-Bultmann approach to the New Testament, with its massive concentration on *Predigt* as a key term to cover all the activities of the early church. For Martin Dibelius and Rudolf Bultmann, *Predigt* was not only a term which covered the church's efforts to convert to its own specific message, it also covered the activity of the first Christians in proclaiming their message in the course of liturgical worship. Not the least of Stendahl's services to the field of New Testament studies was in drawing attention from real or supposed Greek sources and focusing attention instead upon what was then becoming known of the work of the Essenes at Qumran.

In short, Stendahl's thesis is that in Matthew—and *pari passu* also in the other gospels—there are manifest signs of what he describes as "school-activity." From the Dead Sea Scrolls it is clear that we have a firsthand insight into the workings of a Jewish *habûrah,* or brotherhood, contemporary with the intertestamental writings as well as with the New Testament period. In the work known as "The Manual of Discipline" (1QS), and also in the Commentary on Habakkuk (1QpHab), we see the *habûrah,* after it had expanded into a community or "congregation," interpreting the aims and aspirations of its founder(s). Stendahl believes that this kind of consideration profoundly affects our understanding of Luke and his work.

This understanding Stendahl finds in Luke's use of the word *hupēretēs* (usually in English "eyewitnesses"). Not only is the word used in Luke's preface to his Gospel (Luke i 3) but it is also to be found in Acts xiii 5, where John Mark is *hupēretēs* for Paul and Barnabas in preaching—and there the word can hardly mean "eyewitness." In the New Testament as a whole, the word is plainly capable of far more precise definition. Significantly, Luke uses the word to denote the *hazzân* of the synagogue, and the term "official" is probably the best English rendering for such instances as are to be found in Matt v 25, xxvi 58; Acts v 22, 26, xxvi 16; and I Cor iv 1.

If all these considerations are correct, then what we are dealing with in Luke i 3 (as Stendahl suggests) are "instructors." The bearing of this interpretation, not only on the gospels, but also on Acts, can be seen to be far-reaching. For we are then in a position to lay siege to the form-critical belief that the content of Christian faith in the early ages was formed simply by the *Predigt.* Quite to the contrary, assuming that *hupēretēs* = *hazzân* ("assistant") is a valid equation, it is possible to say that the four gospels may have taken shape in a discipline as exacting as that of the interpreters and scribes of Qumran or the formal circle of the Pharisee synagogue.

We know that there were no fine lines of distinction drawn between the functions of the synagogue as school and place of worship, and with Qumran as a present example, it would be astonishing to find that the early Christian communities differed substantially from contemporary Jewish practice. The concentration of scholarship on missionary activity as the driving force which formed and shaped the gospels (and other New Testament material, too) has led to some very odd and even naïve statements, and every conceivable manifestation of Hellenistic life and culture has been pressed into service to man the bastions of the *Formgeschichte* theory. Munck's steadfast refusal to be stampeded by this whimsey was by no means the least of his services to sound scholarship.

C. S. Mann

III. PENTECOST IN ACTS

The late Johannes Munck, both in his commentary and introduction, held to what may for convenience be called the "traditional" view of the phenomena associated with the day of Pentecost in Acts ii. In this view, a result of the outpouring of the Holy Spirit was the ability of the apostles to address the crowd in foreign languages. Much of Munck's "traditional" view may not unfairly be described as a minority view, and I shall attempt here to reappraise the evidence presented to us in Acts ii.

That something paranormal happened on that Pentecost, and which the crowd witnessed, is plain; and some attention must be paid to the manifestation of ecstasy which drew from some onlookers the accusation that the apostles were drunk.

Group excitement is far too well attested in the literature of all peoples, ancient and modern, to be dismissed as of no account. That it has been used to condition the participants to the acceptance of certain beliefs, or to implant suggestions for future conduct, is equally well known; and the evidence in our own time is too overwhelming to permit any doubt. It has been used in every area, political and religious, Christian and non-Christian, and is known to us in a pejorative sense as "brainwashing." Moreover, group suggestibility is not the perquisite of any single Christian group—it has been just as much at home with the *Spiritual Exercises* of St. Ignatius Loyola as among revivalist preachers in nineteenth-century American camp meetings. Group therapy and related techniques are used in our own time with clinical detachment by the psychiatrist. Group suggestibility, the reactions produced by strong emotion (or by a sense of liberation from some inhibiting fear) are phenomena to which we are all subject in greater or lesser degree. Ecstatic behavior and wild enthusiasm (such as are sometimes associated with pop singers and their fans) may be dangerous if held back too long or too rigidly, though for most people the barriers imposed by what Freud called the "moral censor" operate most of the time.

All these phenomena, by no means confined to the unsophisticated, uneducated, or primitive, have been investigated and classified by William Sargant in a most important book, *Battle for the Mind,* London, 1957. To this book, with all its implications for our understanding of emotional motivation in religious behavior, we refer the reader.

It has been commonly asserted that the events described in Acts ii are best seen as manifestations of the kind of wild enthusiasm frequently associated with some wholly new religious or ideological movement, and that such enthusiasm does often produce an apparently uncontrolled or even uncontrollable "speaking with tongues." This is by no means limited to a religious context, as was emphatically illustrated by the incantation-like recitations at Nazi rallies at Nürnberg in pre-1939 Germany. The apostle Paul was quite familiar with such phenomena, as we see from I Cor xiv 6–31, where he emphasized that without careful control and acceptable interpretation the practice could do much harm. In recent years, there has been a revival of it among Protestants in Europe and America, though it must be added that its defenders are more given to pious platitudes than to specifically Christian commitment or action.

We may admit at once that there *was* a scene of wild enthusiasm at Jerusalem on the part of the apostles, at the first recorded post-resurrection Pentecost. But we may be justified in offering a new partial explanation which was not possible twenty years ago. If, as Krister Stendahl and Oscar Cullmann (among others) have urged—and as we have urged in Appendix IV—the infant church based its institutions on the best available model (that of Qumran and the Essenes), then it may be that the Jerusalem community kept Pentecost as a feast of the Covenant. But in the case of the infant Christian community, this would not have been a feast of Covenant-renewal, such as was kept by the Essenes, but a feast of the *New* Covenant (cf. Matt xxvi 28; Mark xiv 24; Luke xxii 20; I Cor xi 25). Paul's letter to Corinth, written before the gospels, links the Eucharist to the New Covenant in the blood of Jesus, and this is also the tradition of the synoptic evangelists. Matthew connects the New Covenant in the blood of the Messiah with the forgiveness of sin, thus fulfilling Jer xxxi 31–33. It is not easy for us, at this remove, to appreciate the intense excitement and ecstasy which such consciousness of a New Covenant might produce in the mind of a receptive first-century Jew.

There is another difficulty in our received tradition of that first Pentecost as Luke records it. It is said that there were "Jews, devout people out of every nation" (Acts ii 5), who saw and heard the apostles at Pentecost, and that some of them accepted the apostles' words as being "in their own tongues." We must first call attention to the apparent surprise which these Jews expressed, in remarking that the men whom they heard speaking were "all Galileans" (Acts ii 7). Since it is quite certain that there were then converts in Judea as well as in Galilee, this cannot be a mere geographical designation. Pagans were still accustomed to call Christians "Galileans" as late as the fifth century; cf. Gregory of Nazianzus (*Orations* IV) on Julian the Apostate. This can be paralleled from the *Acts* (fourth century A.D.?) of Theodotus of Ancyra (XXI), where it is said that pagans called Jesus a "ringleader of the Galileans." At a much earlier date Epictetus (ca. 50–120) speaks (*Dissertations* iv.7.6) of men who would rather die than offer sacrifices: "Can then anyone behave in such a way because of madness, and the Galileans because of settled conviction?" Justin Martyr (about A.D. 140 in the *Dialogue with Trypho* 80) speaks of a sect known as the Galileans, to which he denies the name "Christian" (cf. Josephus *Ant.* XVIII.i.1; *Jewish War* II.viii.1). Moreover, about the middle of the second century A.D., Hegesippus (Eusebius *Ecclesiastical History* IV.xxii.7), lists Galileans among *Jewish* sects. However, there was confusion in this area; e.g., Epiphanius (fourth century) speaks of a sect of "Nazarenes," who were followers of John the Baptist but had their name applied to Christians. Epiphanius was evidently referring to the Hebrew-Christian sect whose teachings have been recently recovered from a medieval Arabic manuscript of the tenth-century Muslim theologian Abd ul-Jabbar.

In the New Testament, "the Galilean" *may* be a term for locality of origin at Matt xxvi 29 (cf. xxvi 71), and so also with "the Nazarene" in Mark xiv 70. But Mark xiv 70 may easily be a recognition of group allegiance ("you are a Galilean"). Luke xiii 1, 2 probably refers to Galilean zealots, and the victims of Herod's wrath are simply called "those Galileans." Luke xxix 60 does, however, appear to be an accusation of allegiance: the contrast with Luke xxiii 6, where in the Greek it is used as an adjective ("a Galilean man") is most marked. John iv 45 is not clear: it may be a note of the home territory of the men who came to the feast, or it may also refer to Galilean zealots. Acts i 11 does not use the

plural "Galileans" alone—it adds "men," "you Galilean men." Acts
v 37 speaks of Judas the Galilean, an allusion which would not have
been lost on those who remembered the abortive revolt. What, then,
is meant by "Galileans" in Acts ii 7?

Among the finds in the caves of Wadi Murabba'at were two
letters from Bar Cochba, dating between A.D. 132 and 135 written
in unskilled hands. The nationalist leader writes (translation of W. F.
Albright) to his lieutenant, Jeshua ben Galgola: "I solemnly swear
by Heaven (that if) any one among the Galileans who saved you
(pl.) suffers property loss (hefsed), I will put your (pl.) feet into
fetters, just as I did to Ben Aphlul." (The rendering will be discussed elsewhere in detail.) The proposal by J. T. Milik, when he
first published the letter in 1953 (Revue biblique 60, 276–94), to
recognize Jewish Christians here, though based on a preliminary
reading of the letter and incomplete documentation, was quite correct. Some of his critics went so far as to insist that Bar Cochba's
followers came from Judah and that the Jews of Galilee were
therefore under suspicion. But the movement was actually far from
limited even to Palestine!

The only suggestion which will fit the available evidence is then
that these men were Hebrew Christians. They can hardly have
been numerous; we have already called attention to the large numbers of Christians who left Palestine before the first Jewish revolt
of A.D. 66–70. It seemed to many Jews of all sects that Bar Cochba
was indeed the Star (Kokhbâ) under whom Israel's fortunes would
be restored. That the first followers of Bar Cochba also included
Jewish Christians who were unsure of their affiliations seems entirely reasonable.

Before making suggestions as to how the equation "Galileans=
Christians in Acts ii 7" materially affects our understanding of the
Pentecost narrative, we must notice the references to Christians in
Acts under another generic term. Acts xxiv 5 uses a word which
refers to Christians as Nazarenes and which is found only here in
the New Testament. But here it is introduced into the narrative
with no sense of needing explanation. "The Nazarene," as applied
to Jesus, is common in the New Testament.

There would appear to be three possible explanations of the reactions of the crowd that witnessed the events of Pentecost, and
heard the apostles. The first is that of Munck, which we have already described as being a "minority" view: that the apostles were
speaking to the crowds in foreign languages. The second possibility

(one which takes on heightened probability if the supposition about the translation of *Galileans* is accepted) is that surprise was expressed by the onlookers that members of a sect which already enjoyed some notoriety should address them in *Hebrew;* see Appendix IX. The Greek *pōs hēmeis akouomen hekastos tē idiā dialektō hēmōn en hē egennēthēmen* could bear the meaning "How do we hear, each one of us, in the language which is our native inheritance?" There is a third possibility, one to which the writer is inclined. In 1957 G. J. Sirks (*Harvard Theological Review* 50, 77–89) suggested that the word usually translated "tongues" may not mean *languages,* but *interpretations,* and that "speaking" in Acts ii 11 does not mean wild and uncontrolled utterance, but an ordered recitation of appointed passages. On this view, the crowd of diaspora Jews gathered outside the building where the apostles were assembled was taken aback and some members of it shocked into mockery by an interpretation of the liturgical lessons for Pentecost which (the apostles asserted) pointed to a dying and rising Messiah. Much of this hypothesis, while it rids us of the necessity of miraculous speaking in foreign languages not known to the speakers, must remain *sub judice.* We have little evidence for Jewish liturgical usage at this period. But granted our suggestion that the word "Galileans" must in Acts ii be rendered "Christians," then we appear to have wonder on the part of the onlookers that these sectarians should venture to interpret, or reinterpret, the traditional Pentecost theme.

In conclusion, the reader is reminded that John's view of the outpouring of the Spirit is difficult to harmonize with the tradition which we have here examined in Acts. (Cf. the writer's discussion in *Theology* 60, 1959.)

C. S. Mann

IV. THE ORGANIZATION AND INSTITUTIONS OF THE JERUSALEM CHURCH IN ACTS

Considering the number of books and articles which have dealt, in one way or another, with the theme of this note, especially since 1950, I propose only to provide some guidelines. I shall try to look at the way in which the Jerusalem church appears to have conducted its affairs and at its characteristic institutions, though they were not necessarily peculiar to it. Much light has been thrown on both by the discoveries in the Judean desert since 1947.

1. ORGANIZATION

A prime requirement here is objectivity. All scholars bring to the study of New Testament origins and history preconceptions from their own confessional background, though it is fair to say that this field is at the moment characterized by a somewhat illusory atmosphere of irenic calm among Christian scholars. It ought not to be assumed, by way of contrast, that non-Christians are of necessity less biased than those committed to Christian belief; the very reverse has often been the case. As far as we can, in the brief compass of this appendix, we shall examine the organization of the Jerusalem church, as described in the Acts of the Apostles, in the light of the one Jewish body (sectarian, like the apostolic church itself) which had a ready-made system of government—that of the Essenes of Qumran. Sherman Johnson, followed by Oscar Cullman, was the first to see the bearing of the Qumran discoveries for the early institutional history of the church, and since 1950 a great many studies (learned and otherwise) have been devoted to the subject.

It is true that the beginnings of what later came to be known as the monarchic episcopate can be found in the letters to Timothy and Titus, though it is necessary to qualify this statement by including the functions of the "elders," *presbuteroi,* which supplemented those of the "bishops," *episkopoi*. As far as the somewhat elusive evidence of Acts carries us, this hierarchic principle appears to have centered at Jerusalem at one time around the person of Peter, and then later around James (who according to both Josephus and Eusebius remained head of the Jewish Christians until his death in A.D. 64). Why this transfer of authority took place, we do not know. If we can find a hierarchic authority in the Jerusalem church, it is also fair to say that we also find ecclesiocratic structure: Acts i depicts the church as administered by the eleven (later, by election, twelve) apostles. The subsequent establishment of a welfare committee of seven (the members of which do not seem to have confined their energies to this kind of work) may have had its origin in a feature of Jewish administration which we do not know otherwise. In addition to this hierarchic structure, we find "elders" helping in the administration (Acts xi 30, xv 2–22); when first mentioned they represent the congregation, and the apostles are not mentioned at all.

In considering the outline of the apostolic organization of the Jerusalem church, it is important to bear in mind that the congregation also had an important role to play. At the election of a successor to Judas (Acts i 15–25), the whole congregation was represented by 120 men, in spite of the fact that the meeting was essentially one convened by, and concerning, the apostles. (See Strack-Billerbeck, II, pp. 194 ff., for the legal significance of "120" in rabbinic usage.) Whatever the influence of Peter (or James), or of the Twelve, the *presence* of the congregation was held to be essential. We recall that in Acts xv 22 the decision of the council was accepted by "the whole church." It is worth emphasizing here that the Greek word *plēthos* (and *polus* which does duty for it occasionally) is a clear translation of the technical term *rabbîm*, "the Many," in the Manual of Discipline, where it is used of the whole gathering of the faithful. In Acts vi, for example, the "Many" gather to assist in choosing the committee of seven.

Plainly, no Greek model (still less a Roman one) will do to explain the kind of organization which the Jerusalem church set up. No possible Greek model will explain the speed and ease with which (according to Luke) the apostles—and the congregation— set up the constitution of the infant church in Jerusalem. Evidently there was a very mixed constitution in the "political" sense. We have used the words "monarchic," "hierarchic," and "ecclesiocratic," and perhaps for good measure (bearing in mind the ratifi-

cation expressed by the whole congregation, the *plēthos*) we ought
also to add that there was a strong element of the "democratic."
These words will serve, for want of better, but it is of the highest
importance that we do not interpret them in a modern political
sense. We use them here in order to make a rough identification
of elements in the Jerusalem church. There is more to be added.
The local congregations could identify themselves with the whole
body of believers, and could consider themselves, their resolutions
and decisions, as being a manifestation of divine will. We may recall Paul's action in I Cor v 3–5: the decision of the apostle to
excommunicate has to be done with the acquiescence of the "spirits"
of the gathered congregation, along with Paul's "spirit," brought together by the Lord. The apostle may use "monarchic" authority,
but it cannot operate without the congregation. On the whole, the
best word we can use to describe the state of affairs that Acts
demonstrates for us is the word "hierarchic" (which does have the
advantage of being free from political overtones).

If there is no Greek model to which we may turn for enlighten-
ment, then it is wholly natural that we turn to Jewish models for
what assistance they can render. We need look no further than the
sectarians of Qumran for background to much of the material in
Acts. There has been a good deal of speculation about the precise
connection, if any, between the infant church and the Essenes of
Qumran. There is no call to add to the quantity of sheer guesswork
which has already taken place. But it is a reasonable hypothesis,
bearing in mind the ease and speed with which the church in
Jerusalem organized itself, to suppose that the earliest Christians
modeled themselves on the one ready-made example near to hand
—that of the Essenes. It is a reasonable hypothesis because (*a*)
so much vocabulary in the New Testament was evidently commonplace among the sectarians, and (*b*) the evidence now available
of the crossing of "party" lines in Judaism makes it inherently
likely that the church (itself a "sect" of Judaism) would have
found some kind of sectarian organization congenial.

We know from both the Damascus Document (CD) and the
Manual of Discipline (1QS) that the Essenes had a carefully
graduated hierarchic society. The entire congregation formed a
corporate body united by a covenant, with priests at the head and
Levites next in order of function. At the annual covenant feast all
members were very precisely graded, each man with his own place
in his own group. Basic to the whole concept of this covenant com-

munity was the responsibility each member owed, not only to the "sons of Zadok" (i.e. the legitimate priests) but also to the whole community. The deciding authority, especially in all matters of admission to the community, rested with the whole congregation of priests and laymen. We have already noticed this concept of corporate responsibility, of a congregational hierarchy, in the Jerusalem church of Acts as well as in the Pauline church of Corinth. At Qumran, the sense of corporate responsibility by no means indicated an absence of differentiation, for every section of the community had its own priests in the first rank, followed by the "elders" (*zeqēnîm* = *presbuteroi* > "priests").

For present purposes, it is interesting to note that all negotiations about new members and business in general were under the direction of the *mebaqqer*, whose basic function was exactly that of the New Testament *episkopos* ("overseer," later "bishop"). This identification of name and function was made by J. Jeremias (in G. Kittel's *Theologisches Wörterbuch zum Neuen Testament*, II, 614 ff.), from the Damascus Document, long before the discovery of the Qumran material. Some have disputed the identification, seeking to connect the *episkopos* with Hebrew *pāqîd*, since (in translation) there is often equivalence between some verbal forms of *pāqîd* and *episkopos*. But this is to make of the *episkopos* an ordinary official (which he was not), and to confuse his functions with those of the *pāqîd* (who was an official). This is not to say that there were never occasions when a *pāqîd* was also a *mebaqqer*, but it does have to be emphasized that the *episkopos* had a well-defined function and was not merely someone with an official post. (Incidentally, it is at least possible that discussions in our own time on the nature of the Christian ministry would often have been less confused and more productive had there not been centuries of identification of episcopal "office" and "function.") Now that we possess such pre-Christian evidence for this hierarchical structure at Qumran, it is both unnecessary and unwarranted to insist on a late date for the references to *episkopoi* and *presbuteroi* in the Pastoral Epistles.

One important item of information about the conduct of affairs at Qumran concerns the council of the community. This consisted of twelve men (1QS viii 1) and three priests. The exact relationship of the three to the twelve is at present impossible to determine. It *may* indicate that the three were given the title "priest" as a mark of honor, and not that they were drawn from outside the twelve. It is difficult to avoid noting the analogy between the twelve of Qumran and the twelve apostles of the New Testament: it also helps our understanding of the anxiety expressed in Acts i that the number should be made up after the defection of Judas. More than this: the number "three" reminds us of the privileged position of Peter, James, and John among the twelve apostles. Here the parallels between Qumran practice and the evidence of the New Testament are so close as to make some connection quite certain. This is not all. In both the New Testament and the Essene material, the Twelve are said to stand for the twelve tribes of Israel and to have functions vis-à-vis those tribes. Again, the Manual of Discipline (viii 5–10) speaks of the council of twelve as a "foundation," and the significance of this kind of terminology for the New Testament understanding of the apostles is immediately apparent. Variously, the apostles are "pillars," "foundations," in Gal ii 9; Eph ii 20; I Tim iii 15; and Rev xxi 14. The function of the twelve in judging (1QS viii 6) calls to mind the same function assigned to the apostles in Luke xxi 30. Elsewhere it is said that the function of the twelve at Qumran is to work for "reconciliation," a notion wholly in accord with Paul's view that the apostolic function is that of the "ministry of reconciliation" (II Cor v 18—it is quite clear from the context that it is the apostolate which Paul has in mind).

Only by a perversity of scholarship is it possible to deny that the Jerusalem church (and the Corinthian church, at least, too) received its structure from Essene models. The Essene community at Damascus appears to have had a slightly different organization from that of Qumran, which may possibly throw some light on the emergence of what has come to be known as the monarchical episcopate. In the Damascus Document the mebaqqer is far more than a mere overseer: he has become judicial authority, preacher, father, and shepherd to his flock. Even here, however, it is significant that there are controls and sanctions in the choice by the assembly of a council of "judges" to assist the mebaqqer. Perhaps here we are entitled to infer that the Damascus community represents a type of organization necessary in the case of a settled congregation in a large city.

2. INSTITUTIONS

It would be unfair to the evidence of Acts, as well as to proper understanding of Christian origins, to leave out such information as the Essenes may provide about some of the institutions of the early church.

a. We are all familiar with the experiment in common living which was a feature of the Jerusalem church, but one of apparently short duration. Now whereas the community of property which obtained at Jerusalem would appear to have been a voluntary arrangement (cf. Acts v 4—which would have to be balanced against Acts iv 32), albeit with penalties attaching to dishonesty in the matter, the communal holding of property at Qumran was monastic in character, and was compulsory. It may be observed here that the parallels between Essene and Christian monasticism have been the subject of some lengthy examination, but it has to be remembered that Christian monasticism began as groups of solitaries, and only later (under Cassian, Basil, and Benedict) did monastic *communities* arise. It must also be emphasized here that the Qumran community stressed community of property rather than poverty (in much the same way as the Rule of St. Benedict in later ages). As far as the New Testament is concerned, compassion for the poor springs from Old Testament roots and from the remembered sayings of Jesus. It is important, in making any evaluation of this New Testament concern, to reckon with the possibility that Christians may have made their way to Jerusalem as a pious exercise (like Jews in more recent times), and then later have become dependent on the local Christian community. This would have served to exacerbate the situation produced by the famine of A.D. 46.

b. We propose next to discuss baptism, both in Essene practice and in the early Christian community at Jerusalem. Before doing so, however, we may include here some evidence which throws light on the possible origins of the Essenes. (For this evidence I am indebted to W. F. Albright, who has kindly allowed me to use this material.) The first Isaiah scroll from Qumran (1QIsa^2) stems from a *Babylonian* recension, as shown by the fact that Assyro-Babylonian names and words are correctly vocalized with vowel letters, whereas they are quite wrongly vocalized in the Greek, Syriac, and Hebrew texts. Essene theology is directly influenced by

Zoroastrian thought, probably in its Zervanite form, and Iranian culture is also reflected in the fragments from a divinatory treatise later attributed to Zoroaster. Add the fact that there are a fair number of Iranian but no Greek loanwords in the material so far published from Qumran, and we have a powerful argument for predominance of Iranian influence on the background of the early Essenes.

There is, however, much more to be learned than this. The important place given by the Essenes to frequent lustrations in "living (running) water" (cf. later Christian canonical requirements for baptism) cannot well have had its origin in Palestine, where climatic conditions do not favor such emphasis. But the Babylonians, with a much warmer climate and with elaborate canal and irrigation works, were familiar with frequent washings, ceremonial and otherwise. In the pagan Babylonian religion, great stress was laid on ceremonial lustrations—actually much more than in Egypt. The Parthian invasions about 140 B.C., with the resulting disruption of ordered life, meant that the old irrigation systems could no longer be maintained, and the complex system of retaining dikes (levees) quickly broke. As a result, the Euphrates and Tigris rivers both changed their courses. This disastrous break with previously ordered ways of life—dated by the sudden end of cuneiform inscriptions at such sites as Erech—must have brought with it wholesale emigration of Jews. This date fits in remarkably well with the presumed date of the foundation of the Essene communities, according to the highly probable correlation of Frank M. Cross, Jr.

The baptism of John, as recorded for us in the New Testament (where it is said to be a "token of repentance") manifestly owes its origin to the Essenes, however reinterpreted. (The evidence for Jewish proselyte baptism is tenuous, and there appears to be no indisputable evidence for such usage before the second century A.D.) It may be safely supposed that many baptist sects which we know to have existed in Judaism after the New Testament period had their remote origins in Essene practice. The ritual baths of the Essenes were an outward manifestation of a spiritual cleansing already accomplished; they were self-administered, and there is no evidence that they were reckoned to have any sacramental efficacy in any sense understood by Christians. At the same time, the language used of them makes it clear that the moral qualities demanded to make them effective correspond to the language recorded in the New Testament as used by John the Baptist. The sectarians provided the background of John's baptismal teaching, so far as known to us, in much the same way that John's baptism provided the ground for the once-for-all baptism of the Christian church. There is no indication whatever in the New Testament that John's baptism was ever meant to be a single initiatory rite, and in so far as the Mandaeans preserve anything whatever of Johannine practice their frequent lustrations may indicate that John's baptism might be, and perhaps was, repeated. The close connection in the New Testament sources between baptism and the passion of Christ established general norms for Christian practice very early, and *eph' hapax* was the keynote for baptism as well as for the passion.

The Essenes have provided us with the exegetical background to Matt iii 11–12, for the Habakkuk Commentary (1QpHab iii 28 ff.) speaks of the *river of fire,* a linking of water-and-fire lustration with judgment which had previously been merely an hypothesis. Where previously we had a connection (Dan vii 10) of somewhat dubious character between Persian thought and Judaism in the "fiery river of judgment," we now have a connection which is certain. Qumran has, moreover (1QS iv 21), given us the prototype of Mark's usage of baptism "in the Spirit" (Mark i 8). What is wholly lacking, as far as our present knowledge goes, is any link between baptism (however understood) and any manifestation of "the Spirit" in the sense in which Luke in Acts links the two.

c. The common meals at Qumran immediately suggest the common meals of the early Christians as we know them from Acts in Jerusalem, and also at Corinth from Paul's first letter. 1QS vi 1–6 gives us basic information about the manner in which the common meals of the Essenes were eaten, with insistence upon ritual baths beforehand, exclusion of the uninitiated, hierarchic order of seating, and priestly blessing of bread and wine. There is enough here, of course, to provide a rough analogy with baptism and the Eucharist, but there are some caveats. Although 1QSa (a two-column document from Cave 1 at Qumran) indeed speaks of the cult meal in an eschatological way, as presided over by the Messiah of Aaron (who is an eschatological figure), and therefore to some extent reminiscent of I Cor xi 26, there is no suggestion whatever that the Essenes thought that the Messiah of Aaron (the spiritual head) or the Messiah of Israel (the political head) had already come. But it was acceptance as Messiah of Jesus, born of Mary, which was central in Christian belief, however varied the statement of the confession might be. Furthermore, however much the last supper of Jesus with his *habûrah* may have been indebted to sectarian Jews either in its framework or in its calendric observance, it was indissolubly linked with the self-oblation of Jesus in a new covenant of forgiveness. For the Essenes, this was emphatically not true. For them, the meal had no link with any *person*, living or dead; there was, as far as our present evidence goes, no memorial of the ministry and death of the founder of the group (still less of his resurrection and exaltation), though all New Testament sources agree that it was central to the Eucharist. To what extent common meals persisted among Christians beyond the Apostolic Age, we do not know with certainty. All we know is the importance which the Apostolic Age attached to them (cf. Acts ii 42, 46), and that in Corinth the common meals were associated with the Eucharist (cf. I Cor xi 20 ff.). From time to time, attempts have been made (presumably on account of the use of the phrase in the Didache) to equate "the breaking of bread" in Acts with the Holy Communion. There is no clear evidence for the equation. It is, however, quite likely, in view of the character of common meals in a *habûrah*, that the Jerusalem church invested common meals with a quasi-sacramental meaning as in some way manifesting unity. Evidently, for Paul, Peter's conduct at Antioch (Gal ii 11 ff.) was reprehensible simply because the character of the common meal had been put in jeopardy by Peter's hesitation to share it with Gentiles.

This survey has necessarily been brief, but it may indicate some of the ways in which the discoveries at Qumran have illuminated our understanding of the New Testament, and of Acts in particular. It is of paramount importance not to be stampeded by popular journalism or semipopular *vulgarization* into assuming parallels where none exists. The following books are recommended:

Raymond E. Brown, S.S., *New Testament Essays,* Milwaukee, 1965.

Frank M. Cross, Jr., *The Ancient Library of Qumran and Modern Biblical Studies,* New York, 1958.

Jean Daniélou, S.J., *The Dead Sea Scrolls and Primitive Christianity,* tr. by S. Attanasio, Baltimore, 1958.

C. H. H. Scobie, *John the Baptist,* Philadelphia, 1964.

Krister Stendahl (ed.), *The Scrolls and the New Testament,* New York, 1957.

Translations of the material so far available from Qumran can be found in Géza Vermès, *The Dead Sea Scrolls in English,* Baltimore, 1962.

C. S. Mann

V. STEPHEN'S SAMARITAN BACKGROUND[1]

Stephen was a Samaritan according to the native tradition preserved by Abul-Fath (Vilmar edition, 1865, p. 159). Acts vii 2–50 confirms this, for it depends on the Samaritan Pentateuch and reflects Samaritan views of Old Testament history. Following are our chief arguments from Stephen's speech in Acts vii.

(a) In the Masoretic text (Gen xi 32) Terah lived 205 years, surviving by sixty years Abraham's departure from Harran (cf. Gen xi 26, xii 4). But Stephen's report that Abraham left at his father's death (vii 4) is in harmony with the Samaritan text in which Terah lived for only 145 years.

(b) God promised Abraham the land but "gave him no inheritance in it, not even a foot of ground" (vii 5); this is based on Deut ii 5b. But in the Masoretic text the noun "inheritance" is found only in ii 5c; in the Samaritan text, however, it also appears in ii 5b.

(c) God told Moses, "I am the God of your fathers" (vii 32); this is based on Exod iii 6. The Masoretic text reads "father"; the Samaritan reading is, however, in the plural.

(d) Stephen's history from Abraham through Moses depends on Genesis and Exodus. Hence vii 37, mentioning a future prophet like Moses, is not based on Deut xviii 15—which would be an intrusion—but on the Samaritan Book of Exodus which contains a pericope (after xx 17) composed of passages from Deuteronomy and called by the Samaritans the tenth commandment.

[1] This appendix is a condensation of much more extensive material prepared by Dr. Abram Spiro at the editors' request. We had hoped that he might write the final draft of our condensation himself, but a long absence in Greece (1966) made this impracticable. Dr. Spiro presented a paper on the subject at the Chicago meeting of the American Oriental Society (April 14, 1965) and is now working on a substantial volume. We wish to thank him heartily for his generosity. Great care has been taken to assure the accuracy of our presentation but we, not Dr. Spiro, are responsible for errors or deviations from his views.

W.F.A. and C.S.M.

(*e*) The six-times-repeated demonstrative "this" (vii 35–40) is a Samaritan formulary construction. A Samaritan liturgical poem has survived in which dozens of lines begin with "this is he" and end with "this is Moses the son of Amram." Stephen's identification of Palestine as "this land in which you are *now* living" (vii 4), inapplicable in Jerusalem to the Sanhedrin, shows that Stephen composed this tract for use among newcomers, that is, for the men of the Diaspora synagogue(s) in Jerusalem (vi 9 ff.).

(*f*) With the story from Abraham through Isaiah's oracle he glorified the Samaritans and denounced the Jews. Conversely, the Jewish writer Eupolemos (second century B.C.E.) showed in his story from Moses through Solomon the harmonious and victorious life of the Jews whose piety culminated in the building of the temple. Another Jewish writer, Pseudo-Philo (first century C.E.), tells the story from Adam to the last days of Saul, thus linking up with Chronicles which begins at this juncture, carrying the account until Cyrus' edict of restoration. These examples show that ancient writers, like Stephen, used slices of history as frameworks for their respective chosen messages.

(*g*) We may, then, proceed as follows: Harran (Haran), relatively insignificant in Hebrew tradition, is central in Samaritan lore, where in an ordeal by fire the sanctity of Gerizim and the Samaritan Pentateuch were demonstrated; Stephen mentions Harran twice (vii 2, 4).

(*h*) Shechem (NT Sichem), the only other city mentioned by Stephen, is the Samaritan counterpart of Jerusalem (vii 16), and he transfers there the cave of Machpelah from Hebron (Gen xxiii 1–20, xlix 31) by stating that Jacob and his sons were buried in the tomb which Abraham had bought; this assumes that Abraham and Isaac were likewise buried there.

(*i*) Abraham's seed shall "worship me in this place" (vii 7). These words echo two half verses, in one of which God spoke to Abraham (Gen xv 14) and in the other to Moses (Exod iii 12), and Stephen's tradition altered a "mountain" (vii 7) to a "place." Moreover, he combined two appearances of God to Abraham—one at Shechem (Gen xii 7) and the other at an unnamed locality (Gen xv 1–21)—into one and placed it at or near Shechem. Since the Old Testament term "place" for a shrine is standard Samaritan usage—appearing innumerable times in their literature and in the New Testament on the lips of Samaritans (John iv 20 and Acts vi 14 in Stephen's words)—it follows that God ordained the shrine ("place") of Shechem, that is, Gerizim.

(*j*) In Exod xxxii 32–34, Moses pleaded with the Lord either to forgive Israel the sin of the golden calf or to blot out his name from the Lord's book. The Lord replied that he would blot out only the sinners, and bade Moses lead the people to its destination, "nevertheless in the day when I visit, I will visit their sin upon them." Stephen asserts (vii 41–43) that Amos identifies the saints and the sinners (Amos v 27) by explaining that the divine visitation means the Babylonian exile, for since Judah was exiled into Babylon it follows that the sins of her ancestors had been visited upon her. It also follows that the Jews, descendants of the Judeans, are the progeny of sinners who had already rebelled against Moses when still in Egypt (vii 25–29, 35–40). Stephen or his Samaritan precursors accomplished this revision of history by changing "Damascus" into "Babylon" in the text of Amos, thus making the prophet speak of the exile of Judah.

(*k*) In contrast to the sinners, the saints had a tabernacle of witness made on a heavenly pattern and brought it into Canaan under the leadership of Joshua (vii 44–45)—the Samaritan hero next in importance to Moses. Samaritan tradition maintained that Joshua established the cult of Gerizim, basing this assertion on Joshua xxiv by altering the "sanctuary" (vii 26) to a tabernacle— the standard Samaritan name for their shrine—and transferring it from Shechem proper (vii 1, 25) to nearby Gerizim. Hence Joshua and the saints fulfilled Stephen's version of God's proclamation to Abraham (vii 7).

(*l*) "So it was until the days of David, who found favor in the sight of God and sought leave to find a habitation for the house of Jacob" (vii 45–46). This depends on Ps cxxxii 4, where David swears not to rest "until I find a place [*māqôm*] for the Lord, a dwelling place for the Mighty One of Jacob." David's seeking a "place" the Samaritans regarded as heresy, for the Lord himself had founded it (vii 7), so Stephen followed Samaritan tradition by only using the second half of the verse and changing it: instead of "the Mighty One (i.e. God) of Jacob," he has "the house of Jacob." Thus David did not seek to establish a "tabernacle" (*skēnē;* cf. vii 43–44) for God, but a "dwelling place," *skēnōma*, for Israel. That is, David sought and found Jerusalem as the secular capital; Shechem remained the sacred one. The Samaritans relate that David was anointed at the foot of Gerizim and sent his offerings

to the "place." His advisers had importuned him to build a temple
in Jerusalem, but the Samaritan high priest dissuaded him.

(m) Solomon's temple was not only in the wrong "place" but
was of human construction (vii 48–50). Because of its heavenly
pattern (vii 44) the Gerizim tabernacle was *not* considered so built.
The Old Testament makes clear, however, that heaven *was* involved in the building of Solomon's temple (II Sam xxiv 18; I Kings
xviii 24, 38; I Chron xxi 18–26, xxviii 19; II Chron iii 1, vii 1;
Ps lxxviii 68–69). But the sanctity of a temple is a relative matter,
depending on whose temple it is and who the witnesses are. According to the Samaritans, the tabernacle of Gerizim was not made by
human hands because the witnesses to its heavenly pattern were
Samaritans, as they infer from the Samaritan Pentateuch, which
alone they consider canonical. Solomon's temple was a human construction because it was a Jewish temple and because the witnesses
to its heavenly origin were Jewish, that is, the testimony is found
in texts which only the Jews consider canonical.

(n) Stephen, who was following Samaritan usage, could not denounce Solomon's temple in the king's own words (I Kings viii 27);
he therefore used Isa lxvi 1–2 but altered the text: (i) He placed the
prophet's opening words, "Thus says the Lord," after the question,
"What house will you build for me?" (omitting "thus"), thereby
making the Lord's question more emphatic. (ii) He changed the
declarative into a question, "Did not my hand make all these
things?" He thus obtained three questions. (iii) His tradition altered the twice-repeated "what manner," *poios,* of the Septuagint,
employing "what manner" in the first question and "which" or
"where," *tis,* in the second one.

To grasp the purpose of this exegesis it should be pointed out
that, in contrast to the Samaritan "place," the Jewish cultic term
was "the house." The prophet thus uses here the Jewish and
Samaritan cultic terms. The interpretation followed by Stephen
makes Isaiah prophesy against the postexilic Jews, trying to dis-
suade them from rebuilding the temple. (i) What manner of temple
("house") will you build for me, says the Lord? Will it be of brick
and stone and other durable material, or will it be a less permanent
tabernacle? (ii) Which (or where) is the place, *māqôm,* of my
rest? Is the "place" Mount Zion or Mount Gerizim? (iii) Did not
my hand make all these things? The answer to this third question,
a rhetorical one, is "Yes," for God had designated to Abraham the
"place" of Gerizim (vii 7) and by an angel to Moses the "taber-

nacle" (vii 44). Thus Solomon's and Zerubbabel's temples are of
human construction, of the wrong material, and in the wrong
"place." Stephen asserts that "the Most High, *hypsistos,* does not
dwell in houses made with hands" (vii 48). He uses "Most High"
as a synonym for God because this term is used in the story of
Melchizedek, the Samaritan hero, king of Shalem (Gen xiv 18–
22), near Shechem in their opinion. Thus the God of Gerizim ("the
Most High") does not dwell in a handmade temple. The Samaritan
Pseudo-Eupolemos (second century B.C.) calls Gerizim the "mount
of the Most High."

In Stephen's view God dealt in person with Abraham (vii 2),
but with Moses through an angel only (vii 30, 35, 38, 44), which
is a departure from the Old Testament (Exod xxxiii 11; Num xii
8; Deut xxxiv 10). The story from Abraham through Isaiah's
oracle provided him with the framework for a glorification of the
Samaritans and a denunciation of the Jews. Conversely, the Jewish writer Eupolemos (second century B.C.E.) showed in his story
from Moses through Solomon the harmonious and victorious life
of the Jews whose piety culminated in the building of the temple
(*apud* Eusebius *Praep. ev.* IX.30). Again, Pseudo-Philo begins
with Adam and terminates with Saul, leaving him on the battle-
field about to die and with a message to David (LXV.1–5), thus
linking up the account with Chronicles where, when the curtain
rises, we find the Lord slaying Saul for his sins (I Chron x 1–14).
Thus the combined account of Pseudo-Philo and Chronicles shows
the lot of the sinner and the portion of the saint—Saul and David,
respectively. Moreover, the combined account presents a revision
of history from Adam through the fall of Judah to Cyrus' edict
of restoration, written in the spirit of the laws of Moses. These
examples illustrate the use by ancient Judeo-Samaritan polemic
writers of an historical framework for their messages. Stephen
acted similarly, and his composition (vii 2–50) seems to have
survived substantially intact.

The downgrading of Moses implies a similar treatment of the
Law. Stephen devotes to the Law, given by an angel on Sinai,
just one verse (vii 38), with the result that it becomes unimportant
by contrast with the Old Testament account of Sinai (Exod xix
16–xx 18)—and subsequent Jewish literature—where one finds
a dazzling array of color and sound and the suspension of the
laws of nature at the momentous hour of the cosmic event, when
on Sinai God gave the Law which was meant to last for all eternity.

Circumcision, in contrast to the laws of Moses, was ordained by God himself to Abraham, and Stephen strongly emphasizes it (vii 8). We thus see that Abraham and his institution are superior to Moses and his laws. Not only was the Law given by an angel, but the heavenly pattern of the tabernacle of witness was likewise communicated to Moses by an angel (vii 44). This is again a divergence from any known Jewish recension of the Pentateuch, where God himself shows the pattern to Moses (Exod xxv 9, 40).

Stephen had no interest in the cult. He used the argument of the illegitimacy of the Jerusalem temple as a polemic against the Jews, to show that they deluded themselves in seeking salvation in the temple, for salvation lay elsewhere. In general, Judeo-Samaritans of that time looked for a Messiah who would avenge the wrongs of Israel and restore Palestine to its rightful owners. Yet, while the Jews could find such a Messiah in the rich imagery and sweep of Prophets and Psalms, the "orthodox" Samaritans had to seek him in the narrow confines of the Pentateuch, which was not easy. They had to utilize the idea of a future prophet like Moses (Deut xviii 15) and make it part of their tenth commandment, though they were not in need of another Moses. Long ago their ancestors had come from Egypt, had crossed the Reed Sea, had received the Law, and had wandered forty years in the wilderness under Moses. Now they were subjugated and despoiled in their own land into which Joshua had brought them and which he had conquered for them. In Stephen's time the Samaritans needed another Joshua to reconquer the land for them by driving out the Romans. Hence their *taheb,* the "One Who Returns," became, despite Deut xviii 15, 18, a composite figure combining the features of Moses and Joshua. In one tradition he is even called "Joshua," while in another he was to die upon completion of his lifework and be buried near Joshua.

Stephen's address makes a composite figure of Moses by borrowing motifs from Joshua. According to Stephen, Moses was a fighter and would-be liberator when still in Egypt. But, alas, the ancestors of the Jews failed to recognize his messianic role (vii 25, 35, 39). Though he dismisses Sinai in one verse (vii 38), he devotes seven to retelling the story of Moses' intervention in two street brawls: in one of these an Egyptian strikes a Hebrew, and in the other a Hebrew strikes a fellow Hebrew (Exod ii 11–15). Stephen's speech transformed the Old Testament account, taking it out from the merely trivial, recasting it typologically, and giving it a messianic significance. Social terms—missing in the Old Testament account—are introduced (vii 23–29). He writes that the Israelite was "being treated unjustly" or "wronged," *adikoumenon,* by the Egyptian and "oppressed," *kataponoumenō,* by him (vii 24). Thus the Egyptian personifies the unjust Egyptian oppression and the Israelite represents the oppressed people of Israel. Even though the Egyptian used no physical violence in Stephen's account, Moses slew the oppressor. Stephen rightly interprets the social aspect of the matter: "Moses went out to his people and looked on their burdens; and he saw an Egyptian beating a Hebrew" (Exod ii 11).

Stephen's exaltation of Abraham and downgrading of Moses represents an early stage in Samaritan attachment to Israel. Beginning with the fall of Israel in 722/21 B.C., several Assyrian rulers had successively brought Samaritans to northern Palestine, where they accepted Yahweh along with their ancestral divinities. Zerubbabel considered these syncretists unworthy to participate in the restoration of the temple, and an enmity developed between the pure and the polluted Yahwists. The governor of Samaria in the fifth century B.C., Sanballat—though he still bore a pagan name —gave his sons Yahwist names and gave his daughter in marriage to the grandson of the high priest in Jerusalem. Nevertheless, Nehemiah still considered them non-Israelites and expelled Sanballat's priestly son-in-law from Jerusalem. As a delayed consequence, the Samaritans—evidently led by Sanballat's descendants, especially the children of his Judean son-in-law—about 389/88 B.C., erected on Mount Gerizim a temple ("tabernacle") to rival that of Jerusalem.[2]

Yet the laws of Moses were slow in becoming a vital force among the Samaritans. For one thing, even postexilic Jerusalem was lax in observing the laws, and it was only through the powers that Ezra had received from the Persian authorities that the laws were enforced. But Sanballat's descendants were not armed with such power and did not seek it, inasmuch as their ancestor Sanballat in opposition to Nehemiah, seems to have been motivated by hostility to the rigor of the laws. Furthermore, the Yahwistic activities of Sanballat and his family did not convert the whole Samaritan community at once. When the royal family of Adiabene accepted Judaism in the first century C.E., it did not make Jews

---

[2] For the date, see A. Spiro, *Proceedings of the American Academy for Jewish Research* xx (1951), 312 ff.

of the people of Adiabene. Similarly, when in the Middle Ages
the Khazar ruling family adopted Judaism it did not convert the
people. But unlike the situation in Adiabene, Yahweh was not a
foreigner in Samaria but master of the land, and the Samaritans
spoke the languages of the land, Hebrew and Aramaic.

Since the Samaritans derived their knowledge of the heroes and
lore of Israel—Abraham, Moses, Egypt, Sinai—largely from the
oral traditions of the North Israelites among whom they had been
settled, Moses and his laws, known to them chiefly from the
Pentateuch which they had imported from Jerusalem, made relatively slow progress with them. Moreover, Abraham was intimately connected with Shechem, where he made his first stop in
Canaan, saw God in a vision, and built an altar (Gen xii 5–7).
Furthermore, he is said to have been the ancestor of a multitude of
nations (Gen xvii 4–5), and through the ages proselytes attached themselves to him and bore his name. Because of Abraham's association with their own Mesopotamian home the people
of Samaria preferred Abraham to Moses. He became both their
ancestor and their founding father. Josephus testifies that they
called themselves "Hebrews" (*Ant.* XI.viii.6). This testimony
is confirmed from all branches of Samaritan literature where the
self-designation "Hebrews" appears scores of times. It may also
be inferred from Jewish literature. Obviously, the Samaritans chose
the name "Hebrews" because of "Abram the Hebrew" (Gen xiv
13). Apparently as early as the third century B.C. they called
themselves "Hebrews," as may be inferred from the Septuagint
(Gen xiv 13) where "Abram the Hebrew" is translated "Abram
from beyond (the river)," a departure from the standard practice of the Septuagint which always transcribes "Hebrew" as *He-
braios* except where it differs from the Masoretic text. The deviation in the case of Abraham is apparently Jewish polemic against
the Samaritans, who had laid claim to "Abram the Hebrew."
Thus in the first centuries of Samaritan teaching it tended to center not on Moses and his laws, but on Abraham, who had ordained
the cult of Mount Gerizim and had demanded that they circumcise
their sons. But this demand was not too burdensome, inasmuch
as many of their Palestinian neighbors practiced circumcision. The
Jews reacted to the notion of a Yahwism without laws, based
on Abraham, by holding that in reality Abraham, and in fact
Adam before him, had observed the Jewish laws, which were not

innovations in the days of Moses but only *renewed* at that time (cf. the account in the Book of Jubilees).

In the course of time, Samaritan attachment to Israel became more solid and the Samaritans appropriated a much wider range of Israelite tradition. Since they lived along the borders separating Ephraim from Manasseh, they began calling themselves "Sons of Joseph," or, in the fuller form, "Sons of Ephraim and Manasseh" (Josephus *Ant.* IX.xiv.3; XI.vi.8, and frequently in their own literature). This is also reflected in Stephen's speech, one fifth of which is devoted to the section on Joseph, in which Joseph's brethren who were "jealous" of him and "sold him into Egypt" are not even mentioned by name (vii 9–18). Thus in the first century of our era the Samaritans had advanced considerably beyond their primitive attachment to "Abram the Hebrew." Nevertheless, their alien origin weighed heavily on them and gave them a sense of inferiority, as may be inferred from Stephen's monotonous repetition of the phrases "our father," "our fathers," and "our race" (vii 2, 11–12, 15, 19, 38–39, 44–45); the Samaritan woman who spoke to Jesus was likewise fond of "our father" and "our fathers" (John iv 12, 20). These tireless assertions had the effect of silencing their own alien voices that came from within and the Jewish taunts that came from without. But even after they had appropriated the history and lore of Israel, the Samaritans were much slower to accept and live by the rigors of the laws of Moses. Josephus writes that "whenever anyone was accused by the people of Jerusalem of eating unclean food or violating the Sabbath or committing any other such sin, he used to flee to the men of Sichem" (*Ant* XI.viii.7). But the dominance of Moses reached great heights among the Samaritans in the centuries that followed Stephen, for the longer they lived under the Law, the deeper became their attachment to it, and the higher Moses rose in their estimation. It was not dissimilar from the situation that prevailed among the Jews, except that with the Jews the process started centuries earlier.

The examination of Stephen's missionary discourse (or tract) in Acts vii 2–50 is relatively easy because it was transmitted faithfully by Luke. It is more difficult to analyze chapter vi, the remainder of chapter vii, and the beginning of chapter viii, because of Luke's share in them. A mere glance suggests that Luke wrote chapter vi on the basis of sources different from those behind the first five chapters. (The use of the word "source" does not necessarily indicate exclusively written or exclusively oral sources; the writer may have had access to both.) (*a*) "Hebrews" is not found in the Gospels or elsewhere in Acts. (*b*) "Hellenists" occurs for the first time here. (*c*) In addition, a number of other linguistic idiosyncrasies occur in the very first verse and still others in subsequent verses of chapter vi.

Since Stephen is the main hero of chapter vii—his missionary discourse (vii 2–50) as well as the story of his death (vii 54–viii 2) is embedded in it—it follows that for it Luke drew upon Samaritan Christian sources well acquainted with the circumstances. Some of the terms employed bear this out. (*a*) As we saw above, the Samaritans called themselves "Hebrews" for centuries. By contrast, the Jews of the first century C.E. did not call themselves "Hebrews," nor did the Gentiles call them "Hebrews." (Some writers when they wanted to archaize or use elevated style occasionally employed "Hebrews" in literary compositions. "Hebrews" as a synonym for Jews came into use only with the second century C.E., and then only in Christian writers.) It is therefore clear that the "Hebrews" of vi 1 are Samaritan Christians. (*b*) As seen earlier, "place," *topos*, for a shrine was a favorite Samaritan term. Now Stephen is reported to have used it (vi 14) even though his words are based on the *logion* of Jesus (Mark xiv 58 and par.; cf. John ii 19), who used "temple," *naos*, not "place." When Jewish witnesses quoted Stephen indirectly, they spoke of the "holy place" (vi 13). The addition of the adjective "holy" shows that "place" was not then a Jewish technical term, as can also be seen from the words of Jesus (Matt xxiv 15). That the Jews had given up the archaic "place" is also shown by its absence in the Mishnah. The great care in the use of "place" in Acts vi shows that it came from a source in which this cultic term was significant.

Several charges are made against Stephen. (*a*) Members of the synagogue(s) of the Freedmen secretly instigated witnesses who said, "We have heard him speak blasphemous words against Moses and God" (vi 11). (*b*) "False witnesses" testified before the Sanhedrin that, "This man never ceases to speak words against this holy place and the Law; for we have heard him say that this Jesus of Nazareth will destroy this place, and will change the customs which Moses delivered to us" (vi 13–14). The first charge, used to incite the people, is neutral with regard to Stephen's Christianity. The second charge, stated as testimony before the Sanhedrin, consists of two divergent parts, which have been linked by the Greek connective *gar,* "for"; it has specifically Christian color only in the second part. In the first part Stephen is said to speak against the "Law," *nomos,* whereas in the second part the "customs," *ethē,* of Moses are in danger of being changed. Yet "Law" is not identical with "customs." We have not merely two but three charges against Stephen: blasphemy against Moses and God (vi 11); speaking ceaselessly against the temple and the Law (vi 13); asserting that Jesus would destroy the temple and change the customs which Moses had delivered (vi 14). Only the last charge has Christian coloring.

The first, the charge of blasphemy, we shall analyze later; here we shall deal with the second, the charge that, "This man never ceases to speak words against this holy place and the Law" (vi 13). This charge is fully justified in the light of our commentary on the missionary tract, in which he argued that the temple was made by hands, of the wrong material and in the wrong "place." Furthermore he downgraded Moses, with whom God dealt only through an angel, and downgraded the Law, which he dismissed with a verse (vii 38), indicating that Stephen paid only lip service to tradition by mentioning the Law and Sinai. Acts vi 13 states that Stephen spoke ceaselessly against law and temple, whereas his missionary discourse in Acts vii is full of hints and implications but no direct statements. Obviously, in his own circle he spoke explicitly about these matters.

The third charge accuses Stephen of having said, "this Jesus of Nazareth will destroy this place, and will change the customs which Moses delivered to us" (vi 14). The first half of this charge may have had some basis (cf. John ii 19; Mark xiv 58) in the *logion* of Jesus, with a change of "temple" to the Samaritan technical term "place." (When the Jewish witnesses did not quote Stephen directly they employed "holy place" [vi 13]; they added the adjective "holy" because "place" was not a Jewish cultic term.) It is clear that the first half of the third charge, in the form of a direct quotation of Stephen, was found in Luke's Samaritan-Christian source. The second half of the charge is not given in the form of a direct quotation of Stephen, as may be seen from the words "which Moses delivered to us," that is, to "us" Jews; thus the witnesses are represented as reproducing Stephen's views in indirect quotation.

In their zeal for the new faith, Christian missionaries made concessions to the customs and ways of life of the varied groups to which they brought the Gospel. Paul takes pride in having "become all things to all men, that I might by all means save some" (I Cor ix 22). To a lesser degree, Peter and Barnabas acted likewise, though Paul berates their inconsistency (Gal ii 11–14). It is, therefore, quite conceivable that, on the analogy of Paul, Stephen may have acted and spoken like a Samaritan when he was preaching the Gospel to Samaritans. He may have expressed his grief at the sight of the flourishing, handmade and illegitimate "place" of Zion while the legitimate "tabernacle" of Gerizim was lying in ruins after its destruction by the Jewish king John Hyrcanus in 129/28 B.C., and he may have promised them that the Messiah would bring better days and restore their "tabernacle." In the year A.D. 35, a Samaritan messianic figure assembled a large armed throng of Samaritans and bade them ascend Mount Gerizim to recover the cultic vessels buried there. Though not stated, the vessels were obviously needed for a restored "tabernacle." We do not know whether the "tabernacle" was supposed to have been rebuilt by this messianic figure or by God himself. But the movement ended in disaster. Pilate blocked the route to Gerizim with cavalry and heavily armed infantry, and in a pitched battle many Samaritans were slain and others fled. Moreover, "many prisoners were taken, whose principal leaders Pilate put to death along with those who were most influential among the fugitives." This massacre caused a furor and brought about Pilate's dismissal (Josephus Ant. XVIII.iv.1–2). The episode shows how eager the Samaritans were to restore their "tabernacle" on Mount Gerizim.

The Samaritans claimed that Moses had identified Mount Gerizim as the future shrine (Deut xxvii 4) and said that the reading Mount Ebal of the Hebrew Bible was a Jewish forgery. Accordingly, the Samaritan reading in all the pertinent passages in Deuteronomy which speak of the shrine is the place which God "has chosen." The Hebrew Bible reads, however, "which God will choose," for the Jews argued that Moses left the matter to future generations to decide according to the Jews. Yet though Moses had not identified the shrine explicitly, tradition had it that Jerusalem was meant—a meaning which could be inferred from the text. Thus, the shrine on Mount Gerizim is a violation of the "customs which Moses delivered," and the text of Luke merely a circumlocution on the lips of the Jewish witnesses against Stephen, who testify to Stephen's views in indirect quotation. Likewise, Luke carefully chose his words, using the noun "customs" and the verb "change," for the latter may refer only to a change in particulars of the ritual rather than to the abolition of the Law.

We shall now turn back to the first charge: "We have heard him speak blasphemous words against Moses and God" (vi 11). On the surface the charge of blasphemy seems a puzzle. It might be argued that Stephen's speaking against the Law was considered blasphemy against Moses. Paul *is* accused of having taught "everywhere" against the Law (Acts xxi 28; cf. xv 2, 5, xxi 21, xxv 8, xxviii 17), but he is not charged with blasphemy against Moses. Commentators cite the words of Jesus in Mark (ii 23 ff., iii 2 ff., vii 14 ff., x 5; cf. Matt v 17), yet no charge of blasphemy against Moses is mentioned in the trial of Jesus. Again, it is said that blasphemy against God is supposed to be based on Stephen's words that Jesus would destroy the temple—the temple being, allegedly, synonymous with God. But Stephen's words are based on the *logion* of Jesus, yet though this *logion* is brought up in the trial of Jesus (Mark xiv 58 and par.) he is not accused of blasphemy because of it. The charge that Stephen blasphemed against Moses could perhaps be explained in the light of our demonstration that in his discourse he downgraded Moses. But what was Stephen's blasphemy against God? It might be argued that the charge of blasphemy against God was not found in Luke's source but is his own formulation on the strength of Stephen's subsequent words that he saw Jesus at the right hand of God (vii 56). In other words, Luke might have followed the account of the trial of Jesus, in which he is reported to have been condemned for blasphemy because of his assertion that he would be sitting at the right hand of God (Mark xiv 64; Matt xxvi 65–66), even though no witnesses on blasphemy had been brought against him. One might continue to argue that for this reason Luke or a precursor mentioned a charge of blasphemy as being the means by which the people were incited, but did not describe it as a testimony before the court, though Stephen was stoned because of this alleged blasphemy. Yet this is scarcely a valid argument, because in Luke's version the words of Jesus were not regarded as blasphemy but as an open avowal of his Messiahship (Luke xxii 71). We must, therefore, assume that the charge of blasphemy is not a Lucan formulation but was found in his source.

Just as Acts vii 2–50 was not a speech before the Sanhedrin but was Stephen's missionary tract, the charges against Stephen (vi 11–14) were not testimonies before the Sanhedrin—for Stephen was never on trial—but a summary of Stephen's real or alleged views. An irate mob thus presumably lynched Stephen not because of his Christianity but because he had carried on Samaritan propaganda in Jerusalem. Unlike Peter and Paul who frequented the temple, Stephen—having been a Samaritan—stayed away from the temple but preached against it among the Jews who had come to Jerusalem with pious devotion to the temple. He met his antagonists among these Jews (vi 9–14).

The stoning of Stephen had repercussions: "And on that day a great persecution arose against the church in Jerusalem; and they were all scattered throughout the region of Judea and Samaria, except the apostles" (viii 1). Since Luke drew on Samaritan-Hellenist sources, the report that "they were all scattered" evidently refers to the members of Stephen's circle. The Jewish Christians remained, however, and their leaders, the apostles, continued working in Jerusalem. This is confirmed by a number of subsequent passages in Acts, from which we see that the apostles remained in Jerusalem (viii 14, 25, ix 27, xi 1–2) as well as the rank and file of the church (ix 26, 31, xi 2). This is also implied in the words "those who were scattered because of the persecution that arose over Stephen" (xi 19). The words "those who were scattered" show that not all were scattered.

The sources which Luke used had no kind words for Paul at this point. We hear first that the witnesses "laid down their garments at the feet of a young man named Saul" (vii 58). Subsequently we are told that "Saul was consenting" to Stephen's death (viii 1). Thereafter, we are told that "Saul laid waste the church, and entering house after house, he dragged off men and women and committed them to prison" (viii 3). Thus we see the contrast between Stephen and Paul. Paul was a bitter enemy of the Samaritan-Hellenist group. Therefore, the source which related the martyrdom of Stephen contrasted the first martyr with Paul, whose fanaticism it related and perhaps exaggerated. Indeed, in II Cor xi 22 ff., Paul inveighs against Samaritan Christian missionaries: "Are they Hebrews? So am I. Are they Israelites? So am I. Are they descendants of Abraham? So am I. Are they servants of Christ? I am a better one." As we have seen above, "Hebrew(s)" was a Samaritan self-designation. Thus these missionaries were Samaritan Christians. This is also evident from the continuation of Paul's words. "Five times I have received at the hands of the Jews forty lashes less one." This shows that the terms "Hebrews" and "Jews" were not synonymous. To ward off charges that his opposition to the Samaritans was motivated by his interest in advancing the Jewish cause, Paul informs his readers that he is *persona non grata* with the Jews. Thus it is not Jewish interests that he is defending. He is engaging in polemics against those who preach another Jesus and another gospel. He writes: "if some one comes and preaches another Jesus than the one we preached, or if you receive a different spirit from the one you received, or if you accept a different Gospel from the one you accepted, you submit to it readily" (II Cor xi 4). Again: "such men are false apostles, deceitful workmen, disguising themselves as apostles of Christ. And no wonder, for even Satan disguises himself as an angel of light. So it is not strange if his servants also disguise themselves as servants of righteousness" (II Cor xi 13–15). Paul, the Jew, was hurt by the anti-Jewish propaganda of the Samaritan Christians, and it galled him to see that they had laid claim to Jesus, making him either a Samaritan or a champion of Samaritan causes. Corinth had a synagogue of the Hebrews, that is, a Samaritan synagogue. The Samaritan missionaries of Corinth presumably used this synagogue as their base of operations. Not only were "Hebrews" Paul's enemies, but also the allies of the "Hebrews," namely, the "Hellenists." We are informed of Paul soon after his conversion that "he spoke and disputed against the Hellenists; but they were seeking to kill him" (Acts ix 29).

After reading Acts vi–viii, based on Samaritan-Christian sources, where we find literary skill, subtlety, legalistic precision, and repeated polemic against the Jews, one cannot help feeling the contrast they present to the first five chapters, which are based on the experiences of the Jewish Christians in Jerusalem. It is fashionable nowadays to dismiss the first five chapters of Acts as worthless for the historian, but this is unwarranted. To be sure, they contain fact and wishful thinking, a reverence toward the past which adorns humble facts and small events by enlarging them and generalizing from them. The speeches attributed to Peter have an involved history. Some elements may be Petrine, others are the *kerygma* of the primitive church, still other elements may be Lucan —though Luke's contribution is much smaller than is commonly supposed. But our interest at this point is not in the verification of every single recorded event. Ancient and not-so-ancient writers used facts loosely when they conveyed a message. But only rarely did they call night day, or call darkness light, or convert a chamber of horrors into a near paradise. Our interest is in the mood that permeates the recollections of the Jewish Christians. They did not remember large-scale persecutions, continuous harassments, or a hostile Jewish populace. They did not recall that they had to live in hiding, had to avoid the light of day, or that they had to carry on their missionary activities in secret. The report in Acts v 13, "None of the rest dared join them, but the people held them in high honor," if it is not out of context, refers to missionary activity in an area which was under the jurisdiction and supervision of avowed enemies, the priests. That it does not imply fear of joining the followers of Jesus is clear from the verse immediately following: "And more than ever believers were added to the Lord, multitudes both of men and women." But even the fear of public identification with the followers of Jesus in the temple precincts seems to have been temporary, for the temple was the scene of Peter's triumphs as well as his occasional setbacks. Assertions that the church had endured a long unbroken chain of suffering in Jerusalem and that its missionary activity had to be conducted in the greatest secrecy are based on the ill-founded notion that Luke, when writing Acts, acted like a writer of an historical novel and invented situations, events, speeches, and created a picture of the primitive church *ex nihilo*. This is manifestly impossible, for the style, manner, and interests of these chapters fly in the face of such assertions. Ancient writers, by and large, were slaves of their sources. They did introduce editorial retouches here and there, they did occasionally alter details, they did transpose. Nevertheless they reproduced the basic texts at their disposal and, fortunately, left enough telltale marks to enable us often to identify the alterations. Luke has not created texts in his Acts; he wrote like other Hellenistic writers who had texts at their disposal. When he found a text which was too unorthodox he left it out of his account. If the text could be salvaged by minor alterations, he edited it and made use of it.

VI. "HELLENISTS" AND "HEBREWS" IN ACTS VI 1

Dr. Spiro's material (Appendix V) has put beyond question the interpretation of *Hebraioi* ("Hebrews") as "Samaritans" or "Samaritan Christians." It is therefore necessary to ask again what explanation may be found for the term *Hellēnistai*, "Hellenists." Both groups are to be distinguished from the Jews depicted for us in the Pentecost story in Acts ii who (from the evidence of that chapter) understood, even if they did not speak, Hebrew, and who came chiefly from regions identified by name, most of which were not under direct Hellenistic influence.

It is not enough to translate the term *Hellēnistai* by "Greek-speaking Jews," for in the circumstances of the time the mere business of daily living demanded a certain competence in Greek, especially for the merchant classes. Many Jews in Palestine, unless living far from cities, would be more or less at home in the vernacular Greek of the time (*koinē*).

Linguistically the verb *hellēnizein* as used by Plato meant "to speak good Greek," but it eventually came to mean "to imitate Greek manners and customs," and so acquired in some quarters a derogatory meaning. This change in meaning was vastly accelerated by the missionary zeal of the Seleucid kings after Alexander. Along with the determined campaign of the Seleucids to spread, and eventually to impose, Hellenistic culture throughout their dominions, there went a deliberate policy of suppressing all native Semitic literature (as is illustrated by the absence of Semitic inscriptions in the directly governed Seleucid dominions of this period). Hellenistic culture was urban, and this fact was at once its strength and its weakness: its strength, in that it was easily assimilated by transient merchants and intellectuals; its weakness, in that it fell before the resistance of the agricultural peasantry. The Jews of the Diaspora were peculiarly exposed to the full force of Hellenistic culture. Living as they did in cities, congregated in small groups for social, occupational, and religious reasons, by inheritance resisting accommodation with the religious syncretism of other peoples, they nevertheless felt the strong attraction of a more cosmopolitan way of life. Even in Jerusalem, as we know, there was some dispute among the rabbis as to how useful a knowledge of Greek literature might be. The Pharisees, not otherwise distinguished for their devotion to Hellenism, were subject to that culture in their adoption of the hermeneutical methods of Alexandrian Judaism.

Although the traffic was not all one way, and Livy (38.17) could complain that Greek colonists in Syria, Parthia, and Egypt had themselves assimilated native manners and customs, the inroads of Hellenism among Jews must still have been extensive. We know, for example, that the rigid predestinarianism of the Essene sects was Iranian in origin, and the interest of other Jewish sectarians in astrology—an interest which Josephus tells us found expression even in the temple—was derived ultimately from Babylon. It is not difficult to see that Jews in Greek cities, although managing to preserve the religion of their fathers, became more submerged in their Greek environment. Such men of the Diaspora, and their families, would have been subject to some degree of suspicion, if not of positive hostility on the part of Palestinian (especially Jerusalem) Jews when they ventured back to the land of their fathers. Palestine had bitter memories, many of them recent, of oppression, of resistance and foreign domination, and the presence in or near Jerusalem of Jews whose only language was Greek might have been more than enough to inflame resentment and even passion. To use a loose analogy, it is likely that the charge of being a "Hellenist" in first-century Judea was equivalent to a charge of being a foreign agent—a common situation in most areas of the world today.

The best translation of *Hellēnistai*, "Hellenists," for the widows of Acts vi 1 is perhaps "Hellenized Jews." "Greek-speaking Jews" simply will not do, for reasons already given. *Hellēnistai* as used in Acts refers to Jews (widows, especially, in this instance, though the term also occurs in Acts ix 29) whose whole cultural and linguistic background was Greek. At what time these people were first drawn into the church we cannot know; some may have joined before Pentecost, more in connection with Pentecost, and most as a result of subsequent missionary work.

Certainly it would appear from Acts that these Hellenized Jews together with the Samaritans, formed the two most significant mi-

nority groups in the early Jerusalem church. The Samaritans would
have turned with relief to a movement which rid them of the
great confusion of sects, claims, and counter claims among them
at that time, while the Hellenized Jews may well have found the
church a haven where their essential share in the inheritance of
Israel was not questioned. The importance attaching to the Samaritan group of Christians is plainly evidenced by the evangelis-
tic efforts of Peter and Philip in Samaria. Perhaps in all our
thinking about Samaritan Christians we have been unconsciously
influenced by the verdicts of the Church Fathers on Simon Magus,
a man of no mean ability, and certainly a Samaritan.

The lines of demarcation—if such they can be called—crossed
and recrossed many times on the margins of Jewish groups and
sects, and while Samaritan and Hellenist Christians could alike
embrace enthusiastically the messianic confession of the primitive
Christian community, it is more than likely that a simple domestic
issue like that of "welfare" would have caused old rivalries to
break out. Minorities intimately bound up with, but distinct from,
a majority are always liable to prove fissionable material, a fact
which can be amply illustrated in the later history of the church.
It was, for example, the rise of Cistercianism, and the subsequent
decline of Benedictinism, which led to the very unedifying and
inflammatory quarrels between Benedictines and Augustinians in
Europe. Later, when the rise of the friars had reduced Cistercianism in its turn to the status of a minority among the religious orders, the Cistercians exhibited the same intrafamily quar-
relsomeness which led to a good many new foundations, set up
on the flimsiest pretexts. In post-Reformation England, the confrontation of the Puritan sects by a monolithic establishment produced not unity, but bitter controversies which gave birth to yet
more sects. In these instances, the quarrels were about peripheral
matters, at least in the beginning. The combative religious orders
were united in their adherence to their religious vows, and the
Puritans were united in opposition to the Elizabethan establishment. Instructive and even closer parallels to the friction between
the Samaritan and Hellenist groups in the Jerusalem church may
also be drawn from the experience of differing ethnocultural back-
grounds of immigrants to the United States: Germans against Irish,
Irish against Italians, Germans against Slavs, and all against
Puerto Ricans, yet all within the organizational framework of the
same church. Indeed, the complaints of one group against another

concerning schools, languages in pastoral ministration, distribution
of charity, etc., would have seemed quite natural to the author of
Acts.

It is important that we do not exaggerate the dimensions of
the quarrel between the Hellenist and Samaritan Christians in Jerusalem. United in their confession of Jesus as Messiah, it was
their very minority status which provoked the dispute which Luke
records.

C. S. Mann

VII. SIMON MAGUS AS "THE GREAT POWER OF GOD"

The passage in Acts viii 9 ff. which describes the career of Simon Magus does not seem to have been clearly understood by commentators. I have employed the translation "the so-called great power of God" for the Greek *hē dunamis tou̯ theou hē kaloumenē megalē*. In Greek the participle *kaloumenos* appears repeatedly from Anaximander in the sixth century B.C. to Plato in the fourth century, in the meaning "called," "so-called," "said to be." This sense is mentioned briefly by H. G. Liddell and R. Scott (*A Greek-English Lexicon*, 1940 ed.); the other references Dr. Mann and I have collected from various sources. It must be remembered that the expression did not necessarily have a pejorative meaning, as in French *soi-disant* and nearly always in English, but it is used more as in German, where *sogenannt* can have both a favorable and an unfavorable sense. Probably both the neutral and the pejorative meanings underlie the use of this expression in Acts. No biblical translation we have consulted seems to give it, but the meaning has been recognized here by a few previous writers (e.g. by H. Leisegang, *Die Gnosis* [1924], p. 61). Since the expression "great power of God" is very strange when applied to a man and is scarcely possible in either a polytheistic Greek or a monotheistic Jewish milieu, it must probably be explained as Aramaic *ḥaylâ rabbâ d'Elâhâ*. *Ḥaylâ* may refer to an angelic being: note Samaritan *ḥaylîn* of a class of angels; the expression is parallel to *kâhnâ rabbâ*, "high priest," etc. It therefore means something like "chief (angelic) power." Since Simon was himself a Samaritan, born at Gitta (modern Jett), as already stated in our oldest source (Justin Martyr, ca. A.D. 140), this is quite natural.

Another characteristic of Samaritan and some late Jewish tradition is the interposition of an angel or angels between God and Moses or another outstanding saint, as pointed out above by A. Spiro. The role of angels in Simonian teaching is stressed by Epiphanius, bishop of Salamis, in the fourth century A.D. In his

Panarion xxi.2.4, he quotes Simon as writing: "In every heaven I took another form . . . according to the form of beings in each heaven in order to remain hidden from the angelic powers and come down to the *Ennoia* [Thought], which is also called . . . 'Holy Spirit,' through whom I have created the angels, but the angels have created the cosmos and men." It may be added that according to all the heresiographers, including Irenaeus (late second century A.D.), the Simonian "Holy Spirit" was incarnated in the person of a prostitute named Helena whom Simon is said to have found in a Tyrian brothel. We now know, thanks to the discovery of the Chenoboskion codices, containing part of the long-lost early Gnostic literature, that the Church Fathers Irenaeus, Hippolytus, and Epiphanius were in general extremely accurate in their reports on the Gnostics, but natural prejudice may easily have crept in and the teachings of Simon may not have been so immoral as they state. It is to be noted particularly that the use of angels by Simon stems from Judeo-Samaritan tradition, whereas later Gnostics nearly always use the Greek term *archontes,* "rulers" (Heb. *sārîm*) for the powers controlling the planets and other phenomena of nature.

The meaning is, in any case, obvious: Simon, as the incarnation of the "great power of God," was sometimes, according to the Church Fathers, identified with God and sometimes with the chief angelic power who created the subordinate angels and through them created the cosmos and mankind. The ideas are wholly Gnostic and do not correspond to anything in the Dead Sea Scrolls or the New Testament (except, e.g., that the term *archons* refers to the angels who are in charge of astronomical and other phenomena of nature).

In early Christian tradition, especially in the so-called Clementines (second century A.D.), Simon became a magician and sorcerer who debated with Peter and Paul and died in Rome when his magic failed. None of these legends can be taken as historical. That he was actually the first Christian Gnostic, as held by all the Church Fathers, is an entirely reasonable assumption, for with him we see true Gnosticism in its earliest and rawest manifestations. That he was obviously an unlettered man is no argument against a native talent for speculation, or against his great significance as founder of the movement. He would not be by any means the only uneducated man in history with a bent for innovation as well as skill in organization (cf. Mohammed and Joseph Smith); he was more than a mere charlatan (cf. among comparable cases Paracelsus and Madame Blavatsky). Allowing for his heretical Samaritan background (allegedly Dosithean), he might be expected to react against both Judaism and the Christianity which he had briefly espoused.

a. He rejected the Hebrew Bible, like his fellow Samaritans, but he went much farther than they did by rejecting most of the Judeo-Samaritan tradition. A corollary of this rejection was his view that the Creator of the Old Testament was not God at all, but was rather a fallen angelic power.

b. He tried to circumvent the astral determinism which was part of his background as a professional diviner (hence called Magus) by turning the angelic hosts of Judeo-Samaritan angelology into creatures which he himself had created and could therefore presumably control, as the "Great Power of God."

c. He took over from somewhere the old myth or allegory of the divine Wisdom who came down to dwell with men but could not find a home, so she returned to heaven, which he modified by identifying this Wisdom (see my book *From the Stone Age to Christianity* [1957], pp. 367–71), with the woman he had, according to the statements of the Church Fathers, found in a Tyrian brothel. In identifying the woman with Helen of Troy and following this up with all sorts of extraordinary combinations with pagan mythology and popular Greek philosophy, he showed undoubted ingenuity but no real learning.

d. He capped his structure by identifying himself with God Almighty and Helen with the Holy Spirit. This may have been an aberration of his later years and it was not, at all events, imitated by the other Gnostics, so far as we know.

By identifying his harlot (*prounikos*) with Divine Wisdom, Simon originated the widespread Gnostic myth of the Fallen Sophia, who was sent down by the Supreme Being to save mankind, but who besmirched her skirts in the *hulē* (material world) and had to be rescued by the Savior—in this case Simon himself. Simon thus appears to be directly responsible for two of the most persistent doctrines of the Gnostics—one, the later Marcionite separation between God as the Supreme Being and the Old Testament God as Creator, and two, the role of Divine Wisdom in fall and redemption. Jean Doresse (*The Secret Books of the Egyptian Gnostics* tr. by Philip Mairet [New York, 1960], pp. 328–32) has pointed out that fragments of original Simonian teaching may be preserved among the Chenoboskion finds of early Gnostic treatises (now in course of publication). More such material is likely to be identified among the now extensive debris of Gnostic literature, both published and unpublished.

W. F. Albright

VIII. PAUL'S EDUCATION

In Acts xxii 3, Paul is quoted by Luke as saying to the Jewish throng in Jerusalem, "I am a Jew, born in Tarsus in Cilicia, brought up in this city (namely, Jerusalem), strictly trained by Gamaliel himself in the ancestral law." An exhaustive study of pagan and early Christian Greek literature by W. C. van Unnik in his *Tarsus and Jerusalem,* which originally appeared in the publications of the Royal Dutch Academy of Sciences and Arts, 1952, and later was published in English translation, London, 1962, has cleared a great deal of superfluous undergrowth from our field of vision. The three Greek verbs used by Paul (*gignomai, trephō* or *anatrephō,* and *paideuō,* or the corresponding passives of the last two), are found together many times in Greek literature from Plato to third-century Christian writers. As van Unnik points out, the word *trephō* is used specifically for "bring up, take care of (a child)."

Our information about the ages of students who passed through the entire course of education in Greek and Jewish circles is unfortunately rather meager, but what we have is instructive and agrees completely with the processes of physical and mental growth in minors. Our best information probably comes from Josephus, who in his *Life* claims to have been already outstanding in his knowledge of Jewish law at the age of fourteen (A.D. 51–52). At sixteen he had completed his academic courses and had begun his adventures with the three leading Jewish sects, followed by a period with the hermit Bannus. He claims that these *Wanderjahre* occupied three years. Later Rabbinic literature (dating in its extant form chiefly between the second and the fourth centuries A.D.) is less than clear; it mentions beginning elementary education at six to seven and higher education at sixteen to seventeen. In other words, empirical observation had shown that the average age at which boys could begin their elementary education was just what it is now (if we leave out nursery school and kindergarten). Higher education began just after puberty, where it does now for the normal boy. We must remember, of course, that Josephus claims to have been a precocious youth. For pertinent rabbinic citations, see Nathan Drazin, *History of Jewish Education from 515 B.C.E. to 220 C.E.,* Baltimore, 1940. One must beware of Drazin's attempt to show that there was universal compulsory education for boys before the end of the Second Temple, for this inference goes far beyond any concrete evidence and is intrinsically most improbable.

Greek education was undoubtedly uneven, varying greatly at different places and in different times. In Athens in the fourth century B.C. the elementary school age was in general from six to fourteen and the secondary school from fourteen to eighteen, after which the young Athenian became for two years an ephebe—that is, a youth of eighteen to twenty theoretically taking military or other training for adult responsibilities.

In any case, the education of youths, whether we look at the Mediterranean civilization of that day from the viewpoint of Greeks or Jews, required ten or twelve years, during which time the youth would study all necessary subjects related to his intended career. It must not be supposed that there was any difference between this situation and that in the second millennium B.C. or in mediaeval times, since the quantity of material to be mastered changed very little between Twelfth-Dynasty Egypt or the nearly contemporary First Dynasty of Babylon and the Middle Ages. We now have, for instance, a detailed synopsis of the examinations which a future scribe was required to pass at the end of his school years in the reign of Ammisaduqa of Babylon in the early sixteenth century B.C. The young scribe had to pass grueling tests in both Sumerian and Akkadian, as well as in other areas of knowledge, including music. It is certainly not necessary to dwell on the mediaeval *trivium* and *quadrivium,* which are generally well known, since they must be surveyed in every course in the general history of education.

Thanks to the work of Saul Liebermann (see especially his *Hellenism in Jewish Palestine,* New York, 1950) and other students of the origins of rabbinic law, we now know that it was Gamaliel's grandfather Hillel the Elder, just before the Christian era, who introduced Greek logic into rabbinic teaching in the form of the Alexandrine hermeneutic principles in use at that time. (The Alexandrine hermeneutics was a rather rigorous logical discipline, which had nothing in common with the allegorical interpretation taken over from Middle Platonism by Philo of Alexandria, who was an older contemporary of Paul.) The key designations for the *middôt* in Tannaitic literature are direct Hebrew translations of the corresponding Greek terms, and the remaining designations are adapted to these key terms. In this way there was gradually created a general practice of using literal, logical interpretation of Scripture or tradition in order to develop new legislation at the same time that the old hermeneutic methods of midrashic type were kept for more hortatory exposition. (See Samuel Rosenblatt, *The Interpretation of the Bible in the Mishnah,* Baltimore, 1935.)

We know from the Dead Sea Scrolls that the earlier Jewish hermeneutics, which was sometimes very far-fetched, was already in normal use in the biblical commentaries preserved in more or less fragmentary form at Qumran. Krister Stendahl has pointed out in *The School of St. Matthew,* that in the Gospel of Matthew we have survivals of the older school of biblical exegesis. (We have equally far-fetched hermeneutic practice in some existentialist exegesis of today, so we can scarcely scorn the Essene commentators!)

In reaction against the attempts by H. Böhlig and more recent writers to show that Paul was well educated in Greek, there have been recent second thoughts (see above, on van Unnik). Of course Paul could speak everyday Greek fluently (see Appendix IX by C. S. Mann on "The Customary Languages of the Jews," below). Paul's language cannot however be used directly as evidence for his knowledge of Greek, since he emphasizes repeatedly his poor writing and he also states that he used amanuenses in preparing his letters. The recent attempt to prove by use of computers that he composed only Romans, Galatians, I and II Corinthians, is absurd on the face of it. Different amanuenses with different degrees of knowledge of Greek and different ideas of how much they might correct their master's dictation would inevitably produce quite different Greek, ranging all the way from ordinary *koinē* to quite literary Attic.

In Paul's letters there is a clue to his education which is often overlooked. It is his frequent insistence on his signature. Not only is he anxious to guard against false teaching contained in forged letters (II Thess ii 2), not only does he want his letters to have wider circulation beyond the community to which a letter is addressed (Col iv 16), but also, by means of his well-known signature, to secure prompt compliance with his wishes (II Thess iii 14). Paul's signature was apparently well known—a kind of trademark

(I Cor xvi 21; Gal vi 11; Col iv 18; I Thess iii 17). But we wholly misconceive the meaning of Gal vi 11 if we assume that Paul's eyesight was in some measure responsible for his "large letters." Rather, it was that the apostle's signature was not the well-formed and precise calligraphy of the professional scribe. In many spheres of Paul's time the possession of a carefully acquired script was not only a matter of great pride, but also a prime necessity in securing some of the most sought-after areas of employment, and ultimately of influence (an important factor). This situation persisted right down into the nineteenth century in Europe. In the Middle Ages, the possession of a "chancery hand," not to mention a copyist's hand, was the sign of an educated man, such as a canon lawyer. The ability to write easily and legibly in the hand required by the courts and the keepers of records was highly esteemed. In Paul's time and for many centuries afterward, there were whole realms of employment denied to those who could not write with the requisite skill or delicacy. Within living memory in England, advertisements used to appear on behalf of law offices offering employment to those with "a good book hand," or "a good legal hand." Some idea of the status in mediaeval Europe of those who could write well is evidenced by the statutory title of a priest of the Church of England: "Clerk in Holy Orders."

There is absolutely nothing in Paul's references to popular philosophy or in his rare use of Greek aphorisms or of common rhetorical devices to indicate that he had ever received a secular Greek education. The total lack of evidence that Paul knew the Greek classics is alone conclusive proof that he had never studied Greek formally—at least beyond an elementary school. That he could speak Greek fluently and without an Aramaic accent, I do not dispute for a moment.

W. F. Albright

IX. THE CUSTOMARY LANGUAGES OF THE JEWS

How complicated the language patterns of Palestine could be in the first century of our era may be illustrated by the words borrowed from other languages which are found in New Testament Greek. Some loanwords, in view of the nature of the New Testament material, we should expect to find (military and administrative words, for example), but there are some thirty-two words borrowed from Hebrew and Aramaic, and about thirty from Latin, excluding proper names in both cases. This, in miniature, gives a picture of the fluid state of spoken languages in Palestine in the period of the compilation of Luke-Acts. Incidentally, it warns us against exaggerating the Hebrew-Aramaic contribution to New Testament Greek *as such.*

Perhaps it is the Greek of the New Testament *koinē,* which has suffered most from commentators and scholars—Arthur Darby Nock, for example, quotes an eminent classicist (Eduard Norden) as saying that he would find Paul's language hard to deal with (*St Paul,* London, 1938, p. 236). By and large, where *koinē* has not been dismissed as a kind of marketplace slang, it has been shrugged off as not worthy of the attention of the serious linguist. However, there are signs that *koinē* is beginning to be taken far more seriously than it was at the beginning of this century. Radermacher's *Koinē* (Vienna Academy, *Phil.-Hist. Klasse,* 1947) is a case in point, and Saul Lieberman's *Hellenism in Jewish Palestine* has served to widen our horizons for its influence on early rabbinic literature.

What we have become accustomed to call *koinē* cannot in the nature of the case have been of sudden growth, and there are numerous foreshadowings of it in the classical period: in fact, there are inscriptions in Attic Greece which can only properly be called *koinē.* It was, however, the proselytizing zeal of Hellenistic culture which was more than anything else responsible for the rapid spread of *koinē.* The impetus given by the conquests of Alexander and

Philip to the acceptance of Greek culture and customs demanded the use of a lingua franca throughout the Mediterranean world. *Koinē* became the common language of almost every department of life and commerce, demonstrating in the process an extraordinary power of assimilating local vocabulary and usage, and an ability to deal with new forms of knowledge, which gave it a long life.

It is important to avoid the suggestion—too easily made—that *koinē* was classical Greek in decline. Radermacher rightly observes that the expression "classical Greek" is very loose, for there were several different dialects, including Ionic, Doric, and Attic (which asserted itself most strongly), as well as survivals from Homeric Greek. What we have essentially in *koinē* is a dominant Attic, with strong crosscurrents from Ionic. This is precisely what we would expect, for whereas in older Greek expansion the Greek colonies had been single language outposts, cities founded by Alexander and his successors were made up of widely varying linguistic groups.

The rise of the Roman imperial system made very little difference: it is clear that Latin had importance only in the army, in central administration, and in central legal enactments. For all purposes of everyday administrative affairs, the Roman provincial official had to have a working knowledge of Greek. Perhaps the best modern parallel is to be found in the position of English in Egypt, or French in Lebanon, up to the end of the Second World War. This was by no means the only way in which Greek penetrated the Roman world of the first century. We know from various sources that even in the district of Rome it was considered "chic" to speak Greek, and the cultivation of that language among Romans produced some odd phenomena, such as an over-frequent use of the optative, or grammatical errors on a par with "This was given to my wife and I" in English. What we have become accustomed to describe as classical Greek was by the first century a consciously cultivated style. We may apply here a rather loose analogy in modern terms. The explanations offered by a present-day physician to a scientific friend differ radically from those offered to an unlettered patient, and in both those cases the language would be different again from what the physician would employ in composing a paper to be delivered before a learned society. In the last case, the language would be the most consciously formed and polished.

Classical scholars of the nineteenth century found the language of the New Testament odd—almost as though it were a Jewish "dialect." But then the whole outlook was changed by the dramatic discovery of *koinē* papyri in Egypt. Up to the discovery of these documents from the scrap heaps of Hellenistic Egypt, it had been assumed that even if the Greek of the New Testament were allowed to stand in its own right, it was nevertheless wholly different from secular speech. Adolf Deissmann (1866–1937) and J. H. Moulton (1863–1917) were among the first to demonstrate that this thesis was wholly inaccurate; that many words and expressions which had up to that time been dismissed as "New Testament" Greek were in fact part of the normal secular tongue of the day. The elaborate style of classical Greek was unknown to the writers of the New Testament, and the writings of the first century B.C. known to us are almost painfully elaborate (with the possible exception of Strabo and Diodorus). Before the time of the *Corpus Hermeticum* there was no single philosophical or metaphysical text in simple Greek. The discovery of the papyri in the Fayyum was therefore a link of capital importance between the world of New Testament writers and the surrounding secular culture.

When we turn our attention to the Palestinian Jews of the first century, the picture is somewhat confused. Lieberman has pointed out that for all the orthodox prejudice against Greek, it was necessary not only to conduct business with non-Jews, but that it was not unknown for the sons of priestly families to learn Greek in order to deal with secular authority. The same author mentions the interesting fact that while Rabbi Akiba might hold Ben Sira to be unlawful study, as being an uncanonical book, the same ban did not apparently hold for Homer, who was too remote to be the subject of sectarian Jewish controversy. How far *formal* Greek education might go, we do not know precisely, even among the Romans. We do know, however (through Plutarch and Pliny), that Cato approved of a working knowledge of Greek literature. But in spite of all the energy which has attended the search for Greek literary patterns in the New Testament, the significant fact remains that there are very few allusions, direct or indirect, to Greek literature. Such as there are might as easily be found in any other collected material of the time—such, for example, as Paul's lists of "virtues and vices," which would have been almost as commonplace as the proverbs current wherever English is spoken.

The assumption that Jesus and his disciples spoke only or chiefly Aramaic has been under attack lately, notably from H. Birkeland in "The Language of Jesus" (Norwegian Academy, *Avhandlinger,*

1954–55). Aramaic became an official language, the language of
administration and law, in the Semitic countries of the Middle East,
and rapidly became a lingua franca in the entire East. It seems
likely that the Jews who returned from the Babylonian exile spoke
and used both classical Hebrew and Aramaic, but Aramaic was
essentially the tongue of both upper classes and administrators,
however much it may have been assimilated by ordinary folk. Even
this picture is complicated by the fact that in the first century
Aramaic was fast becoming fragmented into a number of dialects
and was ceasing to be a lingua franca. The discovery of the Dead
Sea Scrolls has, however, made one point absolutely clear—far
from being in any sense a dead language, Hebrew was more and
more cultivated. Most of the Qumran material so far found is in
Hebrew, and Aramaic is relatively little represented. (The newly
found Ben Sira, for example, is in Hebrew.) This in itself would
be emphatic proof of the use of Hebrew as a living language, but
we now have in addition letters from Bar-Cochba (hardly to be
described as a learned man!), and they are in semiliterate Hebrew.
The position of Mishnaic Hebrew is not very clear; it was coming
into use before the end of the Qumran period, but was apparently
confined to legal and quasi-legal texts (like the Copper Scrolls).

Against this background, it is perhaps fair to say that Birkeland
makes an interesting case for his view that Jesus spoke Hebrew. He
overstates his thesis, but in the light of the knowledge which we
now have, it simply will not do to suppose that when Acts speaks
of Paul addressing a crowd in Hebrew (Acts xxii 2) the text really
means Aramaic. Josephus is clear (*Wars* V.2; VI.2.1) about the
difference between Hebrew and Aramaic, even if (owing to the
Aramaizing of vocabulary) he occasionally calls an Aramaic word
"Hebrew."

In a recent number of the *Expository Times* (Vol. 77, No. 1,
1965) Matthew Black, in reviewing Max Wilcox's *The Semitisms
of Acts,* Oxford, 1965, returns to a theme which has occupied him
for some time—namely, that the language spoken by Jesus and the
disciples, which underlies the earliest traditions of the New Testament, was Aramaic. (Wilcox does not mention the varying types
of non-literary Greek, and often draws conclusions on the basis
of faulty induction.) Black's case is always persuasively argued,
but in the light of present evidence it must be said that the place
of Aramaic is no longer as secure as it formerly was. Black does
provide us, however, with a useful phrase, which—rigidly controlled

as to meaning—characterizes New Testament Greek as "Jewish Greek." The expression does not, of course, mean that Jews in first-century Palestine used a recognizably peculiar Greek, an odd form of *koinē,* but that given the theological material the New Testament uses, with all its undertones of Old Testament (Hebrew and Septuagint) thought, we should expect to find, and do find, Semitisms in the meaning of words and constructions, and even new idioms to deal with Christian experience. As Nock pointed out (*St. Paul* [New York, 1938], pp. 233 ff.), Paul was able to employ such bold constructions in Greek as "the gospel of the circumcision."

It can be a disservice to the New Testament to compare it with classical Greek, and to condemn it for an excessive use of *kai,* "and". The now customary stylistic analysis of individual books, which often results in a refusal to accept traditional attribution to given authors, is useless unless it takes account of the different amanuenses authors such as Paul employed. Furthermore, this procedure often fails to recognize our lack of knowledge of the history of oral tradition before it was committed to writing.

In addition to the material cited above, the reader is referred to Chapter 1 of R. Knopf, H. Lietzmann, and H. Weinel, *Einführung in das Neue Testament,* Berlin, 1949, and to the article by E. C. Colwell, "Greek Language," in *The Interpreter's Dictionary of the Bible,* New York, 1962.

C. S. Mann

KEY TO THE TEXT